Additional praise for Rabbi Shai H

"Shai Held is an extraordinary figure in the world of Torah. Combining deep knowledge of classical Judaica, wide and insightful reading from the religiously diverse world of biblical and theological scholarship, and a keen sense of the human heart, he has produced a set of essays that people from a wide range of affiliations will find well worth reading and pondering."—JON D. LEVENSON, Albert A. List Professor of Jewish Studies at Harvard Divinity School and author of the National Jewish Book Award–winner *Resurrection and the Restoration of Israel: The Ultimate Victory of the God of Life*

"Whatever your level of Torah proficiency or your religious outlook, *The Heart of Torah* will make you think, ask questions, revisit familiar understandings, and gain a new appreciation for the ability of our written and oral tradition to surprise, elevate, and challenge us all. Rabbi Held consistently sheds new light on seemingly familiar texts—his interpretation of 'an eye for an eye' alone is worth the price of the volumes—and insistently prods us to become better Jews and better human beings. If you want solid scholarship, you will find it here; if you want religious inspiration, you will find it here, too. That all-too-rare combination makes *The Heart of Torah* precious indeed."—RABBI ASHER LOPATIN, president of Yeshivat Chovevei Torah Rabbinical School

"The greatest Jewish books arise from authors who combine deep learning in traditional sources with a keen awareness of the intellectual, moral, and spiritual currents of their time and place. Such is Rabbi Shai Held's breathtaking new commentary on the Torah. Expertly weaving together a tapestry of core stories from the Hebrew Bible with their interpretive trajectories over the ages, he has created a masterful compendium brimming with immediate relevance to the contemporary reader. Wherever you place yourself on the Jewish spectrum—or beyond—you will rise from reading this extraordinary work renewed, challenged, and deepened."—RABBI AARON PANKEN, president of Hebrew Union College-Jewish Institute of Religion

"Shai Held's commentary on the weekly Torah portion sets a new standard for our time. He deftly distills a richness of traditional rabbinic commentary, biblical scholarship, modern theology, moral sensitivity, and psycho-spiritual acumen to illuminate a vital core idea or problem at the heart of the parashah that is truly relevant to modern readers. The result is a synthetic tour de force." —RABBI NANCY FLAM, co-director of programs at the Institute for Jewish Spirituality

"This deeply integrative volume provides a beautiful gateway into Torah study for any serious reader, Jewish or Christian. Drawing widely on rabbinic commentary, ancient to modern, as well as contemporary biblical and pastoral studies, Rabbi Shai Held makes his own creative contribution in demonstrating that the ultimate goal of scriptural interpretation is human transformation in community." —ELLEN F. DAVIS, Amos Ragan Kearns Professor of Bible and Practical Theology at the Divinity School, Duke University

"Rabbi Shai Held's superbly crafted reflections on Torah texts from Genesis to Deuteronomy dazzle with insight, practical wisdom, and scholarly erudition. These essays are a model for both Jews and Christians on how to read the Bible with intellectual integrity, religious significance, a mind open to an array of dialogue partners, and a generous spirit that celebrates the love of God and the repair of human dignity in our world today. Highly recommended!" —DENNIS OLSON, Charles T. Haley Professor of Old Testament Theology at Princeton Theological Seminary

"Through Shai Held's original, honest, astute, and humane interpretations, we experience the strong moral voice of the biblical text. He makes it possible to reread our tradition, and thus *stand again at Sinai*." —TOVA HARTMAN, author of the National Jewish Book Award–winner *Feminism Encounters Traditional Judaism: Resistance and Accommodation*

"Shai Held is a remarkable and unique resource for the religious and the secular alike. A serious scholar and a dedicated man of faith, he submits the weekly parashah to piercing scrutiny and polymathic learning as he also simultaneously reaffirms the eternal religious truths he locates inside the text. Any reader with even the slightest interest in Torah or even the life of the religious mind will find not only moral and intellectual challenge but wisdom and wonder in these pages for years to come." —ERIC ALTERMAN, City University of New York Distinguished Professor of English and Journalism at Brooklyn College

"Through its rare combination of literary nuance, historical depth, and ethical concern, *The Heart of Torah* has the potential to contribute to the renewal of faith communities—both Jewish and Christian— that care about the theological and ethical claims of this ancient and sacred text." —J. RICHARD MIDDLETON, professor of biblical worldview and exegesis at Northeastern Seminary

"Held's deep immersion in the Jewish commentary tradition and his appreciative grasp of contemporary Christian biblical scholarship provide a model for how members of both religious traditions can explore the richness of Scripture together to mutual enrichment." —J. GERALD JANZEN, author of *At the Scent of Water: The Ground of Hope in the Book of Job*

"This book is gold. You hold a treasure in your hand. Shai Held's brilliant thought and passionate writing open the door to transformation of character and society, which truly is the heart of Torah." —RABBI BRADLEY SHAVIT ARTSON, Roslyn and Abner Goldstine Dean's Chair at the Ziegler School of Rabbinic Studies, American Jewish University

"The Bible has much wisdom to impart, but it is not easily accessible, clothed as it is in its ancient garments. A lover of Torah, Rabbi Held shows us how close attention to the text yields interpretive jewels. He opens the Bible's witness in surprising and compelling ways, revealing to us its profound truths about God's concern for the whole world, and our responsibilities in it." —JACQUELINE LAPSLEY, associate professor of Old Testament at Princeton Theological Seminary

The Heart of Torah, VOLUME 1

The Jewish Publication Society expresses its gratitude for the generosity of the following sponsors of this book:

DANIELLA FUCHS AND JEFF WECHSELBLATT in memory of our beloved grandparents and Jeff's father Herb Wechselblatt and in honor of Shai Held's effort to teach a Torah of love and hesed.

MORRIE KLEINBART in memory of his beloved aunts and uncles, Claire and Nathan Snow and Gertrude and Leon Kleinbart.

University of Nebraska Press

Lincoln

The Heart of Torah,

VOLUME 1

Essays on the Weekly Torah Portion:
Genesis and Exodus

RABBI SHAI HELD

Foreword by Rabbi Yitz Greenberg

The Jewish Publication Society
Philadelphia

An earlier, shorter version of "Whom Do We Serve?
The Exodus toward Dignified Work" appeared in *Sh'ma*
(September 2013) (http://shma.com/2013/09/from-
avdut-to-avodah-between-slavery-and-service/). Parts
reprinted with permission.

Library of Congress Cataloging-in-Publication Data

Names: Held, Shai, 1971– author.
Title: The heart of Torah: essays on the weekly
    Torah portion / Rabbi Shai Held; foreword by
    Rabbi Yitz Greenberg.
Description: Philadelphia: Jewish Publication Society;
    Lincoln: University of Nebraska Press, [2017] |
    Includes bibliographical references and index.
Identifiers: LCCN 2016039785 (print)
    LCCN 2016040496 (ebook)
    ISBN 9780827613034 (cloth: alk. paper)
    ISBN 9780827612716 (pbk.: alk. paper)
    ISBN 9780827613058 (gift set: alk. paper)
    ISBN 9780827613331 (epub)
    ISBN 9780827613348 (mobi)
    ISBN 9780827613355 (pdf)
Subjects: LCSH: Bible. Pentateuch—Commentaries.
Classification: LCC BS1225.53 .H445 2017 (print) | LCC
    BS1225.53 (ebook) | DDC 222/.107—dc23
LC record available at https://lccn.loc.gov/2016039785

Set in MeropeBasic by Rachel Gould.

Contents

Foreword

RABBI YITZ GREENBERG

This is the golden age of the *parashat ha-shavua* (weekly Torah portion) commentary. Once treated as ephemera, Torah commentaries are increasingly being published, studied, and returned to again and again. Important rabbis and scholars have written substantive, sophisticated essays. These, in turn, are read and discussed in many synagogues on Shabbat mornings, distributed by the thousands and tens of thousands to their followers via the Internet, and, sometimes, published in written form.

This only points up the remarkable achievement of R. Shai Held, whose *parashat ha-shavua* commentaries are gathered and published in this volume. When the history of rabbinic literature of this era is written, R. Held's contributions will be acknowledged as the brightest stars in this new galaxy of Torah teaching. To paraphrase the classic Jewish joke, Shai is a captain among the captains of Torah wisdom in this age.

Why? What distinctive qualities make this work so rich and enriching?

It starts with his remarkable gift for a fresher and deeper *peshat* (plain-sense meaning) of the verse. See, for example, his exploration of the wide spectrum of meanings and expressions of the Fifth Commandment, "honor your father and mother"—including that the range includes extraordinary efforts to fulfill their wishes but does not spell automatic obedience. Similarly, he describes the many interpretive traditions of demands to meet parental needs and expectations—yet not to the point of parents thwarting their children's well-being (Yitro #2). Consider his treatment of the Israelites' complaint, "when we sat by the flesh pots, when we ate our fill of bread"—which in fact reveals that they could only look at the meat. Their masters would not let them eat from the flesh pots. Held adds that the passage not only reveals the retroactive rose coloring of the oppressive Egyptian experience, but also "illustrates the attraction of the regime of oppression and the way even slaves trying to escape from it still are held in its moral grasp."

Held repeatedly focuses on the many Torah commandments to care for the vulnerable and the needy. One of his more innovative treatments is his explication of the thanksgiving sacrifice where uniquely there is a ritual requirement to consume it completely on the very day it is offered. The Torah is instructing, almost forcing, the donor to invite family and friends and outsiders to share in the feast, because thanksgiving should be accompanied by generosity. "Gratitude and hoarding are incompatible." Similarly, the prohibition of leaving over any of the paschal sacrifice "at least in part, reminds us that those who are hungry are our responsibility, that we are to open both our hearts and our homes to them." See also his explication of the often overlooked connection the Torah makes between closeness to God and joy.

In Torah portion after portion, Held picks not the obvious verse but the overlooked gem. Yitro (Yitro #2), the portion of the Ten Commandments, becomes the occasion to show the Torah's profound, if subtle, pushback against generalizing the preceding story of the war with Amalek as proof that the whole world hates the Jews. And Yitro's advice to Moshe reminds us that there is wisdom among gentiles, and that possession of divine revelation should not divert us or close us off from other sources of understanding.

Yet another enrichment is Held's constant conversation with commentators, medieval and modern. He mines the Talmud and midrashim for insights. He draws upon a wealth of Christian, mostly Protestant, commentators who have great exegetical talents, especially so in their ability to employ modern critical and comparative approaches without losing the sacred, transcendent dimension of revelation and interactions with the Divine.

Held also enters into dialogue with the great theologians and writers of world literature in order to illuminate a passage or to highlight a contrasting view of the same conundrum. One brilliant example: In the middle of a breathtaking exposition of the religious weight of *hakhnasat orchim* (hospitality), he counterbalances Kierkegaard's explanation of the *Akedah*. The great Dane justifies Abraham's willingness to override morality and human dignity and obediently kill his own child with the famous suggestion that this submission constitutes a "teleological suspension of the ethical." In response, Held points to Abraham's turning away from his God encounter in order to offer hospitality to three strangers, explaining that Abraham tells God to wait because in the Torah's values, upholding the worth and dignity of human lives takes precedence over attending to God.

Held wittily calls this Jewish supremacy of ethics "an ethical postponement of the theological" or, better still, "an ethical realization of the theological." He understands Abraham's protest to God, as the Patriarch tries to save Sodom from destruction, as a deeply Jewish balancing of obedience and conscience. In so doing, he breaks through the simple binary of absolute obedience to God versus supremacy of the ethical.

Take, too, Held's positive reflections on the blessings of material well-being—so often invoked and promised in the Torah—combined with his guidance on avoiding the pernicious slide into materialism, which shrinks one's universe of moral responsibility and one's ability to center in God. Consider his multifold treatments of leadership: the moral call to take responsibility for others; the value of knowing one's limits; and the need to possess dialectical strengths—both the drive to take charge and a healthy dose of hesitation, both the determination to accomplish and the readiness to prepare the next generation to achieve what they had deeply hoped for but could not achieve in their lifetime.

By consistently holding conflicting ideas in tension, time and again Held reveals richer, more nuanced Torah. Abraham's protest at Sodom is not simply an act of autonomy; it is solicited by God. "Love your neighbor as yourself" necessitates a balance of emotion and action. While emotion can't be commanded, it can be advanced or induced by action. God's love for Israel is unlimited, as the prophets confirm: It continues even when the people have betrayed the relationship. God's love is unlimited in another sense, too: It extends beyond Israel. Balaam is neither the wicked seer of midrash, nor the obedient man of God in the text's surface. He is a real prophet who misses the deepest point of prophecy—that God cannot be manipulated or magically controlled by ritual gestures.

Another recurrent and distinctive Held theme is moral spiritual development within the Torah itself. This then becomes the model for ongoing unfolding of Jewish tradition. In Deuteronomy he describes the inner movement from addressing and turning to God for instruction to turning to the Torah text and judicial interpreters. Characteristically, he shows the duality: This increases human autonomy and participation in unfolding revelation—yet also magnifies the people's risk of losing sight of the connection and relationship to God, their primary guide to action. He draws attention to a subtle divine shift. The Ten Commandments at Sinai proclaimed God's overflowing *hesed* (lovingkindness), which extends to "those who love Me and observe my commandments." In the darkest post–Golden Calf moment, the Lord self-defines as "the compassionate and gracious . . . overflowing with *hesed* (lovingkindness) and truth," but here there is no limiting phrase; that is, the lovingkindness is extended to all.

Held also points to a broadening treatment of human rights. In Exodus we learn that the status of a woman sold into servitude is ameliorated through marriage. Her sale is conditioned: It is permitted only to a person who wishes to marry her. Once married she must be treated as a free woman, with all the rights of a free wife. Nevertheless, despite being lifted out of servitude, her "acquisition" lasts for a lifetime. In Deuteronomy we are told that Hebrew men and women both have a term limit of six years. His many examples along these lines impart another vital message: In essence, the Jewish people's continued moral upgrading of laws and practices to this day constitutes carrying on a great tradition and an intrinsic part of Revelation from the beginning.

What is the secret of Shai Held's countless insights and unfailing choices of texts and values to highlight? I submit that what lifts this book from being an outstanding Torah commentary to a great work of religious thought and human moral development is Held's profound theology that the heart of Judaism's religious life lies in our relationship to God and fellow human beings.

In his portrait a deeply caring, life-affirming God loves Israel and humanity and knows and accepts their limits without settling for their present state or the status quo. God is constantly present but not controlling. God gives and instructs, commands and seeks—yet wants human agency, leaving room for it, respecting it, critiquing it, and applauding it.

In this theology humans are subject to all the flaws of finite flesh—yet they dream of better. The Torah's characters—the founding figures of Jewry and Judaism after all—are remarkably imperfect. They grow and (sometimes) rise to greatness. They fail. They forgive. They grow strong and (sometimes) overreach. They are sustained by God, by relationship, by community, by tradition. Frequently they grow in wisdom. Through Torah they are instructed to choose life and given nurturing religious traditions, institutions, and behaviors. Deeply human, they serve as role models for developing our own humanness.

There's Joseph the needy, indulged child, evolving—in no small measure because of his suffering—first into a self-centered ambitious young man and then into a mature statesman able to forgive his brothers while centering his life and success in God. Then there is Judah. He starts as a callow bystander and opportunist—but after he endures tragic loss, his own (acknowledged) moral failure, and the appropriation of his father's travail, he becomes a compassionate leader, an owner of responsibility, a redeemer willing to sacrifice his own life to save his brother.

Held's extended portrait of Moses brings out his greatness, warts and all. Moses: the modest person who overcomes his natural shrinking tendencies in order to stand up to Pharaoh—and to God—for the sake of his people. Moses: the trusting, dependent brother who rises above his siblings' competitive betrayal to pray for and work with them. Moses: the ever-patient, "nursing mother" leader who runs out of patience, burns out, is unfit to continue, and so tastes the bitterness of being deprived of his ultimate hope to enter the land of Israel. Moses: who then performs a magnificent, magnanimous act of self-abnegation, immediately picking his successor to assure not even a moment of vacuum or panic among the people of Israel.

Shai Held's theology raises every mitzvah, event, and character to its greatest possibilities. When imbued with such life wisdom, Torah serves as our ennobling guide to good living.

In July 1855 the American essayist and poet Ralph Waldo Emerson received an about-to-be published book, titled "Leaves of Grass," from a then unknown poet, Walt Whitman. I am not a public intellectual, as Emerson was; nor is Shai Held unknown. Nevertheless, I quote from Emerson's fan-letter response to Whitman, because it so captures my feelings upon reading *The Heart of Torah*: "I am very happy on reading it, as great power makes us happy. . . . I give you joy of your free and brave thought. I have great joy in it. I find incomparable things said incomparably well. . . . I greet you at the beginning of a great career."

Shai Held has already established himself as an important theologian with his book *Abraham Joshua Heschel: The Call of Transcendence*, a spiritually rich and profound treatment of Heschel's theology. Now *The Heart of Torah* makes clear that Held's own theology is a treasure trove for this age. He will undoubtedly publish more work directly expositing his own thought. I feel further joy knowing that his humane, human, spiritual, and ethical understanding of Judaism will light the path of Jewry in the generation to come. Echoing Emerson I say: If you know my work or trust my judgment, take this book into your life. Read it, absorb it, and share it. It will help you become a more compassionate parent and person, a wiser leader and follower, a more discerning friend and coworker, a better *mentsch*.

Acknowledgments

R. Yitz Greenberg has been a revered teacher, trusted mentor, and cherished friend for more than two decades. His theological vision has deeply influenced the way I think, the way I read texts, and the way I understand my work in the world. I am grateful to Yitz for his Torah, and for penning such a generous foreword to these volumes.

Professor Jon Levenson has likewise long been a teacher, mentor, and friend. His scholarship on Tanakh is consistently bold, insightful, and religiously alive; I can only hope that some small part of his gift for reading texts has rubbed off on me. On so many levels, I am profoundly in his debt.

In building Mechon Hadar with me, Elie Kaunfer, Ethan Tucker, and Avital Hochstein have been nothing less than partners in a dream. In ten short years, Mechon Hadar has gone from an overly bold idea to a major center for Jewish education and Jewish ideas with a national and international reach. Elie, Ethan, and Avital have been steadfast supporters of my work; my life and my career have been immeasurably enriched by their vision, their friendship, and their example.

Andrew Belinfante has the unenviable task of translating many of my half-cooked ideas into real-life programs, which he consistently does with both grace and aplomb; Rebecca Cushman helps manage my workload with dedication, efficiency, and genuine good-heartedness. To them, and to the entire faculty and staff at Mechon Hadar: Thank you for everything you do, and for everything you are.

Elie Kaunfer, Jon Lopatin, and Jeremy Tabick read just about every one of these essays in draft—sometimes multiple times. Their criticisms, suggestions, and requests for clarification have made this a far richer and more readable work. Jeremy also prepared the essays for their first, online publication each week, always with great skill and good cheer. Gabriel Seed has been an industrious research assistant for many years now; his patience with my endless stream of requests is remarkable. Together with Joel Goldstein and Nina Kretemer, he also patiently prepared the bibliography. Elie, Jon, Jeremy, and Gabe each have a real share in this book, and I am deeply indebted to them.

Jeffrey Wechselblatt read and commented on several of these essays in draft form and offered both warm encouragement and productive criticism. For that, and for much else besides, I am in his debt.

With her characteristic diligence and grace, Maya Rosen checked to ensure that references to classical sources were correct. She saved me from countless errors, and I am extraordinarily appreciative.

I am extremely grateful to the thousands of people who read these essays week after week; knowing that they were out there inspired me to work harder, to think more deeply, and to write more passionately and more clearly. To them, and to those who took the trouble to write with questions, comments, or rejoinders: Thank you.

R. Barry Schwartz, director of the Jewish Publication Society, believed in this work from the very beginning. Carol Hupping and Joy Weinberg, former and current managing editors, shepherded the volumes to publication with warmth, *mentschlichkeit*, and exquisite attention to detail. To them, and to the University of Nebraska Press, and especially to Sabrina Stellrecht, my sincerest thanks.

My late father, Moshe Held, was a renowned Bible scholar. In the twelve short years we had together, I had the privilege of watching him pore over texts with great passion and exquisite care. Though his method of reading and mine are miles apart, I have no doubt that he'd have appreciated how deeply his love of Torah affected me and shaped me. I am only sorry he will never hold this book, or any of my books, in his hands.

My children, Lev Moshe, Maya Aviva, and Yaakov (Coby) Carmel Zvi, are my treasures. Their playfulness, their zest for life, their incessant questioning, their kindness, and their gentleness of spirit are wonders to behold each day. I only hope that the words contained here will one day touch their beautiful souls.

Rachel has been my love, my partner, and my rock for almost a decade now. Sharing a life and a home with her has been my life's greatest blessing. This book, like so much else, is for her.

A Note on Translations

In presenting translations of biblical verses, my default position has been to cite the NJPS translation. However, for accuracy and felicity of expression, I have also regularly consulted the NIV, NRSV, and Alter translations and have at times followed their renderings; in addition, some translations are my own. On Deuteronomy I have also benefitted from the translations of Richard Nelson in *Deuteronomy: A Commentary*. Occasionally, in order to render a Rabbinic interpretation more comprehensible, I have translated verses in accordance with traditional Rabbinic readings.

Introduction

"O how I love Your Torah," declares the psalmist; "I meditate upon it all day long" (Ps. 119:97). "Were not your Torah my delight," he adds, "I would have perished in my affliction" (119:92).

I begin with these words from the psalmist because they give powerful voice to the enchantments of learning and teaching Torah. Writing the essays that make up these two volumes has been a labor of abiding love; it would be impossible for me to convey the joy and delight I took in producing them week after week. I pray that my love for Torah is evident in these essays; more than that, I pray that this love is contagious.

Readers will undoubtedly come to these volumes with very different assumptions and convictions about the origins of Torah and about what it means to affirm—or, for that matter, to deny—that the Torah comes from heaven (*Torah min ha-shamayim*). Ultimately I am in agreement with R. Abraham Joshua Heschel (1907–72), who taught that "more decisive than *the origin of the Bible in God* is *the presence of God in the Bible*."[1] Or, as he puts it elsewhere, "the way to faith in the 'Torah from Heaven' (*Torah min ha-shamayim*) is the preparation of the heart to perceive the heavenly in the Torah (*shamayim min ha-torah*). Such a perception may be momentary; it may happen in the mere blink of an eye. But all of life is scarcely worth that momentary gift of heaven."[2] I hope that readers may now and again catch a glimpse of heaven as they read, as I was blessed to catch them as I wrote.

Many years ago I heard R. Levi Lauer say that one of the greatest contributions the Jewish people have made to civilization is the gift of the close reading. And indeed, Jews have traditionally displayed their love of Torah, and in turn deepened it, by reading texts with exquisite care and attention to detail. In writing these essays, I did not start out with an agenda, deciding what I wanted to say and then searching for a peg on which to hang a predetermined idea. Instead I tried to listen to the text, and to the history of its interpretation, and to see what emerged from the encounter. (Of course what emerged was no doubt shaped at least in part by my own interests and predilections.) Each of these essays thus stands alone, independent of the others. And yet, not surprisingly, certain key themes, fundamental to Torah and to my own religious vision, emerge again and again.

II

Biblical texts tell a story about a God who loves. The covenant between God and the Jewish people is, in part, a love affair — a stormy, tempestuous love affair, to be sure, but a love affair nonetheless. God is frequently exasperated by the people's recalcitrance and by their ceaseless turning to idols, but though tempted at times to abandon them, God always welcomes them back. The prophet Hosea makes the stunning claim that God does not abandon the people because, given the depth of God's love, God simply *cannot* abandon them.[3] And so, whenever there is devastation in Israel, whenever the covenant seems in danger of final rupture . . . there is always also hope, because underneath all of God's interactions with the people lies God's unfathomable and inexhaustible love.

God loves before God commands.[4] As the evening liturgy puts it, "With everlasting love have You loved Your people, the house of Israel. You have taught us Torah and mitzvot." The priority of love over commandment is subtly but powerfully conveyed by God's instructions that Aaron place a jar of manna before the ark even before the Ten Commandments are revealed at Sinai (Exod. 16:32–34): "Before the ark receives the tablets, it receives the jar. That is, in terms of the ark's contents, Scripture first tells us about a God of manna before it tells us about a God of mandates, a God who graciously provides before a God who lays down the law."[5] God wants Israel to know God's love before it learns God's will.

But the Torah worries that Israel will misinterpret God's love. First, the people might think that God loves them because of their own merit, thus opening the door to arrogance and a superiority complex. So the

Torah tells them that they did nothing to earn God's love;[6] divine love is a function of grace rather than merit.[7] Second, the people might imagine that God's love gives them a moral blank check: If God loves us, they might think, then we can do whatever we want. So the prophet Amos shocks them with his insistence that "Israel's great privilege of election by God . . . exposes them to judgment rather than exempting them from it."[8] Finally, the people might assume that God's unique love for them means that God is indifferent to the fate of other peoples. So the Torah emphasizes God's deep concern for a lone Egyptian slave suffering at the hands of an Israelite master,[9] and it carefully reminds us that "other communities from the seed of Abraham have been kept by [God's] providence; other communities have been given place to live by [God]."[10]

God's love is closely entwined with God's mercy, without which the world could not endure: The Torah presents the continued existence of humanity in the wake of the flood as a manifestation of divine mercy.[11] Similarly, Israel's sins are forgiven again and again because of God's great mercy. The book of Jonah goes even further, forcefully insisting that God's mercy extends even to the least righteous of peoples. It is, for many of us, a difficult lesson to absorb: God's love may extend even to people we (perhaps legitimately) cannot stand.[12] So vast are God's love and mercy that, according to at least one arresting midrashic passage, not even biblical texts can fully comprehend or contain it.[13] To worship the God of Israel is to worship a God of love and mercy—and thus, as I will suggest later on, to commit to interpreting Torah accordingly.

The God of love is also a God of life.[14] The foundational narrative of the Jewish people tells the story of a cruel tyrant at war with the forces of life itself: Just as God's blessings of fruitfulness begin to be realized among the Israelites, Pharaoh sets out to undermine them (Exod. 1:8–22). The early chapters of the book of Exodus thus tell the story of Pharaoh, eager to thwart life ("pen yirbeh," lest Israel grow—1:10), at war with God, committed to affirming it ("ken yirbeh," the more Israel grew—1:12).[15] Tanakh is in part the story of God's struggle to subdue the forces of chaos, both cosmic and historical, so that human life can flourish. One of the most remarkable—and for some traditional believers, one of the most surprising—aspects of Tanakh is its willingness to confront the painful, and at times unbearable, reality that the forces of chaos have not yet been firmly and finally defeated. Yet the prophets insist that the cosmic victory of order over chaos will one day come.[16]

God's commitment to life is thoroughly entwined with God's affirmation of human dignity. The trajectory of Exodus is unmistakable. When the book begins, the people are enslaved to a merciless despot who refuses to grant them even a moment's respite (Exod. 5:5); when it ends they are serving the God of creation and covenant, who mandates and regularizes periods of rest (35:2). The mitzvah of Shabbat thus helps move the people from "perverted work, designed by Pharaoh to destroy God's people ... [to] divinely mandated work, designed to bring together God and God's people, in the closest proximity possible in this life."[17] God rejects servility: whereas "Pharaoh places the Israelites under a backbreaking and soul-crushing yoke ... God invites them to stand tall."[18]

From the perspective of Jewish ethics, there are few (if any) graver crimes than violating the dignity of another human being. "In hurting another person I am not just running afoul of the will of God—though I am also surely doing that. At some level, I am also assaulting God, who, Jewish theology insists, is profoundly invested in the dignity of God's creatures."[19] Conversely, as R. Abraham Paley (twentieth century) teaches, "being careful with and attentive to the honor of your fellow is the acceptance of the yoke of the kingdom of heaven."[20] The Musar master R. Yeruham Levovitz (1873–1936) explains that "one who honors people honors God, literally (*mamash*) ... [because] the honor of the image of God is the honor of God, literally."[21]

Affirming the dignity of every human being we encounter is foundational to Jewish ethics, but the Torah pays especial attention to preserving the dignity of the vulnerable. Thus, for example, the special charge not to "insult the deaf or place a stumbling block before the blind" (Lev. 19:14) works to rein in "the temptation to see people with disabilities (and, perhaps, the vulnerable more generally) as less human than 'we,' and therefore as less deserving of dignity and protection."[22]

Deuteronomy makes a startling claim about God: "For the Lord your God is God supreme and Lord supreme, the great, the mighty and awesome God, who shows no favor and takes no bribe, but upholds the cause of the fatherless and the widow, and loves the stranger, providing him with food and clothing" (Deut. 10:17–18). Note well: God's greatness, mightiness, and awesomeness consist not of God's having created the world, nor of God's having demonstrated God's power to destroy hateful enemies. God's greatness consists, rather, in God's fairness—in the fact that God "shows no favor and takes no bribe"—and in God's love for the vulnerable and downtrodden. God actively loves those whom society tends to abuse and demean.

The God of Torah is the God of the oppressed, the God who remembers the abandoned and sees those whom others neglect. Thus, for example, though Abraham and Sarah treat Hagar as a nameless servant, a womb without her own identity as a person, the very first word the angel of God utters when he finds her in the wilderness is her name: "Hagar" (Gen. 16:8). Though Abraham and Sarah may not see it, God affirms that, like all of us, Hagar is a human being. Not surprisingly, Hagar in turn names God "El-Ro'i, the "God of seeing," or the "God who sees me" (16:13).[23]

God's concern for the forgotten extends to the political realm as well: The God of Israel will not tolerate the oppression of widows and orphans. The Torah minces no words: Those who exploit the powerless will incur the wrath of God. As parashat Mishpatim warns, "You shall not oppress any widow or orphan. If you do oppress them, I will hear their outcry as soon as they cry out to Me, and My anger shall blaze forth and I will put you to the sword, and your own wives shall become widows and your children orphans" (Exod. 22:21–23). As I've written, "Just as God is moved to respond by the suffering inflicted *upon* Israel, so also is God moved to respond by the suffering inflicted *by* Israel." The God of human dignity summons Israel to build an alternative to Egypt, "a society in which the weak and defenseless are protected rather than exploited, loved rather than degraded."[24]

Marching through the desert, the Israelites are beset by anxiety:

"Is the Lord present among us or not?" (Exod. 17:7). Exodus, and the Torah as a whole, answer with a resounding yes: God is with the people, accompanying them on their journey.[25]

But God's closeness has its dangers, and the Torah insists that even as God is present, God remains, always, transcendent. The yearning to be close to God is arguably fundamental to God-centered religion, but it is also fraught with peril, since "consciously or not, people all too often try to domesticate God, to reduce God to something they can comprehend, predict, and even control."[26] Lest our theology "deteriorate into a cozy over-familiarity,"[27] the Torah reminds us again and again that human temptations (or illusions) notwithstanding, God cannot be possessed or manipulated. God is loving and present, but God is still God.

III

If Jewish theology is grounded in God's love, it is equally focused on human responsibility.

In most ancient Near Eastern myths, human culture is a gift from the gods; in the Torah, in stark contrast, "early humans develop their own culture. The human being, a creature created by God, is the initiator and creator of its own culture."[28] From the earliest chapters of Genesis,[29] human agency is given a privileged place in Jewish theology. Even when God liberates the Israelite slaves from slavery amid a miraculous display of divine power and sovereignty, God summons the people to reject passivity and to learn to act on their own behalf.[30] Human beings are thus asked to play a major role in shaping the world and their own lives within it.

With agency comes responsibility. According to the dominant strand in biblical scholarship, this is what it means for human beings to be created in the image of God: We are God's "vice-regents" and "earthly delegates,"[31] appointed by God to rule God's creation in ways that enable it to flourish and thrive.[32] We are responsible for the world, but we are also responsible — and accountable — for our own actions. For the talmudic sages, "to be human is to be accountable. In contrast to (other) animals, the Mishnah teaches, human beings are always held responsible for our actions" (Mishnah, Bava Kamma 2:6). When Jacob deceives his father and devastates his brother, he pays for his actions for the rest of his life.[33] His mother Rebekah, who hatches the devious plan that she and her son enact, is likewise punished severely.[34] Jacob and Rebekah have reasons for what they do: "It is God who loves Jacob and wants him to be heir of the covenant; perhaps Jacob believes he is only effecting God's will." But the Torah is emphatic: "Sacred ends do not justify crooked means."[35]

We are also responsible, the Torah insists, for one another. Cain may be right that he is not intended to be his brother's "keeper"—in Tanakh, it is God who is people's keeper—but he is intended to be something else: his brother's brother.[36] This is a lesson and a mandate many of us struggle to internalize—and when we do internalize it, we often do so only sporadically and erratically. In the face of all our hemming and hawing, all our evading and looking away, the Torah presses: "The meaning of human freedom is not that we can decide whether or not we are responsible for others; the meaning of human freedom is that we can decide whether or not to live up to that responsibility."[37]

In one of the Torah's most dramatic moments, God teaches Abraham to speak out in the face of injustice—even when he thinks that the perpetrator is God (Gen. 18:16–33). Crucially, God wants Abraham to "instruct his children and his posterity to keep the way of the Lord by doing what is just and right" (18:19). In mentioning Abraham's descendants, the Torah emphasizes that "it is not just prophets who must step forward; what is true of Abraham and Moses ought to be true of us as well."[38] To be part of the Jewish tradition is to "argue for justice and plead for mercy. If, following Abraham's example, Jews are asked to argue with God, how much the more so are we called to speak up in the face of human injustice."[39] R. Abraham Ibn Ezra (1089–1167) takes this to a daunting extreme: One who witnesses oppression and says nothing, he insists, will meet the same fate as the oppressor himself (shorter commentary to Exod. 22:20–22). According to Jewish ethics, then, "in a society where some are oppressed, all are implicated. There are no innocent bystanders."[40]

The Torah places great weight on human responsibility, but it harbors no illusions about human nature. This is most powerfully—and tragically—evoked by the book of Numbers: What begins as a story about a people perfectly committed to enacting the will of God (Numbers 1–10) quickly devolves into "a dreadful tale of distrust, disloyalty, disappointment, and, ultimately, death." Just as the next stage of redemption appears on the horizon, human fear, stubbornness, and recalcitrance carry the day (Numbers 11–25). Numbers introduces a sober—even a somber—note to Jewish theology: "For all its centrality in Jewish thought and spirituality, change is extremely—and sometimes excruciatingly—hard to achieve."[41]

From its very beginnings, the Torah subtly warns us against Pollyannaish notions of moral progress: The same man who invented cities, we learn, also invented murder.[42] Cultural progress is often coupled with moral deterioration (Gen. 4:17–26): Where Cain succumbs to moral failure, his descendant Lemekh positively exults in it (Gen. 4:23–24).

According to Jewish theology, God believes in our ability to renew ourselves, and to make real and deep contributions to realizing a more just, decent, and compassionate world. Participating in those grand visions, in fact, is a large part of what it means to be human. But we are all also asked to live with our eyes open, in full view of just how complicated both we and the world are, and thus of how hard and elusive moral progress really is. We can and must improve ourselves, but we cannot perfect ourselves. We can and must improve the world, but we cannot perfect it. That's part of what it means to wait for the Messiah rather than pretend that we *are* the Messiah.[43]

None of this should be taken as an excuse for despair. Even in the face of failure and heartbreak, there is always the possibility of working, and building, and repairing. In more traditional Jewish language, the door to *teshuvah* (repentance, return) always remains open. Clear-eyed as it is about the limits of human nature, even Numbers refuses to let tragedy have the final word. In the final eleven chapters of the book, a new generation emerges, and with it new hope and possibility. Between naïveté and fatalism lies the possibility of covenantal living:

a commitment to serving God, and when that fails, a commitment to getting up and trying again.

IV

Herein lies the audacity of Jewish theology: Despite how stubborn we are, God enlists us as God's partners; despite how easily seduced we are by vanity and idolatry, God demands that we cast away our false gods; despite how callous we are to other people's suffering, God beckons us to care for the hurting and the aggrieved. To embrace the covenant between God and Israel is to be summoned to embody the good and the holy.

The Torah lays out a blueprint for what such a life ought to look like. Pivotally, what we find in Torah is not privatized religion but a social vision, not ascetic distancing from the world but a deep engagement with, and enmeshment in, the messy realities of living together day in and day out. Reading of Moses's unprecedented encounter with God on Mount Sinai, we perhaps expect him to return with an ethereal vision for how earthly angels ought to worship their Creator. But instead we find this: "When a man's ox injures his neighbor's ox and it dies" (Exod. 21:35). To be sure, Moses does instruct the people in how to worship God, but he also teaches them torts, because biblical religion is, to a great extent, about learning to live with others.

The Torah's vision extends to politics and economics as well. The Israelites are called to build a society in which the weak are protected from those who would prey on them;[44] in which poverty is "robbed of its tyrannical power";[45] and in which the people see one another, across lines of wealth, prestige, and status, as family.[46] Israel's fidelity to Torah will be measured, in large part, by the kind of society, and by the kinds of social relations, it creates.

Ultimately, the character of Israel's life is intended to reflect the character of the God it worships. In other words, who God is has implications for who we are intended—and summoned—to be. After telling us that God loves the stranger, Deuteronomy immediately declares: "You too must love the stranger (*ger*), for you were strangers in the land of Egypt" (Deut. 10:18–19). Subtly but powerfully Deuteronomy issues a call to *imitatio dei*, the imitation of God: God loves the stranger, so we must too. We must love the stranger because of what we ourselves have been through, but also because of who God is. If you want to love God, the Torah teaches, love those whom God loves—the widow, the orphan, and the stranger.[47]

Loving the stranger is part of the broader ethos Torah seeks to instill: a commitment to kindness.[48] When all is said and done, religion is, in large part, about softening our hearts[49] and learning to care, about cultivating generosity and an eagerness to share one's bounty.[50] As the talmudic sage R. Simlai notes, "The Torah begins with an act of lovingkindness (*gemilut hasadim*) and ends with an act of lovingkindness" (BT, Sotah 14a). The heart of Torah is *hesed*—love and kindness.

Concrete actions are necessary but not sufficient; Torah also makes a claim on our inner lives. The focus of Jewish ethics is on both conduct and character. As Ibn Ezra forcefully avers, "the main purpose of the all the commandments is to straighten the heart" (commentary to Deuteronomy 5). To take what may well be the most important example: Called to a life of *hesed*, we are asked both to behave in compassionate ways and to cultivate compassionate character. The two are mutually reinforcing. Ideally, "compassionate character yields compassionate behavior, which in turn deepens compassionate character, and so on in a virtuous cycle."[51]

Covenantal living involves both action and emotion: Loved by God, we are asked to love God in return. More than that, we are asked to love those whom God loves: the neighbor and the stranger. The essence of Torah is a God of love and kindness who calls Israel to love and kindness.

V

Judaism dreams of a world in which human dignity is real and the presence of God is manifest. And yet the world as we know it all too often makes a mockery of that dream: Human dignity is trodden and trampled upon in countless ways, and God seems far away, absent, even nonexistent. How do we go on hoping in a seemingly hopeless world? Torah offers a series of answers: Once a week Jews undertake the radical experiment of living in the redeemed future right now. Shabbat offers us an anticipatory glimpse of another reality. Religion offers us "another world to live in"[52] and thereby transforms our experience of this one. Through the experience of Shabbat "human dignity becomes a little bit more real, the presence of God becomes a little bit more manifest, and Judaism's dream gains in both vitality and plausibility."[53]

Although entering its precincts is now possible only as an act of the imagination, the *mishkan* (tabernacle) functions in much the same way: In a world overrun by chaos, the *mishkan* serves as an island of perfect order in which God's will is obeyed fully and perfectly. Worship in the *mishkan* is thus "intended [as] a counterworld to Israel's lived experience, which is dangerous and disordered. The counterworld offered in the tabernacle holds out the gift of a well-ordered, joy-filled, and peace-generating creation."[54] Experiencing Shabbat, or entering the *mishkan*, we discern that another reality is possible; we understand that appearances notwithstanding, suffering and chaos are not ultimately all there is.[55]

VI

In writing these essays, I have not shied away from admitting when texts seem morally or theologically disturbing. Thus, for example, I ask how the Torah, which usually challenges us to overcome our fears and visit the sick, can stigmatize the *metzora* (one afflicted with a scaly skin disease) and bar him from the camp;[56] I consider the distressing possibility that, from a modern perspective at least, the Torah might sanction marital rape of a captive bride (Deut. 21:10–14);[57] and I probe the question of how the Torah can extend beyond abhoring Amalek's inhumanity to condemning all Amalekites, present and future, as eternal enemies of God.[58] I cannot offer easy answers where none are available. My concern is less with defending the Torah than with understanding it, and wrestling with it.

But in every instance, I have chosen to read as humanely as possible. So I suggest ways that even troubling texts can be understood to teach compassion,[59] and to mandate soul searching and introspection.[60] I read this way not to engage in apologetics but because I believe that this is a mandate derived from Torah itself. Writing in 1945, the religious Zionist leader Moshe Unna (1902–89) insisted that Jewish educators strive to instill "Jewish humanism" in their students. Jewish humanism, he taught, "is humanism with a Jewish character, which springs from Jewish feeling and is learned from our Torah." According to Unna, "there is a need to emphasize the word 'humanism'; it is not enough just to state 'according to the Torah,' for from the Torah one can learn many different things. . . . One can even learn from it an obligation to engage in terror. . . . The word 'humanism' serves to explain and clarify on the basis of which values, of the many found in our literature, we seek to establish Jewish education."[61] Unna frankly admits that sacred texts can be marshaled to sanction cruelty and inhumanity and places the burden on the interpreter to choose another path. Whether we admit it or not, all interpreters of Torah choose to read some texts in light of others; the question is not *whether they have interpretive principles* but rather *which interpretive principles they have.* My own readings reflect my belief in a God who prioritizes the ethical[62] and by Rabbinic tradition's own claim that love of neighbor and affirmation of every human being as an image of God are the "great principles of the Torah" (PT, Nedarm 9:4).

In a similar vein, I have tried to read the stories of the Patriarchs and Matriarchs honestly. As many talmudic sages and medieval commentators readily acknowledge, the Torah presents them in all their complexity, with both heroic strengths[63] and all-too-human weaknesses.[64] I would emphasize that their imperfection is of great theological significance, because it suggests that God, the Creator of Heaven and Earth, chooses to enter into relationship not with ministering angels but with flesh-and-blood human beings. One of the crucial implications of this is that God can use any of us, even the most flawed among us, to accomplish God's ends.[65]

Explaining his decision to quote liberally both from traditional Rabbinic sources and from Greek and Arabic philosophers, Maimonides (Rambam, 1135–1204) establishes one of the pillars of his approach to life and learning: "Accept the truth from wherever it comes" (foreword to the Eight Chapters). Accordingly, in attempting to understand and interpret biblical texts, I have cast a very wide net, appealing to talmudic sages and medieval commentators, and also to modern academic scholars, both Jewish and Christian. I have found it enormously fruitful to have Rashi talk to Patrick Miller, Ibn Ezra to Terence Fretheim, and R. Akiva to Jacob Milgrom. I do not pursue eclecticism for its own sake, but time and again I have found that by examining a wide range of commentaries from a broad array of contexts, I understand texts better and more clearly.

So, too, I bring together literary, psychological, and philosophical-theological approaches to Torah. I focus not just on *what* texts say but also on *how* they say it, and in particular on how biblical texts talk to one another. I attempt to understand how texts address the complexity and intractability of the human spirit. And I ask, always, what the text intends to say about God—and by extension, about what it means to live life in service of that God.

This book of collected essays is called *The Heart of Torah*. My hope is to get at the very heart of the Torah's vision of God, Israel, and humanity; and to make the point, sadly neglected in many popular presentations of Judaism, that "the Merciful One desires the heart."

Jews have been reading and rereading the Torah for thousands of years. I regard it as an immense privilege to be able to read the same texts as countless generations before me have read, and to contribute a link, however small, to a sacred chain of interpretation. I pray that my readers will find in these essays ideas to challenge and inspire them, spiritual sustenance to nourish them, and provocations to unsettle them.

יִהְיוּ לְרָצוֹן אִמְרֵי־פִי, וְהֶגְיוֹן לִבִּי לְפָנֶיךָ:
יְהֹוָה, צוּרִי וְגֹאֲלִי.

"May the words of mouth and the integrity of my heart be acceptable to You, O Lord, my Rock and my Redeemer" (Ps. 19:14).

The Heart of Torah, VOLUME 1

GENESIS

Bere'shit #1

What Can Human Beings Do, and What Can't They?
Or, Does the Torah Believe in Progress?

What can human beings accomplish in the world? According to the Torah, an awful lot. But not quite as much as many myths of human progress would have us believe.

According to a variety of ancient myths, culture and civilization were gifts from the gods. Human beings were seen as recipients, not initiators, of skills like agriculture, animal husbandry, and the ability to build cities. In the myths of Mesopotamia, for example, the basic institutions of civilization were all founded by mythical, semidivine beings; Bible scholar Tikva Frymer-Kensky explains that according to these stories, "humanity did not develop any aspect of human culture."[1] Another scholar adds that "in the ancient Mesopotamian view every aspect of human society was decreed by the gods. . . . Everything in the universe, material or immaterial, human or divine, was laid down by decree."[2]

The Torah's understanding is totally different. Cain, we are told, was the first to build a city (Gen. 4:17). Several generations later, three brothers, descendants of Cain, also make major contributions to civilization. Yaval, we learn, invented the herding of livestock; Yuval invented music; Tuval-Cain invented metallurgy (4:20–22). In a brief genealogy of Cain's brother Seth, we learn of Enosh, who introduced the worship of God (4:26). Later we will discover that Noah planted the first vineyard (9:20) and that Nimrod became the first hunter and empire builder (10:8–10).

Where the origins of culture are concerned, there is an enormous chasm between Genesis and many ancient myths. "In ancient Near East myths," Frymer-Kensky writes, "the gods provide humanity with all the essentials of human civilization. By contrast, in the Bible, early humans develop their own culture. The human being, a creature created by God, is the initiator and creator of its own culture."[3]

But as much as it takes human initiative seriously, Genesis hardly advocates a simpleminded celebration of human cultural or technological progress. As always the biblical text is far more subtle than a simple surface reading might lead us to believe. On the one hand, as we've just seen, Genesis emphasizes that the foundations of human culture and civilization are the products of human discovery and ingenuity. But attributing these developments to people of such dubious origins as Cain and his descendants may be the Torah's way of reminding us that technological advancement and moral progress are two very different things. (After the horrors of the twentieth century, we shouldn't need any more reminders of that sad and sobering fact.) What better way to dismiss naive faith in progress than to inform us that the man who invented cities also invented murder? "What becomes clear from the primeval history," a contemporary scholar writes, "is that the cultural achievements of the human race testify not only to a God-given human power and agency, but also to the possibility of using that power/agency to accomplish evil. Specifically, the culture that humans develop is profoundly intertwined with violence."[4]

Genesis pulls the cord at both ends. On the one hand, the Torah makes a tremendous amount of space for human initiative and achievement. On the other hand, it implies that we should pay careful attention to where this story of ostensible progress ends up. We learn about Lemekh—father of Yaval, Yuval, and Tuval-Cain—who seems to rejoice in his own capacity for violence. Lemekh speaks words to his wives that are notoriously difficult to understand, but one widely accepted possibility is that he is boasting: "I have slain a man for wounding me, a lad for bruising me. If Cain is avenged sevenfold, then Lemekh seventy-sevenfold" (Gen. 4:23–24).

What has happened over the course of these seven generations, then, is that technology has progressed, but so too has the human propensity toward violence. Not only is Lemekh violent, but he celebrates his barbarity, gloating over the fact that he has killed a boy merely for wounding him. Bible scholar Derek Kidner explains: "Cain's family is a microcosm: its pattern of technical prowess and moral failure is that of humanity. . . . Lemekh's taunt song reveals the swift progress of sin. Where Cain had succumbed to it (4:7), Lemekh exults in it; where Cain had sought protection (4:14–15), Lemekh looks round for provocation: the savage disproportion of killing a mere lad for a mere wound is the whole point of his boast."[5]

All this is extremely relevant for understanding the much maligned biblical law of *talion*, or "an eye for an eye." According to Exodus, if an injury takes place during a violent confrontation, "the penalty shall be life for life, eye for eye, tooth for tooth, hand for hand, foot for foot, burn for burn, wound for wound, bruise for bruise" (Exod. 21:23–25). Popular misconceptions notwithstanding, the point of the law was decidedly not to encourage violence, but rather to dramatically restrict it; it was an attempt to introduce a degree of equity into otherwise unrestrained blood feuds, "as if to say, '*Only* an eye for an eye, *only* a wound for a wound.'"[6]

How do we know this? Note the two final clauses in the law, "[Only] a wound for a wound, [only] a bruise for a bruise" and compare them to Lemekh's crude swagger: "I have slain a man for wounding me, a lad for bruising me." Not coincidentally, the key words in each are the same—"wound" (*petza*) and "bruise" (*haburah*)—suggesting that the law of *talion* is an attempt to set limits on the kind of savage behavior exemplified by Lemekh. So far from advocating the taking of an eye for an eye, the Torah is actually limiting what can be taken, and thus attempting to place a bridle on the culture of brutality and barbarism.

Historians and philosophers never tire of arguing about human progress. Speaking of notions like equal rights and free speech, linguist Steven Pinker lauds what he sees as "radical breaks with the sensibilities of the past." Political philosopher John Gray, in contrast, insists that "outside of science, progress is simply a myth." Moral achievements are tenuous and tentative, always subject to setback and reversal. What is the Torah's view of all this? At the very least, I think, Genesis wants to disabuse of us of Pollyanna notions about progress. Seven generations of achievement have passed since Cain's killing of his brother, and yet, Lemekh teaches us, people are more bloodthirsty, not less. Progress in civilization and progress in cruelty are manifestly not mutually exclusive. People can adore Mozart even as they murder innocent children.

The Torah asks us to embrace complexity, and to reject one-dimensional understandings of human potential. On the one hand, people are given awesome responsibility: We are asked to give shape to our own lives; are summoned to work for the flourishing of all creation; are given vast room to create and develop culture and civilization; and are beckoned by God to participate in building the kind of world God dreams of. And yet God is anything but naive, and the Bible does not hold inane ideas about human progress or an inherent goodness of humanity. The Jewish view is neither that human beings are inherently good nor that we are inherently bad. The Jewish view is that human beings are inherently complicated, pulled in many directions at once, capable of breathtaking kindness as well as horrific cruelty and staggering indifference.

Jewish thought steers a course between two equally simplistic conceptions of human nature. It refuses to assume that people are so irredeemably sinful that we're incapable of accomplishing anything, but it just as passionately dismisses the fantasy that we are so good-natured at heart that if we just held hands and swayed lovingly, human life would be perfect, and lions and lambs would lie down together.

Judaism's view is that we are called to be world builders; God believes in our ability to renew ourselves, and to make real and deep contributions to realizing a more just, decent, and compassionate world. Participating in those grand visions, in fact, is a large part of what it means to be human. But we are all also asked to live with our eyes open, in full view of just how complicated both we and the world are, and thus of how hard and elusive moral progress really is. We can and must improve ourselves; but we cannot perfect ourselves. We can and must improve the world, but we cannot perfect it. That's part of what it means to wait for the Messiah rather than pretend that we *are* the Messiah. But waiting for the Messiah is not an excuse for fatalism or despair. On the contrary we wait by working, and building, and dedicating our lives to causes and realities greater than ourselves.

Bere'shit #2

Created in God's Image

Ruling for God

Genesis famously tells us that human beings are created in the image of God (Gen. 1:26–27). But surprisingly it does not tell us what this means. Both Jewish and Christian commentators have offered an array of interpretations, often seeking to identify a particular human quality as the image of God within us. For Maimonides (1135–1204), for example, the image of God is reason (*Guide of the Perplexed*, 1:1); for R. Meir Simha of Dvinsk (1843–1926), it is free will (*Meshekh Hokhmah* to Gen. 1:26,31); for R. Eliyahu Dessler (1892–1953), it is the capacity to give freely and generously.[7] And yet fascinating as many of these interpretations are—if nothing else they tell us what aspect of human being Jewish thinkers tend to hold most sacred—there is nothing in the Torah itself to support them. So what does the Torah mean when it tells us that we are created in God's image?

Among Bible scholars one of the most common interpretations is that being created in the image of God means being given the special role of "representing . . . God's rule in the world."[8] The Torah's view is that people are God's "vice-regents" and "earthly delegates,"[9] appointed by God to rule over the world. One traditional Jewish commentator, R. Saadia Gaon (882–942), anticipated this understanding of Genesis, arguing that being created in the image of God means being assigned to rule over creation (Saadia Gaon, commentary to Gen. 1:26).

The ancient Near Eastern context sheds remarkable light on the audacity of the Torah's message. In the ancient world, various kings (and sometimes priests) were described as the images of a god.[10] It is the king who is God's representative or intermediary on earth, and it is he who mediates God's blessings to the world.[11] In dramatic contrast to this, the Torah asserts that ordinary human beings—not just kings, but each and every one of us—are mediators of divine blessing. "The entire race collectively stands vis-à-vis God in the same relationship of chosenness and protection that characterizes the god-king relationship in the more ancient civilizations of the Near East."[12] Genesis 1 thus represents a radical democratization of ancient Near Eastern royal ideology. We are, the Torah insists, all kings and queens.[13]

The Torah's assertion that every human being is created in the image of God is a repudiation of the idea, so common in the ancient world, that some people are simply meant to rule over others. If everyone is royalty, then on some level, when it comes to the interpersonal and political spheres, no one is.

Assigned the role of God's delegates, human beings are told to "be fertile and increase, fill the earth and master it . . . rule the fish of the sea, the birds of the sky, and all the living things that creep on the earth" (Gen. 1:28).[14] The mandate expressed here has been the subject of enormous controversy: Some environmentalists have placed the blame for the modern West's despoliation of the earth squarely at the Bible's feet. Thus, for example, one influential writer charges that according to Christian (and by implication, Jewish) thinking, "God planned all of this explicitly for man's benefit and rule: No item in the physical creation had any purpose save to serve man's purposes." The environmental crisis, he insists, was rooted in religious "arrogance towards nature" and the only solution, therefore, lay in moving beyond these patently damaging and outdated ideas.[15]

But does the Torah really think that creation exists in order to serve humanity, and that that is the only source of its value? Again and again in Genesis 1, as days of Creation come to an end, the text announces that "God saw that it was good" (ki tov) (1:4,10,12,18,21,31). As Maimonides points out, creation is declared good prior to, and separate from, the arrival of human beings onto the scene (Guide of the Perplexed, 3:13). (If anything it is striking that the Torah never describes God looking at human beings in particular and proclaiming them good—perhaps, in the Torah's eyes, where humanity is concerned, the jury is still out.)

What's more, Genesis 1 repeatedly emphasizes and seems to revel in the fact that God created both vegetation and creatures "of every kind." This is true of seed-bearing plants and fruit-bearing trees (1:11); of living creatures of the sea and of birds (1:21); and of wild beasts and cattle (1:25). God blesses the creatures of the sea and the birds of the sky with some of the same words God uses for humanity: "Be fertile and increase and fill" (1:22).[16] Among other things, then, the biblical . . . creation story is like a hymn to biodiversity, which is seen as unambiguously good in its own right.

For the Torah, then, creation is precious in its own right. Humanity is given the task of ruling over it—and yet many of us are uneasy about seeing human beings through the lens of royalty. We think of monarchy as an oppressive institution, and of kings and queens as abusers only too willing to exploit their vulnerable subjects.

But is this how the Tanakh imagines a king ought to behave, and if not, what is the alternative it envisions? Ezekiel reports that the prophet is sent by God to castigate the kings of Israel, who are intended to be like "shepherds" to Israel, but who instead tend only to themselves. "You have not sustained the weak," Ezekiel charges, "healed the sick, or bandaged the injured; you have not brought back the strayed, or looked for the lost; but you have driven them with harsh rigor" (Ezek. 34:1–6). Selfish rulers who do not care for the lost, ill, and vulnerable come in for God's withering disapproval.

Much the same vision of kingship is expressed in Psalm 72, a prayer on behalf of the king. What are the desirable attributes and characteristics of royalty? The king should be blessed with "justice" and "righteousness"; "Let him," prays the psalmist, "champion the lowly among the people, deliver the needy folk, and crush those who wrong them." Let him behave in such a way that "the righteous may flourish in his time, and well-being abound." The king, we learn, "saves the needy who cry out, the lowly who have no helper. He cares about the poor and the needy; he brings the needy deliverance" (Ps. 72:2,4,7,12–13).

If Genesis 1 teaches that human beings are meant to be kings and queens over creation, Ezekiel and the psalmist make abundantly clear what kind of kings and queens we are summoned to be: "The task of a king is to care for those over whom he rules, especially for the weakest and most helpless. . . . This means that humans are expected to care for the earth and its creatures. Such is the responsibility of royalty."[17] What we find in Genesis 1, then, is not a license to abuse and exploit but a summons to nurture and protect.

Human sovereignty over creation is far from absolute; it is God's will for creation, and not our own, that are we are directed to enact. Commenting on Psalm 115's affirmation that "the heavens belong to the Lord, but the earth He gave over to humanity" (115:16), R. Abraham Ibn Ezra (1089–1164) writes: "The ignorant think that humanity's rule over the earth is the same as God's rule over the heavens. But they are mistaken, because God rules over everything. The meaning of 'but the earth He gave over to humanity' is that the human being is God's steward (*pakid*) over the earth and everything that is on it, and she must act according to God's word." Even as kings and queens, we remain servants of God—and thus stewards, not owners.

To take Genesis 1 seriously, we have to be willing to hold two realities together simultaneously. On the one hand, according to the Torah, there is a hierarchy between human beings and animals: Human life takes precedence. As the Christian theologian Michael Welker writes, "We cannot use the justification for letting our neighbors starve the argument that we must first feed the animals in our own house. We cannot let our children be endangered by wild animals. Human beings have primacy over animals. For this reason the language [of dominion in Genesis 1] is completely unambiguous. In no case may an animal be given higher status than a human being."[18]

Yet on the other hand, human primacy comes with enormous responsibility—to be masters over creation in a way that embodies (like Psalm 72's image of the king) responsibility and caretaking. There is no contradiction here, only nuance.

The problem with the notion of human stewardship over creation is not that it authorizes human exploitation of the earth and abuse of the animal kingdom—which, as we have seen, it emphatically does not. The problem is, rather, that we have not really taken it seriously enough to try it. In modern times, amid an almost manic need to produce and consume more and more, we have all too often lost sight of what has been entrusted to us.[19] What we need is not to abandon Genesis 1 but to return to it and to rediscover there what we have forgotten or failed to see altogether. We are created in the image of God and are thus mandated to rule over creation; this is a call to exercise power in the way Tanakh imagines the ideal ruler would, "in obedience to the reign of God and for the sake of all the other creatures whom [our] power affects."[20]

The approach laid out here overcomes one form of anthropocentrism—the crude notion that everything exists for us, and that we are therefore free to consume and dispense with it as we will—while affirming another: In contrast to the rest of creation, human beings are responsible and answerable for our actions.[21] This is another way to understand the democratization of the image of God: Every human being, each and every one of us, is responsible for his or her actions.

Theologian Norman Wirzba captures this point beautifully: "Despite the desire that many have for greater species equality, the fact of the matter is that we are, because of our spiritual endowment or potential and our technological prowess, masters of this earth. The issue is not how we will shed ourselves of our unique potential and responsibility, but how we will transform it for good."[22] We have both enormous responsibility and awesome power. "It is up to us to determine if we will make of ourselves a blessing or a curse."[23]

Noaḥ #1

Before and After the Flood

Or, It All Depends on How You Look

Something very strange happens after the great flood in Noah's day.

Let's look closely at what happens "before" and "after" the storm. Genesis 6 reports that the earth "became corrupt before God" and "filled with lawlessness" (Gen. 6:11). God is disappointed and gives up on humanity: "The Lord saw how great was man's wickedness on earth, and how every plan devised by his heart was nothing but evil all the time" (6:5). The forty-day flood comes, bringing death and devastation in its wake.

Noah emerges from his ark and offers a sacrifice to God, and then things take a very surprising turn. Now that the deluge is over, God seemingly has a change of heart and decides "never again to destroy every living being" (Gen. 8:21). The reason given, though, is baffling: "Never again will I doom the earth because of man, since the devisings of man's heart are evil from his youth" (8:21). Whereas Genesis 6 suggests that God floods the earth because of humanity's sinfulness, Genesis 8 tells us that God commits never to flood the earth again . . . because of humanity's sinfulness. The reason for God sending one flood has now mysteriously become the reason for God *not* sending another.

Some scholars try to wriggle their way out of what seems like a contradiction by translating the Hebrew *ki* as "since" in chapter 6 but as "although" in chapter 8 (yielding "Never again will I doom the earth because of man, although the devisings of man's heart are evil from his youth"). Although this is a plausible rendering of the Hebrew (*ki* can have either meaning, though it usually means "since"), the text is much richer and more interesting if we wrestle with the paradox rather than attempting to dissolve it. How can humanity's problematic nature serve as grounds both for God's harsh judgment and for God's overwhelming mercy?

The text wants us to know that human nature has not changed after the flood—nor, seemingly, will it in any eon we could recognize. What has changed after the flood is not human nature but God's attitude toward it. The very same shortcomings that had called forth doom and denunciation now elicit forbearance and generosity instead. Judgment gives way to mercy, condemnation to compassion. The crucial lesson is that the same attribute that we see as cause for reproach can often serve as a basis for forgiveness as well; this seems to be what God learns after the flood, and, as we shall see, it is something we should learn as well.

The same striking dynamic is at play in God's response to the Israelites after the sin of the Golden Calf. First, God bitterly condemns the Israelites three times for being "stiff-necked" (Exod. 32:9; 33:3,5). But then Moses appeals to God's mercy, and what is the basis of his plea? "Moses hastened to bow low to the ground in homage, and said, 'If I have gained your favor, O Lord, pray, let the Lord go in our midst, since this is a stiff-necked people. Pardon our iniquity and our sin and take us for Your own" (34:8–9). God is now being asked to forgive for the very reason God condemned. Here again, some scholars scramble— the NJPS translation, for example, reads: "Pray, let the Lord go in our midst, even though this is a stiff-necked people."

Here too, though, the simple meaning is that the basis of condemnation is now appealed to as grounds for mercy instead. Whereas until this moment God had denounced, now God forgives. What has changed is not who and what the Israelites are; they remain just as sinful as before. What has changed, rather, is how God views the same persistent human failure. What is true of God's relationship with humanity as a whole is true of God's relationship with the Israelites in particular: If judgment is the only lens through which God sees the world, it has no future (nor should it). But God chooses otherwise, and sees the world through the lens of compassion and forbearance instead.

Imagine someone you know who struggles with impulse control. Some days you are tempted to write her off as totally hopeless, and maybe even to dismiss her as utterly unworthy of your concern or affection. But then there are moments when the very same deep failing elicits something very different in you, and you find yourself viewing her with compassion rather than judgment. Maybe the fact that she doesn't seem able to control herself calls for mercy rather than derision. "She just can't seem to control herself" first draws forth judgment but then gives way to something very different.

It is always worth being conscious of the ways we tend to dismiss people we don't like for the very same shortcomings we readily forgive in people we do — or, for that matter, in ourselves. (For some people the reverse is just as hard to internalize: We sometimes mercilessly condemn ourselves for failings we might well regard as eminently forgivable in others). Maybe, like the God of this story, we need to learn that our evaluations of people depend on more than just the facts about their nature or character; they also depend on what posture we adopt toward those facts.

Needless to say, it is not always easy to know when judgment is appropriate, or when mercy should trump it. The tension between judgment and mercy is one that Judaism imagines even God finds difficult to negotiate, so there is no reason to expect that we will find it simple. But God's change of heart after the flood reminds us of something crucial: Where there is judgment, there is often also the possibility of compassion.

But our parashah teaches us more than just that we can be forgiving toward people for the same reasons we are inclined to condemn them — though that in itself is actually quite a lot. Genesis also wants us to think about who and what God is in relation to us. God allows the world to persist after the flood not because human beings are so wonderful — or because God is so naive — but because God is compassionate and merciful. As Bible scholar Walter Brueggemann memorably puts it, "The only thing the waters of chaos and death do not cut through (though they cut through everything else) is the commitment of God to creation."[24] The world (and the covenant) endures because of divine mercy. From a religious perspective, the creation of the world is a manifestation of divine grace and generosity — but so also is the persistence of it in the face of so much cruelty and callousness. The fact that the world continues to exist is thus grounds for deep gratitude.

From the Torah's perspective, as Bible scholar Walter Moberley wisely observes, "humanity remains undeserving of the gift of manageable life in a regular world order; but the gift is given nonetheless. . . . [God's] forbearance, rightly understood, should lead not to complacency . . . [but] to the living of life in a way that recognizes its quality as gift."[25]

Noah #2

People Have Names

The Torah's Takedown of Totalitarianism

The Tower of Babel is among the best known and most frequently cited stories in the Torah. And yet most of the conventional interpretations of the narrative are, I think, mistaken. Genesis 11 is not a simple morality tale about a human attempt to storm the heavens and displace God. Nor, conversely, is it a primitive allegory about an insecure deity who is so threatened by human achievement that God needs to wreak havoc on the best-laid human plans. The narrative is also not placed where it is in the Torah in order to explain the vast multiplicity of human languages. Nor is it a lament about some lost primeval unity. The story of Babel is, I would suggest, about something else: the importance of individuals and the horrors of totalitarianism.

The fact that the nine verses that make up the narrative are often described as the "Tower of Babel" story is misleading, since the crime of the builders at Babel is not their desire to build a tower. "A tower with its top in the sky" (Gen. 11:4) is not, in and of itself, any kind of assault on God's authority. The term is, rather, simply a biblical Hebrew expression for a very tall building, what we would similarly call a "skyscraper"—it does not actually scrape the sky; it is just extremely tall.[26]

If we read closely, the text itself tells us that the tower is not the issue: "Thus the Lord scattered them from there over the face of the whole earth; and they stopped building the city" (Gen. 11:8). It seems clear, therefore, that "the building of the city, and not the tower per se, [is what] provoked the divine displeasure."[27]

So why does the construction of the city disturb God so much?

The punishment that God metes out to the builders offers a clue. In an otherwise brief and laconic story, we are nevertheless told twice that God scattered the builders "over the face of the whole earth" (Gen. 11:8,9). But there is something odd about this. When God first created the first man and woman, God blessed them: "Be fertile and increase, fill the earth" (1:28). And after the flood, God blessed Noah by reiterating the very same words: "Be fertile and increase, and fill the earth" (9:1). If a key part of God's primordial blessing and charge to humanity is that we spread out and fill the earth, how can God's scattering humanity be a punishment?

It isn't, exactly.

God's foundational blessing, coupled with God's interruption of the builders' plans, may offer us a first glimpse of what's wrong with their behavior. God had made it clear that the divine vision is for humanity to spread out and fill the earth, yet the builders want to stay put, to congregate in one place. In fact their resistance to God's blessing is clear: They explicitly declare their intention to build their city, and the tower within it, out of fear "lest we be scattered all over the world" (Gen. 11:4). What they most fear is what God most wants. God's "punishment," then, may not ultimately be a punishment at all, but a reaffirmation of the initial divine blessing in the face of human refusal and obstruction. What this story ends with, then, is not just judgment but also, and primarily, "an enforced return to the path of blessing."[28]

But why is the builders' desire to stay huddled together in one place so problematic? And, conversely, why is God so committed to dispersing people in the first place?

The first verse of our story is telling: "Everyone on earth had the same language and the same words" (Gen. 11:1). Genesis starts out describing what seems like a story of human unity, of people living together and successfully communicating with one another. Considering that the story is usually regarded as a tale of human failure, failure so profound that God feels it necessary to put a stop to their labors, this seems like a strange way to begin. What's so bad about human unity? Isn't it a worthy aspiration?

A great deal depends how we understand unity. If everyone speaks "the same language" and utilizes "the same words," then perhaps by implication they think the same thoughts and hold the same opinions. Perhaps, then, this story isn't really about unity but about uniformity, which is much different.

R. Naftali Tzvi Yehudah Berlin (Netziv, 1816–93) observes that although the opening verse tells us that the builders all had "the same words," it never tells us anything about what those words actually were. That, he argues, is precisely the point: "God was not distressed by what they said, but by the fact that their words [and by implication, their thoughts] were all the same" (*Ha'amek Davar* to Gen. 11:1).[29] God finds this unanimity alarming, because total uniformity is necessarily a sign of totalitarian control—after all, absolute consensus does not happen naturally on *any* matter, let alone on *every* matter.

Soon enough, the Netziv tells us, God's concerns prove to be well founded: The builders refuse to let anyone leave their city ("lest we be scattered all over the world"). "This was certainly related to the 'same words' they all shared," the Netziv argues; "they feared that since not all human thoughts are alike, if some would leave they might adopt different thoughts. And so they saw to it that no one left their enclave." The builders wanted Babel to be the capital of the world, the Netziv contends, and the center of ideological enforcement: "It is inconceivable that there would be only one city in the whole world. Rather, they thought that all cities would be connected and subsidiary to that one city in which the tower was to be built." This enforced consensus, he says, explains the building of the tower: The skyscraper would serve as a watchtower from which to monitor the residents and keep them in line (*Ha'amek Davar* to Gen. 11:4).[30]

An inevitable consequence of uniformity is anonymity. If everyone says the same words and thinks the same thoughts, then a society emerges in which there is no room for individual tastes, thoughts, and aspirations, or for individual projects and creativity. All difference is (coercively) erased. The text before us, and the larger context in Genesis where it is found, signal that this is precisely what happened at Babel. Strikingly, no names are mentioned in the story of Babel—there are no names because there are no individuals. This is especially ironic (and tragic) in light of the people's express wish to "make a name" for themselves (Gen. 11:4).[31]

Immediately before our story, we read a long genealogy of Noah's various children, and their children, and their children after them; we are bombarded with names (Gen. 10:1–32). And what comes right after our story? Another long genealogy, with another proliferation of names (11:10–30). Adding irony to irony, this second genealogy, immediately following our nameless story, begins by saying: "This is the line of [Noah's] son Shem" (11:10). Shem means "name" in Hebrew; contemporary interpreter Judy Klitsner points out that in order to make sure we notice that the story we have just read contains no individuals, the Torah hits us over the head by following our story with an introduction of a man named Name.[32]

Let's turn back to the first long genealogy, in chapter 10. This marathon of names interrupts itself repeatedly to let us know that cultural and linguistic diversity has already been achieved (10:5,20,31), and that people have already "branched out" and "scattered"—the same word for what the Babelites resist and God forcibly enacts (10:5,18,32). Compared with what follows, then, chapter 10 is like an ode to diversity, which is unmistakably part of the divine plan. More important, the multiplicity and variegation reported in chapter 10 shed crucial light on chapter 11: Our story is not about the loss of some primordial human unity lost in the mists of time, but on the contrary, about an active attempt to undo a divine plan for diversity that has already begun to come to fruition. God's dispersal of the people and multiplication of languages thus represent the restoration of blessings already in the process of being fulfilled.[33]

When people are anonymous, they are reduced to insignificance. If no one is anyone in particular, then who cares what happens to them? The talmudic sages poignantly dramatize this concern. According to R. Pinhas, if one of the builders would plummet to his death from the enormously tall tower, no one would pay any attention. But if one of the bricks would fall and break, they would "sit and cry and lament: 'When will we have another one to replace it?'" (*Pirkei de-Rabbi Eliezer*, 24). The builders care about the collective project. But the individuals who (in theory) make up the collective are utterly irrelevant; the value of their individual lives has been obliterated.

So which one is it—is the story of Babel about an attempted assault on God or about an all-out attack on human uniqueness? That is precisely the point: An attempt to root out human individuality is an assault on God. Jewish theology affirms that each and every human being is created in the image of God, and that our uniqueness and individuality are a large part of what God treasures about us.[34] To try and eradicate human uniqueness is to declare war on God's image and thus to declare war on God. The story of Babel ends with God's "reversing an unhealthy, monolithic movement toward imposed homogeneity,"[35] and thus with God's reaffirmation of the blessings of cultural, linguistic, and geographical diversity.

We should not make a fetish out of nonconformity, which can easily become just another form of narcissism and self-involvement. But neither can we ever accept enforced uniformity, the coupling of unanimity and anonymity that is the hallmark of totalitarian movements. We are relational, communal beings, and that is a fact to be cultivated and treasured. But we are also individuals, summoned to think and act for ourselves.

Lekh Lekha #1

Are Jews Always the Victims?

Biblical texts talk to each other, often in subtle but startling ways.

In Genesis 15, Abraham[36] gets both good news and bad. The good news is that he will have abundant offspring, as numerous as the stars in heaven (Gen. 15:5), and that they will one day inherit the land (15:18–21). The bad news is that Abraham's descendants will first have to endure a prolonged period of suffering in a strange land (15:13). Only after their prolonged travails will Abraham's children receive the fullness of God's blessing.

The progression of events here does not seem coincidental; it does not just so happen that first Abraham's progeny have to suffer, and only then will the divine promises be realized. It seems, rather, that there is something intrinsic here, that from the Torah's perspective, suffering and blessing are somehow inextricably linked. Bible scholar Tikva Frymer-Kensky notes that biblical texts seem to suggest that "the way to God's reward is through the margins of society and the depths of degradation." She observes that this troubling pattern "remains as an unexplained aspect of God's behavior in the world."[37]

This biblical motif seems to echo a deep truth that many of us know from experience: The deepest blessings we experience often come on the heels of profound and protracted suffering. We may wish it were not the case, we may even rail against God and the universe that it has to be so, and yet somehow blessings often do follow upon harrowing afflictions. This is the experience both of individuals and of the Jewish people as a whole. As the talmudic sage R. Shimon bar Yohai says: "The Blessed Holy One gave Israel three precious gifts, and all of them were given only through sufferings. These are: the Torah, the Land of Israel, and the world to come" (BT, Berakhot 5a).

In our story God tells Abraham, "Know well that your offspring shall be strangers in a land not theirs, and they shall be enslaved and oppressed four hundred years" (Gen. 15:13). Three terms are used to describe the distress and hardship they will undergo: They will be strangers (*gerut*), they will be enslaved (*avdut*), and they will be oppressed (*innui*).

The importance of these terms, and of the experiences they represent, is made clear at the beginning of Exodus, when God decides to redeem the Israelite slaves and take them to the land of Israel. We learn first that the Israelites were "oppressed with forced labor," burdened with building garrison cities[38] for Pharaoh (Exod. 1:11). Immediately thereafter we are told that the Israelites were "enslaved," their lives ruthlessly embittered by the Egyptians (1:13–14). In the next chapter, Moses has a child and names him Gershom, from the word for stranger (*ger*), and explains that "I have been a stranger in a foreign land" (2:22).

Exodus thus begins with the fulfillment of the bad news that Abraham had been given by God. His seed suffers the triple-fate God had decreed: They are strangers, enslaved, and oppressed. And sure enough, the reader is meant to anticipate, the promise that comes after the affliction will soon be fulfilled. In fact there is something ironic at play at the beginning of Exodus: by echoing God's covenantal promises to Abraham, the terms used to describe Israel's suffering in Egypt also serve to reassure the reader that, appearances notwithstanding, God has not abandoned God's people. Soon enough, God will redeem them as promised.

So crucial are these experiences to the way the Israelites understand themselves that when Deuteronomy instructs pilgrims to bring the first fruits of the harvest to the Temple, the formula they are commanded to recite pivots on the same three terms: "My father was a fugitive Aramean. He went down to Egypt with meager numbers and sojourned there (lit. 'was a stranger there'—*vayagor*). . . . The Egyptians dealt harshly with us and oppressed us (*vaya'anunu*); they placed hard servitude (*avodah*) upon us" (Deut. 26:5–6).[39] Not surprisingly these verses from Deuteronomy, and the words for affliction they contain, form a core part of the Seder, the ritual of remembering and reenacting slavery and liberation from Egypt.

But Israelites aren't the only ones to endure this fate, nor are they the only ones to be abundantly blessed after their sufferings. Fascinatingly, the Torah subtly tells us that someone else has already experienced this excruciating triple fate. This time it is not Israelites who suffer at the hands of Egyptians, but rather a vulnerable Egyptian who suffers at the hands of a powerful Israelite:[40] Here it is not Abraham's descendants who endure affliction, but rather his Egyptian concubine-wife Hagar.

In Genesis 16, the chapter immediately following God's covenant ceremony with Abraham, the text tells us of Hagar, an Egyptian maidservant (*shifhah*, meaning a female slave, parallel to the word *eved*, or male slave). Employing a word that cannot be coincidental, Genesis tell us that Sarah, Abraham's wife, "oppressed her" (*va-te'anneha*, from *innui*, or oppression, Gen. 16:6). Although the text does not specify precisely how Sarah mistreated her, it does make clear that Sarah treated Hagar exceedingly harshly.

The role reversal is stark: An Israelite mistress subjugates her Egyptian slave, and the term used to describe the slave's experience is a word almost always associated with what the Israelites suffer at the hands of Egypt. And by a simple shift in vowels, the Egyptian slave's name, Hagar, becomes "Ha-Ger," the stranger. *Gerut* (being a stranger), *avdut* (being a slave), and *innui* (being oppressed) are here the fate of an Egyptian, exposed to the cruelties of her Israelite mistress.

Why does Genesis go out of its way, in the very first chapter after the terms of the covenant between God and Abraham are set, to tell us of an Egyptian slave being oppressed by an Israelite? In order to teach us, I think, that the role of victim and victimizer are not set in stone. Israelites are not always victims, any more than Egyptians are always victimizers. Perhaps the Torah is nervous about crudely triumphalistic interpretations of the covenant, according to which being God's chosen people somehow implies moral blamelessness. (If you are too sure of your own blamelessness, eventually you may grant yourself a moral blank check.) Not so, says the very first narrative after the covenantal promises are given to Abraham: Israel, too, can sin, and it too is held to account by God.[41]

Perhaps the Torah also worries about the psychological consequences of profound suffering: The victim runs the risk of seeing herself as always and everywhere the victim. So even before the Israelites go down to Egypt, the Torah warns us: Don't forget just how easily roles can be reversed.

The Torah also warns against another form of triumphalism. Perhaps the Israelites will assume that being God's elect is equivalent to being the only people about whom God cares. So again, right after the blessings are first expressed to Abraham, the text tells us that God promised Hagar, as God promised Abraham, abundant offspring, too numerous to be counted (Gen. 16:10).

The text gives voice to God's concern with the Egyptian slave with great poignancy. Abraham and Sarah never refer to Hagar by name; to them she is always just the slave girl, a womb without her own identity as a person. So it is extremely striking that the very first word the angel of God utters when he finds her in the wilderness is "Hagar" (Gen. 16:8). The Egyptian slave, nameless to her Israelite masters, has a name. Hagar, in turn, gives God a name, El-Ro'i, the "God of seeing", or perhaps, the "God who sees me" (16:13). (If I am not mistaken, she is the only character in the Bible who gives God a name).[42]

The Torah thus tries to nip two forms of triumphalism and self-congratulation in the bud. Israelites are not the only victims; just like anyone else, they can all too easily become victimizers. And God may love them uniquely, but God does not love them exclusively. God also loves and sees those whom the Israelites, for whatever reasons, do not.

What is true of Israel as a whole is true of individuals as well, which is perhaps why the Torah tells us about the oppression of a single Egyptian by a single Israelite, who herself has endured vast pain and suffering. Perhaps Sarah, who had been taken by Pharaoh against her desires and had presumably been exposed to the fear and vulnerability (and unwanted sexual relations?) that that entails (Gen. 12:14–15), feels that, having earned the status of victim, she is entitled to act against anyone who slights her. Perhaps she feels that barrenness is such a burden that she cannot possibly be accountable for how she treats a preening pregnant woman. Yet the Torah describes her actions without equivocating: "And Sarah oppressed her" (16:6), and oppression, we know, is unacceptable no matter how much the culprit herself has suffered, no matter how deeply she has internalized the status of victim.

How many of us have known someone who understands himself, always and in every situation, only as a victim? (How many of us have gone through phases in our lives when we have been that someone?) No interpersonal rupture can possibly be his fault, since, after all, he is the victim. (One can almost hear the indignation: "I was abused as a child; how dare you accuse me of abuse?")

Conversely, how many of us have known someone (or again, at times been someone) who imagines himself, always and in every situation, as the culprit? Every interpersonal rupture must be his fault, since, after all, he can do nothing right. In the face of all of these perfectly understandable but also totally destructive dynamics, the Torah comes along and says: Never forget that moral life is far more complicated than that. Victims can all too easily become victimizers. We need vigilant self-awareness lest we, like Sarah, end up victimizing as one more tragic result of our own past victimization.

Lekh Lekha #2

Between Abram and Lot

Wealth and Family Strife

Genesis 13 tells the story of a family in the process of falling apart. God's bountiful blessing of wealth paradoxically leads Abram and Lot, the Patriarch and his nephew, into deep conflict. Having returned to Canaan together, the two now part ways: Abram remains in the land of Canaan, while Lot departs for Sodom.

But the separation between Abram and Lot is not just geographical; it is also characterological. In the hands of the narrator, Abram and Lot become paradigms for two very different ways of perceiving and responding to abundance and wealth. Where Abram is portrayed as the man of faith and trust, able to see clearly even in the face of increasing prosperity, Lot is depicted as the opposite, a man blinded by materialism and an unquenchable hunger to acquire more. A careful reading of their story offers a remarkable window into the Torah's approach to receiving and responding to God's blessing.

Genesis 12 had informed us that there was a severe (*kaved*) famine in the land, which lead to Abram's "descent" into Egypt (Gen. 12:10), where his family was rent asunder by his fear that Pharaoh would kill him and take Sarai. Genesis 13 provides a stark contrast: Although the nuance of the Hebrew is impossible to capture perfectly in translation, the text tells us that now Abram is "severely (*kaved*) wealthy" (13:2). In this chapter too, the family is torn apart, only this time the problems are induced by prosperity. In its careful choice of words, the Torah hints that if scarcity can tear families apart, so too, assuredly, can abundance.

Summoned by God to head toward the Promised Land, Abram begins his journey: "Abram took his wife Sarai and his brother's son Lot, and all the wealth that they had amassed . . . and they set out for the land of Canaan" (Gen. 12:5). Faced with famine, Abram soon departs Canaan and heads to Egypt. After a tempestuous sojourn there, he returns to Canaan. Subtly the text suggests that while Abram and his nephew had been on close terms in the past, by the time of their return to the land, something has come between them: "From Egypt, Abram went up into the Negev, with his wife and all he possessed, together with Lot" (13:1). "By placing [Lot] last in the list, after Abram's possessions, the text hints at a degree of estrangement."[43]

What now stands between Abram and Lot? Read the verse closely, and it tells us: wealth and property[44]—the verse literally places the issues that drive them apart between their names. The breach between Abram and Lot is amplified in the following chapter: When Lot is taken into captivity, we learn that "the [kings of Sodom and Gomorrah] also took Lot, and his possessions, the son of Abram's brother" (Gen. 14:12). The unusual formulation is extremely suggestive: Lot's possessions are what stands in the way of his relationship with his uncle.[45]

So plentiful is Abram's and Lot's wealth that "the land could not support them staying together, for their possessions were so great"; perhaps in order to emphasize that the land's resources has other claimants as well, the text adds that "the Canaanites and the Perizzites were then dwelling in the land" (Gen. 13:6–7). Abram's herdsmen and Lot's begin to quarrel. Wishing to avoid conflict, Abram speaks to Lot: "Let there be no strife between you and me, between your herdsmen and mine, for we are kinsmen" (13:8).

Genial as they are, Abram's words may convey a subtle critique of Lot. The usual word for strife in situations such as these would be *riv*, or quarrel (Gen. 13:7), but Abram speaks instead of (the linguistically closely related) *merivah*, or strife (13:8). Bible scholar Nahum Sarna notes that "it cannot be fortuitous that all other usages of *merivah* in biblical Hebrew refer exclusively to the controversies and grumblings of the people against their leader and against God over the lack of water during the wilderness wanderings." Abram's choice of words may thus contain "the submerged judgment of base ingratitude on the part of Lot."[46]

Nevertheless, in his offer to Lot, Abram is "magnanimous in the extreme":[47] "Is not the whole land before you? Kindly part from me: If you go north, I will go south; and if you go south, I will go north" (13:9). Abram's magnanimity is enormously important and instructive: "His trust [in God's] promise makes him gracious and generous."[48] Abram believes what God has told him—the land will one day belong to him and his descendants—but he does not insist that the promise must be fulfilled in its entirety at the present moment.

Some modern Jewish thinkers insist that the religious person "discerns in every divine pledge man's obligation to bring about its fulfillment, in every promise a specific norm."[49] But Genesis 13 has other ideas, emphasizing instead that sometimes the appropriate religious posture is patience and a willingness to wait. Abram understands that, ultimately, the land is a gift,[50] not an earthly possession—and so he refuses to grasp it too tightly.

The land has been promised to Abram by God, and yet he is willing to let go of part of it in the interest of peace. Abram treasures the land, but he trusts in God so deeply and values family concord so highly that he lets go of precisely what is so precious to him. Strikingly, Bible scholar Victor Hamilton notes, Abram "is prepared to sacrifice what has been promised to him, as he will later willingly offer Isaac who has been promised to him."[51] Jon Levenson insightfully adds: "Since Abraham is finally again promised the lands he ceded to Lot, the chapter has a certain parallel with the *Akedah*, in which Abraham gets back him whom he gave up and receives anew the promises that depend on the would-be offering."[52]

Immediately after Abram and Lot part ways, God reiterates the promise of land and even intensifies it. Abram is to receive "the whole land . . . through its length and its breadth." And now it is Abram himself, and not just his descendants, who will inherit the land (Gen. 13:14–17). Bible scholar Gordon Wenham observes that "the reiteration of the promises puts the divine seal of approval on Abraham's treatment of Lot."[53]

What is the nature of the gap between Abram's character and Lot's? When Abram returns from Egypt newly "very rich with cattle, silver, and gold" (Gen. 13:2), the Torah tells us that "he proceeded by stages from the Negev as far as Bethel, to the place where his tent had been formerly, between Bethel and Ai, the site of the altar that he had built there at first; and there Abram invoked the Lord by name" (13:3–4). By indicating that Abram returned to his familiar routine — the same home and the same devotion to God — the text hints that Abram has returned home unchanged by his newfound wealth; he is the same person now as he was before he grew prosperous.[54] The fact that Abram invokes God's name is telling, since Lot evinces no signs of piety or gratitude to God.[55] Moreover, when Abram offers Lot whichever part of the land he wants, Lot chooses the area near Sodom, which is beyond the borders of the Promised Land. Abram amasses wealth and remains pious and humble, ever aware of the fact that what he has been given is a gift; Lot amasses wealth and hungrily seeks out more, so much so that he leaves the Promised Land in search of a place he finds materially more appealing. Lot thus anticipates the decision of the tribes of Reuben and Gad, who similarly choose to dwell outside the land because they are drawn to "cattle country."[56] In an understated way, the Torah even ties the two stories together: The land inhabited by Reuben and Gad borders on the home of the Ammonites and the Moabites, Lot's descendants.[57] Reuben and Gad, too, are Lot's (spiritual) descendants.

Lot's decision demonstrates just how alluringly deceptive appearances can be and how blinded we can be by our own acquisitiveness: "Lot looked about him and saw how well watered was the whole plain of the Jordan, all of it — this was before the Lord had destroyed Sodom and Gomorrah — all the way to Zoar, like the garden of the Lord, like the land of Egypt" (Gen. 13:10). Lot sees how beautiful the land near Sodom is, but pays no attention at all to the character of its inhabitants. Note the narrator's ominous warning in our verse, as well as the Torah's simple declaration that "the inhabitants of Sodom were wicked sinners against the Lord" (13:13). "Dazzled by the surface appearance of prosperity, he pays no heed to the moral depravity of his future neighbors."[58] Lot sees that the land in the valley is reminiscent of Egypt, but given Abram and Sarai's recent experience there, this should not necessarily be an attraction.

The Torah subtly juxtaposes Abram's character and Lot's. Despite being the elder, Abram self-effacingly defers to Lot, allowing him to choose whichever part of the land he desires. Lot does not respond in kind. "Courtesy demands that Lot defer to his uncle, but shockingly, he agrees to make the selection himself. He promptly (and discourteously) chooses the Jordan valley, leaving the dry and rocky hill country to his uncle.... He chose the best for himself without hesitation or apology."[59]

Abram's magnanimity notwithstanding, the text gives us no indication that the two men reconcile. Lot simply sees what he wants and journeys toward it (Gen. 13:11). The Torah deftly uses geography to dramatize the contrast between Abram and Lot: As the chapter draws to an end, "Abram [is] on the heights, Lot down on the sunken plain."[60]

Va-yera' #1

The Face of Guests as the Face of God

Abraham's Radical and Traditional Theology

Parashat Va-yera' begins with a stunning scene. God appears to Abraham as he sits at the entrance of his tent. Receiving a visitation from God is obviously an awe-inducing experience, and yet Abraham does something very strange. He leaves God and runs to greet three passing travelers, warmly inviting them to eat and rest.

Not for nothing is Abraham held up by Jewish tradition as the very paradigm of *hakhnasat orchim*, welcoming guests into one's home. Here he treats seemingly random guests like royalty. They appear at the most inconvenient possible moment—it is the hottest part of the day, and in any case, he is in the middle of an encounter with God. Yet he wastes no time in graciously greeting them. Moreover, where in Gen. 18:5, NJPS has "seeing that you have come your servant's way," the King James translation offers "for therefore are ye come to your servant" instead. If we take the King James seriously,[61] Abraham also insists that their arrival is a result of divine providence—the very reason they are passing by is so that he may welcome and serve them. Furthermore Abraham humbly underplays his own generosity: He speaks of providing a bit of water and a morsel of bread, but in the passage that follows, he and Sarah prepare a lavish and sumptuous feast for their guests. Not surprisingly, then, a midrash sees him as the embodiment of the ethical principle of "say little and do much" (*Avot de-Rabbi Natan*, version A, ch. 13).

But what is Abraham doing? How can he just turn away from God and go greet human guests instead?

A medieval midrash imagines that as Abraham sees the men approaching, he turns to God and "says, with purity of heart, 'Master of the world, let the Shekhinah (the divine presence) wait for me until I welcome these guests.' And that is what happened" (*Midrash Ha-Gadol* to Gen. 18:2). But even if, as the midrash suggests, Abraham first excused himself, his actions remain perplexing: What allows Abraham to ask God to wait, and what leads God to agree to do so?

Citing our parashah, the Talmud records a striking statement. "R. Judah said in Rav's name: 'Welcoming guests is greater than welcoming the presence of the Shekhinah, for it is written, "My lords, if it please you, do not go past your servant," etc.'" (BT, Shabbat 127a). Now we are on more interesting and provocative ground: Basing himself on our biblical verses, a talmudic sage here declares unequivocally that hospitality is so important a value that it is considered even greater than welcoming the very presence of God. And yet still we are left to ask just how and why this should be the case.

One might think of our passage as a kind of counterweight to Kierke-gaard's notion of the "teleological suspension of the ethical"—that is, the idea that at the *Akedah* (the binding of Isaac), Abraham rightly decides to fulfill his duty to obey God over against both his duty not to take an innocent life and his commitment to the well-being of his own son. Here, one could argue, is something we might call "the ethical postponement of the theological." Faced with the presence of God, Abraham finds the audacity to ask God to wait because he has an immediate interpersonal obligation to attend to.

But I would argue that this notion of the ethical postponement of the theological is an inadequate explanation of what happens in this extraordinary moment between Abraham, God, and his guests. The truth is far more radical than that. What in fact takes place is not a postponement at all. Instead it is a signal case of what I would call the ethical realization of the theological.

Commenting on Rav's statement in the Talmud, R. Judah Loew of Prague (Maharal, 1520–1609), explains that "welcoming guests is tantamount to honoring God. To welcome a guest into your home and treat him with respect because he is created in the likeness and image of God—this is considered like honoring the Shekhinah itself." Besides, the Maharal adds, we can't actually see the Shekhinah, but when a human guest stands before us, we have the potential to attach ourselves completely to the image of God standing right before us (Netivot Olam, Netiv Gemilut Hasadim, ch. 4).[62] In other words welcoming a guest is not a postponement of the theological at all; it is, rather, part and parcel of the theological, and quite possibly its highest manifestation.

R. Abraham Noah Paley, a twentieth-century teacher of Musar (Jewish ethics and moral self-cultivation), says something breathtaking about the relationship between loving God, on the one hand, and loving other human beings, on the other. R. Paley is puzzled by a seeming contradiction in Jewish law. Discussing the obligation to "accept the yoke of the kingdom of heaven" by reciting the *Shema* and the blessings before and after it as part of the daily liturgy, the Shulkhan Arukh rules that it is totally impermissible to communicate with others while reciting the *Shema*. One may not even wink or gesture with one's hands, because interruptions of any kind while accepting the yoke of the kingdom of heaven are prohibited (Shulhan Arukh OH 63:6). A prominent commentator adds that these modes of communication are impermissible even if they are intended to help fulfill another commandment (Magen Avraham to OH 63, #9). And yet, Paley notes, the Mishnah itself teaches that one may interrupt the recitation of Shema in order to return the greeting of a human being (Mishnah, Berakhot 2:1).

Why, Paley asks, are we prohibited from interrupting the *Shema* for any other commandment, while we are permitted to do so in order to show honor to another human being? "It must mean," he concludes, "that the commandment to 'love your neighbor as yourself,' is a reflection of the commandment to 'love the Lord your God,' and that both are one."[63]

Paley's comments can shed powerful light on what Abraham does when he seemingly walks away from God and toward his guests. Abraham is not postponing the theological at all; rather he is fulfilling it in all its depths. Walking toward one's guests is walking toward God, and in that sense Abraham goes from one form of greeting God to another. As Paley himself writes, "Being careful with and attentive to the honor of your fellow *is* the acceptance of the yoke of the kingdom of heaven."[64]

We are obligated to treat other human beings not just with the honor and respect due to human kings, Paley argues, but with the honor and respect due to the ultimate king, to God. In loving his neighbors, Abraham is not delaying loving God; rather he is loving God at that very moment and in that very action.

None of this means, as some modern Jewish thinkers have suggested, that God is merely a metaphor for, or a way of talking about, the ethical. According to Jewish theology, God is real, and our relationship to God is not exhausted by our ethical obligations, vast and urgent as these are. But the God of Judaism embraces the ethical and always sends us back to it. God asks us to honor our fellow human beings just as we honor God, and to welcome them just as we would welcome God. We serve God in the very act of serving the neighbor who stands before us.

Commenting on Abraham's delay of his direct encounter with God, R. Elazar says: "Come and see how the ways of the Blessed Holy One are not like the ways of flesh and blood. With flesh and blood one could not say to her superior, 'Wait until I return to you,' whereas with the Blessed Holy One [we see that God consented to wait for Abraham]" (BT, Shabbat 127a). God waits for Abraham because God understands that Abraham's apparent *turn away from* God is in the deepest sense a profound *turn to* God.

Va-yera' #2

In Praise of Protest

Or, Who's Teaching Whom?

It is, by all accounts, one of the most remarkable stories in the Torah. Appalled by the corruption and lawlessness of Sodom and Gomorrah, God is moved to respond. But before taking action, God makes a choice to consult with Abraham. Alarmed at the prospect of God acting unjustly, Abraham protests, demanding to know whether God will "sweep away the innocent along with the guilty" and asking indignantly, "Shall not the Judge of all the earth deal justly?" "Far be it from You," Abraham twice boldly admonishes God (Gen. 18:23,25).

There is much that is striking, even captivating about this story: a God who has so much respect for human beings (or at least for the prophets among them) that God will not act without consulting with them; a man who has so much confidence in his moral intuitions that he insists God live up to them; and a God who listens to and engages with God's bold, presumptuous covenantal partner. And yet familiar as the story is, a close reading suggests that it is at once subtler and more radical than is conventionally assumed.

How are we to understand the respective roles of God and Abraham in the narrative? Bible scholar Walter Brueggemann writes that "it is as though Abraham is [God's] theological teacher. . . . He does not flinch from urging God and even offering himself as a theological teacher to God so that God may think more clearly and responsibly about his own vocation. . . . We must not miss the point. This revolution in the heart of God is because Abraham intervened."[65] Although there is something deeply moving about the image of an audacious Abraham confronting an educable God, Brueggemann's interpretation is, in my view, unpersuasive, dependent upon a misreading of what God is really doing in the story.

Rather than emphasizing Abraham's initiative in challenging God, the text indicates that God actively seeks out an argument from Abraham: "Now the Lord had said, 'Shall I hide from Abraham what I am about to do?" (Gen. 18:17). Why should God share God's plans with this mere mortal? "For I have singled him out, that he may instruct his children and his posterity to keep the way of the Lord by doing what is just and right, in order that the Lord may bring about for Abraham what [the Lord] has promised him" (18:19). In light of this introduction, it seems odd to imagine that Abraham here serves as God's "theological teacher," as if God needs to be taught the very way the text identifies as God's own way![66] So what is going on here?

God wants Abraham to train his descendants to do what is just and right, but Abraham cannot teach what he himself has not yet learned. Abraham needs to learn how to stand up for justice and how to plead for mercy, so God places him in a situation in which he can do just that. Subtly the text communicates a powerful lesson, one that is learned all too slowly, if at all, by those of us blessed with children: We cannot teach our children values that we ourselves do not embody. If Abraham is to father a people who will stand up for what is good and just, he will first have to do so himself.

So Brueggemann, it seems, has it backward: It is God who is Abraham's teacher, educating him so that he, in turn, can instruct (and serve as a model for) his offspring.

In the first part of Genesis 18, three men approach Abraham to inform him that after many long years of infertility, Sarah will soon have a son (Gen. 18:1–15). Immediately thereafter we hear of God's concern about Sodom and Gomorrah and of God's plans to consult with Abraham (18:16–19). The text then informs us that "the men went on from there to Sodom, while Abraham remained standing before the Lord" (18:22), at which point Abraham steps forward and begins to intercede with God on Sodom's behalf.

Remarkably, however, the text in front of us, describing how "Abraham remained standing before the Lord," may not be how the Torah originally read. As a midrash reports, "R. Simon said: 'This is a revision of the Scribes (*tikkun soferim*); it was in fact the Shekhinah (divine presence) which was actually waiting for Abraham'" (Genesis Rabbah 49:7). In other words, R. Simon contends, the verse originally read, "The Lord remained standing before Abraham,"[67] but the Scribes found the image so disturbing that they emended the text to affirm that Abraham waited for God and not the other way around.[68]

Brueggemann interprets the "original" text (with God waiting for Abraham) as follows: "The picture is one which agrees with our comment about Abraham as [God's] theological instructor. It is as though Abraham were presiding over the meeting." Brueggemann adds that "the earlier version suggests with remarkable candor what a bold posture Abraham assumes and how presumptuous is the issue he raises."[69]

But again, I think, Brueggemann has it backward. The point of what he assumes is the original version is not—and, in any case, surely not only—that Abraham is audacious in confronting God. The point, rather, is how far God will go in teaching Abraham to speak up in the face of injustice. God is willing to humble Godself by standing and waiting for Abraham in order to make sure that he intervenes on behalf of the innocent. "If Abraham remained standing before [God], as the Masoretic text reads, Abraham is the one who wanted to say something. On the other hand, if [God] remained standing before Abraham, as the original would read in case of an authentic scribal emendation, [God] appears to wait for Abraham to talk."[70] The startling statement about God waiting for Abraham thus tells us more about God than about Abraham—it teaches us what God wants from Abraham and how far God is willing to go in order to teach him. Genesis 18, then, is a story in which God, "'the ultimate sage and teacher,' waits for Abraham, the divinely chosen teacher of righteousness and justice, to engage the deity in a conversation about righteousness and justice. . . . It is almost as if Abraham is put to the test, to see if he would fulfill his function as a . . . prophet."[71]

R. David Hartman (1931–2013) finds in Genesis 18 a key to Jewish theology as a whole. "The God of nature," he writes, "acts alone. The God of covenantal history, however, acts in a relational context. . . . Abraham represents the shift from God the solitary Creator of Nature to God the self-limiting covenantal Lord of history. Abraham is not simply an instrument of the omnipotent Master of Nature; he stands over and against God as an other; his importance as a historical figure is marked by divine self-limitation."[72]

This stunning story makes clear that from God's perspective, this self-limitation is not a concession. On the contrary this is how God wishes to operate: God wants—indeed, God actively solicits—the intercession of the prophets. Argue with Me, God says; stand up to Me and persuade Me.

Something similar seems to happen between God and Moses after the incident of the Golden Calf. God instructs Moses to go down from the mountain, "for your people, whom you brought out of the land of Egypt, have acted basely." God continues, detailing the treachery the Israelites have committed against God (Exod. 32:7–8). But then something strange—and extremely subtle—happens. God goes on speaking, but the text first inserts the words, "The Lord said" (*va-yomer*). Apparently, God pauses after verse 8, seemingly waiting for a response from Moses—but Moses remains silent.[73]

Now, however, God drops a less subtle hint of the kind of response God wants. God condemns the people for their "stiff-neckedness" and then continues: "Now, let Me be, that My anger may blaze forth against them and that I may destroy them, and make of you a great nation" (Exod. 32:9–10). Pamela Reis astutely asks: "Why is God telling Moses to let him alone? Moses has been letting him alone." Moses now picks up on what God wants and "steps nimbly into the breach between God and the sinning Hebrews." Moses "implores" God and, "pointedly changing the antecedent of the pronoun God had used," he begs God to relent of God's anger against "Your people, whom You have delivered from the land of Egypt." Moses intersperses an array of appeals—the Israelites are, despite everything, God's people; the Egyptians might well say that God has taken the people out only to slay them; and God would do well to recall God's promises to the forefathers (32:11–13).[74] Sure enough God "renounced the punishment [God] had planned to bring upon [God's] people" (32:14).

What is the connection between the two parts of Genesis 18—the announcement that Abraham and Sarah will soon have a child (Gen. 18:1–15) and the divine-human exchange over the fate of Sodom (18:16–33)? The first part of the chapter is concerned with the wondrous fact that Abraham and Sarah will finally have a child together; the second part insists that the blessing comes with a challenge. God is concerned that Abraham "instruct his children and his posterity to keep the way of the Lord by doing what is just and right." Our covenant with God is not just about having children; it is also about the kind of children we have. Abraham is promised a son, but he must raise him with a passion for what is good and just. The continued flow of divine blessing depends on it (18:19).[75]

Why is this so important? The Torah wants us to know that it is not just prophets who must step forward; what is true of Abraham and Moses ought to be true of us as well. Even "the children of prophets," as the Talmud calls the Jewish people (BT, Pesahim 66a), must argue for justice and plead for mercy. If, following Abraham's example, Jews are asked to argue with God, how much the more so are we called to speak up in the face of human injustice. As the Talmud startlingly puts it, "Whoever is able to protest against the transgressions of his own family and does not do so is held responsible for the transgressions of his family. Whoever is able to protest against the transgressions of the people of his community and does not do so is held responsible for the transgressions of his community. Whoever is able to protest against the transgressions of the entire world and does not do so is held responsible for the transgressions of the entire world" (BT, Shabbat 54b).

If Sodom is characterized by *tze'akah* (outcry), Abraham and his descendants must evince *tzedakah* (righteousness).[76] This subtle wordplay serves to teach us that the Jewish people are in the world at least in part to embody a radical alternative to the brutal cruelty of Sodom. We are charged never to go along to get along; in the face of injustice, we are challenged by God to speak up.

Ḥayyei Sarah #1

Isaac's Search

On the *Akedah* and Its Aftermath

After the *Akedah*, Isaac seems to disappear.

At the opening of the story, as Abraham and Isaac journey toward the land of Moriah at God's command, the Torah takes special care to tell us that "the two of them walked on together" (Gen. 22:6). And yet after the intense drama of the *Akedah*, after the angel has stayed Abraham's hand, we hear only that "Abraham then returned to his servants" (22:19), with whom he travels home to Beer-sheba. The sensitive reader cannot help but ask: Where is Isaac?

The next time we meet Isaac, in this week's parashah, we are told that he "had just come back from the vicinity of Be'er-lahai-roi" (Gen. 24:62). Where is Be'er-lahai-roi, and more important, *what* is it? A few chapters earlier, when Hagar had been cast out by Abraham for the first time, an angel had discovered her and promised her vast offspring, including a child who could fend for himself and could not be easily victimized or enslaved (16:11–12). The angel informs Hagar that "God has heard your suffering" (16:11). She names God "El-Roi," the God of seeing, and the place where God has seen her "Be'er-lahai-roi," the meaning of which is hard to decipher but which has something to do with seeing or being seen by God. Cast out, alone in the desert, Hagar discovers—or better, is discovered by—a God who regards the unregarded, who remembers those whom others have forgotten.

By telling us that Isaac has gone to Be'er-lahai-roi, the text subtly tells us something extremely important. Where does Isaac go in the aftermath of the *Akedah*? To the place where Hagar met God. Sure enough a midrash observes that when we encounter Isaac coming from Be'er-lahai-roi, he has just come back from a mission: "He had gone to bring Hagar home, the one who sat by the well and said to the

Life of the World (*Hei Ha-Olamim*): 'See (*re'eh*) my humiliation'" (Genesis Rabbah 60:14). And when we hear in the next chapter that after Sarah's death Abraham takes a new wife named Keturah, a midrash insists that Keturah is really Hagar (Genesis Rabbah 61:4). In the Rabbinic imagination, in other words, after Sarah's death, Isaac arranges for his father to marry Hagar.

But why did Isaac go to Be'er-lahai-roi? Why does he want and need to find Hagar?

Perhaps Isaac, newly traumatized, goes to find comfort in his father's other wife, undoubtedly bearing some deep traumas of her own. Perhaps, newly traumatized, Isaac also has newfound compassion for Hagar's predicament and seeks not only to be consoled but also to offer consolation. Having been made to suffer at Abraham's hands, he has a newfound capacity to embrace those who have endured a similar fate.

Arguably, though, something even deeper is going on here. Isaac has just come from a terrifying encounter with God's mysterious, uncompromisingly demanding side. Much of what had guided him has been called into dramatic and excruciating question: Who is Abraham, a father who declares his presence to Isaac and yet agrees to sacrifice him? And who is the God who demands such behavior of Abraham?

Isaac—confused, troubled, likely somewhat lost—heads for the one place he knows where a very different face of God has been revealed: Be'er-lahai-roi, the place where God sees and hears those who have been cast out. Isaac goes to Be'er-lahai-roi, then, for three intertwined reasons: to comfort Hagar, to be comforted by her (and in the process, to bring together a fractured family), and to rediscover a face of God that has been eclipsed for him—the God of mercy and compassion rather than stern judgment (or sheer inscrutability).

Sometimes we imagine God too intimately, as if God were all sweetness and light. This is what the prophet Jeremiah rails against: "Am I only a God near at hand—says the Lord—and not a God far away?" (Jer. 23:23). And yet just as often, we imagine God too far away, all distance and unapproachability. Isaac has just experienced the terror of an utterly mysterious God, and now, to preserve both his faith and his sanity, he goes in search of the tenderness of an utterly loving One.

Perhaps Isaac can remind us, too, of the possibility of being met by the God who saw Hagar, by the God of compassion who never forgets us, no matter how downtrodden and cast off we may sometimes feel.

Ḥayyei Sarah #2

People Are Complicated

Or, Sensitivity Is a Dangerous Thing

Human beings are complex creatures, capable of deep kindness and stunning selfishness. In the span of just three chapters of Genesis, one biblical character scales the heights and plumbs the depths of human behavior. One of the Matriarch Rebekah's great virtues is her ability to discern what a vulnerable, reticent man wants but cannot ask for. But that very insight is also dangerous, because it comes with an ability to manipulate, to utter just the right words in order to get what she wants. As we shall see, Rebekah can care for her husband Isaac, but she can also play him. Rebekah's gift for identifying people's vulnerability is a sign of her greatness; it is also, tragically, her undoing.

Sent to the land of Abraham's birth to find a suitable wife for Isaac, Abraham's servant devises a test to determine suitability. Standing by the spring as the young women come out to draw water, the servant prays, "Let the maiden to whom I say, 'Please, lower your jar that I may drink,' and who replies, 'Drink, and I will also water your camels' — let her be the one whom You have decreed for your servant Isaac'" (Gen. 24:14).

Although some traditional commentators insist that the servant is engaged in some form of divination,[77] the simple meaning of the text is that he has crafted a test of character. Rashi (1040–1105) explains that the purpose of the servant's test is to identify a woman committed to performing acts of lovingkindness (*gemilut hasadim*), since only such a person "is fit to enter the house of Abraham" (commentary to Gen. 24:14). Recall that when Abraham had seen three men standing near him in the heat of the day, he had run to greet and feed them (18:6–7). Bible scholar Meir Sternberg observes that Abraham's servant thus crafts "a shrewd character test. What touchstone could be more appropriate than the reception of a wayfarer to determine a woman's fitness to marry into the family of the paragon of hospitality?"[78]

The test is demanding in the extreme. A single camel "requires at least twenty-five gallons of water to regain the weight it loses in the course of a long journey," and the Torah informs us that Abraham's servant has no fewer than ten camels with him (Gen. 24:10)! One scholar estimates that dozens of trips (and presumably several hours) would have been required to fully quench the animals' thirst.[79]

To be sure, the test the servant constructs works to establish "nobility of character. The ideal wife must be hospitable to strangers, kind to animals, and willing to give of herself to others."[80] But it also checks for energy, industriousness, and raw physical strength.[81] As Sternberg notes, "It is a stiff test . . . since it would require far more than common civility to volunteer to water 'ten' thirsty camels."[82]

All of this is obviously important, but I suspect something deeper may underlie the servant's test. He plans to ask the young woman for water, but the real measure of her appropriateness for Isaac is whether she offers to water the camels without his prompting. On one level, of course, this is simply a test of her generosity: She is so kind that she does more than she is asked, and beyond her concern for people, she cares also for the needs of animals. But at another level, the servant may understand something critical about traumatized, taciturn Isaac: He is not capable of asking for everything he needs. A suitable wife for Isaac will need not only to listen to what he says, but also to try and intuit what he cannot say. The servant's test is about compassion, but it is also about sensitivity and discernment, about responding to unspoken needs and yearnings.

The young woman whom the servant encounters—the narrator tells us that her name is Rebekah, and that she is Abraham's grandniece (Gen. 24:15)—passes the test with flying colors. She encounters the servant and immediately launches into a whirl of activity, which the text conveys with a flurry of active verbs: "She said, 'Drink, my lord,' and she hurried and lowered her jug upon her hand and let him drink. She let him drink his fill and said, 'For your camels, too, I shall draw water until they drink their fill.' And she hurried and emptied her jug into the trough and she ran again to the well to draw water and she drew water for all his camels" (24:18–20). Rebekah's actions "dramatize a single point: That the young woman's performance surpasses even the most optimistic expectations."[83]

The Torah tells us that Rebekah "hurried" (*va-temaher*) (Gen. 24:18,20) and "ran" (*va-tarotz*) (24:20,28) to be of service to the servant. These words call to mind Abraham's own generosity in welcoming strangers: He, too, "hurried" (*va-yemaher*) (18:6,7) and "ran" (*va-yarotz*) (18:2,7) to ensure that his guests were properly greeted and fed.[84] Rebekah thus proves herself worthy not only of marrying into Abraham's family but also of being of his ethical and spiritual heir: She, like him, is committed to a life of lovingkindness (*hesed*).

Rebekah's mirroring of Abraham runs even deeper. Asked whether she will delay or go to Canaan with Abraham's servant right away, Rebekah answers simply, "I will go" (*eilekh*) (Gen. 24:58). Her terse response is a clear echo of God's initial call to Abraham, "Go" (*lekh*) (12:1). Like Abraham—but unlike Isaac, who stays put in the land—Rebekah embarks on the long journey to the land of promise. "Rebekah rather than Isaac parallels Abraham; she continues the faithful response of leaving home and family that furthers God's purposes."[85]

As she is about to set out for Canaan with Abraham's servant, Rebekah receives a blessing from her family: "O sister! May you grow into thousands of myriads; may your offspring seize the gates of their foes" (Gen. 24:60). The blessing given to Rebekah is strikingly reminiscent of the blessing given to Abraham after the *Akedah*:[86] "I will bestow My blessing upon you and make your descendants as numerous as the stars of heaven and the sands of the seashore; and your descendants shall seize the gates of their foes" (22:17). Rebekah thus both "follow[s] exactly in Abraham's footsteps and . . . receive[s] the same blessing."[87] She is "a kind of Abraham-figure in her own right."[88]

Remarkably, then, it is Rebekah rather than Isaac who is described as living out Abraham's legacy—she is the continuator of his kindness and hospitality; she undergoes a journey directly parallel to his; and she is blessed with the very same words as he. With total fidelity to the text, we could easily speak of the God of Abraham, Rebekah, and Jacob.[89] Exploring the Torah's portrayal of Rebekah, Bible scholar Mary Donovan Turner writes, "we may be encouraged to lay aside our exclusive designation of the patriarchal narratives of Abraham, Isaac, and Jacob, and more appropriately refer to them as stories of our ancestors."[90]

The Rebekah of Genesis 24 is a model of spirited generosity. But we soon encounter another, very different side of Rebekah. Overhearing Isaac planning to bless Esau, Rebekah immediately launches into action. Working to thwart her husband's plans, she displays her characteristic alacrity and decisiveness, only this time in the service of a duplicitous and destructive plot.[91] Rebekah forcefully commands her favored son Jacob to heed her words and deceive his father, thus wresting the coveted blessing away from his older brother (Gen. 27:8,13).

We should avoid oversimplifying a complicated text. The Rebekah of this story is not an odious villain. She must contend with a husband who favors his eldest son for the most superficial of reasons, namely that he likes the game that son hunts for him (Gen. 27:4). It is not just that Isaac "gives priority to his physical appetite over his spiritual discernment";[92] in so doing he tries to obstruct God's plans for Jacob to be the bearer of divine election (25:23). In insisting on blessing Esau, Isaac goes against Rebekah's wishes, but also, crucially, against God's.

And yet Isaac's blindness—in this story physical blindness is at least in part a symbol of spiritual blindness (Gen. 27:1)—does not justify Rebekah's underhanded plot. "Her spiritual values are sound," one Bible scholar comments, "but her method is deplorable."[93] Another notes: "To exploit a man's blindness was not only prohibited on grounds of humanity; God himself watched over dealings with the blind and deaf (Lev. 19:14; Deut. 27:18)."[94]

Rebekah's plot advances the divine plan, but it also sows enduring discord and brings devastation in its wake. Rebekah "arranges the fulfillment of the divine plan . . . [but] in a manner that is morally offensive to a high degree."[95] She pays a steep price: After sending Jacob away, she never sees him again. And strikingly, the text simply ignores her death (Gen. 35:8).[96]

How can Rebekah behave this way? Her family has fallen apart, and so, it seems, has her marriage. The story is structured as a set of seven dialogues: Isaac and Esau (Gen. 27:1–4); Rebekah and Jacob (27:5–17); Isaac and Jacob (masquerading as Esau) (27:18–29); Isaac and Esau (27:30–40); Rebekah and Jacob (27:41–45); Rebekah and Isaac (27:46); and Isaac and Jacob (28:1–5). Crucially, Jacob and Esau never interact, and Rebekah and Isaac communicate only briefly, after the blessing has been stolen, and then only so that Rebekah can manipulate him into aiding Jacob's escape from his infuriated brother (27:46). Typically in biblical narratives only two characters engage in dialogue at one time. "Here, however, the number of separate meetings and their manner imply intentional exclusion and reflect the deep division within the family." This is a family "wrecked by jealousy, deception, and power struggles."[97]

Rebekah and Isaac do not communicate at all; they have fallen far indeed from the days when Isaac prayed on behalf of his wife, and in her presence (Gen. 25:21).[98] Why does Rebekah not speak to Isaac? R. Naftali Tzvi Yehudah Berlin (Netziv, 1816–93) suggests that their lack of communication is rooted in the fact that Rebekah holds Isaac in awe (*Ha'amek Davar* to Gen. 24:64–65), but it seems more likely that the opposite is the case: Rebekah does not speak to Isaac because she has lost all respect for him. Perhaps his passivity and weakness, coupled with his stubbornly superficial reasons for preferring Esau over God's chosen Jacob, have alienated her. A woman in awe of her husband does not play him for a fool (27:5–17); a woman who thinks little of her husband just might.

The first psalm distinguishes starkly between "the way of the righteous," on the one hand, and "the way of the wicked," on the other. But the truth is that most of us are neither purely righteous nor totally wicked; we are capable of both deep kindness and staggering selfishness. We may be tempted to believe that attunement to other people's vulnerabilities leads ineluctably to care and concern for them. But emotional sensitivity is no guarantee of kindness; the ability to understand other people's experience can elicit generosity, but it can also enable scheming and manipulation — often in the very same person. In its portrayal of Rebekah, the Torah presents a sobering reminder of what is perhaps the simplest and deepest truth we know about ourselves: People are complicated.

Toledot #1

In Praise of Isaac

The Bible's Paragon of Marital Empathy

Does Abraham understand Sarah's importance? Are the covenantal promises his alone, or does God want Sarah, too, to be the bearer of blessing?[99]

After mandating that Abraham and his offspring keep the covenant by circumcising every male, God tells Abraham that his wife Sarah, too, will be abundantly blessed: "I will bless her; indeed, I will give you a son by her. I will bless her so that she shall give rise to nations; rulers of peoples shall issue from her" (Gen. 17:16). Abraham seems to find this absurd and falls on his face in laughter. And then he adds words — one wonders whether she can hear them — that appear to represent a complete abandonment of Sarah: "Would that Ishmael might live in Your favor!" (17:18).

Conscious of both his old age and Sarah's, Abraham seems reconciled to having had his one child with Hagar. After all his years of marriage to Sarah, after all their journeys and travails together, Abraham seems willing for Ishmael — Hagar's son, the text emphasizes, rather than Sarah's (Gen. 16:15–16) — to be his sole heir. But God reminds Abraham that this is not the divine plan, and that in fact Sarah will soon bear him a son, Isaac (17:19). By accepting the notion that Ishmael will be his heir, Abraham signals that he thinks that the covenant is his and not Sarah's — and God takes the trouble to correct him.

One wonders to what extent Sarah is aware of Abraham's (mis)perception of the covenantal dynamic. In the previous chapter, Sarah had given her maidservant Hagar to Abraham in the hopes of "being built up through her" (Gen. 16:2) — that is, of having a son, with Hagar serving as a kind of surrogate. When, upon conceiving, Hagar had treated Sarah with less than adequate respect (the text does not tell us precisely what took place between them), Sarah had exploded at Abraham: "This outrage against me is because of you!" (16:5). On the face of it, Sarah's fury at Abraham is perplexing: Just what had Abraham done wrong? Why does he merit such harsh words from his wife? In light of Abraham's later response to God—"Would that Ishmael might live in your favor!"—one can speculate that perhaps Sarah has always known that although Abraham would *prefer* her to be the biological mother of his covenantal heir, his preference is merely that: a preference, perhaps even a strong preference, but no more than that.

Sarah's situation appears even more poignant if we pay close attention to a seemingly stray detail that appears in a later story about her and her husband. A few chapters later, Abraham passes Sarah off as his sister, and Avimelech king of Gerar has her brought to him. God punishes the king, threatening him with death for taking another man's wife. When Avimelech protests his innocence—after all, Abraham had told him that Sarah was his sister—God concedes that he behaved "with a blameless heart" (Gen. 20:6). Abraham prays on Avimelech's behalf, and we are told that as a result, "God healed Avimelech and his wife and his slave girls, *so that they bore children*" (emphasis mine) (20:17). Abraham's prayers, it seems, can heal and enable barren women to give birth. And yet, astoundingly, he has apparently never chosen to intervene for Sarah. Couldn't he have—*shouldn't* he have—prayed for Sarah rather than (or at least before) consenting to take Hagar into his bed?

Sarah is childless despite her deepest yearnings—a painful fate in any context, let alone in a cultural context in which so much of a woman's value is understood to derive from bearing and rearing children. If we read the cycle of stories about Sarah and Abraham closely, we cannot help but wonder whether beyond her deep sadness and disappointment, she also feels profoundly alone—and justifiably so. Abraham seems to display no empathy for her predicament and, despite his power to intercede with God, he fails to implore God for children on her behalf.

If Abraham's response to his wife's barrenness is problematic, his grandson Jacob's behavior in a similar situation is even more so. When his beloved Rachel expresses the depth of her desperation to have children — "Give me children," she tells him, "or I shall die" — Jacob berates her: "Jacob was incensed at Rachel, and said, 'Can I take the place of God, who has denied you fruit of the womb?'" (Gen. 30:1–2). In place of empathy, Jacob responds with defensiveness and harsh dismissal.

In this light the Isaac of parashat Toledot seems like a hero — a paragon of marital empathy, relatedness, and kindness. Like her mother-in-law Sarah and her daughter-in-law Rachel, Rebekah is childless, but her story plays out very differently from theirs. Genesis tells us simply that "Isaac pleaded with the Lord *lenokhakh* his wife, because she was barren; and the Lord responded to his plea, and his wife Rebekah conceived" (Gen. 25:21). Most commentators, traditional and modern, take the Hebrew *lenokhahh* in our verse to mean "for," or "on behalf of."[100] The contrast between Isaac's response to Rebekah's barrenness and Abraham's response to Sarah's could not be more clear. Very simply, Isaac prays for his wife. He wants to have children with her, and her barrenness is unequivocally *their* problem, not hers alone.

But the Hebrew *lenokhakh* has another, more literal meaning: It means "in front of," "in face of," or "opposite." Isaac praying on behalf of his wife may be the primary meaning of this verse, but we should not lose sight of the literal meaning: Isaac prays not alone *for* his wife, but also *in front of her*, in her very presence. Isaac acts on Rebekah's behalf, but crucially, he also makes sure that she is aware of his presence and his care, and of his total commitment to her as the mother-to-be of his covenantal heirs.

In this context it is worth noting that Isaac is the first man of whom the Torah says that he loved his wife (Gen. 24:67),[101] and it is also telling that he alone among the forefathers takes only one wife. Isaac is married to Rebekah, loves her, and wants only her. Subtly the text informs us that Isaac and Rebekah were married for twenty years without children — compare 25:20 and 25:26 — and yet he does not seem to consider taking another wife.

None of this is coincidence — Isaac does not just happen to behave more lovingly and empathically toward his wife than does his father (or his son). On the contrary, it is likely that Isaac learns from and seeks to correct his father's mistakes.[102] This is all the more striking given how much of Isaac's life is a mere replay of scenes from his father's (Genesis 26). He is the passive son, the one whose life recapitulates his much more powerful father's—except in this one extremely crucial regard: He prays for—and in the presence of—his beloved—only—wife.

R. David Kimhi (Radak, 1160–1235) asks why Genesis feels the need to tell us that Isaac loved his wife (24:67). Do not most men love their spouses? Evidently, he says, Isaac loved Rebekah even more than is usual because he was so moved by her exceptional qualities. Not surprisingly Radak comments: "Isaac prayed abundantly for his wife to bear children because he loved her so much. Because of his great love for her, he did not want to take another wife in addition to her, or to marry one of her maidservants" (Radak to Gen. 25:21). He prays *lenokhakh*, on behalf of his wife, that she should bear children and that thereby she should remain his only wife.

A Rabbinic interpretation amplifies the deep connection Isaac and Rebekah share. Picking up on the word *lenokhakh*, which I have already suggested can mean "opposite" or "in face of," a midrash comments: "This teaches that Isaac prostrated himself [in prayer] here and she there [opposite him], and he prayed: 'Master of the World, may all the children you grant me be from this righteous woman.' And she likewise prayed: 'May all the children you will one day grant me be from this righteous man'" (Genesis Rabbah 63:5). *Lenokhah*, opposite, is here understood expansively to suggest that not only was Isaac praying in Rebekah's presence, but that they were praying opposite one another and even offering parallel prayers. The midrash, it seems, wants us to know how deep are the love and mutual commitment they share.

As we have already noted, in comparison with both his father and his son, Isaac can appear to lack independent will. It often seems as if things simply happen to him, that he is not a significant actor in the unfolding of his own life. It has also often been noted that Isaac appears bumbling and confused at times[103]—how, for example, can he possibly miss all the signs that Jacob is deceiving him and attempting to take Esau's blessing for himself?

And yet in one crucial respect, Isaac is very much "his own man": He is a husband who loves his wife and is utterly committed to her, who learns from his father's mistakes how both to communicate empathy and to act on it. In this moment he is a hero of genuine love and relatedness.

Toledot #2

Between God and Torah

Judaism's Gamble

During much of the biblical period, Tanakh tells us, people spoke to God, and God spoke back. More, God actively sought people out and communicated God's will to them. But by the end of the biblical period, the line of direct divine communication had largely dried up. Instead of seeking direct dialogue with God, people began to seek guidance and inspiration in God's teachings—that is, in Torah. Insisting that God's will and presence could be found in Torah was one of Judaism's greatest innovations and achievements. It was also one of its greatest gambles.

Suffering terribly as a result of her children "crushing one another in her womb," Rebekah "went to inquire of the Lord" (*lidrosh et Hashem*) (Gen. 25:22). Scholars struggle to explain just what inquiring of the Lord consists of, and where Rebekah goes to do it. Most assume that Rebekah must have gone to consult with an oracle or a diviner; as one scholar explains it, Rebekah "traveled to either a prophet, a priest, or a special shrine where she might receive a word from God."[104]

But others see no reason to imagine the involvement of an intermediary; as Bible scholar Tamara Eskenazi notes, "The text pointedly omits any mention of mediated communication, which suggests that Rebekah addresses God directly, and that God responds to her with equal directness."[105] In general, Erin Fleming observes, the events described in Genesis take place in "a time generally without prophets, when the characters have more direct access to [God]. . . . Adam, Eve, Cain, Noah, Abraham, Sarah, Hagar, and Jacob all definitely experience direct communication with [God] without an intermediary." So it is quite likely, Fleming suggests, that Rebekah had the same direct access to God. If anything, she argues, the example of Rebekah indicates that "women as well as men could have direct recourse to the deity through divination."[106]

In general, though, to inquire of God was "to seek divine guidance in a moment of great perplexity and anguish. Generally one would go to a specific sanctuary or to some charismatic personage of recognized authority."[107] But the term eventually acquires "a legal nuance with the sense of 'seeking a judgment or decision,' 'making judicial inquiry.'"[108]

To take the best-known example, Moses explains to his skeptical father-in-law why "the people stand about [him] from morning until evening": "It is because the people come to me to inquire of (*lidrosh*) God" (Exod. 18:14–15). The people come to Moses, Bible scholar John Durham explains, when they have a question (or a dispute) about what God requires of them. "God is the origin of the requirements and instructions, so God must give the explanatory application of them, and Moses is the medium of access by whom the people may approach God with problems of this kind." At this moment in Israel's history, Durham adds, "no one but Moses has had the privilege of such consultation."[109]

In Genesis and Exodus, then, Rebekah and her descendants "inquire of the Lord"—and God responds, either directly or by intermediary. By the time of Ezra the Scribe, however, something dramatic has changed. Describing Ezra's qualifications to lead the people, the book that bears his name tells us that he "had dedicated himself to study [*lidrosh*, the same Hebrew word rendered as "inquired" above] the Teaching of the Lord (Torat Hashem) so as to observe it, and to teach laws and rules to Israel" (Ezra 7:10).[110]

A remarkable transformation thus takes place over the course of biblical history. Whereas in earlier books, "the root [*d-r-sh*] is used to refer to the act of seeking out God's will, particularly through consulting a figure like Moses or a prophet or another type of oracular authority, by the end of the biblical period, the locus for that search appears to have settled on the text of the Torah, where, it was now believed, God's will for the present moment was to be found."[111] Instead of inquiring of God directly, people now seek guidance through studying God's Torah.

Psalm 119 speaks of the immense delight that can be found in engaging with God's Torah.[112] So powerful is the psalmist's connection to Torah that he uses expressions ordinarily reserved for faithfulness to God to express his passion for God's teaching.[113] The psalmist laments that he is "a sojourner in the land" and implores God, "Do not hide Your commandments from me" (Ps. 119:19). Alienation from God is usually expressed as God's hiding God's face; here God's commandments (mitzvot) have taken the place of God's face. Describing the path he has taken in life, the psalmist declares: "I have chosen the way of faithfulness; I have set (shiviti) Your rules before me" (119:30). Elsewhere, in a verse that has had deep impact on the history of Jewish spirituality, the psalmist says that he "has set (shiviti) the Lord before [him] always" (16:8). Where we would expect to find God, we now find God's rules (mishpatim).

The psalmist continues, affirming that "I cleave to Your decrees (davakti ve-eidotekha), O Lord" (119:31). The notion of cleaving to decrees is found nowhere else in Tanakh; what we do find is that a person cleaves to God (Ps. 63:9); indeed Deuteronomy commands Israel to do just that (Deut. 10:20). Undoubtedly the most "astonishing"[114] move in this psalm, though, placing God's commands where we would expect to find God is this one: "I raise my palms (esa kapai) to Your commandments, which I love; I study Your laws" (Ps. 119:48). To raise one's palms — or, as some prefer to render the Hebrew, to stretch out one's hands — is to engage in a gesture of prayer![115]

In this stunning verse, the psalmist seems to pray to God's commandments rather than to God! In every other instance where we encounter the raising of palms, the gesture suggests a moment of prayer addressed to God.[116]

What is going on here?

Bible scholar Moshe Greenberg observes that "there is a new religiosity in this psalm. Religious sentiment, religious emotion — love, delight, clinging to — are now focused on the Torah, the Teaching." But does this not open the door to a kind of idolatry — to worshiping Torah instead of God? Greenberg notes that God is in no way "displaced" in the psalm; "on the contrary, the entire psalm is addressed to God. 'You' in the psalm is God, and 'Your Torah,' 'Your precepts,' 'Your commandments' are praised. The Torah does not come between the psalmist and God; it serves to link them." So far from exiling God, Greenberg argues, Torah makes a deep and abiding connection between God and Israel possible: "God's Torah, [God's] commandments, rules, precepts, testimonies, words—all these are available on earth to the . . . Israelites, enabling them at all times to feel contact with God. God's presence is assured within the human community through [God's] Torah that [God] has bestowed on Israel."[117]

Standing in the presence of Torah, we sense—and when we do not quite sense, we nevertheless affirm and yearn to sense—that we are standing in the presence of God. Consider the mottoes often inscribed above Torah arks, or on their curtains. "Know before Whom you stand" (BT, Berakhot 28b) we read, or "I have set the Lord before me always" (Ps. 16:8). "These mottoes imply," Bible scholar Jeffrey Tigay notes, "that when participants in worship face the Ark, they are in the presence of God."[118]

There is something enormously compelling about all this: So deep is the Jewish people's love of Torah[119] and so confident are we that Torah mediates both God's will and God's presence, that even in the darkest moments in Jewish history, when God seems entirely absent, God's presence can nevertheless be found in Torah.

There have been times in my own life—and the older I get, the more frequent they are—when the world seems utterly devoid of God's presence. But in learning Torah, I still sense a hint of a glimmer of a presence, and I discern a small, subtle voice. To a Jew in search of God, that textual cord uniting heaven and earth can be the most precious thing in the world.

But the Torah's standing between God and Israel can also be dangerous: Whatever mediates God can also come to displace God. We can become so focused on Torah that we lose any sense of the reality of God, let alone of God's commanding presence. And then we run the risk of being text worshipers rather than God worshipers.

A midrash teaches: "They asked wisdom: What should be the punishment of a sinner? And wisdom said: 'Misfortune pursues sinners'

(Prov. 13:21). They asked prophecy: What should be the punishment of a sinner? And prophecy said: 'The person that sins shall die' (Ezek. 18:4,20). They asked The Blessed Holy One: What should be the punishment of a sinner? And God said: 'Let him repent and he will be atoned for'" (PT, Makkot 2:6). Commenting on the midrash, R. Abraham Joshua Heschel (1907–72) writes, "Prophecy is superior to wisdom, and God's love is superior to prophecy.... God is infinitely more sublime than what the prophets were able to comprehend, and the heavenly wisdom is more profound than what the Torah contains in its present form."[120]

Heschel implicitly ties God's sublimity to God's mercy; God's love is so vast that not even the books of prophecy can fully comprehend or contain it. If we interpret Torah without a sense that we are serving a God of love and kindness, our Torah may become stale at best and cruel at worst. Torah is (supposed to be) a bridge connecting us to a compassionate God, but we can become so focused on the bridge itself that we simply forget about what (or Who) stands on the other side.

The author of Psalm 63 declares, "I call You to mind upon my bed... I think of You in the watches of the night (*ashmurot*)" (Ps. 63:7). But the author of Psalm 119 spends his nights somewhat differently: "My eyes greet each watch of the night (*ashmurot*), as I meditate upon Your word" (119:148). Between Psalm 63 and Psalm 119 a distance has been traveled — from thinking about God to contemplating God's teachings. This shift is, in some sense, the beginning of Rabbinic Judaism — finding God through attending to God's word. Every student of Torah has moments of wanting to proclaim with every fiber of his or her being, "How I love Your Torah, it is my meditation all day long! ... Were not Your Torah, my delight, I would have perished in my affliction" (119:97,92).

But this is also Judaism's gamble. When it works, Judaism's text-centeredness renders our connection to God portable; we can have access to God in every conceivable circumstance. When it doesn't, it makes God marginal. We can forget whom we serve because we love the Torah more than God. The talmudic sage R. Hiyya b. Abba imagines God saying of the Jewish people: "If they forsook Me, I would forgive them, because they might yet keep My Torah. If they forsook Me but kept My Torah, the light that is in it would bring them close to Me" (PT, Hagigah 1:7).

R. Hiyya's point is both clear and powerful: Even in moments when we lose God, we still have Torah. But Torah is not an end in itself; the purpose of Torah is to bring us (back) to God. Rebekah seeks out God, and we study the Torah's report of that seeking. In both cases, though, it is God's closeness and God's guidance for which we yearn.

Va-yetse' #1

Can We Be Grateful and Disappointed at the Same Time?

Or, What Leah Learned

It's not often that a biblical character makes you want to cry, but if you pay careful attention to the Matriarch Leah, she can break your heart.[121] Leah is married to Jacob, a man who does not love her—indeed who barely notices her. According to Genesis, Jacob arrives at Laban's house and is soon smitten with Laban's younger daughter Rachel, who is, the text tells us, "shapely and beautiful." As for Rachel's older sister Leah, we are told only that she had "weak eyes"—and Jacob pays her no attention at all (Gen. 29:17).

Jacob works almost breathlessly for the right to marry Rachel; the seven years he serves in order to win her hand "seemed to him but a few days because of his love for her" (Gen. 29:20). But Laban deceives him, and Jacob ends up married to Leah, whom he does not love, and does not want. After arguing with Laban over being tricked, Jacob agrees to work for seven more years so that he can be with Rachel, his true love.

Imagine Leah's predicament, and her humiliation. She is older and less physically attractive than her sister. While Rachel presumably has suitors, Leah remains alone, with no sense that this situation is likely to end happily, or soon. Perhaps her father thinks he is doing his elder daughter a favor, protecting her honor by deceiving Jacob into marrying her. Perhaps Leah herself harbors the fantasy that Jacob will learn to love and appreciate her. Imagine her feelings when, on the morning after her wedding, her husband's only response to discovering that she, rather than her sister, is his wife is an excruciating mix of outrage and disappointment: "What is this you have done to me?" he demands of Laban. "I was in service for Rachel! Why did you deceive me?!" (Gen. 29:25).

Perhaps we have sympathy for Jacob, and perhaps also for Rachel—

lovers unjustly kept apart by a father's machinations. But what of poor Leah, so undesired, and likely feeling so utterly undesirable? Jacob is now married to two sisters. The text makes no secret of his preferences, and neither, ostensibly, does he. Genesis tells us simply that Jacob "loved Rachel more than Leah" (Gen. 29:30).

But then something happens, the pathos of which is almost unbearable. God sees that Leah is unloved and blesses her—but not her sister Rachel—with children. Leah has several children in succession, and as she names each one in turn, her loneliness and her yearning come bursting forth. She names her first son Reuben, declaring that the name means: "'the Lord has seen my affliction (ra'ah ... b-onyi/Reuven)'; it also means, 'Now my husband will love me (Ye'ehevani/Reuven)'" (Gen. 29:32).

One can almost feel Leah's plaintive wish: Maybe now that I have given my husband a son, he—like God—will actually see me, pay attention to me, love me. But nothing changes. The text's silences speak volumes: Leah expresses a heartfelt hope for love, but Jacob is simply nowhere to be found.

So Leah tries again. Bearing a second son, she names him Simeon, declaring: "This is because the Lord heard (shama/Shimon) that I was unloved and has given me this one also" (Gen. 29:33). Like Hagar before her, Leah is unseen and unheard by her husband but is vividly seen and heard by God.[122] Yet the earthly love she so longs for continues to elude her, and we can almost taste her desperate longing. Again things remain as they have always been, and Jacob's silence grows louder and louder.

Leah soon bears a third son, names him Levi, and declares: "This time my husband will become attached (yilaveh/Levi) to me, for I have borne him three sons" (Gen. 29:34). Notice that when her first son was born, she had the temerity to hope that his arrival would elicit Jacob's "love"; by the time the third is born, it seems she would settle for her husband's "attachment" to her. By this point the reader is ready to cry for her. What ensues, predictably, is more of the same: Jacob is absent, and Leah remains forsaken and forlorn.

But now something seemingly inexplicable happens. Leah bears a fourth son, and we wait for yet another expression of her sadness and desolation, and perhaps also of her wish that her husband finally care for her. But something else entirely occurs: "She conceived again and bore a son, and declared: 'This time I will praise (odeh) the Lord.' Therefore, she named him Judah (Yehudah)" (29:35). What has happened here? How does a woman mired in such deep misery, languishing in such excruciating lovelessness, suddenly do a total about-face and express gratitude rather than longing?

Leah has somehow found the courage to accept that her life is not going to turn out as she had hoped. She has spent years aching for the love of her husband, repeatedly convincing herself that perhaps it is just around the corner. But now, suddenly, she sees that this constant yearning will only generate more fantasy, and illusion, and the steadily mounting pain of a dream dashed time and time again. Something inside of her shifts, and rather than sinking in the sorrow of what she does not have, she is able to embrace the beauty and fullness of what she does. She is the mother of four children, and they will beget an entire nation, the people of God's covenant.

It is crucial to emphasize that Leah's gratitude does not magically set everything aright and banish every other feeling she has. Her disappointment is real, and deep: She will never have the kind of love, or the kind of marriage, she has so fiercely hoped for. In its inimitably understated way, the Torah tells us that even after Leah's death, Jacob still does not betray even a modicum of marital love for her. Instructing his sons to bury him in the cave Abraham had bought long ago, he remarks: "There Abraham and his wife Sarah were buried; there Isaac and his wife Rebekah were buried; and there I buried Leah" (49:31). The reader waits in vain for Jacob to refer to Leah as his wife, but he cannot bring himself to do so. In death as in life, Leah remains unloved.[123]

Leah is disappointed, and as we have seen, she has every right to be. But she is also grateful—despite the intensity of her pain, she, too, has her blessings. (Recall that when she utters these words, Rachel has Jacob's love, but no children. Even Leah's beautiful and beloved sister has her share of pain and disappointment.) With the birth of Judah, Leah has discovered the awesome capacity to feel grateful even amid her sorrows.

A talmudic sage makes a surprising, even jarring statement about Leah. R. Simeon b. Yohai says that Leah was the first person in the history of the world who ever expressed gratitude to God (BT, Berakhot 7b). What could this possibly mean? Of course other people before Leah had offered thanksgiving to God. An impulse to gratitude is part of the human condition, at least as natural as the urge to suppress it. According to the Rabbinic interpretation of Psalm 139, Adam expressed profound gratitude to God for how wondrously he was made (Ps. 139:14). What makes Leah's gratitude unique; what is it that establishes her as the first truly grateful person?

It is one thing to be grateful when everything is wonderful, when all our dreams have been fulfilled and all our hungers sated. But it is quite another to be grateful when life is complicated, when some of our most cherished dreams have remained painfully unrealized, when some of our yearnings are so intense that they threaten to burn right through us. Leah is the first person to feel and express gratitude even and especially amid profound sorrow and enduring disappointment.

Strikingly, the name Leah gives her fourth son, Judah, meaning "I will praise" or "I will express gratitude," becomes the name of the Jewish people as a whole (Jew—Yehudi, comes from the name Judah—Yehudah). Who is a Jew? One who discovers the possibility of gratitude even amid heartbreak. That is why we are given the name that expresses Leah's courage, and her achievement: A Jew is, ideally, a human being who, like Leah, can find her way to gratitude without having everything she wants or even needs.

Disappointment need not preclude gratitude, nor need gratitude crowd out the very real possibility of disappointment. Judaism does not ask us to choose one feeling or the other but rather makes space—indeed seeks to teach us to make space—for the sheer complexity and contradictoriness of human experience. Who better than Leah to teach us that a broken heart can also have moments of profound fullness.

Va-yetse' #2

No Excuses

Jacob's Sin and Its Consequences

To be human is to be accountable. In contrast to (other) animals, the Mishnah teaches, human beings are always held responsible for their actions (Mishnah, Bava Kamma 2:6). The Torah seeks to impart this lesson through the often sordid story of the Patriarch Jacob.

One day, as Jacob is cooking a lentil stew, he is approached by his exhausted older brother, who asks, "Give me some of that red stuff to gulp down, for I am famished" (Gen. 25:30). Esau is presented as brutish and uncouth—he does not care how or what he eats, as long as it fills him—but Jacob comes across as coldhearted and conniving. He responds to his brother by demanding, "First sell me your birthright." Bible scholar Yair Zakovitch notes that "we would have expected Jacob to try to alleviate his brother's distress quickly, to give him food and drink with no conditions and without (it goes without question) expectation of payment. Not only is this not the case, but Jacob demands the highest price—the birthright—for a simple bit of food."[124] Jacob's "lack of compassion and hospitality stand in stark contrast to that of his grandfather Abraham (18:1–8)"[125] and his mother Rebekah (24:15–27).[126]

Esau responds impetuously, willingly accepting Jacob's offer. But Jacob still does not share his stew, insisting that his brother first swear to surrender the birthright. Esau again consents. The text then informs us that Esau "ate and drank and rose and went away and spurned the birthright" (Gen. 25:32–34). The barrage of five consecutive verbs draws out "Esau's earthly, bestial nature as a man who does not pause to consider his actions."[127]

The picture of Esau presented in the text is disturbing, but the portrayal of Jacob is worse. As R. Isaac Abravanel (1437–1508) comments, "Had Jacob been blameless and upright, how could he have dared to tell his older brother to sell him his birthright for . . . a contemptible price such as a bowl of lentil stew." Esau's boorishness does not excuse Jacob's greed: "If Esau is a foolish man, Jacob should have been a just man and not tricked him."[128]

What comes next is even more distressing. Concerned that her husband is going to bestow his blessing on Esau, Rebekah hatches a plot for Jacob to trick his father into blessing him instead. Rebekah will cook a meal like the one Isaac expects from Esau, and then Jacob will impersonate his brother by donning Esau's clothes. Rebekah covers Jacob's hands and neck with the skins of kids, gives him the food to present his father, and things unfold as planned. Both Isaac and Esau condemn Jacob's trickery. Isaac informs his elder son that "your brother came with deceit and took your blessing." Esau responds by connecting Jacob's name (Ya'akov) with his actions—he cheated (va-ya'akveini) me these two times! First he took away my birthright and now he has taken away my blessing" (Gen. 27:35-36).

When Jacob was born, his name was explained as deriving from the word heel (Ya'akov-akev), one who grabbed his brother's heel (Gen. 25:26). But now Esau offers a brutally critical alternative etymology: Ya'akov, he implies, derives from the word akov and means "crooked one" (27:36). As if the condemnations were not enough, the text also vividly elicits the reader's pathos: Esau "burst[s] into wild and bitter sobbing" and pleads like a small child, "Bless me too, Father" (Gen. 27:34).[129]

Based on a series of subtle textual clues, R. Ya'akov Zvi Mecklenberg (1785-1865) argues that Jacob was "uncomfortable" with Rebekah's plan and that he acted as he did only because he "felt compelled to do his mother's bidding" (Ha-Ketav V-ha-Kabbalah to Gen. 27:12,14,16).[130] Yet the simple meaning of the text suggests otherwise. Jacob hesitates to carry out his mother's wishes only because he is afraid of getting caught: "If my father touches me," he says, "I shall appear to him as a trickster and bring upon myself a curse, not a blessing" (Gen. 27:12).

Jacob does not worry about how his deception will hurt his brother or humiliate his father, nor does he evince concern for how his actions will reflect upon his character. As Bible scholar Victor Hamilton acidly notes, "He who is later capable of wrestling with God wrestles little with his mother or with his conscience."[131]

The Torah takes an extremely dim view of Jacob's trickery; he is made to pay for his deception for the rest of his life. Parashat Va-yetse' reports that after working seven long years in order to marry his beloved Rachel, Jacob is deceived by his father-in-law Laban, who gives him his elder daughter Leah instead of the younger Rachel. When Jacob discovers the deception, he is outraged, demanding of Laban, "What is this you have done to me? I was in service for Rachel! Why did you deceive me?" (Gen. 29:25).

A midrash imagines Jacob lambasting Leah as well: "You are a lying daughter of a liar! During the night did I not call out 'Rachel' and you answered me?'" Leah's response to Jacob is searing: "Is there a school without students? Did your father not call out to you, 'Esau,' and you answered him?!" (Genesis Rabbah 70:19).

Infuriated by the deception, Jacob is nevertheless silenced: "Laban indeed cheats Jacob, but how can the scheming Jacob protest, Jacob whom his own father has described as having 'come with deceit and taken your blessing' (27:35)?" This is a clear case of poetic justice, or measure-for-measure (*midah ke-neged midah*). Zakovitch notes the painful symmetry between what Jacob does and what is now done to him: "In the story of the stealing of the blessing, the mother, Rebekah, took advantage of the father's blindness to replace his firstborn son with the younger one. In the parallel episode, the father, Laban (who is Rebekah's brother), takes advantage of darkness . . . to substitute his younger daughter with the firstborn."[132] Terence Fretheim rightly observes that "in matching deception for deception, the narrator must have understood Jacob's activity in Genesis 27 as reprehensible. Jacob must now know something of how Esau felt."[133]

Laban none-too-subtly reminds Jacob that he has no leg to stand on in protesting fraud. "Laban said, 'It is not the practice in our place to marry off the younger before the older'" (Gen. 29:26). The word *bim-komeinu*, in our place, is no doubt intended to sting. "'In our place' —

Laban pronounces — matters are not conducted as they are in Canaan, where a younger sibling can bypass the firstborn and steal his rights."[134]

Years later Jacob's sons sell his beloved Joseph into slavery. Then they dupe their father into believing that Joseph is dead: "They took Joseph's tunic, slaughtered a kid, and dipped the tunic in blood . . . they said, 'We found this. Please examine it; is it your son's tunic or not?" (Gen. 37:31–32). Again, poetic justice: "His sons' cruel trickery represents [another] measure-for-measure punishment for Jacob's having procured his brother's blessing: He cheated his father by using his brother's garments, now his own sons cheat him by using the garment of their brother."[135] As a Hebrew aphorism puts it, "Jacob betrayed with garments, and his sons betrayed him with a garment."[136]

Esau is not alone in his evaluation of Jacob's behavior. Suggesting that Jacob's duplicity goes all the way back to his time in his mother's womb, the prophet Hosea proclaims: "In the womb he deceived (akav) his brother" (Hos. 12:4). In contrast to Genesis, where, as we have seen, Jacob's name is said to derive from the fact that he grabbed his brother's heel, in Hosea his name at birth is already a denunciation of his character.[137]

Jeremiah goes even further. Excoriating the people for their perfidy and corruption, he accuses them all of being Jacobs: "Beware, every man of his friend! Trust not even a brother! For every brother acts deceitfully (akov ya'akov), every friend is base in his dealings. One man cheats the other, they will not speak the truth. . . . You dwell in the midst of deceit (mirmah) [the same word Esau uses in decrying Jacob's actions]; in their deceit, they refuse to know Me — declares the Lord" (Jer. 9:3–5).

But "crooked" is not Jacob's only name. He is also called Yeshurun, which sounds like yashar, meaning straight or upright.[138] Moreover, when the gentile prophet Balaam blesses the Israelites, he ties another of Jacob's names, "Israel," to the same root (Num. 23:10). It is as if there are two impulses in Tanakh, one that castigates Jacob for his treachery, and another that seeks to rehabilitate him.

Strikingly, though, the very first invocation of this alternative name drips with irony. Moses accuses the people of forgetting God: "So Yeshurun grew fat and kicked—you grew fat and gross and coarse—he forsook the God who made him and spurned the Rock of his support" (Deut. 32:15). The very name suggesting Jacob's straightness is thus used to accuse his descendants of crookedness.

The Torah is unsparing in its criticism of Jacob's conduct. Esau is a problematic character; perhaps Jacob thinks his brother deserves what he gets. But theft is a crime even if the victim is no saint. The Torah describes Rebekah as the chief instigator and schemer; indeed she tells Jacob that if he gets caught the curse will be upon her (27:13). Perhaps Jacob feels he is only fulfilling his mother's wishes.

But Jewish ethics is unequivocal: We may not obey our parents when they tell us to do something morally or religiously forbidden (*Midrash Sifrei*, Kedoshim, Parashat 1). It is God who loves Jacob and wants him to be heir of the covenant; perhaps Jacob believes he is only effecting God's will. But sacred ends do not justify crooked means, and even those who enact God's will are punished for their sins (Gen. 15:14).

Most of us are not consciously defiant when we go astray; we do not explicitly think, "I know this is wrong, and I don't care." We are not brazen sinners—but we are inveterate rationalizers. We tell ourselves that what we did was not actually so bad or that it was not really our fault. Like Jacob, perhaps, we think the person we mistreated had it coming to him or her; or we insist that someone else—a parent, a mentor, a supervisor—is ultimately the one responsible; or we construct a narrative showing that what we did was necessary in order to achieve some compelling goal. In the face of all this the Torah declares: You cannot "spin" your way out of moral responsibility, even when something as important as God's blessing is on the line.

Our patriarch Jacob tragically learns this the hard way.

Va-yishlaḥ #1

The Fear of Killing

Jacob's Ethical Legacy

What is the Jewish attitude toward violence and military force? One crucial window into that extremely important question is provided by a Rabbinic interpretation of parashat Va-yishlaḥ.

Jacob had long ago left home after taking his brother's blessing in a morally compromised fashion (Genesis 27). Now, finally on his way back home, he faces the fearful scene of Esau coming toward him with four hundred men (Gen. 32:7); in that moment Jacob no doubt recalls Esau's desire to kill him (27:41–42). All that he has built and acquired in his time of wandering seems poised to be taken from him; his life, and the life of his family, appear to be in grave danger.

When he hears of Esau's approach, the Torah tells us, "Jacob was greatly afraid, and he was distressed" (Gen. 32:8). Rabbinic tradition is confused by this seemingly unnecessary doubling of language: If Jacob was greatly afraid, then surely he was also distressed. What does the latter phrase tell us that the former does not? (This question is rooted in the assumption of the sages that the biblical text does not waste words. An apparent excess of words, they assume, serves to teach us something we might otherwise not know.)

Citing a midrash, Rashi (1040–1105) comments: "Jacob was greatly afraid lest he be killed, and he was distressed lest he kill others." Faced with what he imagines is a grudge-bearing brother approaching with an army, Jacob is doubly anxious. So far from exulting in the thought that he might emerge victorious in battle, Jacob fears that either outcome, victory or defeat, will yield disastrous consequences. The talmudic sage R. Judah b. Ilai suggests that as Esau headed his way, Jacob thought, "If he prevails against me, will he not kill me; while if I am stronger, will I not kill him?" (Genesis Rabbah 76:2).

In Rashi's version of the midrash, found in several manuscripts as well, Jacob is first and foremost worried about being killed, but he is also afraid of becoming a killer himself. It is only natural, a commentator on the midrash notes, to be more afraid for your own life than for anything else.[139] But in other versions of the midrash, the order is reversed: "Jacob was greatly afraid lest he kill, and he was distressed lest he be killed." In this rather startling formulation, Jacob is even more worried about taking a life than he is about having his own taken.[140]

Not surprisingly Jacob's fear of slaying someone—even, critically, someone who (so he believes) wants to slay him—is coupled with an aversion to violence and a disdain for weapons. Jacob blasts his sons Simeon and Levi for slaughtering all the inhabitants of the city where their sister Dinah had been raped (Gen. 34:30–31) and repeats his condemnation near the end of his life, declaring his desire to be distanced from these two sons and what they represent: "Simeon and Levi are a pair; their weapons are tools of lawlessness. Let not my person be included in their council, let not my being be counted in their assembly. For when angry they slay men, and when pleased they maim oxen. Cursed be their anger so fierce, and their wrath so relentless" (49:5–7).

A midrash explains what Jacob intended to communicate to his sons: Weapons are worthy of Esau, but not of you (Genesis Rabbah 98:5),[141] and a modern commentator elaborates: "In reality [your embrace of weapons] is not your way, and it represents a departure from your values."[142] Since in Rabbinic tradition Esau is the paradigmatic enemy of the Jews,[143] it seems fair to conclude that according to these midrashim, weapons are worthy of Israel's enemies but not of Israel itself.

The Rabbinic antipathy to weapons finds expression in a well-known debate over the laws of Shabbat. A mishnah teaches that a person may not go out on Shabbat bearing a sword, a bow, a shield, a lance, or a spear, and it adds that if one did go out with one of these weapons, one is liable for a sin offering, because the laws of Shabbat prohibit carrying in the public domain (Mishnah, Shabbat 6:4). R. Eliezer demurs, suggesting that such weapons are like a person's "ornaments." In other words they are like jewelry, which one is permitted to wear on Shabbat, and it should therefore be permissible to wear them as well. But the sages will have none of R. Eliezer's argument, and their words are fierce and impassioned: A person's weapons, they aver, "are nothing else than a reproach, for it is said, 'And they shall beat their swords into plowshares and their spears into pruning hooks. Nation shall not take up sword against nation; they shall never again learn war'" (Isa. 2:4).

The sages want nothing to do with a view that regards swords or lances as ornaments. On the contrary, if Shabbat is the time during each week when we experience a foretaste of what the redeemed world will one day look like, and Isaiah teaches that in that ideal future there will be no more weapons, then few things would represent a greater assault on Shabbat and the dream it expresses than parading around wearing weapons and pretending that they are like jewelry.

To be clear: The Jewish tradition is far from pacifistic. On the contrary a significant principle of Jewish law and ethics asserts that "if someone comes to kill you, hasten to kill him first" (BT, Berakhot 58a). Thus in our case, had Esau in fact intended to kill Jacob, Jacob would have been obligated to attempt to slay him first. But even so R. Judah b. Ilai imagines Jacob tormented by the thought that he would need to take a life. Justified violence is nevertheless tragic, a manifestation of a world still agonizingly far from perfection.

In light of all this, what happens when you realize that you want (or need) to build a modern state? After all, one of the characteristics and prerogatives of a state is that it claims the right to use violence systematically in its defense and in defense of its people. From the very beginning, rabbis who embraced Zionism therefore had to wrestle with the vexed question of Judaism's relationship to modern military force. The two most influential founding figures of religious Zionism, Rabbis Isaac Jacob Reines (1839–1915) and Abraham Isaac Kook (1865–1935), refused to countenance the notion that aspiring to statehood entailed taking up arms. A Jewish army, they felt, was a contradiction in terms.

R. Reines insisted that Judaism is a culture of the book which stands in stark opposition to the culture of the sword that so dominates human life and history. Judaism's dream, Reines writes, is the eradication of the "rule of force and fist" and its replacement by the rule by reason. Reines is unrelenting: There is no middle ground at all, he taught, between the culture of the book, on the one hand, and the culture of the sword, on the other. That is why, he argues, the sages insist that it is forbidden to bring a weapon into the *beit midrash* (the study hall) (BT, Sanhedrin 82a)—the presence of the former makes a mockery of the latter and everything it stands for. Playing with Isaiah's classic image, Reines imagines a time when swords will be melted into pens, "pens of scribes who write the principles of Torah and wisdom, to increase peace and salvation in the land."[144]

In a similar vein, R. Abraham Isaac Kook, first Ashkenazic Chief Rabbi of Palestine, insisted that violence was anathema to Judaism. In an essay written during World War I, R. Kook went so far as to argue that although exile had been forced on them, on some level the Jewish people had assented to it, because they did not want to wield power until such time as "government could be conducted without ruthlessness and barbarism." "It is not appropriate," Kook maintained, "for Jacob to engage in political life at a time when statehood requires bloody ruthlessness and demands a talent for evil."[145]

So how could Jews have a state of their own? With hindsight Rabbis Reines and Kook can seem so hopelessly optimistic as to be divorced from reality. Reines seemed to believe that the British would protect the Jews, while Kook, who was certain that the Messianic Age was upon us, believed that statehood would now be possible because the world was in the process of being utterly transformed. "The day has come," he wrote, "it is very near—when the world will grow gentler (*ha-olam mitbasem*); we can begin to prepare ourselves, for it will soon be possible for us to conduct a state of our own founded on goodness, wisdom, justice, and the clear Light of God."[146]

In the hundred or so years since Kook wrote these words, the world has become no gentler—the Shoah, for example, happened after he was writing, not before—and statecraft has required more than its share of violence and bloodshed. In a century's retrospect, Kook's words seem almost excruciating in their naïveté.

And yet Reines and Kook should continue to serve as important voices, correctives to a tendency in recent religious Zionism to revel in military force and even confer the status of the sacred on it. R. Zvi Yehudah Kook, son of R. Abraham Isaac Kook and spiritual father of the settlement movement, for example, wrote: "A country needs a military, and so the military is holy."[147] Elsewhere he shockingly adds that "every Jew who comes to the land of Israel, every tree that is planted in the soil of Israel, every rifle added to the army of Israel is an additional stage, truly spiritual, another step of redemption, like glorifying and magnifying Torah by multiplying yeshivot."[148]

In thinking about a Jewish approach to military power, neither Reines nor the elder Kook, on the one hand, nor the younger Kook, on the other, help us all that much. The fantasy that statehood is possible without anyone getting hurt is precisely that — a fantasy, entirely unmoored from this-worldly reality. And yet the full-throated embrace of militarism represents a dramatic departure from normative Jewish ethics as it has been understood for millennia. Having a state means having an army, but that is a tragic necessity rather than a revelation of the holy.

Even as Jews traditionally refuse pacifism, we ought to remember our ancestor Jacob, who was tortured by the thought that he might have to kill. An unavoidable tragedy is nevertheless a tragedy.

Va-yishlaḥ #2

The Power of Compassion
Or, Why Rachel's Cries Pierce the Heavens

Devastated by her barrenness and immensely jealous of her sister, Rachel starkly demands of her husband Jacob, "Give me sons or I shall die" (Gen. 30:1). She does eventually give birth to a son, but evidently she means what she has said: Rachel wants sons, in the plural—one will not suffice. So she names her eldest son Joseph ("may God grant more"), thus giving voice to her fierce desire for another (30:24). Sure enough she conceives again, and while traveling on the road toward Efrat, Rachel goes into labor. Labor is extremely difficult, and her midwife tries to comfort her by telling her that her wish has been fulfilled—she is having the second son she has yearned for. But in a painfully ironic twist, Rachel, who had insisted that she would die if she did not have sons, now dies in the very process of having one. With her last breath, Rachel names her son Ben-Oni, "son of my misfortune." Attempting to create some distance between his new son and the tragic circumstances of his birth, Jacob renames him Benjamin, or "son of my good fortune" (35:16–18).[149]

As always, the Torah is laconic about emotion; we are told nothing explicit about what Jacob feels as he buries his wife. But since Rachel is "the treasure of Jacob's life,"[150] we imagine that he is grief stricken. Rachel is buried on the road to Efrat,[151] and to memorialize her, Jacob sets up a pillar on her grave; the text adds that "it is the pillar at Rachel's grave to this day" (Gen. 35:20). Alone among the Matriarchs, Rachel is not buried in the cave of Makhpelah, which is also Jacob's burial place. "Such perpetual separation is ironic, given [Jacob's] intense love for Rachel."[152]

Since Rachel's last words are filled with such sorrow, she becomes associated in the Jewish imagination with weeping and lament. Yet Jewish tradition focuses neither on the tears Jacob likely sheds for

Rachel nor on the tears she may well have shed for her own pain, but rather on the tears she sheds for her descendants who are later forced into exile. As the prophet Jeremiah reflects upon the destruction of the northern kingdom, dominated by the tribe of Ephraim, he is reminded of Rachel, Ephraim's grandmother. Jeremiah invokes Rachel to express the grief felt by mothers for their lost and exiled children. "Thus said the Lord: 'A cry is heard in Ramah[153]—wailing, bitter weeping—Rachel weeping for her children. She refuses to be comforted for her children, who are gone'" (Jer. 31:15).

According to Genesis, when he thought his beloved son Joseph had died, Jacob had "refused to be comforted" (Gen. 37:35). Here Jacob's inconsolable grief over the fate of his son is transferred to his beloved wife, who similarly refuses consolation over the loss of her children.[154] Rachel's lament elicits a divine response of "presence, concern, intervention, and rescue." God is so moved by Rachel's tears that God promises to bring all the tears to an end: "Thus said the Lord: 'Restrain your voice from weeping, your eyes from shedding tears; for there is a reward for your labor'—declares the Lord—'they shall return from the enemy's land. And there is hope for your future—declares the Lord—'your children shall return to their country'" (Jer. 31:16–17).[155] Sorrow will be replaced by joy, exile by homecoming; "the gift of hope overrides the despair of the lamenter."[156]

What does God mean when God tells Rachel that there is reward for her "labor" (pe'ulateikh)? A remarkable midrash imagines Abraham, Isaac, Jacob, and Moses all pleading with God to no avail concerning the sin of King Manasseh, who placed an idol in the Temple. But then Rachel steps forward and asks, "Master of the World, whose mercy is greater, Your mercy or the mercy of flesh and blood? You must admit that Your mercy is greater. Now, did I not bring my rival [that is, her sister Leah] into my home? Jacob worked for my father for years, only to be with me. When I came to enter the bridal canopy (huppah), they replaced me with my sister." Rachel reminds God that she did not protest; on the contrary she actively aided Leah, sharing with her the sign she had given Jacob to enable him to distinguish between the two of them. Now she entreats God for a similar display of heroic mercy: "You, too, if Your children brought Your rival into Your house [that is, brought an idol into the Temple] keep Your silence for them." Despite being unmoved by all the appeals preceding hers, God is stirred by Rachel's words. "God said to her, 'You have defended them well. 'There is reward for your labor'—that is, for your righteousness, that you gave your sign to your sister'" (Rashi to Jer. 31:14).[157] In another, more expansive retelling of this exchange, Rachel tells God that "I extended kindness (*gamalti hesed*) to [Leah] and was not jealous of her, and did not allow her to be shamed," averring that if she, a flesh-and-blood person with a real rival, reined in her feelings and prevented her rival's disgrace, how much the more so should God ignore God's jealousy. After all, in contrast to Rachel's, God's purported rival, the idol, is of no substance at all (Lamentations Rabbah, Petihta 24).

According to this midrash, the strategies that the other supplicants use are also related to their life stories. Abraham appeals to his ability to conquer his mercy at God's command (at the *Akedah*), Isaac to his willingness to be slaughtered; Jacob insists that he risked his life to save his children from Esau, Moses that he has served God faithfully for four decades. Yet only Rachel's words pierce the heavens because she herself has displayed such remarkable mercy. As a talmudic sage teaches, "One who is merciful to others, mercy is shown to him by Heaven" (BT, Shabbat 151b). According to Jewish theology, many things are precious to God, but compassion and kindness are precious above all else.

Rachel does more than behave compassionately toward someone who finds herself in a vulnerable situation. She musters empathy and mercy even in a situation where her own needs and desires are at stake, and where great pain and destructive rivalry are at play. If there were ever a moment when it would make sense for self-assertion to crowd out the possibility of compassion, it is surely this one: After years of longing, Rachel is finally about to be with the man she has yearned for— and yet, in order to prevent Leah's being disgraced, she lets her sister's needs trump her own. In the eyes of the midrash, this is the kind of compassion that changes the divinely guided course of Jewish history.

The sages tell another remarkable story about compassion in difficult circumstances and its power to move God. The land of Israel is enduring a drought, so the people go to the sage R. Tanhuma and ask him to proclaim a fast.[158] He declares one fast day, then another, and then a third—and yet no rain falls. R. Tanhuma gets up and begins to preach: "My children! Be filled with compassion for one another, and then the Blessed Holy One will be filled with compassion towards you." Seemingly moved by his words, the people begin distributing alms to "their poor."

Even as they are giving out alms, they see a man giving money to his ex-wife. Outraged, they go to R. Tanhuma and exclaim: "Why do we sit here while such egregious behavior is taking place?" (Although they never explicitly say it, the people clearly assume that the man is paying his ex-wife for sex.[159]) R. Tanhuma asks them, "What did you see?," and they tell him. The sage summons the man and asks him why he was giving money to his ex-wife. The man replies: "I saw her in great distress and was filled with compassion for her." R. Tanhuma looks heavenward and prays: "Master of the World, this man, upon whom this woman has no claim for sustenance, nevertheless saw her in distress and was filled with compassion for her. It is written of you: 'The Lord is gracious and compassionate' (Ps. 145:8). We are your children, the children of Your beloved ones, Abraham, Isaac, and Jacob, how much the more so should you be filled with compassion towards us!" Sure enough "immediately the rain came down and the world enjoyed relief" (Genesis Rabbah 33:3).

The story is fascinating. On one level, of course, the people appear to heed their teacher's words and set about giving *tzedakah*. And yet they are suspicious, even cynical: If this man is giving money to his former wife, they are sure, something illicit and corrupt must be passing between them. We are righteous, they confidently assume; he must be a sinner, and the consequences of his brazen sinfulness fall upon all of us.

But the truth is quite different: They are generous only in the most mechanical way. Their hands are open, but their hearts are decidedly not. R. Tanhuma summons them to be "filled with compassion for one another," but they merely distribute money to "their poor." Even the giving of *tzedakah* can be done as a "purely external and [therefore] worthless act."[160] As the talmudic sage R. Elazar asserts, "The reward of *tzedakah* depends entirely on the extent of kindness in it" (вт, Sukkah 49b).

Notice the stark contrast between the people and the man they condemn: They "see" a man sinning, but he "sees" a woman in pain. Now it is quite possible that the relationship between this man and his former wife is complicated; relationships between former spouses often are. And yet when he sees her—when he really looks and sees her—her vulnerability and suffering render whatever tensions may lie between them irrelevant.[161] He alone, it seems, embodies the kind of compassion for which R. Tanhuma called; he alone embodies the kind of compassion that has the power to move heaven.

"The Lord is good to all, and [God's] mercy is upon all [God's] works," says Psalm 145 (145:9). The verse is usually taken to mean that God is merciful toward all of God's creatures. But the talmudic sage R. Joshua of Sikhnin explains the verse differently in the name of his teacher R. Levi: God is good to all, he teaches, and God has given of God's mercy to human beings. People have the capacity to partake of God's compassion and bestow it upon others, even those with whom our relationships have not always been simple. As we remember Rachel crying for her children, we ought also to recall her making space for her sister. After all, the sages insist, God hears the former because of the latter.

The man in our story's remarkable show of compassion for his ex-wife is reminiscent of Rachel's stunning kindness toward her sister. Rachel's relations with Leah are not smooth; it would be all too easy for Rachel to abandon her. But Rachel nevertheless sees Leah's distress— she is alone and unloved—and responds accordingly. Like the man in our story, Rachel displays compassion even in the face of legitimate, understandable ambivalence—and this singular display of humanity is what enables her to move heaven.

So great is compassion, Jewish theology tells us, that it has the power to break God's heart open.

Va-yeshev #1

Against Halfheartedness

Jealous of his favored status and fed up with his grandiose dreams, Joseph's brothers decide to kill him. Reuben, the eldest, resists their plan and attempts to save him. But something about Reuben's seemingly noble efforts leaves the talmudic sage R. Isaac b. Marion profoundly uneasy.

As soon as the brothers hatch their plot to dispose of Joseph, Reuben intervenes: "But when Reuben heard it, he came to his rescue. He said, 'Let us not take his life.' And Reuben said to them, 'Shed no blood! Cast him into that pit out in the wilderness, but do not lay a hand upon him' — intending to save him from them and restore him to his father" (Gen. 37:21–22).

Meanwhile, the rest of the brothers sell Joseph to some passing Ishmaelites (or possibly Midianites — the story is notoriously difficult to sort out). When Reuben comes back, he is devastated by what he finds. "When Reuben returned to the pit and saw that Joseph was not in the pit, he rent his clothes. Returning to his brothers, he said, 'The boy is gone! Now, where am I to go?'" (Gen. 37:29–30).

It is possible to see Reuben as a paragon of decency and integrity, and arguably even of courage — he sees Joseph in grave danger and rather than stand by passively, he intercedes on his behalf, even at the risk of angering his resentful brothers. But R. Isaac understands Reuben very differently: He sees him as having failed to respond appropriately to the task before him. "When a person does a mitzvah," R. Isaac teaches, "he should do it with his whole heart. For had Reuben known that the Blessed Holy One would record of him [in scripture] 'But when Reuben heard it, he came to his rescue,' he would have carried Joseph on his shoulder and brought him to his father" (Ruth Rabbah 5:6).[162]

In other words, according to R. Isaac, Reuben fails to act decisively. He wants to save his brother, and he takes important steps to try and do just that, but he does not act strongly enough to ensure Joseph's safety. He is undoubtedly well intentioned, but he is tripped up by his own fecklessness.

R. Isaac's is certainly not the only way to interpret Reuben's behavior, and it may seem at first glance that he is being more than a bit ungenerous in his assessment. Indeed it may be that making the homiletical point is more important to R. Isaac than offering an airtight reading of the story. But there is one clause in the text that supports R. Isaac's analysis. Why, one wonders, does Genesis feel the need to add a description of Reuben's motives—"intending to save him from them and restore him to his father"? If his behavior had been more definitive and less ambiguous, the reader would not need additional attestation of his noble intentions.[163] If there is still room to interpret your actions negatively, in other words, perhaps you haven't really done all that you can.

R. Isaac is equally struck by the Torah's strange description of Aaron's response to his brother Moses in parashat Shemot. Frustrated by Moses's repeated refusals to go to Pharaoh, and by his paralyzing anxiety about his difficulties speaking, God gets angry and tells him: "There is your brother Aaron the Levite. He, I know, speaks readily. Even now he is setting out to meet you, and when he sees you, he will rejoice in his heart" (Exod. 4:14). Moses and Aaron are about to set out on a world-historical mission, and what's more, they have ostensibly not seen one another since Moses was an infant, and all God can say about Aaron is that he will rejoice in his heart?! R. Isaac observes: "Had Aaron known that the Blessed Holy One would record of him [in scripture] 'Even now he is setting out to meet you, etc.,' he would have gone forth to meet him with timbrels and dances!" (Ruth Rabbah 5:6).

R. Isaac faults Aaron, like Reuben before him, for acting tepidly and halfheartedly in a moment of truth. Perhaps Reuben is afraid of his brothers; perhaps Aaron is afraid of Pharaoh—and perhaps these fears are understandable. But wholeheartedness requires us to rise above our fears and to act with resolution and determination.[164]

On one level, of course, R. Isaac is talking only about biblical characters, whose fateful decisions are recorded by God in scripture. Surely they ought to have acted ardently. But it would be a mistake to assume that his comments are directed exclusively at those rare few whose stories are told in the Torah. After all, from what he perceives as their failures he explicitly derives a lesson intended for all of us: When a person does a mitzvah, she should do it with her whole heart. R. Isaac wants to reorient each of us by reminding us of what every religious person supposedly knows: that since God watches every decision we make and every action we take, the ways we respond to life really do matter. If we brought God's watchful eye to the very center of our consciousness, then we would not be lazy or listless. We would live—in each moment, and not just in "big moments"—with everything we have and everything we are.

It would be easy to hear this idea as oppressive, or to experience it as a prescription for an unending flow of guilt and self-blame. But I don't think that's what R. Isaac intends. The version of the midrash I have cited, from Ruth Rabbah, has R. Isaac saying that a person should act with his or her whole heart. But another version, cited in Leviticus Rabbah, formulates the lesson slightly differently: "When a person does a mitzvah, she should do it with a joyous heart" (Leviticus Rabbah 34:8).

Perhaps we can understand why God's watching would lead us to act wholeheartedly, but why joyously? The invocation of joy in this context encapsulates one of Jewish theology's most stunning claims: In the deepest sense, the fact that God is watching means that we can live in the profound joy of knowing that we matter, and that our actions matter. In other words our awareness of God's watchful eye—or, in the language of the Days of Awe, of the fact that everyone's signature is in the book God keeps—can be a source of delight rather than anxiety. This is part of what underlies the Rabbinic notion of *simhah shel mitzvah*, the joy of being commanded. We matter to God, and so, therefore, do the decisions we make each day.

Why is it so hard to respond to life with everything we have? Two Musar masters offer two different but intertwined explanations for our habitual halfheartedness. According to R. Yeruham Levovitz (1873–1936), our problem is that we don't believe that every single action we take really matters. We forget—or fail to internalize in the first place—that there is, in his words, "eternity in every action, however seemingly minor." This, he argues, is the source of our deepest spiritual and interpersonal failings: "The whole of Torah testifies to and teaches this foundation—the enormous significance of even one action; and if we do not live with this awareness, that any one of our actions can reach all the way to heaven, what hope do we have—because this is the very essence!"[165]

R. Chaim Zaitchik (1905–89), in contrast, reminds us that at the deepest levels, we constantly sell ourselves short, doubting that we have the power to act forcefully and definitively. We become discouraged and demoralized far too quickly, he tells us, and we thus succumb to exhaustion and lethargy. Our problem, in other words, is that we "lack faith in, and lack consciousness of, the full range of [our] currently latent, hidden capacities." Like Reuben before us, he insists, we are all obligated to assess our abilities expansively and generously.[166] Self-doubt, in other words, is self-fulfilling. If we do not believe in our abilities, we will in fact fail.

What, then, can we learn from Reuben? That it is a religious imperative to believe in our ability to act and to impact the world in significant ways, and that we are obliged to recognize that the moment and the task before us, no matter how seemingly trivial, matter, and matter ultimately.

At first blush it might seem unbearably trite and self-congratulatory to say "you have to believe in yourself." But R. Isaac's approach is a far cry from the pop-culture version of self-affirmation, because whereas the latter is purely self-referential, the former is robustly covenantal: We act with a full heart, and with real presence, because that is what our relationship with God demands. We are not simply acting for ourselves but in the name of our relationship with God.

R. Isaac and his interpreters offer a powerful reminder of our potential, of who we could be rather than who we already are, and of the fact that each moment of our lives calls for us to act with our whole heart.

Va-yeshev #2

Election and Service

What Joseph Learned

Being singled out by God is an enormous privilege, but it also comes with heavy responsibilities.

Already as a teenager, Joseph earns the enmity of his brothers. In their eyes he is guilty of at least three crimes. First, Genesis tells us, he "brought bad reports of them to their father" (Gen. 37:2). It is not clear whether Joseph's reports were true or false, but the Hebrew word used to describe them, *dibah*, elsewhere suggests a false and malicious report.[167] In light of this, Bible scholar Gordon Wenham contends that "it seems likely that Joseph misrepresented his brothers to his father, his father believed him, and his brothers hated him for his lies." But even if Joseph's accounts were accurate, Wenham adds, they "would doubtless have enraged his brothers, especially since their father had never held them in high regard."[168]

Second, Joseph shares his dreams about his entire family bowing down before him (Gen. 37:5–9). When Joseph recounts his first dream, the brothers respond with a pair of angry rhetorical questions: "Do you mean to reign over us? Do you mean to rule over us?" (37:8). Remarkably, despite having incurred their wrath over his first dream, Joseph insists on sharing his second one as well (37:10). The Torah thus subtly informs us that the young Joseph seems oblivious of, and indifferent to, other people's feelings.

Nor is that all. Jacob favors Joseph, and as a sign of their special bond, Jacob makes him an ornamented tunic (Gen. 37:3).[169] As his brothers attacked him, "they stripped Joseph of his tunic, the ornamented tunic that he was wearing" (37:23). Wenham notes that "this unexpected expansiveness slows down the narrative for a moment and focuses on the piece of clothing that was the mark of his father's affection and the occasion of his brothers' hatred."[170]

But one question is as crucial as it is easy to miss—and herein lies Joseph's third offense: Why does Joseph, sent by his father to see how his brothers are faring, insist on wearing the tunic, the potent symbol of their hatred of him (Gen. 37:3–4), when he goes out to see them? Bible scholar Joel Kaminsky writes that "it seems quite improbable that Joseph is wearing the [ornamented tunic] because it is cold out when he shows up to check on his brothers in Dothan in the middle of the day (37:17–23). It is much more likely," Kaminsky suggests, "that Joseph, like many a child who has been given a toy that his siblings have not received, is flaunting his favored status in front of his brothers for his own ego gratification." Thus, even if the brothers' actions against Joseph are "clearly unjustifiable," their hatred of him seems "readily understandable."[171] As Terence Fretheim notes, "no individual in this story emerges innocent. . . . Joseph, though certainly the primary victim, furnishes fuel for his own troubles."[172]

Joseph is not just Jacob's favorite; he is also God's, "as demonstrated by his beauty, his clear leadership qualities, his ability to have prophetic dreams, as well as his wisdom to interpret other people's dreams and to dispense good advice."[173] But at first he uses his gifts only for his own glory. A midrash wonders why, after the Torah has already told us that Joseph was seventeen years old, it adds the seemingly superfluous observation that he was a lad (Gen. 37:2), and answers that "he behaved like a boy, penciling his eyes, curling his hair, and lifting his heel" (Genesis Rabbah 84:7). The teenaged Joseph is spoiled and self-enamored.

Two chapters after his brothers sell him into slavery, we hear of Joseph's remarkable ascent in the house of Potiphar, one of Pharaoh's courtiers. "When the master saw that the Lord was with [Joseph] and that the Lord lent success to everything he undertook, he took a liking to Joseph" and eventually placed him in charge of his whole household and everything he had (Gen. 39:2–6).

Potiphar's wife, too, will soon take a liking to Joseph and attempt to seduce him, but before she engages him, the text stops to note that

"Joseph was well built and handsome" (Gen. 39:6). Why tell us this now, rather than when Joseph was first introduced? Hewing to what seems to be the plain sense (*peshat*) of the text, Nahmanides (Ramban, 1194–c. 1270) and R. David Kimhi (Radak, 1160–1235) suggest that this bit of information is simply a necessary prelude to what transpires between Joseph and Potiphar's wife: He is attractive, and she is drawn to him (commentaries to Gen. 39:6). But Rashi (1040–1105), following (some of) the talmudic sages, sees a hint of something sinister in the timing of the Torah's observations about Joseph's appearance: "As soon as Joseph found himself in the position of ruler, he began eating and drinking and curling his hair. Said the Blessed Holy One: 'Your father is mourning and you are curling your hair?! I will incite the bear [i.e., Potiphar's wife] against you!'" (commentary to Gen. 39:6).[174]

Enticed by power and privilege, Joseph loses his way. The Torah tells us that one day Joseph "came into the house to do his work" while there was no one else at home (Gen. 39:11). One talmudic sage comments simply that the text means what it says: Joseph went into Potiphar's house to take care of his responsibilities. But another is skeptical: Why, knowing the intentions of Potiphar's wife, would Joseph nevertheless allow himself to be alone with her?[175] What the text means, he concludes, is that Joseph "went to satisfy his desires" (BT, Sotah 36b).[176] If the latter interpretation is correct, then it is only at the last moment that Joseph regains his bearings and pulls away from his seductress (39:12).[177]

How did Joseph lose his way? The verses describing Joseph's relationship with Potiphar emphasize repeatedly that Joseph's extraordinary success is made possible only by God's blessing. So blessed is Joseph that even an Egyptian courtier can see that God is with him (Gen. 39:2,3,5). Yet it is the narrator and the courtier who invoke God and sense what really underlies Joseph's success; Joseph, tellingly, makes no mention of God at all. The reader is thus left to wonder whether Joseph "assume[s] that] he attained this position on his own and that his charisma was for no greater purpose than to live a comfortable life."[178]

But Joseph undergoes a profound transformation. Over time—and perhaps as a result of his great suffering—he realizes that "his gifts come from God and are given to him so that he can be of use to others."[179] When Pharaoh's two servants are distraught as a result of their dreams, Joseph responds: "Surely God can interpret! Tell me [your dreams]" (Gen. 40:8). When Pharaoh needs a similar service performed, he tells Joseph that he has heard "that for you to hear a dream is to tell its meaning." But Joseph is careful to correct him, declaring, "Not I! God will see to Pharaoh's welfare" (41:15–16). Again and again, as Kaminsky notes, Joseph mentions God in Pharaoh's presence (41:16,25,28,32),[180] as if to make sure that Pharaoh — and, perhaps he himself — remembers that God is the source of his talents and abilities.

This transformation reaches a climax when Joseph reveals his true identity to his brothers. They are afraid, but he reassures them: "Do not be distressed or reproach yourselves because you sold me hither; it was to save life that God sent me ahead of you" (Gen. 45:5).[181] Now, after all these years, Joseph has come to understand that God singled him out not so that his brothers would bow down to him but so that he could protect and care for them. Kaminsky writes: "The story of Joseph and his brothers affirms that God does indeed mysteriously favor some over others. Yet it also proclaims to both the elect and the non-elect that the divine favor bestowed in election is not to be used for self-aggrandizement. Rather, election reaches its fruition in a humble yet exalted divine service which benefits the elect and the non-elect alike."[182]

Joseph grows to the point of understanding that divine election is not an invitation to egotism and self-adoration. The haftarah for parashat Va-yeshev makes clear, however, that Israel as a whole finds this a hard lesson to learn.[183] Faced with the people's smug self-satisfaction, the prophet Amos proclaims in God's name: "You alone have I singled out of all the families of the earth." One can imagine Amos's hearers nodding complacently, perhaps expecting to hear words of affirmation from their divine patron, but Amos upends their assumptions, thundering: "Therefore I will call you to account for all your iniquities" (Amos 3:2).

Amos's words "therefore" no doubt jolts his listeners. The people may assume that as God's elect they are immune to punishment and entitled to a bounty of privileges. But God is no patron; on the contrary with "great privilege" comes "great condemnation": "Israel's great privilege of election by God and of relationship to him through the covenant . . . exposes them to judgment rather than exempting them from it."[184]

"The Joseph story strongly emphasizes the connection between election and service, stressing that election carries with it a duty to help others."[185] What is true of divine election is true of divine gifts more generally: God's beneficence is intended, at least in part, to enable us to be beneficent ourselves; God gives so that we, too, may become givers.[186]

To know our own gifts and abilities is not arrogance; it is self-awareness. Arrogance is the illusion that we are the sole authors of our talents and that they are therefore our exclusive possession. Spiritual maturity, in contrast, is the understanding that we do not own our gifts. When we acknowledge how much has been done *for* us rather than achieved *by* us, we, like Joseph, grow ready to serve.

Mikkets #1

His Brother's Brother

Judah's Journey

It is a mandate as easy to express as it can be hard to fulfill: We are responsible for the fate of others. As a variety of biblical narratives attest, the Torah is preoccupied with the inescapable fact of human responsibility, but also with the transformative processes by which we can learn to embrace and internalize it.

Cain is brazen in his refusal of responsibility. In one of the most well-known stories in the Torah, Cain and his brother Abel bring sacrifices to God. When God accepts Abel's offering but ignores Cain's, Cain kills his brother. God asks a pointed question: "Where is your brother Abel?" and Cain impudently responds: "I do not know. Am I my brother's keeper?" (Gen. 4:9).

This is a twofold disavowal of responsibility: Cain rejects responsibility for his actions, and just as important, he denies any responsibility for the well-being of his brother. On the one hand, Cain is a murderer without a shred of remorse; he kills and then shamelessly lies about it. But even had he himself not been implicated in the death of his brother, the latter's fate should have been among his highest concerns. With his insolent words, Cain denies a core piece of his own humanity: Whether he likes it or not, whether he rises to the challenge or not, he is, in fact, his brother's keeper. Seven times in ten verses the Torah repeats the word "brother" (*ah*) (Gen. 4:2–11), as if to say, over and over again, "But, Cain, he is your *brother*."

The Torah's broader assumption is that simply by dint of our being human, we are responsible for the fate of others. The meaning of human freedom is not that we can decide whether or not we are responsible for others; the meaning of human freedom is that we can decide whether or not to live up to that responsibility.

Cain's words to God are even more cutting and more rebellious than they appear at first glance. He asks God whether he is his brother's "keeper" (*shomer*). In Tanakh people are not generally described as one another's "keepers." God, and not human beings, is the keeper of human life. When the psalmist turns to God in a moment of crisis, he reminds himself that his "Keeper [or guardian, *shomer*] will not slumber," and declares that "the Keeper (*shomer*) of Israel neither slumbers nor sleeps." He prays that God will "keep (*yishmor*) [him] from all harm, will guard (*yishmor*) [his] life," and that God "will guard (*yishmor*) [his] going and coming now and forever" (Ps. 121:3–4,7–8). When God blesses Jacob after his dream, God assures him that "I am with you. I will protect (keep) you (*shemartikha*) wherever you go" (Gen. 28:15). In a similar vein, when conferring blessing upon Israel, the priests say: "The Lord bless you and keep you (*yishmerekha*)" (Num. 6:24).

So when Cain asks God whether he is his brother's keeper, he assumes that the answer is a resounding no—God, and not he, is supposed to be Abel's keeper. Cain not only abjures his responsibility for Abel's fate, then, he also passes the buck to God: You ask me where Abel is, God, but his fate is more Your problem than mine!

The talmudic sages pick up on Cain's contemptuous words. A midrash teaches that God's exchange with Cain "may be compared to an officer who was walking in the middle of the road, and found a man slain and another man standing over him. 'Who killed him?' he demanded. 'I will ask you that question instead of your asking me,' the other replied. 'You haven't said anything,' the officer retorted" (Genesis Rabbah 22:9).

It is worth lingering for a moment upon the officer's—that is, God's—response. The point of the words "you haven't said anything," I think, is not to dismiss the charge that God's inaction as murder unfolds is potentially a major theological problem. The point, rather, is to teach us something about moral responsibility: The fact that others, too, have duties and obligations does not absolve us of our own. Whatever God's culpability or lack thereof in the story, one thing remains clear: Cain is responsible whether he likes it or not. Every attempt to talk his way out of that fact is destined to fail: No matter what he says, he hasn't said anything.

Cain may be right about one thing—perhaps, as the verses cited indicate, he is not intended to be his brother's keeper. But he is intended to be something else: his brother's brother.[187] And that, too, comes with enormous responsibility. Whether as keeper or as brother, Cain is responsible both for his actions and for the fate of his brother.

Where moral responsibility is concerned, Cain's story is not the Torah's last word. Cain has a successor, Joseph's older brother Judah. Judah's story starts out quite a bit like Cain's: Like Cain, he regards the favoritism shown his younger brother as both inexplicable and unforgivable. And like Cain, he wants to be rid of the source of his hurt and humiliation. Indifferent to both his brother's fate and his father's pain, he hatches a plan to sell Joseph into slavery. Under Judah's leadership, Joseph's brothers abandon him to his fate (Gen. 37:26–28).

But something shifts in Judah, and just a few chapters later, in parashat Mikkets, he seems like a changed man. Faced with a famine so severe that the family's provisions have all but totally run out, Jacob instructs his sons to return to Egypt in search of more food. Judah reminds his father that the viceroy in Egypt—Joseph, who had recognized them, though they hadn't recognized him—will not see them again unless they bring along their youngest brother, Benjamin. Understandably frightened and anxious—and quite possibly distrustful of his sons and their intentions—Jacob resists, whereupon Judah declares: "I myself will be surety for him; from my hand you may seek him: if I do not bring him back to you and set him before you, I shall stand guilty before you forever" (Gen. 43:9). Judah, who had been so utterly indifferent to Joseph's fate, now insists that Benjamin's is his personal responsibility.

And Judah is not finished yet. In the next chapter, as Benjamin seems poised to be imprisoned, thus realizing Jacob's worst nightmare, Judah again steps forward. Standing before the viceroy, he begs to be enslaved in Benjamin's place (Gen. 44:33). The same man who had callously sold one brother into slavery now stands willing to be enslaved lest the same fate befall another. And the same son who had displayed such wanton disregard for his father's suffering now seems unable to bear the thought of his father enduring more pain: "Now, if I come to your servant my father and the boy is not with us—since his own life is so bound up with his—when he sees that the boy is not with us, he will die. . . . Let me not be witness to the woe that would overtake my father" (44:30–31,34). Judah, once the ringleader in brotherly irresponsibility, has now become his brother's keeper—or, perhaps better, he has become his brother's brother.

What happened? How has Judah, once so callous and uncaring, become both responsible and empathic? The text does not explicitly explore this question, but it does offer some clues. Following the sale of Joseph, Judah is confronted with the fact that he has badly wronged another family member. His eldest son, Er, dies childless, and in accord with the laws of *yibbum* (levirate marriage), his second child, Onan, is forced to marry Tamar, his brother's widow. Onan soon dies, too, and Judah concludes that the deaths of his two sons must in some way be Tamar's fault. Fearful for the fate of his third son, Shelah, he instructs Tamar to go and wait until Shelah is old enough to marry her. She waits and waits, but Judah has no intention of ever letting her marry another of his sons. Tamar is chained to Judah's family—not provided with a husband from within, but forbidden by law to marry anyone without. Tamar poses as a prostitute and gets Judah to impregnate her. He leaves his cord, seal, and staff in pledge until he can pay her. Meanwhile, when Judah hears that Tamar is with child, he assumes she has committed adultery and condemns her to death. She sends a message to him, asking, "Recognize, please, whose seal and cord and staff are these?" (Gen. 38:25). Confronted with the evidence, Judah admits that he has behaved poorly: "She is more in the right than I, for did I not fail to give her Shelah, my son?" (38:26).

Tamar's message must have shaken Judah to the core, because the words she uses—"Recognize, please" (*haker na*)—are the very words Judah and his brothers had used in presenting Jacob with his son's bloodied tunic: "Recognize, please (*haker na*), is it your son's tunic, or not?" (Gen. 37:32). From Tamar, and the starkness of the challenge she poses to him, Judah learns to take responsibility for his actions.

And empathy? Having had to endure the agony of burying two of his children—having been through the unimaginable hell of that experience—Judah is now able to muster deep empathy for his father and the torment he has been forced—by Judah himself—to endure. Sobered by life, Judah becomes his brother's brother and his father's son.

But Judah is not the last stop in the Torah's trajectory of fraternal responsibility. There is one more biblical character who seems to understand and accept her responsibility immediately, without needing a long and arduous process of moral and emotional education. Exodus tells us that as her brother Moses is placed in a basket by the bank of the Nile, his sister Miriam "stationed herself at a distance in order to know what would befall him" (Exod. 2:4).

Contemporary interpreter Devora Steinmetz points out that the words used to describe Miriam's mission are chosen carefully. Recall Cain's statement: "I do not know (lo yadati)," and compare Miriam's project: "to know (le-dei'ah) what would befall him." Where Cain does not know and does not care, and where Judah needs a lifetime to come to know and care, Miriam immediately wants to know and thus demonstrates the depth of her care. She is, in Steinmetz's words, an "anti-Cain."[188] She is, from the start, her brother's sister.

For the Torah Cain is the very paradigm of moral irresponsibility, the model of who and what we ought not to be. Miriam at the Nile is his antithesis, the paragon of moral responsibility, standing ready to help save her brother. But the Torah knows that most of us live in the messy and complicated space between Cain and Miriam: We step up to embrace our responsibilities only sporadically and erratically. Even when we accept our duties in principle, we often fail to fulfill them in practice, sometimes egregiously. So the Torah tells us of Judah, the paradigm of a man who is transformed by painful experience, who learns to care and to take responsibility. Through his story, we too are summoned to become our brother's brothers.

Mikkets #2

Reuben's Recklessness

What Disqualifies a Leader?

In ancient societies it was generally assumed that the firstborn son would inherit the mantle of leadership from his father. Yet in one appalling moment Reuben's hopes of one day assuming leadership over his family come crashing down. In telling this sordid story, the Torah offers a fascinating window into the destructive dynamics of Jacob's family and the tortured inner life of one of his sons. But it also imparts a powerful lesson about just how much damage impulsiveness can do—and about why it disqualifies even those with good intentions from positions of leadership.

As Jacob's death approaches, the elderly Patriarch gathers his sons to "bless them" (Gen. 49:28). But "paradoxically, what the narrator calls 'blessings' are often anti-blessings";[189] Jacob's words to his sons "interlace commendation and condemnation."[190] In particular Jacob censures his three eldest sons for their character flaws (49:3-7), paving the way for him to tap the fourth, Judah, as Israel's future leader (49:8-10). In speaking to Reuben, Jacob offers a stunningly stark contrast between what Reuben could have been—what he *should* have been, according to Jacob[191]—and what Jacob thinks he has become: "Reuben, you are my first-born, my might and the first fruit of my vigor, preeminent in rank and preeminent in honor. Turbulent as water, you shall not have preeminence; for when you mounted your father's bed, you brought disgrace—my couch he mounted!" (49:3-4). In these notoriously difficult and elusive words, a lifetime of conflict between father and son reaches its agonized conclusion.

But what has Reuben done to earn his father's ire?

Genesis reports that shortly after Rachel's death, "Reuben went and lay with Bilhah, his father's concubine." Ominously the text adds: "And

Jacob heard" (*va-yishma*) (Gen. 35:22). Elsewhere the term *va-yishma* suggests an impending response,[192] but here Jacob keeps his silence.[193] Bible scholar Gordon Wenham observes that the Torah "leaves us in suspense, wondering how and when the cloud will break." Jacob's "long and eerie silence" about Reuben's offense is broken only as his end nears, in his impassioned denunciation of his eldest son.[194]

But why would Reuben sleep with his father's concubine? The answer may, of course, be lust, and indeed several sources suggest exactly that.[195] But something deeper appears to be at play: Reuben wants to defend his mother's honor.

Sensing that Leah has been unloved and humiliated long enough, Reuben worries that her disgrace will only deepen if Jacob takes Bilhah, Rachel's handmaiden, as his new chief wife. "By violating Bilhah, Reuben makes sure that she cannot supplant or even rival his mother's position of chief wife now that Rachel is dead."[196] As the talmudic sage R. Simeon b. Elazar argues, Reuben "resented his mother's humiliation. He said, 'If my mother's sister was a rival to my mother, must the maid of my mother's sister be a rival to my mother?'" (BT, Shabbat 55b).[197] By having sexual relations with Bilhah, Reuben effectively relegates her to "the tragic status of 'living widowhood'"[198] and clears the path for his mother's preeminence to be clear and unambiguous.

Reuben's intimate involvement in his mother's marriage goes back even earlier. "Once," the Torah tells us, "at the time of the wheat harvest, Reuben came upon some mandrakes (*duda'im*) in the field and brought them to his mother Leah" (Gen. 30:14). In the ancient world, mandrakes were considered an aphrodisiac and were thought to help barren women conceive.[199] Why is Reuben so involved in his mother's marital suffering, so much so that he brings her aphrodisiacs and even seduces her potential rival?

When a first son is born to the unloved Leah, she names him Reuben, which she takes to mean, in part, "Now my husband will love me (*Ye'ehavani/Reuven*)" (Gen. 29:32).[200] Imagine for a moment walking through the world with your mother's plaintive cry for a name: "(Maybe) now my husband will love me." Leah projects her loneliness and sadness, and her yearning for love, onto her eldest son, and that legacy stays with him for the rest of his life. A devoted son, he tries to bring to fruition the wish she expresses upon his birth. Perhaps when Reuben brings Leah mandrakes, he imagines that there is still hope for his father to love his mother. But by the time he beds his father's concubine, he is more likely suing for her honor than attempting to orchestrate marital closeness.

Were he only defending his mother's honor, perhaps Reuben's actions would be (at least somewhat) forgivable. But there is another, more sinister side to what he does. Reuben's act serves not only to eliminate his mother's rival but also, it seems, to stake a claim to being the family leader himself. As Walter Brueggemann notes, "the taking of the father's concubine is an attempt to seize power, claim the leadership, and, in fact, announce that the old man is dead."[201]

A parallel case supports this interpretation: In supporting the rebel Absalom's attempt to dethrone his father David, Ahitophel encourages him to have intercourse with David's concubines (2 Sam. 16:20–22); in doing as David's former counselor suggests, "Absalom is making clear his intentions to usurp his father's royal authority."[202] Here too, it seems, Reuben seeks to unseat and overthrow his father as head of the family.

What drives Reuben to such a drastic act? Why does he want to depose—and if Brueggemann is right, effectively murder—his father? We have already seen that Reuben is fighting for his mother's honor, but he may also be avenging his own. Terrified of his looming reunion with Esau, Jacob does something that likely devastates the children he has had with Leah: "He divided the children among Leah, Rachel, and the two maids, putting the maids and their children first, Leah and her children next, and Rachel and Joseph last" (Gen. 33:1–2).

Bible scholar Yair Zakovitch explains what it is going on here: "With this arrangement Jacob objectifies the sentiment he feels toward his various wives and children. The maidservants and their children are less important than Leah and her children; Rachel and her son, Joseph, are the most precious." Jacob makes no effort to disguise the fact that he cares for some children more than others. "We can only assume,"

Zakovitch notes, "that this was obvious, too, to the women and children who saw how he was ready to endanger them for the sake of Rachel and Joseph's well-being."[203]

In light of this moment—an encapsulation of Jacob's relationship with his sons over the course of their whole lives—one might imagine that Reuben carries a reservoir of anger and hostility toward his father. So in one audacious, presumptuous, and ultimately ill-advised moment, he both fights for his mother and stands up for himself (and his brothers).

On one level, then, Jacob's condemnation of his son represents merely the final stage of a series of family conflicts. Indignant and resentful, Reuben acts against his father, and his father (belatedly) lambasts him. In comparing his son to unstable water, Jacob censures him for "acting in an irresponsible, impetuous manner, casting off all moral restraint, even as a torrent of water rushes wildly headlong."[204] Jacob's words suggest that he sees Reuben as "a man of ungoverned impulse," guilty of "wildness as much as weakness."[205] It may be easier for Jacob to imagine that what animates his son is an unruly libido rather than a conscious rebellion rooted in deep and enduring suffering inflicted by Jacob himself.

Yet it would be a mistake, I think, to interpret Reuben's demotion as rooted exclusively in unresolved family conflict. Perhaps, even apart from their shattered relationship, Jacob sees something even deeper in Reuben that convinces him that the latter is unsuited for leadership. In parashat Mikkets the famine in Canaan grows so severe that Jacob's sons realize that they have no choice but to return to Egypt, but Jacob nevertheless refuses to allow Benjamin to travel with them. With the family stuck at an impasse, Reuben steps forward: "Then Reuben said to his father, 'You may kill my two sons if I do not bring him back to you. Put him in my care, and I will return him to you'" (Gen. 42:37). Jacob simply ignores Reuben's ardent plea, turning to all the brothers and declaring, "My son shall not go down with you" (42:38).

Note what happens here: Reuben sees a problem and acts quickly—quite possibly from pure motives. But his alacrity is sadly matched by his heedlessness: He tries to assure Jacob by offering him the right to put his own grandchildren to death! As a midrash imagines Jacob saying, "This is a foolish first-born son! Are your sons not my sons?" (Genesis Rabbah 91:9).

Judah, in contrast, bides his time; he is not quick, but he is effective. When conditions deteriorate even further, Judah addresses his father: "Send the boy in my care, and let us be on our way, that we may live and not die—you and we and our children. I myself will be surety for him; you may hold me responsible. If I do not bring him back and set him before you, I shall be guilty before you forever" (Gen. 43:8-10). Upon hearing Judah's plea, Jacob relents and agrees to send his beloved Benjamin.

The contrast between Judah's proposal and Reuben's is stark and powerful: Where Reuben begins by introducing the specter of death (and the possibility of even more death as a response), Judah begins by affirming life and assuring his father that they—all of them—will live and not die. Judah works more slowly than his older brother but also more methodically—and intelligently.

The same contrast was already evident when the brothers first hatched a plan to dispense with Joseph. Reuben immediately—and admirably—resists their plans: "When Reuben heard [their plans], he tried to save him from them. He said: Let us not take his life." Reuben goes on: "Shed no blood! Cast him into that pit out in the wilderness but do not touch him yourselves."

Reuben wants to do what is right; the narrator tells us that he "intended to save [Joseph] from them and return him to his father" (Gen. 37:21-22).[206] But here, too, he fails; like his father much later, his brothers simply ignore him. In this instance, too, Judah waits and after a while proposes an alternative to slaying Joseph: "What do we gain by killing our brother and covering up his blood? Come, let us sell him to the Ishmaelites, but let us not do away with him ourselves. After all, he is our brother, our own flesh." Strikingly, though the brothers discount Reuben's protest, they accept Judah's proposal (37:26-27).

Judah's approach diverges from Reuben's in two critical ways: First, he waits until the heat of the moment has passed, when the others are more likely to listen; and second—note the remarkable subtlety of the text—he never distances himself from his brothers: Judah's entire speech is in the first person, as if to suggest that he and his brothers are in their plot together. His language wins their trust and, ultimately, their compliance. Reuben, in contrast, shifts to the second person. On one level the shift is understandable: He wants no part of their nefarious plot. But it is also ineffective, and it erects a wall between him and them. Not surprisingly, his intervention fails.

Jacob understands that Reuben is dangerously impetuous. Even when his cause is just and his motives pure, he operates too hastily—and thus loses the very people he needs to convince. A similar dynamic is at play in Reuben's rebellion against his father. One can imagine a more communicative version of Jacob lecturing his son: "I understand that you were hurt and angry. But you thought that the best way to get back at me was to violate elemental rules of decency?!"[207]

In likening Reuben to "turbulent waters," then, Jacob no doubt refers to his horrific behavior with Bilhah, but he also points to something deeper and more fundamental: His son is reckless, impulsive, and foolhardy—and therefore also totally ineffectual. Reuben's suffering is deep and his anger understandable. Jacob likely does not grasp how much he has hurt his son, and how much desperation he has induced in him. But Jacob nevertheless discerns a crucial truth about leadership: Rashness, no matter how righteous, does not a leader make.

Va-yiggash #1

Humiliation

Judaism's Fourth Cardinal Sin?

In Jewish ethics humiliating another person is regarded as an extraordinarily grave offense, one that we should avoid committing, some rabbis insist, even if our lives depend on it. The talmudic sages learn that lesson from two striking stories in Genesis, each of which, they insist, has dramatic ethical implications.

Parashat Vayeshev tells the story of Judah and Tamar (Genesis 38). Tamar finds herself in an impossible situation, with her life on the line, and the sages are awed by the way she handles herself.

Tamar is married to Judah's first son Er, who dies without having had a child. Because of the requirements of Levirate law (*yibbum*), Er's brother Onan then marries Tamar, but, realizing that any child he and she have will be his brother's heir rather than his own, he carefully avoids impregnating her, and he, too, soon dies. Judah worries that maybe his first two sons have died as a result of their common wife, Tamar, so he tells her to go and wait in her father's house until his third son, Shelah, is old enough for marriage. But as both she and we are given to understand, he has no intention of ever giving his youngest son to her. She is tied down and seemingly helpless—at once forbidden to marry outside Judah's family and prevented from marrying inside it.

Tamar takes matters into her own hands. When Judah has completed the mourning period after the recent death of his wife, she poses as a prostitute, accepts his request for sex, and conceives in the process. (Subtly the text criticizes Judah: Just as soon as he is permitted, he goes looking for sex, the possibility of which he has indefinitely taken away from her).[208] At Tamar's request he leaves his seal, cord, and staff with her (which Robert Alter calls the ancient equivalent of all a person's major credit cards)[209] until such time as Judah can pay her with a kid from his flock. Judah sends a friend to find the prostitute and settle his debts, but the people of her town insist that there has been no such woman among them.

Eventually Tamar begins to show. Judah hears that she is pregnant and condemns her to death by fire. The sages were preoccupied with what happens next. Tamar has evidence that would incriminate Judah and exonerate her—and yet, at least as the sages understand the story, she takes the risk of sending the signs to Judah privately, asking: "See, please (*haker na*) if you recognize to whom these belong." Taking responsibility, Judah acknowledges that Tamar has behaved better than he (*tzadkah mimeni*), and her life is saved (Gen. 38:25–26).

The sages were profoundly moved by Tamar's clear choice: She would rather die than humiliate her father-in-law. Her father-in-law has treated her badly over a long period and has now condemned her to death—and yet still she will not humiliate him, even at the price of her own life. From this a sage (there is some confusion about his exact identity) concludes that "it is preferable for a person to throw herself into a fiery furnace rather than humiliate another person" (BT, Bava Metzia 59a).

This startling principle of Jewish ethics is almost always associated with Tamar. But another Rabbinic sage derives the same conclusion from parashat Va-yiggash. Seemingly still angry at his brothers for long ago selling him into slavery, the now enormously powerful Joseph has made their lives extremely difficult, accusing them of crimes they have not committed and making demands he knows they will find it all but impossible to meet. Finally Joseph orchestrates a scene whereby Benjamin, his younger brother and Jacob's new favorite, will be imprisoned on trumped-up charges. For Judah this is the last straw, and he throws himself upon Joseph's mercy: If Judah and his brothers return to their father without their youngest brother in tow, their father will die of grief, a burden they simply cannot bear. Judah goes so far as to beg to be enslaved in Benjamin's place (Gen. 44:33–34).

Seeing how Judah, who had hatched the plan to sell him into slavery, now stands ready to do anything at all to help Benjamin avoid a similar fate, Joseph is overcome with emotion. What he does next strikes a talmudic sage as exceedingly strange: "Joseph could no longer control himself before all his attendants, and he cried out, 'Have everyone withdraw from me!' So there was no one else about when Joseph made himself known to his brothers.... Joseph said to his brothers, 'I am Joseph. Is my father still alive?'" (45:1,3).

Given his brothers' past history of hatred and violence toward him, is Joseph not acting recklessly? Perhaps, before identifying himself, he ought to have called more attendants into the room rather than sending away the ones already present. R. Samuel b. Nahman comments: "Joseph put himself in grave danger, because if his brothers had killed him, no one would have known whom to blame. So why did he say, 'Have everyone withdraw from me?' This is what Joseph thought: Better that I be killed than I humiliate my brothers in front of the Egyptians" (*Midrash Tanhuma*, Va-yiggash 5).[210]

Joseph, like Tamar just a few chapters earlier, would rather die than humiliate another person. Those whose feelings he wants to protect have hurt him immensely and caused him great pain and suffering. Perhaps, in learning from these biblical models, we are meant to reason as follows: If Tamar and Joseph, each nursing such deep wounds, nevertheless refuse to humiliate those who have aggrieved them, even at the price of their own lives, how much more so must we subdue the impulse to shame and humiliate. We have likely not been condemned to death or sold into slavery, nor is the choice before us shaming another or facing possible death. The message of the sages seems clear: Humiliation is a heinous offense, and there is rarely—if ever—an excuse for it.

Just how literally is this prohibition meant to be taken? Are we really supposed to submit to death rather than bring shame upon another person?

At first glance this seems like a beautiful idea, potentially even a life-transforming one, but undoubtedly also a homiletical one. Our sages want us to know just how serious a crime it is to shame and humiliate another person, so they wax hyperbolic, telling us that we should prefer to be killed rather than commit such an egregious crime. In any case the expression "it is preferable" to act in a certain way sounds much more like advice than like law.

And yet, amazingly, some of the most significant figures in the history of Jewish law insist that our principle is not hyperbole at all, but rather a simple and straightforward statement of legal obligation: We are required by law to die rather than humiliate another person.[211] Ask a reasonably knowledgeable Jew, and he or she is likely to tell you that there are three cardinal sins in Judaism, three offenses one should prefer to die than commit: idolatry, sexual immorality, and murder. But according to these scholars, stunningly, humiliation appears to be a fourth.[212]

Why is Judaism so preoccupied with avoiding humiliation? Rabbeinu Yonah suggests that humiliation has "shades of murder" to it (avak retzihah). If this strikes you as far-fetched, close your eyes for a moment and imagine the moment in your life when you have felt most deeply humiliated. Your body, your blood flow—everything feels terrifyingly off-kilter, almost like a mini-death. How many people have found themselves wishing they could die rather than be humiliated in the same way again? In a similar vein, R. Eliyahu HaKohen of Izmir (1659–1729) suggests that humiliation is actually worse than murder: Murder happens all at once, and then it's over, he says, but humiliation takes place slowly and is torturously painful. Moreover, murder happens once, but when someone is humiliated, he is humiliated anew each time he sees the people who witnessed it, and it is like being killed over and over again.[213]

Why do so many influential rabbinic figures maintain that there is a legal requirement to die rather than humiliate another person despite the fact that the talmudic statement is couched in the language of counsel rather than law?

Everybody knows that people, often despite themselves, tend to take concrete legal obligations more seriously than inspired ideas and high-minded ideals. These legal decisors want the prohibition on humiliation to have teeth, to take hold of us and orient the way we carry ourselves in the world and interact with other people. To state the obvious, though, even those who do not think our statement has the status of law still assign it tremendous importance. There is no question that one may not humiliate another person; the debate is really over whether the prohibition is so serious that one should choose death rather than violate it. According to a variety of Jewish sources, the honor of a person is in many ways akin to the honor of God. The prohibition on humiliation is really just the culmination of Judaism's obsession with human dignity more broadly.

But there is another reason, too. All too often, we tend to rationalize the act of embarrassing people. Sometimes, after speaking abusively to another person, we can almost hear ourselves saying, "It's not like I killed them, is it?" Actually, Jewish ethics reminds us, it is.

Taking inspiration from the examples of Tamar and Joseph, the sages want us to live as if the dignity of the people we meet is the most important thing in the world. Because, according to Jewish theology, it just might be.

Va-yiggash #2

Saving and Enslaving

The Complexity of Joseph

Sometimes the line between heroism and cruelty can be difficult to discern.[214]

Faced with severe famine, Joseph shows himself to be a skilled and effective administrator; with great foresight and planning, he repeatedly brings the Egyptians back from the brink of starvation. Joseph is obviously an adept manager, but he is also seemingly a ruthless one: He saves the Egyptians, but, as we shall see, he also enslaves them. In so doing he runs afoul of the Torah's vision of how an ideal society should function.

As the devastating famine in Egypt persists, the land languishes, and the Egyptians grow progressively more desperate. Joseph provides the people with "rations," in exchange for which he "gathers in all the money that was to be found in the land of Egypt" (Gen. 47:14). The Egyptians' money gives out, but conditions are still terrible, and the people need food. They approach Joseph, saying, "Give us bread; why should we die before your very eyes? for the money is gone" (47:15). Joseph responds by demanding that the Egyptians bring their livestock, and he feeds them "in exchange for the horses, for the stocks of sheep and cattle, and the asses" (47:16–17).

But the livestock too runs out, and, finding themselves in dire straits, the Egyptians approach Joseph again: "We cannot hide from my lord that, with all the money and animal stocks consigned to our lord, nothing is left at my lord's disposal save our corpses[215] and our land." They beseech him, "Why should we perish before your eyes, both we and our land? Take us and our land in exchange for bread, and we with our land will be serfs (*avadim*) to Pharaoh; provide the seed, that we may live and not die, and that the land may not become a waste" (Gen. 47:18–19).

Joseph dispenses food and thereby "gains possession of all the farm-land of Egypt for Pharaoh, every Egyptian having sold his field because the famine was too much for them"; soon enough Pharaoh owns every last inch of the land (Gen. 47:20)—except that owned by the priests (47:22). Joseph "removes the population town by town, from one end of Egypt to the other" (47:21). Reminding the Egyptians that he has "acquired [them] and [their] land for Pharaoh," he disburses seed for them to sow the land. He instructs the people that they may keep four fifths of what they grow, but the remaining fifth is a tax due to Pha-raoh (47:23-24). The people respond with gratitude, declaring, "You have saved our lives! We are grateful to my lord, and we shall be serfs (slaves? Hebrew *avadim*) to Pharaoh" (47:25).

Joseph establishes this as the law of the land "to this very day": A fifth of everything the people grow belongs to Pharaoh (Gen. 47:26). Having surrendered everything—their money, their livestock, their land, and their freedom—to Joseph, the people become Pharaoh's "slaves"—or, as some modern scholars prefer, "tenant farmers of the state."[216]

How does Joseph understand his own behavior? Earlier, in an attempt to alleviate his brothers' distress, Joseph had told them that "it was to save life (*la-mihyah*) that God sent me ahead of you" (Gen. 45:5). At min-imum his words refer to his now having the power and wealth to feed his own family (45:7,11), but Joseph may well think that his mission is grander and more universal: God sent him to Egypt so that he could save the lives of the Egyptians, too. And indeed, when the Egyptians thank Joseph, they use language strikingly reminiscent of Joseph's own: "You have saved our lives (*hehiyitanu*)!"[217]

But how does the Torah view Joseph's enslavement of the Egyptians? And how are we, as modern readers, to understand his actions? Com-menting on Joseph's decision to remove the Egyptian populace from their homes (Gen. 47:21),[218] R. Samuel b. Meir (Rashbam, 1085-1158) and R. David Kimhi (Radak, 1160-1235) powerfully (though probably unintentionally) capture the ambiguity of the text. Rashbam compares Joseph's actions to the Assyrian king Sennacherib's (2 Kings 18:32) and explains that Joseph wanted to make sure that the Egyptians could not claim possession of their lands after having sold them (Rashbam to Gen. 47:21).[219] By comparing Joseph's actions to those one of Tanakh's great villains, is Rashbam subtly condemning them? Or is he merely explaining (one aspect) of what Joseph did by comparing his actions to those of another biblical figure? It is difficult to know.[220]

Radak goes one step further, explaining that Joseph dislocated the Egyptians because he wanted them to be cognizant of their profound indebtedness to Pharaoh, on whose land they are able to dwell their only by his good graces (Radak to Gen. 47:21).[221] Is Radak criticizing Joseph here, or merely uncovering the inner logic of his decisions? Again it is difficult to say.

Some scholars defend Joseph and even heap praise upon him, noting that "each time the citizenry give Joseph something of theirs, he gives back something of value. In exchange for their money, Joseph gives them rations (Gen. 47:14). In exchange for their cattle, he gives them food (47:17). In exchange for their land and persons, Joseph gives them seed (47:23)."[222] Though enslavement "sounds harsh," they argue, "it was in this situation beneficial, for now [the people's] food supply was Pharaoh's responsibility."[223] One scholar insists that Joseph was very far from a "callous, unethical taskmaster": Although the people do give up ownership of their land, Joseph allows them to keep fully 80 percent of their harvest.[224] As another scholar asks, "What kind of 'serfdom' is it that grants four-fifths of the produce to the 'serf'?"[225]

Even some scholars who themselves see Joseph's actions as troubling nevertheless doubt that the Torah shares their perspective. Jon Levenson, for example, avers that "the cruelty of Joseph's enslavement of Egypt does not seem to bother the narrator,"[226] and Robert Alter suggests that "the reduction of the entire population to a condition of virtual serfdom to the crown in all likelihood was meant to be construed not as an act of ruthlessness by Joseph but as an instance of his administrative brilliance."[227]

And yet I wonder. The ironic turns in the text are intense and powerful and thus require explanation: Brought to Egypt as a slave, Joseph now becomes Egypt's enslaver. And soon enough, a new Pharaoh rises and "the House of Israel [finds] themselves once again on the wrong end of the enslavement process."[228] Joseph displays remarkable administrative prowess, but he unleashes forces that eventually end up oppressing and degrading his own people. It is hard to imagine that the Torah makes no moral judgment at all on Joseph's setting this destructive process in motion.

Does this mean that Joseph is no better than the Pharaoh who eventually oppresses Israel? Hardly. The Torah paints a far more subtle and nuanced picture. It is surely noteworthy that while the Israelites groan under their misery (Exod. 2:23), the Egyptians, as we have seen, express gratitude to Joseph for keeping them fed (Gen. 47:25).[229] Not every slaveholder is the same, and not all processes of disempowerment are equivalent. But being better than Pharaoh is not in itself a ringing endorsement. The question is not whether Joseph is the most oppressive figure in the Torah; he most assuredly is not. The question is more modest: How does the Torah evaluate his behavior?

The Torah makes clear that Joseph is not out for his own profit or gain: The text is careful to mention that "Joseph brought the money [he collected] into Pharaoh's palace" (Gen. 47:14), and Nahmanides (Ramban, 1194–c. 1270) astutely explains that the Torah wants to emphasize Joseph's "trustworthiness": He does not create secret storehouses for his own lucre in Egypt, nor does he send the money to Canaan. Rather "he gives it all to the king who trusts him" (commentary to Gen. 47:14).

But faithful service to Pharaoh does not necessarily righteousness make. What of Joseph's treatment of the Egyptian people? Joseph does indeed save lives — no small feat in the midst of a widespread famine (Gen. 41:57). And yet the reader is left to wonder just how many of the steps Joseph takes are really necessary. Feeding the Egyptians is one thing, but progressively stripping them of everything they have is seemingly another. In what is perhaps another irony, the Israelites themselves will soon find out that being fed by one's owner creates an unhealthy and undignified sense of dependence, keeping one bound to one's oppressor (Exod. 16:2–3).[230]

Assume for a moment that Joseph's actions at the moment of crisis itself are defensible. It is nevertheless difficult to understand why he makes the serfdom of the Egyptians permanent, "to this very day" (Gen. 47:26). When the Torah imagines Israel's life in the land of Israel, it prohibits the permanent selling of land (Lev. 25:23); more generally, biblical texts insist that land is a heritage rather than a commodity to bought and sold—let alone for all time.[231] Deuteronomy is especially emphatic that, when the people arrive in the land, debt must be "rob[bed] of its tyrannical power" in order to "limit human misery."[232] In particular slavery must have a built-in limit of six years (Deut. 15:12[233]); permanent enslavement is unthinkable. In other words the Torah passionately prohibits the Israelites from doing to one another what Joseph does to the Egyptian people as a whole.[234] Walter Brueggemann notes that Deuteronomy's legislation is intended to serve as "a contradiction to the economic processes of the state economy in Egypt, in which debt-slaves evidently were so deeply indebted to the state that they were hopelessly and perpetually in bondage."[235]

In light of all this, Brueggemann cuttingly observes that "Joseph may be credited with shrewdness. But for a tradition looking to the Exodus, it is a doubtful credit."[236] I would be inclined to a somewhat more nuanced position: Joseph does save countless lives in a disastrous time and thus brings abundant blessing to the Egyptians. And yet he exacts too high a price from them—everything they have, including their very freedom—and insists on making what should have been at best a temporary arrangement permanent.[237] With those decisions he plays with fire, and that fire will eventually wound his own family in unspeakable ways.

Joseph provides short-term relief in the midst of a ghastly famine, but he also systematically and relentlessly strips the people bare. There is something to be said for administrative aptitude, but it is sobering to realize that it can be coupled with profound shortsightedness. It is also a great virtue to behave honestly and honorably with our superiors. But the greatest test of character may lie elsewhere—in the empathy we display toward those who stand powerless before us.[238]

Va-yeḥi #1

The Majesty of Restraint

Or, Joseph's Shining Moment

Judaism generally urges us to be agents, to be active rather than passive, to take responsibility for our lives and for the world. R. Joseph Soloveitchik (1903–93) goes so far as to insist that "the peak of religious ethical perfection to which Judaism aspires is man as creator."[239] This means that we are often asked to use the power at our disposal both to better our lives and to achieve holy ends.

But sometimes we are challenged to do just the opposite, to know when it is inappropriate to exercise our power. Although Soloveitchik (rightly) emphasizes the dignity of action, it is often no less important to learn the dignity of restraint.

Hurt and humiliated by her maidservant Hagar, Sarah "oppresses" her (Gen. 16:6). Although some traditional commentators defend Sarah's actions,[240] others forcefully accuse her of sin and moral failure. R. David Kimhi (Radak, 1160–1235) explains that Sarah's failure lies in the fact that she exercises her capacity to afflict someone vulnerable: "It is not appropriate," he says, "for a person to do everything she can with what is under her power." Radak cites the poet Solomon Ibn Gabirol (eleventh century): "How beautiful is forgiveness at the moment one has power." The terribly painful story of Sarah and Hagar is included in the Torah, Radak teaches, precisely so that we learn from Sarah's mistakes (commentary to Gen. 16:6).

Joseph starts out following in Sarah's path. At first, it seems, he really wants to make his brothers suffer. But over time something shifts in him—and in them—and that makes possible one of the most moving and remarkable moments of transformation in the Torah.

When we first hear of Joseph's tortured relations with his brothers—of Jacob's favoritism and of Joseph's habit of bringing bad reports about his brothers to his father—Genesis tells us that his brothers "could not speak a friendly word to him" (*velo yakhlu dabro leshalom*) (Gen. 37:2–4). Years later, when the brothers arrive in Egypt in search of food during a famine, Joseph, by now second in command to Pharaoh, recognizes them, although they do not recognize him. Right away the text informs us that Joseph "spoke harshly to them" (*vayedaber itam kashot*) (42:7). Just as they, long ago, could not find a kind word for him, now he will not trouble himself to find one for them.

In what follows, Joseph appears to take revenge. Joseph's brothers had followed Judah's lead and sold him into slavery (Gen. 37:26–28), unleashing the process that led to his imprisonment on false charges (39:17–20). Now, with his brothers in his sights, what does Joseph do? He falsely and repeatedly accuses them of being spies and confines them to the guardhouse (42:9–17). Just as Potiphar imprisoned Joseph for a crime he did not commit, so now he falsely imprisons his brothers.

There is a certain literary elegance to the next stage of Joseph's treatment of his brothers. In that fateful moment when they had decided to finally rid themselves of him, Joseph's brothers had sold him for money (Gen. 37:28). Now, years later, Joseph orders his brothers' bags filled with grain and provisions, but also with the very money they have used to pay for what they need (42:25). Bible scholar Matthew Schlimm notes: "Joseph's brothers once sold him into slavery for financial gain. In an act of symmetrical retribution, Joseph strikes fear into their hearts by giving them silver that they do not deserve and should not rightfully possess."[241] Money had played a key role when they hurt him; now money serves as his method of revenge.

And Joseph is still not done. Once, his brothers had sold him for "twenty pieces of silver" (Gen. 37:28). On their next visit to Egypt, Joseph further confounds his brothers, setting (one of) them up again: Joseph commands his steward to place his silver divination cup in Benjamin's bag and then has him exposed as a thief (44:1–13). The repeated invocation of silver is revealing: Joseph had already tormented his brothers by surreptitiously returning their silver to them (42:25,28,35), and now he furtively plants his silver cup with his younger brother (44:2).

Bible scholar Thomas Broadie astutely explains that "the silver is the symbol of the still-unresolved betrayal" and comments: "Ever since [that betrayal], the silver seems to stick to [Joseph's brothers]. Like Lady Macbeth, unable to get the blood of the murdered king off her hands, they cannot get away from the bloody silver."[242]

Accused of theft, Joseph's brothers return to Egypt, where he confronts them: "What is this deed that you have done?" (*mah ha-ma'aseh asher asitem*) (Gen. 44:15). On the surface, of course, he appears to be asking about the (purportedly) stolen silver cup. But as Schlimm points out, the question has a deeper and more fundamental resonance. Recall God's words to Eve after she and Adam eat of the forbidden fruit in Eden: "What is this you have done?!" (*mah zot asit*) (3:13), and to Cain after he slays his brother: "What have you done?!" (*meh asita*) (4:10). Like God's words in those two foundational stories, "Joseph's question is a call for reflection on all that has transpired, both in the immediate and in the distant past." That is why, Schlimm observes, Joseph speaks in the plural (the Hebrew *atem*, rather than *atah*), even though he claims he is only interested in the one brother who has acted wrongly in this instance.[243]

Joseph thus afflicts his brothers over a period of years, punishing them for what they had once done to him. But he does more than just mete out punishment. He also tries to shock them and shake them, to disorient them so much that they are forced to ask how they ended up in this horrific situation.

The strategy seems to work. After being falsely accused of spying and told that they will have no choice but to bring their youngest brother down to Egypt, they begin to search themselves: "They said to one another, 'Alas, we are being punished on account of our brother, because we looked on his anguish, yet paid no heed as he pleaded with us. That is why this distress has come upon us'" (Gen. 42:21).

Perhaps there is even more: Perhaps Joseph jars and unsettles them in such extreme ways because he wants to see whether they have changed. Perhaps if they have let go of their hatred of him, he can forgive them. In a deeply poignant moment, as soon as he hears them express remorse, Joseph "turned away from them and wept" (Gen. 42:24). The regret on the part of the culprits does not erase past injuries, but it does mitigate the severity of Joseph's pain—or, at very least, it sets that process in motion.

This slow, torturous tale now comes to an astonishing resolution. Faced with the impending unjust imprisonment of his youngest brother, Judah steps forward and insists that he should be incarcerated in Benjamin's place. Having once hatched the plan to sell Joseph into slavery (Gen. 37:26), Judah is now willing to be enslaved rather than allow a "recurrence of past evils."[244] Whereas he and his brothers once displayed brazen indifference to the pain their actions would cause their father, Judah now seems passionately concerned with Jacob's well-being: "For how can I go back to my father unless the boy is with me? Let me not be witness to the woe that would overtake my father!" (44:34). Judah, it seems, is a changed man, a paragon of repentance. Joseph is so moved by this display that he can no longer contain himself—sobbing, he reveals his true identity to them (45:1–4). Stunningly, he encourages them to forgive themselves, averring that God had been working behind the scenes, sending Joseph to Egypt to "save life" and ensure his family's survival in the face of prolonged famine (45:5–7).

In this moment the text, in its quiet, subtle way, signals how much has really changed. Joseph embraces his brother Benjamin, and they both weep. And then, Genesis tells us, "he kissed all his brothers and wept upon them, and afterwards his brothers spoke with him" (Gen. 45:15). Recall how this long and harrowing saga began: Joseph's brothers could not speak a friendly word to him (37:4). Now, finally, it seems, after all the tribulations the family has endured, they do just that.

And then, in parashat Va-yeḥi, comes another exquisitely moving moment. Jacob dies, sending Joseph's brothers into a panic. They again fear that Joseph still bears a grudge against them and will make them pay for their past crimes (Gen. 50:15)—living testimony to just how difficult it can be to believe that those we have wronged have truly forgiven us. They beg for Joseph's mercy and declare, "Here we are, slaves to you!" (50:18). But Joseph's response demonstrates how profoundly he too has changed: "Have no fear! Am I a substitute for God?" (50:19).

We have already seen the depth of Judah's repentance and transformation. Now look at Joseph. As a young man, he had dreamed of his brothers bowing down to him, of being lord over them (Gen. 37:5–11). Now, with the fulfillment of his grandiose dreams before him, he repudiates his dreams and embraces his brothers instead. He makes unequivocally clear that he has no illusions of being God and no need for his brothers to be his servants or slaves. Where they fear he will enact vengeance upon them, he instead promises to support and care for them and their children. Joseph may well have harbored fantasies of hurting his brothers and exacting revenge—and here, finally, is his chance. But with his father dead and his brothers at his mercy, what does he do? He insists that punishment is God's prerogative rather than his. And then, again, the poignant refrain: "He comforted them and spoke kindly to them" (literally spoke to their hearts, *vayedaber al libam*) (50:21). Joseph and his family have discovered the power of comforting speech.

Sarah's failure is Joseph's success; what she forgets, he at last remembers. Fully conscious of his power to wound those who have wounded him, Joseph instead heeds a commandment Moses will soon receive: not to take revenge or bear a grudge (Lev. 19:18). Sometimes people achieve greatness through the use of power. But in this remarkable moment, Joseph models a different kind of greatness: the majesty of restraint.

Va-yeḥi #2

Underreacting and Overreacting

Dinah's Family in Crisis

How do we respond when someone we care about is violated? Genesis portrays both Jacob and his sons responding in ways that are, ultimately, totally inappropriate. The Torah's account of their reactions prods us to imagine how we might respond in the face of such disorienting and infuriating brutality.

As the end of his life nears, Jacob passionately denounces his sons Simeon and Levi: "Simeon and Levi are a pair; their weapons (*mekhoroteihem*)[245] are tools of violence (*hamas*). Let not my person be included in their council, let not my being be counted in their assembly. For when angry they slaughter men, and when pleased they maim oxen.[246] Cursed be their fury so fierce, and their wrath so relentless. I will divide them in Jacob, disperse them in Israel" (Gen. 49:5–7).

The Hebrew is notoriously difficult, but the thrust of Jacob's words is clear: Simeon and Levi are so consumed with anger that they behave in brutal and barbaric ways; they are, as one scholar puts it, "murderous, violent, fiercely angry, arbitrary, cruel, and harsh in their treatment of animals."[247] Because the two sons "uniquely share the same criminal traits of violence, anger, and cruelty, they share the same condemnation and fate."[248] Jacob wants no part of them; he ostracizes them and punishes them with loss of both leadership and land.

Jacob's censure of his sons refers back to the rape of Dinah (Genesis 34),[249] one of the most sordid stories in the Torah. In that squalid tale, Simeon and Levi do indeed behave deplorably, but Jacob's own conduct is arguably no better than theirs.

Genesis tells us that Dinah "went out to see the daughters of the land" of Canaan (Gen. 34:1). Shechem, son of Hamor, one of the leaders of the land, "saw her . . . took her, laid with her, and violated her" (34:2).

But Shechem develops tender feelings for his victim and wants to marry her.[250] He asks his father to "get me this girl for a wife" (34:3-4).

The reader expects that when Jacob hears that "his daughter" has been "defiled," he will be indignant; in a parallel case, when King David hears that his daughter Tamar has been raped, he is "very angry" (2 Sam. 13:21).[251] But oddly, the Torah reports that Jacob "kept his silence until [his sons] came home" (Gen. 34:5). When his sons come in from the fields and hear the news, they grow "distressed and very angry, because [Shechem] had committed an outrage (*nevalah*) in Israel by lying with Jacob's daughter—a thing not to be done" (34:7). The contrast between Jacob's reaction and his sons' could not be more stark: He is silent and passive, while they are—appropriately—incensed.

Jacob's silence reflects poorly upon him. Casting Jacob in a frightfully negative light, some scholars accuse him of "indifference to his daughter's humiliation" and insist that "he does not seem to care about his daughter's honor."[252] Noticing that the text nowhere describes Jacob as summoning his sons home, they conclude that, appallingly, "Jacob does not view [Dinah's having been raped as] important enough to send prompt word."[253]

Jacob's harshest critics may be right, but I am not sure that the patriarch's inner world is transparent enough to convict him of indifference. Rather, as we shall see, cowardice may play a large part in his (non) response. But one thing does seem clear: Jacob's silence and passivity are deeply disturbing.[254]

In contrast to their father, Dinah's brothers spring into action, plotting to avenge the humiliation of their sister. As negotiations take place between Shechem and his father, on the one side, and Jacob and his sons, on the other, the Canaanites shockingly conduct themselves as if nothing untoward has transpired, likely adding to the brothers' rage. An agreement is reached, but Jacob's sons engage in subterfuge: They tell the two Canaanites that they are uncomfortable with the thought of their sister marrying an uncircumcised man, "for that is a disgrace among us" (Gen. 34:14), and declare that they are open to intermarriages with the locals on the condition that "you will become like us in that every male among you is circumcised" (34:15). Shechem and his father readily agree and convince the people of their town to do as asked.

On the third day after their circumcision, as the men are "in pain," Simeon and Levi slaughter them: "Each took his sword, came upon the city unmolested,[255] and slew all the males. They put Hamor and his son Shechem to the sword, took Dinah out of Shechem's house" — only now do we learn that Dinah had been held in Shechem's house the whole time; under the veneer of a good-faith negotiation lies the terrifying reality of a sister still in captivity— "and went away" (Gen. 34:25–26).

In telling a story, it is rare for the Torah to make its moral judgments explicit; it usually conveys its perspective in far subtler ways. And yet here the text takes pains to make its judgment clear and unambiguous, characterizing the brothers' plan as a deception (*mirmah*) (Gen. 34:13), a word whose connotations are always pejorative.[256] This is the word Isaac uses to condemn Jacob's deception in taking Esau's blessing (27:35), and also the one Jacob himself uses to express outrage at Laban's mendacity in substituting Leah for Rachel (29:25). The narrator wants to make sure that even if, as readers, we share the brothers' sense of indignation, we will not be blinded to the nefariousness of their plot. Not only are the brothers dishonest; they also "use religion as a vehicle for their deception."[257]

But of course deception is only the beginning of their crime. Simeon and Levi murder a city full of men for the crime of one of them. That kind of collective punishment is appalling by any moral standard.

Working hard to defend the massacre, Maimonides (Rambam, 1135–1204) argues that the residents of the city, bound as they were by the Noahide laws, were obligated to set up a judicial system to punish crimes such as Shechem's. Their failure to execute judgment implicated them and meant that they deserved the death penalty (*Mishneh Torah*, Laws of Kings and Their Wars 9:14). But Nahmanides (Ramban, 1194– c. 1270) will have none of it, asking why, if the residents of Shechem deserved to die, Jacob did not kill them himself. And if fear is what held him back, why does he so forcefully condemn the actions of his sons? (commentary to Gen. 34:13).

As we have seen, Jacob's sons are at first portrayed far more favorably than their father—they, at least, are indignant about how Dinah has been treated. Yet their ultimate response is arguably even more deplorable than their father's; their moral indignation gives way to "unmitigated violence and shameless barbarity."[258] Lest we worry that this judgment projects a modern sensibility onto the text, Gordon Wenham emphasizes that "a massacre of all the men of the city for one man's sin was as shocking to the narrator as it is to modern ears." Though Simeon and Levi's "motives can . . . be construed as honorable . . . their actions were reprehensible."[259]

But the story is not quite over. Though Simeon and Levi have rescued their sister and departed the city, their brothers now come and plunder the town. They seize everything: "All that was inside the town and outside; all their wealth, all their children, and their wives, all that was in their homes, they took as captives and booty" (Gen. 34:27–29). The text notes that they did all this "because their sister had been defiled"; Nahum Sarna explains that "the narrator is at pains to stress that the brothers were stirred to action because of the defilement of their sister, not simply for the love of booty."[260] But Meir Sternberg suggests that the description of the brothers' motivation may well be ironic, an attempt to contrast "the brothers' fine words and their ugly deeds, between idealistic facade and materialistic reality, between deceit as sacred rage and as unholy calculation."[261]

Finally, as the story comes to an end, Jacob speaks: "Jacob said to Simeon and Levi, 'You have brought trouble on me, making me odious among the inhabitants of the land, the Canaanites and the Perizzites; my men are few in number, so that if they unite against me and attack me, I and my house will be destroyed'" (Gen. 34:30). Jacob's "feeble response . . . is less than noble. He is concerned only about a counter-offensive from an alliance of other Canaanites in the region."[262] Jacob expresses no judgment at all about the moral (in)appropriateness of his sons' behavior; his concerns are, in Nehama Leibowitz's words, "purely utilitarian."[263]

Jacob is, in a word, afraid. The man who had been courageous enough to wrestle with an angel is nowhere to be found in this story. "Of course, fear is natural in such a situation, but the reasons Jacob gives for damning his sons betray him. He does not condemn them for the massacre, for abusing the rite of circumcision, or even for breach of contract."[264] He is frightened of the consequences of his sons' actions — nothing more.

Jacob's sons are no doubt disgusted by his words. "But they answered, 'Should our sister be treated like a whore?'" (Gen. 34:31). Addressing Jacob, they do not call Dinah "your daughter," as we might have expected. "They in effect wrest her out of the father's guardianship: She may not be your daughter, but she certainly is 'our sister,' and no one will treat her like a whore."[265]

Wenham points out that the brothers' furious rhetorical question "could be referring not just to Shechem's treatment of Dinah, but also to Jacob's." Behind the brothers' question, he argues, is a brutal condemnation of their father: "To do nothing about the rape and then to be willing to accept gifts after the event is to act like a pimp."[266] In any event "Jacob here is sadly comparable to the Canaanites. He shows no moral indignation and wants only to solve the matter prudently."[267]

Faced with an assault on their daughter and sister, Dinah's family thus splits into camps, each responding in extremely problematic ways. Jacob and his sons offer only scandalous nonreaction, on the one hand, and murderous overreaction, on the other. Jacob's "sons are rash and unbridled, and he is passive. No one in this story escapes censure"[268] And so, as the story ends, "the appeaser and the avengers, mutually exasperated, and swayed respectively by fear and fury [are] perhaps equidistant from true justice. They exemplify two perennial but sterile reactions to evil."[269]

What does the Torah want to teach us about violence?

When Dinah's brothers first hear of the attack on their sister, the Torah tells us that they were "distressed." The Hebrew word, *va-yit'atzvu*, is extremely suggestive. Looking at the vast wickedness threatening to overrun the earth in the days of Noah, God's "heart was distressed" (*vay-it'atzeiv*) (Gen. 6:6). In contrast to her father, Dinah's brothers respond correctly — like God, they stare evil in the face and are heartbroken.

But that Godlike response is not the end of the story. As we have seen, with death approaching, Jacob finally does express fierce moral condemnation of his sons' savagery. Tellingly he accuses them of *hamas*, violence (Gen. 49:5).[270] That word, too, is enormously suggestive: Why does God give up on humanity in the days of Noah? Because they are guilty of *hamas* (6:11).

With stunning literary subtlety, the Torah thus makes its point: Dinah's brothers are right to respond to evil with sadness and outrage. But in slaughtering an entire population they reproduce and even amplify the very evil to which they respond. In combating evil, the Torah warns us, we must remain ever vigilant lest we become more and more like the enemies we legitimately fight.

EXODUS

Shemot #1

Why Moses?

Or, What Makes a Leader?

What makes a leader? For the Torah leadership is not primarily about methods or tactics; it's about character.

What kind of human being must one be in order to lead on God's behalf? Not surprisingly, the life of Moses offers us some clues.

Exodus 2 recounts three episodes in Moses's life that seem to prepare him to assume the mantle of Israel's leader. First, Moses sees an Egyptian taskmaster beating an Israelite and intervenes on the latter's behalf (Exod. 2:11–12). Not content to defend his fellow Israelites, however, he next tries to adjudicate between them (2:13). Observing injustice on the one hand, and internecine conflict on the other, Moses is not just disturbed or disappointed; he acts to remedy the situation.

How many of us encounter situations of injustice and pretend not to notice — or, just as bad, register the injustice but find a million excuses not to act? And how often do we turn a blind eye to strife that we could ameliorate or even heal, fearing that the burden of getting involved would just be too great to bear? What sets Moses apart is that he does not merely recognize oppression; he also acts unflinchingly to bring it to an end.

Crucially, the circle of Moses's concern does not end there. The Torah tells us a third story, in which Moses sees a group of shepherds mistreating a group of seven young Midianite women. "Moses rose and saved them," the text tells us, "and he watered their flock" (Exod. 2:16–17). Seeing the women being abused, Moses acts resolutely and rescues them.

Why is it so important to the Torah to tell this story? The Torah wants us to know that Moses is not just offended by injustices perpetrated against his own people. Moses also defends foreigners and strangers, and "his passion for justice makes no distinctions between nations."[1]

It is not enough for a Jewish leader to display ethnic solidarity—ethnic solidarity is surely necessary, but it is just as surely not sufficient. In order to be worthy of leadership, one must rebel against wrongdoing, no matter who the victim is.

The word the Torah employs to describe Moses's bold action is highly significant: he is described as "saving" the women (*vayoshi'an*). In the next chapter we learn that God, too, is about to be a rescuer (Exod. 3:8). And in summarizing the miraculous events at the sea eleven chapters later, the Torah announces, in words that echo Moses's own actions, "The Lord saved (*vayosha*) Israel that day from the Egyptians" (14:30). The word used to describe Moses's actions on behalf of the vulnerable women is the same word used to describe God's actions on behalf of the vulnerable Israelites. To side with the oppressed and act against injustice, the Torah subtly tells us, is to be like God (an instance of what philosophers call *imitatio dei*, Latin for the imitation of God). Just as God rebels against injustice and embraces the stranger, so too must the divinely appointed leader.

Moses's heroism in siding with the Midianite women has a fascinating parallel in American history. Frederick Douglass, the great abolitionist and ex-slave, was also an impassioned advocate for women's suffrage. Asked why he, a man, should be so ardently involved in the struggle for women's dignity, Douglass explained: "When I ran away from slavery, it was for myself; when I advocated emancipation, it was for my people; but when I stood up for the rights of women, self was out of the question, and I found a little nobility in the act."

Like Moses millennia before him, Douglass dedicated his life to leading his people out of slavery. And like Moses he understood that fighting for the groups to which he belonged—blacks, men—was ultimately not enough. The God of Israel is against injustice in all its forms, and not just injustice against this people or that (no matter how beloved). Put somewhat differently: what both Moses and Frederick Douglass intuitively understood is that for all the profound importance of ethnic solidarity, a wider human solidarity is also fundamental. One cannot lead this particular people without a concern for justice for all people(s).

Moses is an activist, a person appalled by oppression and persecution. These are, as we've seen, noble qualities — so noble, in fact, that they are associated with God. And yet crusaders against injustice are often consumed by their own indignation; all too often the line between righteousness and self-righteousness all but disappears and indignation crowds out gentleness, or modesty, or even the capacity for intimacy.[2]

So the Torah tells us something else about Moses: He was a shepherd (Exod. 3:1). To perform his duties properly, a shepherd must combine power on the one hand, with gentle attentiveness on the other. He must have the capacity to control and provide for his sheep, but he must also nurture and care for each one. A midrash poignantly evokes Moses's mercy and tenderness: "When Moses our teacher was tending the flock of Jethro in the wilderness, a little kid escaped from him. He ran after it until it reached a shady place.[3] When it reached the shady place, it came across a pool of water and stopped to drink. When Moses approached it, he said: 'I didn't realize that you ran away because of thirst; you must be tired.' He placed the kid upon his shoulder and walked on. Thereupon God said: 'You have mercy in leading a human being's flock; you will assuredly tend my flock Israel'" (Exodus Rabbah 2:2).

Not only must a leader take offense at injustice and act accordingly, in other words; he must also have compassion and act accordingly. Real compassion is not just an emotion — Moses does not just "feel bad" for the kid; real compassion is a weave of emotion and action. God's appointed leader does not merely feel for others. He acts decisively to alleviate their pain.

This is brought home in another Rabbinic interpretation of Moses's formative years. Exodus tells us that when Moses grew up, "he went out to his brothers and saw their burdens" (*vayar besivlotam*) (Exod. 2:11). What, ask the sages, does it mean that Moses "saw their burdens"? That he identified with them, felt for them, and — pivotally — acted to lighten their load: "He would see their suffering and weep, saying, 'Woe is me for you; would that I could die for you.' There is no work more strenuous than working with clay. He used to shoulder the burdens and help each one" (Exodus Rabbah 1:27). A modern commentator clarifies the nature of Moses's "seeing" Israel's burdens: "This seeing penetrated his belly, until his compassion for them brought him to tears. And out of his great compassion, he himself assisted them."[4]

As soon as God gives Moses his world-historical assignment ("Come, therefore, I will send you to Pharaoh and you shall free My people, the Israelites, from Egypt" [Exod. 3:10]), Moses tries to demur and protests: "Who am I that I should go to Pharaoh and free the Israelites from Egypt?" (3:11). God attempts to assuage Moses's anxieties: "I will be with you; that shall be your sign that it was I who sent you."

The second clause is actually somewhat ambiguous; it isn't clear precisely what God is suggesting will serve as a sign to Moses: is it the fact that God will be with him, or the fact that God just appeared to him in the burning bush? Or might it refer to what immediately follows: "When you have freed the people from Egypt, you shall worship God on this mountain" (Exod. 3:12). According to this last possibility, "the sign that it is God Who has sent Moses will be realized [only] when Moses succeeds in the extraordinary undertaking of bringing the Hebrews out of Egypt and leads them all the way to the mountain on which he now stands."[5]

R. Alexander Zusia Friedman (1897–1946) offers a fanciful but beautiful interpretation of what God means. God gives Moses his monumental assignment, and Moses responds by asking, "Who am I?" God then tells him: The very fact that you ask this question, the very fact that you doubt your ability to carry out this momentous mission is itself the sign that it is I who sent you, since I only choose those who are modest and self-effacing to do my work.[6]

As hard as it can be to remember in a culture obsessed with self-promotion, a degree of self-doubt is essential for authentic leadership. Too much self-doubt, and a person ends up paralyzed and fails to step up to the project at hand. Too little, however, and the temptations of arrogance and grandiosity loom large. God tells Moses, in effect: Good that you doubt yourself. Now go . . .

The opening chapters of Exodus paint a portrait of a flesh and blood leader, but they also lay out a template of what kind of human being a leader in the deepest sense should be: one who sees injustice and is compelled to respond; one who is outraged by oppression of any human being, Jewish or not; one who brings together a capacity for indignation with a gentleness of spirit; one who manifests a compassion so deep that he cannot but attempt to aid those in need; and one who remembers to ask, "Really, me?" Those are the signs that it is God who sent him.

Shemot #2

Gratitude and Liberation

Everyone thinks they know the story of the Exodus: No longer able to bear their oppression and enslavement, the Israelites cry out to God, who remembers the covenant and redeems them. The story of the slaves being freed is the foundational story of the Jewish people: Twice a day Jewish liturgy recounts the experience of slavery and liberation, and once a year, at Passover, Jews ritually reenact the journey from bondage to freedom. When God is revealed at Mount Sinai, it is not as Creator of heaven and earth but as the "God who brought you out of the land of Egypt, the house of bondage" (Exod. 20:2; Deut. 5:6). And when the Torah demands that the Israelites take care not to oppress the stranger, they are repeatedly reminded why: "For you know the feelings of the stranger, having yourselves been strangers in the land of Egypt" (Exod. 23:9).

And yet in some Jewish sources, the story takes on a seemingly very different hue. A narrative of subjugation and deliverance becomes, of all things, a tale of gratitude and ingratitude.[7]

The book of Exodus begins on an ominous note: The text tells us that "a new king arose over Egypt who did not know Joseph" (Exod. 1:8). This is a surprising turn of events—according to Genesis, after all, Joseph was enormously powerful, second in power only to Pharaoh himself. He effectively controls the Egyptian economy and amasses tremendous wealth for Pharaoh (Gen. 47:13–27). How is it possible that the new Pharaoh does not even know him?

But Joseph is not the only biblical character whom Pharaoh does not know. A few chapters later, when Moses first conveys God's demand to let Israel go, Pharaoh responds contemptuously: "Who is the Lord that I should heed Him and let Israel go? I do not know the Lord, nor will I let Israel go" (Exod. 5:2).[8]

Commenting on Pharaoh's purported ignorance of Joseph, a midrash asks, "But how can this be, for to this very day, the Egyptians know the kindness Joseph did for them?!"[9] Rather, the midrash answers, "Pharaoh knew Joseph but did not pay him adequate attention, and was ungrateful to him. And in the end, he was ungrateful to God as well, as it says, 'I do not know the Lord.' From this we learn," the midrash adds, "that ingratitude is closely related to rejection of God" (*Midrash Ha-Gadol* to Exod. 1:8).[10] When the Torah tells us that Pharaoh did not "know" Joseph, in other words, it means to suggest not that Pharaoh was unacquainted with Joseph, but rather that he did not acknowledge Joseph and the great debt that Egypt as a whole, and Pharaoh in particular, owed him.

Pharaoh is ungrateful both to Joseph and to God. The midrash insists that these two types of ingratitude are of a piece, and even that one leads almost inevitably to the other. Gratitude and ingratitude are ways of being in the world—the former has the potential to pervade and enrich every corner of our lives, and the latter has the power to metastasize and poison every aspect of our being. Pharaoh's ingratitude permeates his entire world, and it drives his life in endlessly destructive ways.

What does it mean to be ungrateful? At bottom ingratitude reflects an inability—or perhaps an unwillingness—to acknowledge our dependence on, and our indebtedness to, anything or anyone beyond ourselves. To be ungrateful is to be unable—or again perhaps just unwilling—to acknowledge other people, past or present, who have made our lives possible; and, traditional Jewish texts add, to be unable or unwilling to acknowledge God as the source of life. Hence Pharaoh refuses—and maybe at a certain point his refusal is so entrenched that it becomes an inability—to acknowledge his debt, either to Joseph or to God.

The midrash goes on to imagine God exhorting the Jewish people: "Be careful lest you be ungrateful to Me, for one who is ungrateful cannot accept the Kingdom of Heaven." At first glance God's statement may seem like a threat, but it is really a description: If we are ungrateful, if we don't acknowledge the reality of just how much has been given to us rather than made or achieved by us, we will actually be incapable of worshipping anything but ourselves. It is not surprising, then, that the prophet Ezekiel imagines Pharaoh insolently declaring, "The Nile is mine; I made it for myself" (Ezek. 29:3). Pharaoh's statement is the most dramatic denial possible of the fact that he is dependent, that as powerful as he is, he is still a creature, created by and dependent on God. Another midrash imagines Pharaoh disdainfully announcing: "I have no need of God; I created myself" (Midrash Ha-Gadol to Exod. 5:2). I myself am God, Pharaoh implies, and I therefore have no obligations to anything or anyone besides myself.

The midrashic Pharaoh is an extreme, even caricatured case. But you don't need to be Pharaoh to struggle with gratitude—you just need to be human. Very few of us are either brazen or delusional enough to claim that we created ourselves, or that we made the world that sustains us. And yet in smaller, less dramatic ways, many of us resist and struggle against admitting just how dependent and vulnerable we really are— against admitting, in other words, just how much we owe. Pharaoh embodies that problem at its ugliest and most frightening extreme.

Moses provides a striking contrast to Pharaoh.[11] At the beginning of Exodus, God hears the cries of the Israelite slaves and decides to send Moses to free his downtrodden people. Moses soon encounters God at the burning bush, and God summons him: "Come, therefore, I will send you to Pharaoh, and you shall free My people, the Israelites, from Egypt" (Exod. 3:10). Moses hesitates, God insists, and then ... something quite strange happens. Moses has just been assigned a world-historical task. Yet amazingly, he does not immediately head for Egypt to fulfill his mission. Instead Moses returns to his father-in-law Jethro in Midian and asks for permission: "Let me go back to my kinsmen in Egypt and see how they are faring" (4:18).

What is Moses doing? Pharaoh is mercilessly brutalizing the Israelites—according to one midrash, he is slaughtering and bathing in the blood of three hundred Jewish infants each day (Exodus Rabbah

1:34); according to another, when an Israelite slave fails to produce an adequate number of bricks, the Egyptians take his youngest son and use him as brick and mortar (*Sefer Ha-Yashar* to Exod., 69:6–8). Moses has been given the opportunity to free his brothers and sisters, and yet—seemingly inexcusably—he dallies.

A midrash imagines an answer to this question. Upon hearing God's demand that he set out for Egypt, Moses responds, "Master of the world, I can't, because Jethro welcomed me and opened his home to me, and I have become like a son to him. One who opens his home to you—you owe your life to him. . . . Jethro welcomed me and treated me with respect. Should I now leave without his permission?!" (*Midrash Tanhuma*, Shemot 16).

The end of Moses's divine mission mirrors its beginning. According to Numbers, God instructs Moses to fulfill one more task before he dies, to "avenge the Israelite people on the Midianites" (Num. 31:2). But instead of going himself, Moses appoints others: He chooses twelve thousand soldiers for the battle and sends them out under the leadership of his grandnephew Phineas (31:6). A Rabbinic commentary expresses surprise: "God says, 'You go,' and he sends others in his place?!" It then explains: "[Moses did this because] he grew up in Midian, and reasoned, 'It is not right that I afflict them, since they were good to me.' The parable says, 'Do not throw stones into a well from which you have drunk'" (*Midrash Tanhuma*, Matot 3).

Moses displays gratitude when God assigns him his first task, and he does so again when God assigns him his last. Moses's life, the midrash implies, is animated by gratitude from beginning to end.

Quietly, subtly, Rabbinic tradition thus casts the story of Exodus in a dramatic new light. The clash between Moses and Pharaoh is not just a struggle between the Israelite slaves and their Egyptian lords, nor is it just a battle between God and Pharaoh. The clash between Moses and Pharaoh is also a war between gratitude and ingratitude.

When Moses refuses to go to Egypt before he secures Jethro's permission, he is not just fulfilling a personal obligation—though he is surely also doing that. He is tacitly saying: It would be inappropriate for me to lead the Israelites out of this bastion of ingratitude by first behaving like an ingrate myself. I am going to model a radically different way of living; I am going to lead like the anti-Pharaoh and model what a life of gratitude could look like.

This may be precisely why God chooses Moses to lead the Israelites in the first place: In the end only a person who truly understands and embodies the quality of gratitude can lead the slaves out of Egypt, an abyss of cruelty fueled by pervasive ingratitude. God's hope, then, is not just that the Israelites will leave the political oppressions of Egypt, but also that they will leave behind the culture that makes such oppression possible—and for that they need a leader who embodies a life oriented by gratitude.[12]

By this point readers may be tempted to protest that they want their Exodus back! How and why has the Jewish people's grand narrative of slavery and liberation—and, for that matter, western civilization's paradigmatic story of slavery and liberation—been reimagined as a story about something ostensibly less potent and less urgent? What is the relationship between oppression and freedom, on the one hand, and gratitude and ingratitude, on the other? And why has Rabbinic tradition seemingly made a decision to conflate them?

First, recall what I have already suggested: Pharaoh's ingratitude and his inhumanity share the same root, namely his refusal to see other people and to acknowledge the ways that he and his people are dependent upon them. One of the tragic—and potentially horrific—consequences of ingratitude is the sense that nothing outside of me makes a claim on me. Since ingratitude is the insistence that "I don't owe anybody anything," it can blind me to the reality and dignity of other people. Being ungrateful can thus be both a symptom and a cause of inhumanity, and the two have the potential to feed off of one another in a dangerous downward spiral.

Remember the midrash's observation that "one who is ungrateful cannot accept the Kingdom of Heaven." If the Israelites are to accept the Kingdom of Heaven—that is, if they are to serve the real God rather than be enslaved by shameless pretenders—then the leader who guides them must himself embody the character trait that most makes such acceptance possible.[13] No gratitude, no relationship to God.

It is no coincidence that Moses and Pharaoh represent gratitude and its antithesis. The chasm between them is fundamental to the story and part of what gives it life. Unbridled self-assertion and a refusal to acknowledge indebtedness to anyone or anything else are what underlie Pharaoh's rule, and his way of being in the world. Acknowledgment of others and a willingness to face his own indebtedness, on the other hand, are what underlie Moses's leadership, and his way of being in the world.[14]

The liberation of the Israelites from Egypt is a liberation from a mode of seeing the world and living in it at least as much as it is an escape from concrete political circumstances. Moses returning to Jethro before he heads for Egypt, then, is integral to the story of Israel's liberation. They are about to embark on a journey toward a culture of gratitude and reciprocity, and Moses leads the way.

Leaving a place of ingratitude is leaving a place of enslavement in another crucial sense as well. It is not just that those who are devoid of gratitude may feel license to dehumanize others, but also that ingratitude itself constitutes a kind of prison. If we refuse to be grateful, we close ourselves off from the possibility of real relationship and connection to others. To be ungrateful is to be stuck inside ourselves, to be shackled in a prison of our own making; it is like living in a form of solitary confinement.

Conversely to be grateful is a powerful manifestation of freedom—the freedom to live a life infused by mutuality and reciprocity. In allowing ourselves to be grateful, we free ourselves from the prison of our own self-enclosure and become available to meet and be met by others.

Va-'era' #1

The Journey and the (Elusive) Destination

Sometimes we feel we know certain texts so well that we lose the capacity to be surprised and unsettled by them. It is thus easy to forget — or to fail to notice — that two of Judaism's most basic texts are marked by the same oddity: They tell a story whose ending has been lopped off.

The foundational story of the Jewish people is about our ancestors being freed from slavery in Egypt and brought by God to the Land of Israel. And yet, reading the Haggadah at Pesach, we come upon an anomaly: We learn a great deal about the Exodus but hear almost nothing about arriving in the land. Amazingly, in reading the Torah, we encounter much the same thing: We are told quite a lot about the Exodus and the long journey through the wilderness. We hear many details about what is supposed to happen when the Israelites arrive in the land and conquer it, but the Torah startlingly ends before they actually get there. What is going on here?

The Haggadah repeatedly truncates key biblical passages. One of the central texts traditionally studied at the seder is the formula recited by the Israelite who brings first fruit to the Temple. Recapitulating Israelite history, he declares: "My father was a wandering Aramean. He went down to Egypt with meager numbers and sojourned there; but there he became a great and populous nation. The Egyptians dealt harshly with us and oppressed us; they imposed heavy labor upon us. We cried to the Lord, the God of our fathers, and the Lord heard our plea and saw our plight, our misery, and our oppression. The Lord took us out of Egypt by a mighty hand, and by signs and portents" (Deut. 26:5–8). We were enslaved and suffered greatly, the Israelite recounts; we cried out to God, and God saved us. There the Haggadah leaves it.

But this is extremely strange. The Mishnah explicitly instructs us to read the passage from Deuteronomy "until we complete the whole section" (Mishnah, Pesahim 10:4). But we do not in fact complete the section. Curiously, the last verse in the passage is simply omitted: "He brought us to this place and gave us this land, a land flowing with milk and honey" (Deut. 26:9). The final stage of the story, God's bringing the people to the land, has mysteriously been erased.

At the seder we bless God for keeping God's promise to Israel and recall the "covenant between the pieces" (*berit bein ha-betarim*) between God and our forefather Abram. We read of the promises God made on that day: "Know well that your offspring shall be strangers in a land not theirs, and they shall be enslaved and oppressed for four hundred years. But I will execute judgment on the nation they shall serve, and in the end they shall go free with great wealth" (Gen. 15:13–14).

Reading the Haggadah alone, we would think that God's promises had ended there. But a simple look at the text in Genesis shows that this is not at all the case. God goes on: "And they shall return here. . . . To your offspring I assign this land, from the river of Egypt to the great river, the river Euphrates" (Gen. 15:16,18). Once again the conclusion has simply been elided, as if all that God had promised was the Exodus from Egypt. The promise of the land has once again disappeared.

At the beginning of parashat Va-'era', God speaks to Moses and informs him that God has heard the groaning of the Israelites and remembered the covenant (Exod. 6:5). Moses is to speak to the Israelites in God's name, and say: "I am the Lord. I will take you out (*vehotzeti*) from under the burdens of Egypt and I will rescue you (*vehitzalti*) from their bondage. I will redeem you (*vega'alti*) with an outstretched arm and through extraordinary chastisements. And I will take you (*velak-achti*) to be My people, and I will be your God. And you shall know that I, the Lord, am your God who took you out from under the burdens of Egypt. I will bring you (*veheveti*) into the land" (6:6–8).

There are five crucial terms here, suggestive of five stages of divine redemption. These verses are crucial to Pesach, and yet at the seder we drink four cups of wine, which are said to correspond to the four-staged redemption promised by God. Yet again a pivotal biblical text has been truncated, and the last stage of redemption, arrival in the land (*veheveti*), has been totally effaced.

Where has the land of Israel gone? Why is the seder night so focused on the journey and seemingly so uninterested in the destination?

Scholars have offered historical answers to our question — parts of the seder took shape, they remind us, during a time of exile, and it is only natural that a community stripped of access to the land would downplay its centrality. Moreover, there were power struggles between Jewish communities living in Israel and those living in Babylonia, and the latter often triumphed (remember that the core text of much of Jewish culture is the Babylonian Talmud rather than the Palestinian). So perhaps our arrival in the land is absent from the seder because of the historical circumstance in which the Haggadah came together, a reflection of deep-seated communal rivalries.

Perhaps. But there is likely also something deeper at play. Maybe the Haggadah seeks to teach us that the journey is often more important than the destination.[15]

If we look closely at our verses from Va-'era', we quickly realize that the Haggadah is not alone in omitting the promised ending. The Israelites are promised five stages of redemption, culminating in inheriting the land, but the Torah itself ends before that final promise has been fulfilled. On some level the story the Torah tells is incomplete: The promised destination is still out of reach. As Bible scholar Terence Fretheim puts it, "The ending [of the Torah] defers the fulfillment of the promise; it gives to the Pentateuch the character of an unfinished symphony."[16] In leaving out the arrival, then, the Haggadah is in a sense merely imitating the Torah.

Maybe the Torah, too, wants us to know that the journey is not just a means but also an end in itself. The journey does not merely serve to lead us to the land. No, the journey itself is intrinsically holy.

Think for a moment about Judaism's three pilgrimage festivals. Pesach, of course, commemorates the Exodus from Egypt. Shavuot, as our sages understand it, commemorates the revelation at Mount

Sinai. And Sukkot? Sukkot does not recall any earth-shattering or life-orienting events. It merely remembers (and reenacts) the long journey of the Israelites through the wilderness. Remarkably, it is Sukkot that is referred to as *zeman simhateinu*, the time of our joy. The happiest days of the year in Judaism are the days devoted to remembering and reexperiencing the journey.

We can personalize this as well. For many people the experience of a religious quest is more fundamental, and more meaningful, than the (often illusory) sense of having arrived.

Many years ago, when I was a teenager studying in an Israeli yeshiva, I found myself preoccupied by a series of what felt to me like pressing theological questions, mostly about biblical criticism and its implications for faith. I asked several of my teachers for help, but they were uniformly unhelpful: Some confessed ignorance of the issues at hand, while others warned me that my questions posed a danger to the religious welfare of other students.

Quite by accident I stumbled upon a book by the late R. Louis Jacobs (1920–2006), in which he wrestled with precisely some of the questions I found most vexing. As only an angst-ridden adolescent could, I proceeded to write him a fifteen-page handwritten letter about my religious concerns, anxieties, and fears. He was kind enough to respond right away. What stayed with me was how he concluded his very kind note. "Remember always," he said, "that the search for Torah is itself Torah and that in the very search you have already found." Those words have sustained me through periods of great doubt and enabled me to be nourished by the joy of spiritual and intellectual quest.

In a similar vein, the talmudic sage R. Isaac teaches: "If a person tells you, 'I have searched and not found,' do not believe him" (BT, Megillah 6b). The Hasidic master R. Menahem Mendel of Kotzk comments: "Because, after all, the searching is itself the finding."

There is real beauty and profound truth in all this, and yet we should be careful to avoid naïveté. There is something powerful about where both the Torah and the Haggadah end, but there is also something tragic about it. A promise, followed by a journey, and finally . . . a promise left often painfully unfulfilled. This is the stuff of deep spiritual growth, but it can also cause great pain and suffering.

Think of Moses's life: He dies knowing all too well that a journey without an ending can be disappointing and even excruciating. He journeys to the very border of the land and then dies without entering. This is not—or at least is not only—about uplift; it is also about heartbreak and loss.

As the Torah comes to a close, anxiety about the future remains in place. In Fretheim's words, "The promise is left suspended and the people are dispirited and fearful." The future is not simply filled with delights; it is fraught with danger. The people are so stubborn and sinful that the likelihood is that they will be disloyal to God again and again (e.g. Deut. 28:15, 29:17, 30:17, 31:16). In light of all this, Fretheim notes that "Deuteronomy leaves readers wondering what might be in store for this inevitably disobedient people. These negative possibilities create an ending of no little ambivalence."[17]

Had the Haggadah wanted to give us simple, happy endings, we'd have been instructed to stay up long into the night recounting the joys of living in a land flowing with milk and honey. Had the Torah wanted to give us simple, happy endings, it would have contained six books rather than five; it would have ended with the book of Joshua, with its narrative of conquering the land, rather than Deuteronomy, with the people still outside, looking in.

As always Jewish spirituality asks us to embrace complexity rather than eschew it: The journey can indeed be more significant, and more joyous, than arriving at the destination. But the never-endingness of the journey can also exhaust and enervate us. The perpetual elusiveness of our destination can enliven our hearts, but sometimes it can also break them.

Va-'era' #2

Cultivating Freedom

When Is Character (Not) Destiny?

"I have set before you life and death, blessing and curse," says the Deuteronomy; "choose life, that you and your children may live" (Deut. 30:19).

The conviction that human beings have the freedom—and the responsibility—to choose how we will act lies at the very heart of Jewish theology and spirituality. As Maimonides (Rambam, 1135–1204) writes, free will is "a great principle and a foundation of the Torah.... The choice is yours, and anything a person wishes to do, for good or for evil, he can do" (*Mishneh Torah*, Laws of Repentance 5:3). Moreover, Maimonides insists, without a robust conception of human freedom, the whole idea of moral responsibility collapses into incoherence: "If God decreed that a person should be righteous or wicked ... what place would there be for the Torah? By what right or justice would God punish the wicked or reward the righteous? 'Shall not the judge of all the earth deal justly?'" (5:4). No freedom, says Maimonides, no moral responsibility; no moral responsibility, no Judaism.

Not surprisingly, then, commentators both traditional and modern have often found the idea of God hardening Pharaoh's heart—so central to Exodus—deeply disturbing. As God first sends Moses to Pharaoh, God says: "When you return to Egypt, see that you perform before Pharaoh all the marvels that I have put within your power. I, however, will stiffen (*ahazek*) his heart so that he will not let the people go" (Exod. 4:21). Then, as Moses is about to come before Pharaoh a second time, God tells him again, "But I will harden (*aksheh*) Pharaoh's heart, that I may multiply my signs and marvels in the land of Egypt" (7:1–3). Commentators are understandably perplexed: How could God rob Pharaoh of his freedom, they wonder, and then punish him for his deeds? As R.

Abraham Ibn Ezra (1089–1167) asks, "If God hardened his heart, what was his transgression and what was his sin?" (commentary to Exod. 7:3).

Important as Ibn Ezra's question is, it is not where the Torah's attention is focused. Rather, what animates the text is God's desire to make God's sovereignty unambiguously clear. Pharaoh brazenly dismisses God—derisively he asks, "Who is the Lord that I should heed Him and let Israel go? I do not know the Lord, nor will I let Israel go" (Exod. 5:2)—and now he will learn that God is lord and master of creation.[18] Never again, God hopes, will God's power and presence be doubted. As Bible scholar John Durham puts it, God "is orchestrating, in a combination of opposing and unlikely forces, a deliverance that will above all be a proof of [God's] active presence. A reluctant Moses, an unbelieving Pharaoh[;] a crushed and dispirited Israel, a proud and ruling Egyptian people[;] a non-nation against the greatest of nations, are brought together, and the opposing sides are set still more firmly in their respective ways, so that proof of [God's presence] which is to turn everything upside down, may be established irrevocably."[19]

And yet, for many readers, Ibn Ezra's question still demands a response: How can God punish Pharaoh for deeds over which he exercises no control? Jewish thinkers have put forward an array of responses, but one in particular deserves careful consideration.

Although, as we've seen, Maimonides maintains that free will is fundamental to Jewish theology, he nevertheless adds that "it is possible for a person to commit a sin so egregious, or to commit so many sins, that the judgment rendered before the True Judge is that his retribution for these sins, which he committed freely and of his own accord, is that he is prevented from repenting and is no longer able to abandon his evil ways—so that he dies and perishes on account of those sins he committed." This, Maimonides insists, is how we should understand the hardening of Pharaoh's heart: "Since he initially sinned of his own free will and wronged the Israelites who lived in his land . . . justice required that he be prevented from repenting, so that he be punished. This is why the Blessed Holy One hardened his heart" (Laws of Repentance, 6:3).

What does Maimonides mean when he says that sin can lead to loss of freedom? Some interpreters take his words literally—that is, they assume that at a certain point, when a person has persisted in choosing evil, God actively intervenes to undermine his capacity to repent.[20] But this is not a defensible interpretation of Maimonides, who "embraced a naturalistic metaphysics[21] that severely restricted—or even virtually eliminated—instances of direct divine intervention in the universe. . . . Indeed, Maimonides reduced prophetic locutions of the form 'God does x' to statements of the form, 'within the natural order ordained by God, x occurs.'"[22] Moreover Maimonides insists in the *Guide of the Perplexed* that God never interferes with human freedom (3:32), and that divine providence never takes the form of direct divine intervention to punish the wicked (3:18).[23]

So what does Maimonides mean? There comes a point when a person has become so totally entrenched in bad behavior that he simply loses the ability to choose any other path.[24] Crucially, the person remains responsible for his actions even after he has lost his freedom because his consistently bad choices are what led him to his current state.[25] Human nature is such that freedom at a particular time may be constricted by decisions made earlier. God can be said to have hardened Pharaoh's heart only in the sense that God created human nature this way.

Maimonides's interpretation is philosophically and psychologically compelling, but does it find any support in the biblical text itself? Some argue that it does. Despite God's informing Moses at the outset of his mission that God would harden Pharaoh's heart, the fact is that during the first five plagues we hear nothing at all about any divine role in Pharaoh's stubbornness; the text speaks only about Pharaoh hardening his own heart (Exod. 7:13,22; 8:11,15,28; 9:7). Only with the sixth plague (boils) do things change: "But the Lord stiffened the heart of Pharaoh, and he would not heed them, just as the Lord had told Moses" (9:12). The same happens after the seventh (hail) (10:1),[26] the eighth (locusts) (10:20), and the ninth (darkness) (10:27).

In terms that echo Maimonides, Bible scholar Nahum Sarna maintains that the fact that the Torah describes Pharaoh's first five refusals as self-willed and thereafter speaks of them as divinely willed is really just "the biblical way of asserting that the king's intransigence has by then become habitual and irreversible; his character has become his destiny. He is deprived of the possibility of relenting and is irresistibly impelled to his self-wrought destruction."[27]

Is this a convincing reading of the biblical text? I am not sure. Nineteenth-century Bible scholars Carl Friedrich Keil and Franz Delitzsch introduce the helpful idea that for the Torah, there is a "twofold manner [in which] God produces hardness": "permissive" hardness, whereby God "giv[es] time and space for the manifestation of human opposition, even to the utmost limits of creaturely freedom," and "effective" hardness, whereby God "drive[s] the hard heart to such utter obduracy that it is no longer capable of returning."[28] Maimonides and Sarna see only "permissive hardness" in the text, but it seems likely that effective hardness plays some role as well. In other words, God does not merely *allow* something to happen; God actively *does* something.[29]

Whether or not it fully captures the Torah's intentions, Maimonides's interpretation does powerfully evoke a fundamental truth of the human condition. In psychologist Erich Fromm's words, "Every evil act tends to harden a man's heart, that is, to deaden it. Every good deed tends to soften it, that is, to make it more alive. The more man's heart hardens, the less freedom does he have to change, the more is determined already by previous action. But there comes a point of no return when man's heart has become so hardened and so deadened that he has lost the possibility of freedom."[30] Consistently repeated, sinful behavior can take deep and unrelenting hold of us. Piling bad decision upon bad decision deeply compromises our ability to choose a different course.

Sin may have a tenuous hold on us at first, but over time its grip becomes tighter. The talmudic sage R. Akiva observes that "at first sin is like a spider's web, but eventually it becomes like a ship's rope," and R. Isaac adds that "at first sin is like a passing visitor, then like a guest who stays longer, and finally it becomes the master of the house" (Genesis Rabbah 22:6). Repeated often enough, bad behavior can eventually take over our inner world. As anyone who has ever taken the project of repentance seriously can attest, to stop committing sins that have become deeply ingrained habits—speaking ill of others, violating Shabbat, eating unhealthful foods, and so on—can be excruciatingly difficult.

On the surface, at least, there is a tension here between what Maimonides, Sarna, and Fromm say, on the one hand, and what I have written, on the other. Following the biblical narrative, they all speak about losing the capacity to repent and change altogether, while I have suggested that over time change becomes difficult—but not impossible. Yet the tension may be more theoretical than real: Pharaoh is the paradigm of freedom run totally amok, of human evil utterly without trammels or limits.

Most of us are not Pharaoh; even if in certain situations change becomes impossible, it is nevertheless crucial to emphasize that such cases are extremely rare. Most of us are faced with the daily struggle of exercising our freedom in the midst of very real limitations, not least the limitations we ourselves have created. Maimonides writes what he does about Pharaoh in the context of motivating people to change, not dissuading them that it is possible. What the extreme case of Pharaoh is intended to teach is that we should be careful with our choices and not Pollyanna about how we are always and everywhere free without limits.

We often think of freedom as a fact, but it is also—and perhaps primarily—an aspiration. Real freedom requires, R. Joseph Soloveitchik (1903–93) writes, "a continuous awareness of maximal responsibility by man without even a moment's inattentiveness."[31] Mindfulness and constant, exquisite attention are necessary for freedom to flourish. Freedom needs to be nurtured and attended to, not taken for granted.

R. Shlomo Wolbe (1914–2005) adds that "freedom is not at all part of humanity's daily spiritual bread. It is, rather, one of the noble virtues which one must labor to attain. It is not lesser than love, and fear, and cleaving to God, acquiring which clearly demands great effort. We *can* acquire freedom, and therefore we *must* acquire it."[32]

Freedom is, in other words, a spiritual project. In order to thrive, it must be brought into awareness (Soloveitchik) and actively cultivated (Wolbe). Then, and only then, can we soften our hearts.

Bo' #1

Pharaoh

Consumed by the Chaos He Sows

The plagues that God visits upon the Egyptians confuse and disturb many contemporary readers. What are all these "signs and portents" (*otot u-moftim*) meant to accomplish? Is this just an extended revenge fantasy, or is there a deeper meaning here? What does this narrative teach us about the nature of the world?

Imagine living in a world in which violating the laws of morality leads inexorably to consequences in the world of nature. Faced with the fear and pain of living in what appears to be a cold, unfeeling cosmos, where immorality seems to have no inevitable consequence, the possibility of inhabiting such a morally ordered world is appealing. But on another level, faced with the reality of our own failures and shortcomings, the thought of living in such a universe can be, frankly, terrifying. We yearn for such a world, and yet we can't really bear the thought of it.

Large parts of Tanakh describe just such a world. For Tanakh, Bible scholar H. H. Schmid notes, "law, nature, and politics are only aspects of one comprehensive order of creation." Therefore "an offense in the legal realm obviously has effects in the realm of nature (drought, famine) or in the political sphere (threat of the enemy)."[33] A violation in one sphere, in other words, often yields consequences in another.

Sometimes the consequence of sinful action is effected "automatically, by inner necessity." What follows on a human action is natural, intrinsic. Thus, for example, the book of Proverbs teaches, "He who digs a pit will fall in it, and whoever rolls a stone, it will roll back on him" (Prov. 26:27). At other times, however, God actively intervenes to connect an action to its consequence. The story of the plagues is among the most dramatic examples of active divine intervention to ensure that wicked behavior is punished.

Schmid points out that these two modes of act and effect—the automatic and the divinely enacted—are not really contradictory, in that the inner logic of the created world is attributed to God in any case. In other words, since God created the world and established its inner logic, a seemingly automatic consequence is still implicitly an act of God.[34]

But what is God doing in Egypt? What are these shocking, staggering, overwhelming plagues meant to signify? Is God just randomly pulling out all the stops at God's disposal to punish an evil Pharaoh, or is something else less obvious also at play?

The first chapter of Exodus presents Pharaoh not merely as the oppressor of Israel, but as a cruel tyrant at war with the forces of life itself. The text tells us that the Israelites "were fertile (*paru*) and prolific; they multiplied (*vayirbu*) and increased very greatly" (Exod. 1:7). The reader cannot but hear the resonances of God's blessings to humanity in Genesis 1: "Be fertile (*peru*) and increase (*revu*), fill the earth" (Gen. 1:28). God's blessings of fruitfulness and God's commitment to life are being played out among the children of Israel, and seeing this, Pharaoh seeks to thwart the people's growth and, by extension, the divine plan (Exod. 1:8–22). Pharaoh is firmly entrenched on the side of death, while God is lined up on the side of life.

This is expressed beautifully but understatedly in two opposing phrases in Exodus 1. Pharaoh expresses anxiety lest Israel continue to grow in number (*pen yirbeh*) (Exod. 1:10) and moves to oppress and enslave them. But the more he oppresses the Israelites, the text tells us, the more they grow (*ken yirbeh*) (1:12). Citing a talmudic teaching, Rashi comments: "The holy spirit says thus: 'You say, lest they grow (*pen yirbeh*), but I say, the more they grew (*ken yirbeh*).'" The rhyming contrast captures much of what it is at stake in the first four *parshiyot* of Exodus: *Pen yirbeh* versus *ken yirbeh*, an Egyptian ruler bent on death and destruction on the one hand, and the God of Israel, committed to life—and, as will soon become clear, to the liberation of God's people—on the other.

How problematic a figure is Pharaoh? The Bible imagines him as both a historical figure and a mythological one[35]—his arrogance and murderousness represent an assault on creation itself. The prophet Ezekiel imagines Pharaoh brazenly announcing, "My Nile is my own; I made it for myself."[36] Tellingly, God refers to Pharaoh, whom God is about to slay, as "the mighty sea monster" (*ha-tanim hagadol*) (Ezek. 29:3).[37] This starkly mythological image has a very clear meaning: in a variety of (starkly mythological) biblical texts, God establishes the world by slaying the sea monster, who symbolizes the forces of evil and chaos that threaten to overrun God's plans for a good, ordered world.[38]

Pharaoh is thus a living embodiment of everything that works to undermine the world. As Bible scholar Terence Fretheim puts it, "Egypt is considered a historical embodiment of the forces of chaos, threatening to undo God's creation."[39] This is likely also why Exodus imagines God defeating Pharaoh by splitting water (Exod. 14:21–22)—just as God created the world in part by splitting water (Gen. 1:6–7). The defeat of Pharaoh is a victory *of* creation, and *for* creation. It represents the triumph of life over the forces of death.

How is all this related to the plagues? God wants life to thrive and proliferate, and God's blessings begin to be fulfilled among the Israelites. With his genocidal edicts, Pharaoh declares himself an enemy of life and creation. Fretheim astutely analyzes what happens next: "God is portrayed in these texts as active in judgment, that is, in the interplay of Pharaoh's sin and its consequences . . . but in effect God gives Pharaoh up to reap the 'natural' consequences of his anticreation behaviors." In other words, Fretheim writes, "the consequences are cosmic, because the sins are creational."[40] God acts—forcefully and seemingly without restraint—and yet there remains an intrinsic link between the kind of violations Pharaoh commits and the kind of fallout he faces. God uses the forces of nature to enforce the moral law.

The plagues are comprehensive in their scope; they devastate every aspect of creation. God is both undoing creation—the culture of death, God seems to be warning, will reap death—and demonstrating that God, and God alone, is ultimate Master over it.

Recall Ezekiel's portrayal of Pharaoh, insolently insisting that he made the Nile for himself. How does God respond? By turning the Nile into blood. Pharaoh makes the ultimate anti-religious declaration— everything I have, I made for myself. God now starkly reminds him that he did not create the world and does not ultimately control it. Describing the first plague, the text tells us that Aaron is to take his staff and hold out his arm over all the "gatherings" (*mikveh*) of water in Egypt, leading them to become blood (Exod. 7:19).

The text underscores the connection between creation and the plagues. Bible scholar Ziony Zevit draws our attention to the Hebrew word for "gatherings," *mikveh*, and reminds us that we have seen it before, when God splits the waters on the third day of creation (Gen. 1:10–11). This obvious linguistic connection, he argues, "indicates the cosmic import of the plague."[41]

The two final plagues provide the best evidence, I think, for seeing the plagues as God's undoing, or dismantling, of creation. In Genesis the process of creation gets started with God's creation of light (Gen. 1:3). In the penultimate plague, God brings darkness over Egypt (Exod. 10:21– 23), symbolically returning it to a state of primordial chaos. Here nature comes to reflect morality: Moral darkness yields natural darkness.

Perhaps worried that we will miss the connection, Exodus offers another subtle allusion to Genesis. Just as God had separated light from darkness in the creation story (Gen. 1:4), so here also God separates light from darkness: whereas the Egyptians are engulfed in deep darkness, "all the Israelites enjoyed light in their dwellings" (Exod. 10:23).[42]

The last plague is the death of the firstborn, and it will soon be followed by the drowning of all the Egyptians at sea. This constitutes, Zevit suggests, an "obverse echo" of the optimism of Genesis 1. There, of course, God had brought forth human life and blessed it; here God brings forth only death and devastation.[43]

"At the end of the narrative in Exodus," Zevit remarks, "Israel looks back over the stilled water of the sea at a land with no people, no animals and no vegetation, a land in which creation has been undone."[44] For Zevit, the main point of all this is to demonstrate to Israel that God—and not Pharaoh or anyone else—is lord of all creation. That is undoubtedly part of what takes place here, but we should not miss the point with which we started: Pharaoh has sown death and destruction, and he reaps what he sows. The "symbiotic relationship of ethical order and cosmic order"[45] is real and deep; according to the Torah, the implications of that connection cannot be escaped.

Is this interpretation of the plagues obviously correct? I am honestly not sure. It explains many aspects of the plague narratives but certainly not all. I am not sure such a complex and multifaceted narrative can be given a simple, unequivocal interpretation.[46] But something important does seem to be going on here: The forces of death and devastation are met with death and devastation; the forces of chaos are met with chaos and are consumed by the ultimate biblical symbol of chaos — raging water.

We ourselves inhabit a world that seems to run very differently. Ours is a world both far more and far less frightening than that of Exodus: far more, in that life can all too often seem utterly random; far less, in that the connection of action and consequence in our world is far looser than in Exodus, and we do not always face the consequences of our actions (or inaction). We have moved to a world in which God's presence is subtle and elusive rather than thunderous and unmistakable. There are vexing questions here about what has been lost and what gained as a result of this transformation.

But one thing, it seems to me, does remain clear: To worship the God of the Torah is to serve a God who lines up on the side of life.

Bo' #2

Receiving Gifts (and Learning to Love?)
The "Stripping" of the Egyptians

Three times Exodus tells us that as the Israelites were departing Egypt, they "plundered" the Egyptians. Bible scholar Brevard Childs notes that "few passages have provoked such an obvious embarrassment both to Jewish and Christian expositors as this one."[47] And yet unease with the surface meaning of the text has enabled interpreters to uncover deeper and deeper layers of meaning within it. The result has been a stunning array of exegetical and ethical-religious insights.

Pharaoh finally defeated, the Israelites prepare to leave Egypt. But before their departure, we learn, "the Israelites had done Moses' bidding and borrowed (*vayish'alu*) from the Egyptians objects of silver and gold, and clothing. And the Lord had disposed the Egyptians favorably toward the people, and they let them have their request; thus they stripped (*vayenatzlu*) the Egyptians" (Exod. 12:35–36).

Modern interpreter Nehama Leibowitz notes that had these been actions initiated by the Israelites themselves, they would have been understandable, if not exactly praiseworthy; after all, she argues, the people had been "enslaved, exploited, and downtrodden for two centuries," and they had suffered in unspeakable ways. "The Torah describes the generation of the wilderness without any idealization, with all its slave mentality, ingratitude, lack of faith, and longing for the fleshpots. In this too they would have run true to form."[48]

But in fact the plundering of the Egyptians had been a direct response to a divine command. Speaking with Moses at the burning bush, God had told the prophet: "I will dispose the Egyptians favorably toward this people, so that when you go, you will not go away empty-handed. Each woman shall borrow (*sha'alah*) from her neighbor and the lodger in her house objects of silver and gold, and clothing, and you shall put these on your sons and daughters, thus stripping the Egyptians" (Exod. 3:21–22). And then, as God was about to bring the final devastating plague on Egypt, God had reiterated the instructions: "Tell the people to borrow (*ve-yish'alu*), each man from his neighbor, and each woman from hers, objects of silver and gold." The Torah adds that "the Lord disposed the Egyptians favorably toward the people." Moreover, Moses himself was much esteemed in the land of Egypt, among Pharaoh's courtiers and among the people" (11:2–3), all of which facilitated the Israelites getting what they wanted.

But why—why would God mandate that the Israelites despoil the Egyptians on their way out; why this seeming combination of theft and deception?

Since Hellenistic times many interpreters have insisted that in "stripping" the Egyptians the Israelites were merely getting their just deserts. The pseudepigraphic book of Jubilees (second century BCE), for example, explains that the Israelites despoiled their former slave masters "in exchange for the bondage in which they had forced them to serve" (Jubilees 48:18).[49] Faced with a demand by later Egyptians that the Jews return the silver and gold their ancestors had taken from Egypt, the talmudic sage Gebiha b. Pesisa responds: "Pay us for the toil of six hundred thousand men whom you enslaved for four hundred and thirty years" (BT, Sanhedrin 91a). In a similar vein, modern Bible scholar Victor Hamilton sees what the Israelites take as "just compensation for withheld wages. Think of all those free man-hours Pharaoh has obtained from the Hebrews. Surely they are entitled to some financial/material compensation."[50]

But other interpreters see something else at play. God's assurance to Moses that "when you go, you will not go away empty-handed (*reikam*)" (Exod. 3:21) calls to mind the laws of the manumitted slave in Deuteronomy: "When you set him free, do not let him go empty-handed (*reikam*)" (Deut. 15:13).[51] In Exodus, then, God enforces the law as set out in Deuteronomy: When a slave is set free, he is to be given a dignified economic start by his former owner.[52] Moshe David (Umberto) Cassuto notes that a provision for departing slaves "was required by law—that is, absolute justice demanded it—and though no earthly court could compel the king of Egypt and his servants to fulfill their obligation, the Heavenly Court saw to it that the requirements of law and justice were carried out, and directed the course of events to this end."[53] In Deuteronomy the Israelites are charged to "furnish [the slave] out of the flock, threshing floor, and vat, with which the Lord your God has blessed you" (Deut. 15:14). Here, "for the stuffs stipulated by the Deuteronomic law . . . gold and silver and clothing, more conveniently borne across the desert, were substituted."[54]

Why then does God instruct the people to place the items they receive from the Egyptians on their children? Some scholars suggest that the point is "to stress the liberation of the parents along with their off-spring, the latter not to be kept behind by Pharaoh,"[55] but others discern a deeper motivation behind God's command: God is helping the people acquire the ability to care for their children. As Moshe Greenberg writes, "The recovery of dignity by the liberated slaves would be signalized by their being able to provide good things for their children. Of even greater importance than their own enrichment was their capacity to assert parental solicitude toward their children."[56] Again we see that God works to restore the people's freedom but also, crucially, their dignity and self-respect.

But why the deception? Why do the Israelites—on God's command— "borrow" items they have no intention of returning?

The word *sha'al*, rendered as "borrowed" by NJPS (and many other translations), actually has a semantic range that encompasses both "to borrow" and to "ask"; some scholars even suggest that it can mean "to ask for a gift" and maintain that that is what it means in our verses. R. Saadia Gaon (882–942), R. Hananel (990–1053), R. Samuel ben Meir (Rashbam, 1085–1158), and R. Bahya ben Asher (1255–1340) all insist that the Israelites ask the Egyptians for gifts rather than loans (commentaries to Exod. 3:22).[57] Some scholars dismiss this as apologetics, but the fact is that "there is no indication [in the text] that a pretext was involved" in the Israelites getting gold, silver, and clothing from the Egyptians. "The text does recognize that such willingness on the part of the Egyptians to comply with their request is highly unusual, but attributes this response to the intervention of God."[58]

And yet it is worth noting that "in striking contrast to the entire history of exegesis, [the Torah] makes no attempt whatsoever to justify the act."[59] Though the ethical concerns raised by interpreters ancient and modern are undoubtedly important, the Torah's attention appears to be focused elsewhere—on the display of God's sovereign power over human events.[60] According to Bible scholar John Durham, the plundering of the Egyptians "functions as a description of [God's] triumph over Egypt and everything Egyptian"; "the object of the request the Israelites are to make is a further humbling of Pharaoh and the gods who are supposed to be looking after his people and his country." God manifests God's power by causing the Egyptians, who have never evinced fondness for the Israelites, to have favor for them now. As Durham understands the narrative, "the Israelites 'ask,' and the Egyptians, in a kind of trance of affection and trust caused by [God], freely give." The point of these texts, Durham insists, is to portray God's power: "That the Egyptians could be so picked clean is another testimony of [God's] triumph over Pharaoh and all his gods and wizards." From the Torah's perspective, God's act thus "needed no further justification, only proclamation."[61]

Terence Fretheim, too, sees great divine power at work in Exodus but toward very different ends. God has been hardening Pharaoh's heart, Fretheim argues, but God has also been softening the Egyptians': "The Egyptians are not portrayed as gullible; rather, God has been at work among them so that they genuinely view Israel with favor."[62] Perhaps God puts God's power to work not just in defeating the Egyptians but also in transforming them.[63]

Along similar lines Gerald Janzen comments that God's victory "is not only through force." So far from the "trance" that Durham imagines, Janzen envisions a genuine "change of heart within some of the Egyptians." Thus, when the Israelites ask the Egyptians for a "parting gift," "it will be freely given. In such a case, the 'plunder' becomes a token that [God's] might is not simply a matter of 'force.'"[64] A core part of God's immense power, Fretheim and Janzen suggest, is the ability to open and soften callous hearts.

But perhaps the Egyptians are not the only people whose hearts need softening.

Passionately dismissing the recurring citation of this text by those who want to impugn both Jews and Judaism, Bible scholar (and Rabbi) Benno Jacob (1862–1945) sees in our story "the most elevated and spiritual reconciliation among people; it was full of wisdom and love of fellow man." The gold and silver the Egyptians gave were "farewell gifts," Jacob insists, given out of a genuine sense of affection for the Israelites. "This new mood was surprising, but even some of Pharaoh's loyal courtiers [had begun] to see matters differently and respected Moses (Exodus 8:20; 10:7; 11:3)." The gifts given by the Egyptians were thus "a clear public protest against the policies of the royal tyrant. They demonstrated a renewal of public conscience." In words that anticipate Fretheim and Janzen, Jacob adds that this turn of events "was of major importance to the Torah in our drama of liberation, as it showed a moral change; the receptive heart of the Egyptian people was now contrasted to the hard heart of Pharaoh."[65]

On Jacob's account, then, the Egyptians in large numbers have changed. But God does not stop there. God works on the heart of the Israelites, too. Worried that the Israelites might now "feel triumphant and reject the farewell of their former Egyptian neighbors, God wished to win the Israelites to a more generous point of view." As Jacob understands it, God's primary concern during the Israelites' final hours in Egypt was "peace between the two peoples." And this was in fact achieved: "The Israelites stretched out their hands in friendship and the Egyptians responded with farewell gifts." Seeking to ensure that the mandate to love rather than hate would be the lesson Israel learned from its time in Egypt, God commanded in no uncertain terms: "You shall not abhor an Egyptian, for you were a stranger in his land" (Deut. 23:8).[66]

Is Jacob's interpretation convincing as the plain-sense meaning (*peshat*) of the text? I am skeptical. One senses in Jacob's words the insights of a brilliant exegete but also the pain of a rabbi and teacher in a Germany consumed by hate.[67]

But whether it can be understood as *peshat* or not, there is something salutary and enormously important about Jacob's reading. In a world suffused with bigotry and hostility, a world in which people of faith often marshal sacred texts to legitimate acts of cruelty and to extol hatred as a virtue, there is great power in reading Jacob's words and being reminded: At the heart of the religious enterprise is the attempt to soften, and open, one's heart, to God and to one another. If even the Egyptians and the Israelites can be (successfully!) called to love one another, then perhaps, even in the darkest of times, slim glimmers of hope are available to us.

Be-shallaḥ #1

Leaving Slavery Behind
On Taking the First Step

The scene is terrifying. God wreaks a series of harrowing plagues on the Egyptians, and the Israelite slaves finally leave the place of their suffering and degradation. At last admitting defeat at the hands of God, Pharaoh and the Egyptians let the Israelites go and, stricken with fear over what God might do next, even urge them on.

But now, as the Israelites approach the sea, Pharaoh and his minions have a change of heart and set out with a massive force in hot pursuit. The Torah ominously tells us that every chariot in Egypt is enlisted for battle. To make sure we understand that Pharaoh means business, and that the threat he represents is all too real, the text repeats the word "chariot" again and again (Exod. 14:6–9).

Overcome with fear, the Israelites turn on Moses with a vengeance, insisting that continued slavery in Egypt would have been better than being slaughtered in the wilderness. We feel the pathos of the moment: Oppression in Egypt was horrific, but at least it was familiar. Leaving familiar circumstances, no matter how demeaning, is often hard, and sometimes excruciating. Now, liberated from the familiar, the Israelites are forced to confront the terror of uncertainty, and the seemingly very real possibility of imminent death.

Moses responds forcefully to their mix of dread and indignation: "Moses answered the people, 'Do not be afraid. Stand firm and you will see the deliverance the Lord will bring you today. The Egyptians you see today you will never see again. The Lord will fight for you; you need only be still'" (Exod. 14:13–14). Moses tries to reassure the newly emancipated slaves that they have gravely underestimated the power of God, who is on their side, and who will do battle on their behalf. All they need to do in this fateful moment, Moses informs them, is watch as God again saves them from their enemies.

What happens next is jarring, to say the least. God lets Moses have it: "Then the Lord said to Moses, 'Why are you crying out to Me?! Tell the Israelites to go forward!'" (Exod. 14:15). Moses has just called upon the people to have faith in God, to rest assured that God will fulfill God's promises, and God responds with . . . irritation and impatience?[68] What is wrong with what Moses has said? If we can understand the dynamics at play between God, Moses, and the Israelites in this moment, we will have gone a long way toward comprehending the way Jewish theology understands the nature of faith and human responsibility.

Think for a moment about a slave's existence. Robbed of dignity and freedom, the slave has no agency, no capacity to shape his or her own fate. Slaves do as they are told, lest they be beaten or dehumanized further. And although they work hard, they are passive, because in no sense are they the authors of their own lives. In order to go from slavery to freedom—in order to be truly transformed, in other words—the Israelites will need to discover, however slowly and painfully, that they have agency, that they can act in ways small and large to determine their own fate.

Angry, afraid, longing for the familiar, they cry out to God and lash out at Moses. In response, Moses unwittingly gives them instructions that undermine the very journey they are on. He tells them, in effect, "Be passive; sit back and watch what God does."

But being totally passive is not the way to reassert their dignity. Strikingly, the phrase "stand firm" (hityatzvu) is used elsewhere in the Bible to suggest readiness for battle,[69] and what's more, in the previous chapter of Exodus, we had been told that the Israelites left Egypt armed.[70] But here, rather than being urged to fight for themselves, either literally or figuratively, they are told to be still and to wait for God to act. Furthermore, Moses's admonition to "be still" (taharishun) may well suggest not just that the Israelites be silent, but that they adopt a posture of passivity and inactivity.[71]

God rejects those instructions. "Moses," God says in effect, "don't tell them to be passive. On the contrary, tell them to go forward. Otherwise we will never get anywhere in teaching them to be free and helping them to restore their dignity. You can't leave Egypt—not really—until you discover that you can take responsibility for your life and affect your own fate."

Needless to say the story of the Exodus is not primarily a story celebrating human effort and enterprise—it's a narrative of thunderous divine intervention, about a God who enters history to vanquish the forces of cruelty and barbarism. But that is precisely what makes God's words to Moses so powerful: Even—and perhaps especially—in the midst of a story about divine power, the Torah works to make space for human initiative. Only if the Israelites find the courage to move forward will God save them. God's miracles are, in some fundamental sense, dependent upon prior human effort. As Jewish mystics are fond of saying, without a "stirring from below" there will be no "stirring from above."

The Talmud records a remarkable debate about just what took place at the Sea of Reeds. R. Meir argues, "When the Israelites stood by the Sea of Reeds, the tribes competed with one another, each one wanting to descend into the sea first. Then the tribe of Benjamin sprang forward and descended first." According to R. Meir, the Israelites were all eager to go forward; brimming with courage, they yearned to proceed into the unknown. Benjamin was merely the first to take the plunge.

But R. Judah, perhaps possessed of a more sober sense of human nature (and based on what we've just seen about the Israelites complaining to Moses, hewing closer to the biblical text), rejects R. Meir's view out of hand. "That is not what happened," he contends, but rather "each tribe in turn said, 'I will not be the first to descend into the sea.' This continued until Nahshon the son of Aminadav [the prince of the tribe of Judah] sprang forward and descended into the sea first."

Whereas R. Meir imagines myriads of Israelites filled with faith and ready to plow ahead, R. Judah imagines these same masses anxious and afraid, each one eager for someone else to take the first step. Nahshon is the one who rises to the occasion, taking initiative while others dally.

Nahshon's lionheartedness makes him a hero, the paradigm of a person willing to act on faith rather than succumbing to fear. It is because of Nahshon's courage, the Talmud tells us, that he merits numbering David and the kings of Israel among his descendants (BT, Sotah 36b-37a). More, a midrash adds, it was because Nahshon "sanctified God's name at the sea" that he was chosen by his peers to bring the first sacrifice to the newly dedicated tabernacle (Numbers Rabbah 13:7).

Even in an age in which God splits seas, the Torah places tremendous emphasis on human beings taking the first step. God will not save the Israelites unless and until they are willing to go forward into the unknown. The sea will not split until someone is intrepid enough to proceed. It is only once the Israelites act, boldly and dauntlessly, that God's miraculous intervention sets in. In order for the Israelites to leave slavery behind—existentially, and not just politically—they must learn to take their fate into their own hands and thereby to rediscover their capacity to act and make an impact upon the world, and upon their lives within it.

Times have changed. In our own day, God does not split seas or accompany Israel in a cloud. God's presence is more subtle and elusive, God's involvement more mysterious. If, in a time when God's saving presence was manifest, people were nevertheless called upon to take matters into their own hands, all the more so are we required to do so now, in a time when God's presence is hidden, or even absent. What was necessary in biblical times, therefore, is all the more urgent today: People are called upon to refuse passivity as a religious posture.

In the language of our sages, "We do not rely on miracles" (PT, Yoma 1:4).[72] Faith sometimes demands a willingness to let go, but, even more often, it requires the courage to act.

Be-shallaḥ #2

Bread from the Sky

Learning to Trust

Long after liberation, the lingering effects of dehumanization endure. For the people of Israel, a long and tortuous road lies "between bondage and well-being."[73] One of the many things Pharaoh has taken from them is the ability to trust. God's provision of manna (and Shabbat) is intended to restore that ability to the people, and thus to open them to the possibility of healthy dependence and real relationship.

Only days after their liberation from slavery, the Israelites grow thirsty and complain against Moses. God responds by miraculously providing them with drinking water (Exod. 15:22–27). For a brief moment, perhaps, the people learn that God is not only a warrior but also a provider; they will be saved from their enemies, but also nourished and fed.

Yet a few weeks later, they find themselves hungry, and as a result, they grow belligerent. Earlier it seemed that only some of the people were complaining ("the people"—Exod. 15:24); now, the Torah makes clear, everyone is discontented ("the *whole* [*kol*] community"—16:2). The Israelites angrily declare, "If only we had died by the hand of the Lord in the land of Egypt, when we sat by the fleshpots, when we ate our fill of bread! For you have brought us out into this wilderness to starve the whole congregation to death" (16:3). The people insist, in essence, that God "is about to kill them in the wilderness, so he might as well have done the job back in Egypt, where at least they would have died on a full stomach."[74]

A midrash suggests that the Israelites' bellicose words give them away. During the time when they were enslaved, it teaches, "an Egyptian would go into the wilderness, seize a ram or deer, slay it, place it in a pot, cook it, and eat it, while the Israelite would look on and taste nothing." Note carefully the people's words: "'When we sat by the flesh-

159

pots, when we ate our fill of bread!' It does not say 'when we ate from the fleshpots,' but 'when we sat,' because they had to eat their bread without any meat" (Exodus Rabbah 16:4).[75] "In the eyes of its inhabitants," Michael Walzer observes, "the house of bondage . . . was also a land of luxury. . . . No old regime is merely oppressive; it is attractive, too, else the escape from it would be much easier than it is."[76]

With its portrayal of the people's skewed recollection of life in Egypt, the Torah demonstrates just how profoundly fear and anxiety can warp our perceptions. The people had been exploited and degraded in Egypt for generations; they had cried out in anguish from the backbreaking labor brutally imposed upon them. But now, "only a few weeks' distance has given a rosy hue to [Israel's] experience in the slave house."[77] As Bible scholar Walter Brueggemann notes, "Egypt is known to be a place of deep abuse and heavy-handed oppression. Here, however, none of the oppression or abuse is mentioned, only meat and bread." Overcome with hunger—or perhaps with fear of impending hunger—the people can no longer see straight: "Given anxiety about survival, the immediacy of food overrides any long-term hope for freedom and well-being."[78]

God evinces no anger in response to the people's grumblings. Instead God responds by providing food: the mysterious "bread from the sky" (i.e., manna)[79] in the morning and meat in the evening (Exod. 16:4,8). The manna appears each day, steadily sustaining the people through their long years of wandering in the desert (16:35).

But it comes with built-in controls. First, whether one gathers a little or a lot, one ends up only with what one needs to eat; God shrinks the portion of those who take too much and expands the portion of those who take too little (Exod. 16:17–18). And second, the manna must be eaten on the day it is collected; storing and hoarding are impermissible—and, as the people soon discover, impossible (16:19–20).

God also institutes a crucial exception to these rules: On Fridays portions are doubled in anticipation of Shabbat, and the manna that is left over for Shabbat day does not rot as on other days (Exod. 16:22–26). Manna will not be found on Shabbat because the seventh day is God's day of rest (16:25). Note the language the Torah uses: "See, how the

Lord has given (*natan*) you the Shabbat; therefore [the Lord] gives you two days' food on the sixth day" (16:29). "God has given the Sabbath, previously holy only to [God], (Gen. 2:1–3) as a gift to Israel."[80] The people ask for food; God responds with gifts both material and spiritual.

As the story unfolds, it becomes clear that God is not only feeding the Israelites but also attempting to educate them. The people are anxious and fearful; their impulse is to grab and to hoard. Introducing the gift of manna, God tells Moses, "I will rain down bread for you from the sky, and the people shall go out and gather each day that day's portion [or quota] — that I may thus test them, to see whether they will follow My instructions or not" (Exod. 16:4). Rashi (1040–1105) explains that God is testing Israel's obedience, "whether they will keep the commandments connected to [the manna] — not to leave any of it over, nor to go out to gather it on Shabbat" (commentary to Exod. 16:4).

Why would obedience in this instance be hard? R. Obadiah Seforno (1475–1550) suggests that the manna represents a life of ease, and faithfulness can be difficult "when one is provided for with no pain" (commentary to Exod. 16:4).[81] But Seforno's comments retroject God's later fears that Israel will grow spoiled and entitled once it enters the land[82] onto the very different experience of wandering in the desert; he seems to miss the depth of Israel's anxiety, the extent to which it is still struggling to leave slavery behind.

More convincing, I think, are the words of R. Abraham Ibn Ezra (1089–1167), who maintains that God is testing Israel's ability to tolerate "needing [God] each and every day" (commentary to Exod. 16:4).[83] Dependence can be difficult, Ibn Ezra realizes, especially when one has heretofore been dependent upon a merciless tyrant. But God wants to teach the people trust, and genuine trust will require the embrace of healthy dependence.

The real test, Brueggemann argues, is whether Israel can receive bread under "wholly new terms": "The ways of receiving bread in Egypt are completely inappropriate here. Israel will be under scrutiny to see if old ways of receiving bread in Egypt (in anxiety, oppression, hoarding) can be resisted."[84] The people are being taught a new way of being, and a new way of receiving.

The test does not go well. The people "pay no attention to Moses" and try to store manna overnight; it becomes infested with worms (Exod. 16:20). And despite what they have been told, some of the people go out looking for manna on Shabbat, thus eliciting God's anger and frustration (16:27–28). "[God] provides for physical needs each day, only to have some of his people attempt to hoard for the next day. [God] provides for the spiritual growth of his people by setting one day apart as special, only to have some lose the benefit by ignoring the day."[85] Israel's resistance proves stronger than God's command.[86] Trusting God is evidently too frightening; the people want instead "to establish a surplus, to develop a zone of self-sufficiency."[87]

Given their prolonged persecution in Egypt, it is no surprise that the people resist dependence of any kind. But God is not Pharaoh, and gracious gifts should not be conflated with the meager rations supplied by a ruthless despot.

Strikingly, the term "daily quota" (*devar yom be-yomo*) is used in only two contexts in Exodus. As Bible scholar Gerald Janzen explains, "In chapter 5, the people as slaves of Pharaoh must scatter day by day to look for straw with which to make their daily quota of bricks. In chapter 16[, in contrast], the people of God scatter day by day to look for the daily quota of food that God promises to provide."[88]

This stark contrast between God and Pharaoh is amplified by the envelope structure (*inclusio*) of chapter 16 as a whole. While the chapter begins, as we have seen, with Israel's distorted and debilitating memory of past provisions in Egypt, it ends with an attempt to instill a very different kind of memory in the people. Aaron is to put an *omer* (about two quarts) of manna in a jar and place the jar before the ark, "to be kept throughout the ages . . . in order that they may see the bread that I fed you in the wilderness when I brought you out from the land of Egypt" (Exod. 16:32–34). Terence Fretheim explains the point of bracketing the chapter in such divergent memories: "The idealized and unwarranted memories of Pharaoh's food are to be replaced with the genuine memories of the bread from God."[89] This is in many ways the key to the story: The people are to be fed not by a cruel taskmaster but by a loving provider. To be fed by God "requires dependence but does not lead to a fresh bondage."[90]

On the surface there is something odd about the instructions given to Aaron to set the manna in the ark: The ark has not yet been built, and directions for its construction have not yet even been revealed. Why the anachronism?

On one level, of course, the answer may simply be that in dealing with the manna, the Torah includes both the story and its later implications in one place.[91]

But something deeper and more powerful may also be going on: The ark will contain the Ten Commandments, which encapsulate Israel's obligations to God. But crucially the ark contains something else as well—and by the logic of this text, contains it first: "Before the ark receives the tablets, it receives the jar. That is, in terms of the ark's contents, Scripture first tells us about a God of manna before it tells us about a God of mandates, a God who graciously provides before a God who lays down the law."[92] Unlike Pharaoh God is not a stern taskmaster. God first loves and then commands. After generations of hardship and abuse, the people need this subtle reminder: Serving God and serving Pharaoh are utterly distinct and incommensurable.

Religion is about many things—one of them is the aspiration to surrender the illusion of self-sufficiency. We need God, and we need other people. Because we are human, and therefore embodied and fragile, the question, ultimately, is not *whether* we will be dependent, but *on whom*.

The Torah is, in part, a story about leaving destructive dependency (and the toxic memories that keep us in its thrall) and discovering life-affirming dependency as a radical alternative. We should not make an idol of dependency (any more than we should make one of autonomy); there is a dignity that comes from being able to care and provide for oneself (just ask any young child who insists time and again, "I can do it!"). And yet dependency is an irreducible part of the human condition and should be embraced as such.

But Jewish theology takes an even more radical step: It tells us that not only are we dependent on God, but also that on some level God chooses to be dependent on us. There is no symmetry here—God remains God, and we remain human creatures—but a relational God is also, necessarily, a vulnerable and dependent One. The deeper we dig, the more a theology of human dependence on God reveals itself to be a theology of divine-human interdependence, or covenant. There is a courage and a dignity in learning to say "I need you."

Remarkably, Jewish theology teaches, even God decides to say those fateful, liberating words.

Yitro #1

Does Everyone Hate the Jews?

And, Is There Wisdom Outside of Torah?

What should a people repeatedly attacked conclude about the broader world's relationship to it? What attitude should a nation blessed with divine revelation hold toward other potential sources of wisdom? Parashat Yitro subtly offers powerful and surprising answers to these fundamental questions.

The order of events described in our parashat seems jumbled. But the seemingly confusing chronology is meant to teach us a crucial lesson.

Parashat Yitro begins by recounting the story of Moses being visited by his father-in-law, who delights in all that God has done for the Israelites. Bringing Moses's sons and wife with him, Jethro comes to see Moses "in the wilderness, where he was encamped at the mountain of God"—that is, at Mount Sinai (Exod. 18:5).

But at the opening of the next chapter, we learn that Moses and the Israelites have not yet arrived at Sinai—they are still journeying from a place called Rephidim (where chapter 17 leaves off) toward the mountain where they will receive God's revelation (Exod. 19:1–2). Chronologically speaking it seems obvious that chapter 19 should have preceded chapter 18: Surely the story of the journey to Sinai should have been told before the recounting of a significant event that took place at Sinai. So why does the Torah present these stories out of order?

Right before we learn about Jethro's arrival, the text presents a description of battle: The Israelites, thirsty and discontented, are assailed by the Amalekites, and only God's assistance enables them to fend off the marauders (Exod. 17:8–13). Although the story in Exodus offers no details about Amalek's conduct, the version presented in Deuteronomy describes a particularly savage and heartless assault: "Undeterred by fear of God, [Amalek] surprised you, when you were famished and weary, and cut down all the stragglers in the rear" (Deut. 25:18). Knowing no limits to cruelty, Amalek targets the most vulnerable among the Israelites. Whereas God has lined up on the side of the weak and defenseless, Amalek seeks to kill and destroy them. No wonder, then, that the Torah imagines Amalek as an enemy of both God and Israel (Exod. 17:14-16, Deut. 25:19).[93]

R. Abraham Ibn Ezra (1089-1167) suggests that the Torah presents these crucial events in Israel's history out of their proper order precisely in order to draw attention to the stark contrast between them. Amalek seeks to ravage Israel, but Jethro shares in its joy at God's deliverance and offers guidance as to how it can best function as a nation in its newfound freedom (Exod. 18:9-23). "Since Scripture has just mentioned the evil that Amalek did to Israel," Ibn Ezra writes, "it mentions the good that Jethro did as a contrast." Moreover, he adds, just as Israel is enjoined to do battle with Amalek, so is it charged with remembering the kindness of Jethro and cautioned not to harm his descendants (longer commentary to Exod. 18:1).

Bible scholar Moshe David (Umberto) Cassuto (1883-1951) takes Ibn Ezra's insight further. He points out that the Torah provides an abundance of literary cues to draw our attention to the connection between the two stories. The Amalek episode repeats the root for battle (*l-h-m*) over and over again (Deut. 17:8,9,10,16); the Jethro story begins and ends with the word for peace or well-being (*shalom*) (18:7,23). In the Amalek story, Moses "chooses" men for war (17:9); in the Jethro story, he "chooses" men to dispense justice (18:25). When Amalek comes Moses "sits" on a rock to pray for victory in battle (17:12); when Jethro comes he "sits" to judge the people (18:13). In the first story Moses's hands "grow heavy" (17:12); in the second, he is told that the burden of deciding disputes among the people is "too heavy" for him (18:18). And so on.[94]

Such a proliferation of literary links is not a coincidence. The Torah wants to draw our attention to crucial connections between the two stories—Amalek at war and Jethro at peace. But what is at stake here? Why does the Torah deem it so important to juxtapose Amalek and Jethro?

A people that has been brutally oppressed by one nation and then mercilessly attacked by another might well conclude that it has no friends, allies, or well-wishers. Descendants who read about these events might be tempted to conclude similarly. But the Torah wants to preempt this line of reasoning by reminding us that not all non-Jews are Amalek. Not everyone hates the Jews. Indeed Jethro serves as a paradigm of the non-Israelite who can seek the well-being of Israel and acknowledge the greatness of its God.

But there is another reason, I think, why the Torah introduces the story of Jethro before the Israelites encounter God at Mount Sinai. Every religious Jew has probably at least once entertained some version of this thought: "We have received Torah from God. That is not only the most important thing in the world; on some level it is the only thing in the world that really matters. Anything I need to know, I can and should learn from revelation. Everything else is at best an afterthought, and at worst a distraction or an actively dangerous snare. If we have God's word, we simply don't need anything else. The right thing to do, the courageous thing to do, is to shut out everything else lest it lead us astray."

Exodus anticipates this religious posture and tries to nip it in the bud. Right before the Israelites stand at Mount Sinai, they are taught a crucial lesson in the administration of justice by a non-Israelite who has no access to Torah. It is Jethro who tells Moses that the system he has set up for dealing with conflicts among the Israelites is untenable: One person cannot possibly handle such a herculean task alone; he must appoint helpers, "capable men who fear God, trustworthy men who spurn ill-gotten gain" (Deut. 18:17–23). As soon as Jethro has offered his recommendation, the Torah reports simply that "Moses heeded his father-in-law and did all that he had said" (18:24).

Just before a moment of encounter with the magnificent presence of God, just before the revelation of divine guidance for how Israel ought to live, Exodus stops to teach a lesson: There is wisdom among the nations, and there is wisdom to be found through the use of reason to evaluate a situation and the needs of the moment. Torah is incomparable, and it is the axis around which Jewish life should rotate. But Torah is not our only source of wisdom and insight. By telling us the story of Jethro, and by placing it exactly where it is in the narrative structure, the Torah itself here endorses and emphasizes that very point.

How do we know that Exodus is granting its imprimatur to the idea of learning from a non-Jew? Because another, competing view is expressed elsewhere in the Torah. Deuteronomy in general expresses far more anxiety about outside influences on Israel than any other of the Five Books of Moses. Strikingly, when Moses recalls the emergence of Israel's judicial system at the beginning of Deuteronomy, Jethro simply disappears. Moses attributes both the realization that a one-man judiciary is implausible and impracticable, on the one hand, and the construction of an alternative system, on the other, to himself rather than his father-in-law (Deut. 1:9–15).

What we have here, then, appears to be a struggle between two competing impulses and two contrasting conceptions of Israel's relationship to gentile wisdom. Taken together Exodus and Deuteronomy express a significant tension in the religious life — on the one hand, the acknowledgement and endorsement of learning from the broader world, and on the other, an understandable anxiety about that very project. Exodus, in any event, is clear: *yesh hokhmah ba-goyim*, there is important and necessary wisdom among the nations (Lamentations Rabbah 2:13).

Subtly but unmistakably, the opening of our parashat makes two essential points. Although some people undoubtedly do, not everyone hates the Jews. And although Torah is endless in its depth and riches, there is vital wisdom to be found elsewhere, too. The Torah itself teaches that Torah alone is not enough.

Yitro #2

Honoring Parents

(Sometimes) the Hardest Mitzvah of All

The fifth of the Ten Commandments reads: "Honor (*kabed*) your father and mother, that you may long endure on the land that the Lord your God is giving to you" (Exod. 20:12). Noting that we are commanded to "honor" both our parents and God, the Talmud concludes that Scripture equates the honor due parents with the honor due to God (BT, Kiddushin 30b).

And yet the parameters of the obligation are not obvious: What is required by the commandment, and what isn't? And perhaps most significant, what is it about our own time that makes honoring parents at once especially challenging and especially urgent?

The Hebrew word for honor, *kabed*, also means to be heavy, suggesting that what is commanded is for people to "give weight to" to their parents, to "regard [them] as of high value or worth." The commandment's negative counterpart is linguistically parallel: "One who curses (*mekalel*) his father or his mother shall be put to death" (Exod. 21:17). The Hebrew word for curse, or dishonor, *k-l-l*, also means to be light. So the thrust of the Torah's teaching is clear: Do not "make light of" your parents, but give them weight and treat them "with appropriate seriousness."[95]

Neither Exodus nor Deuteronomy fleshes out precisely what honoring parents requires. Through careful readings of other biblical passages about filial duty, some scholars attempt to construct at least a partial picture. "Heed, my son, the discipline of your father, and do not forsake the instruction of your mother" (Prov. 1:8) suggests a mandate to adhere to parental teachings; laws in Parashat Mishpatim make clear that striking or insulting a parent are strongly prohibited (Exod. 21:15,17). Misappropriating parental property is vigorously condemned: "He who robs his father and mother and says, 'It is no offense,' is a companion to vandals" (Prov. 28:24).[96] Moreover, as we see in Ps. 91:15, honoring "has nuances of caring for and showing affection."[97]

In general, Bible scholar Brevard Childs notes, "the choice of the word 'honor' carries with it a range of connotations far broader than some such term as 'obey'"; the Torah's intention is thus "to expand the area covered by the commandment as widely as possible."[98] In a related vein, Terence Fretheim suggests that the Torah's use of a "wide-ranging" verb like "honor" means "that there is no one specific behavior that is commanded. It is an open-ended commandment, inviting children to respond in any way that honors parents. In all dealings with parents, respect, esteem, having regard and concern for, and showing affection, considerateness, and appreciation are the order of the day."[99]

Modern scholars disagree over whether honoring parents entails obeying them. Jeffrey Tigay, for example, writes that "one aspect of [honoring] is respect, which includes obedience to parents,"[100] and Richard Nelson adds that "to 'honor' in this context means to submit appropriately to authority."[101] Walter Brueggemann, on the other hand, argues that "the command does not advocate obeying or being subordinate,"[102] and Terence Fretheim avers that for the Torah, "obedience is not at the center of what it means to honor."[103]

Still other scholars insist that to pose such a question to the Fifth Commandment is "asking too much" of it. Peter Enns, for example, maintains that "the Ten Commandments are consistently ambiguous" and suggests that "this is not just the case for us but for the ancient Israelites themselves." On Enns's account the purpose of the Ten Commandments is "to reveal to the Israelites a bit of who God is, knowledge that must translate into appropriate behavior on their part. In other words, as glimpses into the nature of God and [God's] relationship with [God's] people, the Ten Commandments are not exhaustive pieces of legislation that account for each and every contingency and possibility. They are to be obeyed, but as to how, that is a matter of continual reflection by the Israelites as they continue to live and grow in the shadow of God's love and protection."[104]

And yet *halakhah* (Jewish law) always seeks concrete applications, lest divine commands remain at the level of abstraction, or even platitude. Accordingly, the sages ask, "What is meant by reverence (*mora*)? One should not sit in [the parents'] place or speak in their presence or contradict their words. What is meant by honor (*kibud*)? One should feed them and give them drink, help them get dressed, welcome them when they come home, and escort them when they go out" (Sifra, Kedoshim 1).

Strikingly, nothing is said here about an obligation to obey one's parents. This leaves the interpreter to make a judgment: Does such an obligation not exist in *halakhah*, or, conversely, is its existence so self-evident that it does not need explicit mention?[105]

One thing, at any rate, is clear: Parents cannot demand that their child sin. Commenting on the mandate in Leviticus, "You shall each revere his mother and father, and keep my Sabbaths: I the Lord am your God," a midrash asks, "Could it be that if one's father or mother instructed one to transgress one of the commandments in the Torah, one should obey them? That is why Scripture says, 'and keep my Sabbaths'—you are all obligated to honor Me" (Sifra, Kedoshim 1).[106] And indeed the central code of Jewish law unequivocally insists that "if his father told him to violate the words of Torah, whether a positive commandment or a negative one, even of Rabbinic status, he should not obey him" (R. Joseph Caro, 1488–1575, Shulhan Arukh YD 240:15).

A child's sense of how to best fulfill his religious obligations is also enough to override his parents' express wishes. As R. Joseph Caro puts it, "If a student wishes to move to another place where he is certain that he will benefit greatly from the rabbis there, and his father forbids him to go because he is worried about possible deeds of idolaters there, he need not abide by his father's wishes" (Shulhan Arukh YD 240:25). So also if a person wants to pray in a synagogue where prayers are offered with greater devotion, he may do so even against his parents' wishes (R. Abraham Hirsch b. Jacob Eisenstadt, 1812–68, Pithei Teshuvah YD 240:22).

One could argue that in such cases the issue is a conflict between religious obligations—honoring parents, on the one hand, and other religious requirements, on the other. But a number of Jewish legal sources open the door wider, indicating that parents cannot thwart their child's subjective sense of well-being. R. Moses Isserles (1520–1772), for example, writes that "if a father forbids his son to marry the wife of his choice, the son can disregard the father's instructions" (Shulhan Arukh YD 240:25). More generally a parent cannot demand that one's children carry the parent's grudges indefinitely: "If a father commanded his son not to speak to a particular person, nor to forgive him until after a certain time, if the son wishes to make up with that person immediately, despite the father's command, he may disregard the command" (Shulhan Arukh YD 240:16).[107]

In general some of the most significant medieval rabbinic decisors seem to have held that there is no blanket obligation for a child to obey his or her parents. Obedience, they argue, is simply not what the Torah means by honor.[108]

It is crucial to emphasize this distinction between honor and obedience because relations between parents and children can easily run aground when the two are conflated. Narcissistic parents tend to see their children as mere extensions of their will. When children begin to chafe under that unbearable burden, entire families can begin to unravel. (Needless to say, no one emerges from such a process feeling that his or her dignity is fully intact.)

All of this points to a more fundamental fact about the Fifth Commandment: The contours of what honor requires in specific situations can be enormously difficult to discern, and fulfilling those obligations can be just as (if not more) difficult. Not surprisingly a talmudic sage teaches that the commandment to honor our parents is the most difficult one to fulfill (PT, Pei'ah 1:1).

Yet not being obligated to obey parents does not constitute permission to ignore them.[109] In fact, the commitment not to ignore parents and, as they get older, not to cast them aside, arguably lies at the heart of the Fifth Commandment.

Consider the broader context of the mitzvah: The Ten Commandments as a whole are addressed first and foremost to adults rather than children. (After all, it would make little sense to admonish children not to covet or commit adultery; moreover the Fourth Commandment explicitly requires its hearers to have their own children rest on Shabbat [Exod. 20:10]). It would seem, then, that the central concern of the Fifth Commandment is with how grown children treat their parents.

Some argue that the mandate to honor parents is, at bottom, "a command which protected parents from being driven out of the house or abused after they could no longer work."[110] As Patrick Miller puts it, although "the commandment is addressed to persons of any age whose parents are living, it was not primarily directed to children, to tell them how to treat their parents, but to adults; this means that this commandment has in mind especially how mature adults are to treat their older or elderly parents." Caring for the frail and infirm can be exhausting and enervating, and the Torah worries about the all-too-human temptation to abandon them. The Fifth Commandment thus "focuses on the mature person, no longer under the control of parents and now probably stronger than they are in every way. It has in mind elderly parents, the weaker and needier members of the relationship, who may be regarded by grown children as unimportant [and] burdensome."[111]

Noting that (on his count[112]), of the Ten Commandments, only the fourth and fifth are stated positively, Walter Brueggemann suggests that perhaps this is meant to point to a deep connection between honoring parents and keeping Shabbat. He writes that "the fifth commandment reflects parents who have by aging lost their productive capacity and therefore their social utility. . . . If the circumstance in the command is that the parents have lost social productivity and so are made vulnerable, then it comes close to the Sabbath command that affirms that life does not consist in productivity. Sabbath is the celebration of life beyond and outside productivity."[113]

Taken together, then, the obligations to observe Shabbat and honor parents make a powerful—and in our own time, urgently important—point: Our worth as human beings does not derive from our jobs or from how much we produce, but from the simple fact that we are created in the image of God.

In traditional societies, surgeon and writer Atul Gawande has recently observed, "it was understood that parents would just keep living in their home, assisted by one or more of the children they'd raised." But in contemporary societies, all of that has changed: "Old age and infirmity have gone from being a shared, multi-generational responsibility to a more or less private state—something experienced largely alone or with the aid of doctors and institutions."[114] There are many questions to be answered—about just how and why this happened; about how much of it can and should be reversed; and about how that which cannot be reversed can nevertheless be rendered kinder, gentler, and more humane. "Do not cast me off in old age," the psalmist prays; "when my strength fails me, do not forsake me!" (Ps. 71:9). A midrash imagines King David (to whom tradition assigns authorship of the psalms) praying, "When I was young, I would go out to battle and I gave my life for Your children, but now that I am old, I have no more strength, and they say, 'Until when will this old man go on living?'" (Agadat Bere'shit, ch. 35).

How to affirm the dignity of the elderly and ill is an enormous challenge—psychologically, sociologically, and economically; in many ways we as a society are only at the beginning of a much-needed conversation on care for elders. One religious truth, at least, should serve as a touchstone as we move forward: To take the Fifth Commandment to heart is to understand that no one should ever be made to feel that we as a society are simply waiting for them to die.

Mishpatim #1

Turning Memory into Empathy
The Torah's Ethical Charge

One of the Torah's central projects is to turn memory into empathy and moral responsibility. Appealing to our experience of defenselessness in Egypt, the Torah seeks to transform us into people who see those who are vulnerable and exposed rather than looking past them.

Parashat Mishpatim contains perhaps the most well-known articulation of this charge: "You shall not oppress a stranger (*ger*), for you know the feelings of the stranger, having yourselves been strangers in the land of Egypt" (Exod. 23:9; see also 22:20). By *ger*, the Torah means one who is an alien in the place where he lives—that is, one who is not a member of the ruling tribe or family, who is not a citizen, and who is therefore vulnerable to social and economic exploitation. The Torah appeals to our memory to intensify our ethical obligations: Having tasted the suffering and degradation to which vulnerability can lead, we are bidden not to oppress the stranger.

The Torah's call is not based on a rational argument, but on an urgent demand for empathy: Since you know what it feels like to be a stranger, you must never abuse or mistreat the stranger.

This prohibition is so often cited that it's easy to miss just how radical and non-obvious it is. The Torah could have responded quite differently to the experience of oppression in Egypt. It could have said, Since you were tyrannized and exploited and no one did anything to help you, you don't owe anything to anyone; how dare anyone ask anything of you? But it chooses the opposite path: Since you were exploited and oppressed, you must never be among the exploiters and degraders. You must remember what it feels like to be a stranger. Empathy must animate and intensify your commitment to the dignity and well-being of the weak and vulnerable. And God holds you accountable to this obligation.

On one level, of course, the Torah is appealing to the collective memory of the Jewish people: The formative story around which we orient our collective life is about our harrowing sojourn in Egypt and our eventual miraculous redemption by God. We should not oppress the stranger because we as a people remember what oppression can mean.

But I would argue that we should also individually personalize the Torah's demand that we remember. Each of us is obligated, in the course of our lives, to remember times when we have been exploited or abused by those who had power over us. (Such experiences are blessedly rare for some people. Tragically, they are part of the daily bread of others.) From these experiences, the Torah tells us, we are to learn compassion and kindness.

It may be tempting to imagine a Manichean world in which the "good guys" learn compassion from experiences of vulnerability and suffering, while the "bad guys" learn only hostility and xenophobia. But it is far more honest, I think, to wrestle with the ways that each of us often has both responses at the same time: Part of us responds to the experience of suffering by wanting to make sure that no one else has to endure what we did, but another part of us feels entitled and above reproach. If you had been through what I've been through, we can hear ourselves saying, you would understand that I don't owe anybody anything. As Leon Wieseltier once remarked of the Jewish people, "The Holocaust enlarged our Jewish hearts, and it shrunk them." The Torah challenges us to nurture and cultivate the compassionate response and to make sure that the raging, combative one never becomes an animating principle of our lives.

Where Exodus commands us not to oppress the stranger and ties that obligation to the ways memory can be harnessed to yield empathy, Leviticus goes further, moving from a negative commandment (lo ta'aseh) to a positive one (aseh): "When a stranger resides with you in your land, you shall not wrong him. The stranger who resides with you shall be to you as one of your citizens; you shall love him as yourself, for you were strangers in the land of Egypt: I the Lord am your God" (Lev. 19:33–34). With these startling words, we have traveled a long distance; we are mandated to actively love the stranger.

A lot can be (and has been) said about what the commandment to love the neighbor (Lev. 19:18) does and doesn't mean in Leviticus, but one thing is clear: The love we owe to our neighbor we also owe to the stranger who resides among us. In the Gospel of Luke, Jesus is asked about the reach of the obligation to love your neighbor as yourself: "Who is my neighbor?" (Luke 10:29). Leviticus anticipates the question and offers a stunning response: The stranger is like your neighbor, and what you owe to your own kin you owe to the stranger as well. The Torah forcefully makes clear that the poor and downtrodden, the vulnerable and oppressed, the exposed and powerless are all our neighbors. We are called to love even those who are not our kin, even those who do not share our socioeconomic status, because, after all, we remember only too well what vulnerability feels like.

Deuteronomy subtly introduces still another dimension to our obligation to love the stranger. Along the way it offers a remarkably moving lesson in theology: "For the Lord your God is God supreme and Lord supreme, the great, the mighty, and the awesome God, who shows no favor and takes no bribe, but upholds the cause of the fatherless and the widow, and loves the stranger, providing him with food and clothing. You too must love the stranger, for you were strangers in the land of Egypt" (Deut. 10:17–19). The text begins by praising God as "great, mighty, and awesome." Of what does God's greatness, mightiness, and awesomeness consist? According to these verses, not of God's having created the world, and not of God's having demonstrated God's ability to smite God's enemies. No, God's grandeur is rooted in God's fairness ("who shows no favor and takes no bribe") and in God's championing the oppressed and the downtrodden.

This is reminiscent of a verse from Psalms that we recite every Shabbat and holiday morning. The verse begins, "All my bones shall say, 'Lord, who is like You?'" What is the source of God's incomparable greatness? Again, it is not raw power or might, but rather mercy and care for the vulnerable. "You save the poor from one stronger than he, the poor and needy from his despoiler" (Ps. 35:10). The God Jews worship, in other words, is a God who cares for the distressed and persecuted.

All of this helps us to understand Deuteronomy's presentation of our obligation to love the stranger. Here loving the stranger is a form of "walking in God's ways," or what philosophers call *imitatio dei* (the imitation of God). Just as God "loves the stranger" (Deut. 10:18), so also must we (10:19). The Torah here presents a radical challenge and obligation: If you want to love God, love those whom God loves. Love the fatherless, the widow, the orphan, and the stranger. In other words Deuteronomy gives us two distinct but intertwined reasons for what lies at the heart of Jewish ethics: we must love the stranger both because of who God is and because of what we ourselves have been through.

Exodus teaches us the baseline requirement: not to oppress the stranger. Leviticus magnifies the demand: Not only must we not oppress the stranger, we must actively love the stranger. And Deuteronomy raises the stakes even higher: Loving the stranger is a crucial form of "walking in God's ways."

Literature scholar Elaine Scarry hauntingly asserts that "the human capacity to injure other people is very great precisely because our capacity to imagine other people is very small."[115] By reminding us again and again of our vulnerability in Egypt, the Torah works to help us learn to imagine others more so that we allow ourselves to hurt them less.

The obligation to love and care for the stranger and the dispossessed is a basic covenantal requirement incumbent upon us as Jews. We surely have moral obligations that are incumbent upon us because of the simple fact that we are human beings. In its recurrent appeals to memory, the Torah seeks to amplify and intensify those obligations, to remind us, even when it is difficult to hear, that the fate of the stranger is our responsibility.

This mandate may seem overwhelming at times, and its concrete implications may sometimes be difficult to discern. But loving the stranger is fundamental and lies at the heart of Torah. If we wish to take the obligation to serve God seriously, and to be worthy heirs of the Jewish tradition, we have no choice but to wrestle with these words, and to seek to grow in empathy and compassion.

Mishpatim #2

Hearing the Cries of the Defenseless

Or, We Are All Responsible

Biblical laws make specific, concrete demands upon us. But discerning the meaning of these laws for our own time can sometimes be extremely difficult: How does a law rooted in the ancient world continue to speak, inspire, challenge, and provoke even in our own radically different one? Parashat Mishpatim offers a fascinating case study.

The Torah teaches: "You shall not oppress any widow (*almanah*) or orphan" (Exod. 22:21). According to some scholars, an *almanah* in the Torah is not equivalent to a widow in our modern context. By widow we mean a woman whose husband has died, but in the ancient world, the primary issue is not whether a woman's husband has died but whether there are any male relatives to be responsible for her after his passing. "Ordinarily," Bible scholar Paula Hiebert notes, "the widow's maintenance would have been the responsibility of either her sons or her father-in-law. When these male persons were nonexistent, then the widow . . . became an almanah." The Torah worries that the *almanah* has no one to provide for her, and—worse—that she has no one to protect her from those who would prey on the defenseless, especially since "they fear no reprisals from outraged family members."[116] Both the *almanah* and the orphan "have lost their male advocate and protector and so are exposed to endless social threat."[117]

The Torah's primary concern seems to be with the socioeconomic vulnerability of the widow and the orphan, but, subtly picking up on the Torah's phrasing—"You shall not oppress any (*kol*) widow or orphan"— Maimonides (Rambam, 1135–1204) focuses our attention on their psychological vulnerability as well: "A person must be extremely careful in interacting with orphans and widows because their spirits are very low and their feelings are depressed. This applies even if they are wealthy—

even if they are the widow and the orphan of a king." Maimonides weaves together the Torah's demand for probity in the economic sphere and its concern with emotional sensitivity in the relational one: "How should one interact with them? One should speak to them only gently and treat them only with respect. One should cause pain neither to their body with overwork nor to their heart with words, and one should show more consideration for their financial interests than for one's own." One who oppresses a widow or an orphan, or causes them financial loss—let alone one who beats or curses them—violates the Torah's prohibition, Maimonides emphasizes, but so also does one who vexes or angers them or hurts their feelings (*Mishneh Torah*, Hilkhot De'ot 6:10).

God warns of dire consequences if people mistreat the widow and the orphan: "If you do oppress them, I will hear their outcry as soon as they cry out to Me, and My anger shall blaze forth and I will put you to the sword, and your own wives shall become widows and your children orphans" (Exod. 22:22–23).[118] R. Abraham Ibn Ezra (1089–1167) notes that the text shifts between speaking to the Israelites in the singular and addressing them in the plural—"do not oppress" is in the plural; "if you do oppress" is in the singular; and "I will put you to the sword" is again in the plural—and explains that the Torah expands the circle of responsibility to include not only those who oppress the widows and the orphans, but also "those who see the oppression and remain silent. . . . Therefore it is written, "If you (singular) do oppress them . . . I will kill you (plural)" (shorter commentary to Exod. 22:20–22).[119] In a society where some are oppressed, all are implicated. There are no innocent bystanders.

In the ancient Near East—and indeed, in much of Tanakh—it is the duty of the king to protect those are vulnerable and exposed.[120] In a variety of contexts, the protection of the weak was seen as the will of the god (and, in Israel, of God), and, since the king represented the god's rule on earth, it was he who was tasked with being their earthly protector.[121]

Ibn Ezra's insight thus points to a crucial (but easy-to-miss) dimension of the text: The law of the widow and the orphan in parashat Mishpatim represents a radical democratization of moral responsibility.[122] The whole society—and not just the king—is responsible to ensure that the widow and the orphan are not abused. For the Torah God is the ultimate protector of the powerless, but all Israel must be their proximate protector.

Momentously, God declares of the widows and the orphans that God "will hear (*shamo'a eshma*) their outcry as soon as they cry out to Me" (Exod. 22:2). This language is reminiscent of God's having heard (*va-yishma*) the cries of the Israelites as they moaned under Egyptian bondage (2:24). "The same fate awaits these oppressors as that which fell on the Egyptians."[123] The point is profound and powerful: Just as God is moved to respond by the suffering inflicted *on* Israel, so also is God moved to respond by the suffering inflicted *by* Israel. "As the cry of Israel against Egypt mobilized [God], so now the cry of widows and orphans will mobilize [God] against oppressive Israel."[124]

The prohibition on oppressing widows and orphans is presented in tandem with a similar prohibition on mistreating the stranger: "You shall not wrong a stranger or oppress him, for you were strangers in the land of Egypt" (Exod. 22:20).[125] Taken together these laws point to the heart of the Torah's vision: God wants Israel to create an anti-Egypt, a society in which the weak and defenseless are protected rather than exploited, loved[126] rather than degraded. Accordingly, "God's people must not show any sign that they are becoming like the Egyptians . . . in how they treat others, whether fellow Israelites or aliens living among them."[127]

God's self-identification as the patron of the powerless is central to the goals of the text. The dramatic—and, for a legal code, uncharacteristic—shift from a second-person prohibition ("You shall not") to an impassioned first-person declaration ("I will hear . . . and My anger shall blaze forth") is highly suggestive. First, it points to just how central compassionate treatment of the vulnerable is to God's hopes for how Israel is to live. Indeed, just a few verses later, God says that when someone behaves mercilessly toward the poor, God will respond, "for I am compassionate" (*hanun*).[128] To behave compassionately is thus to walk in God's ways, to participate in some small way in God's own compassion.[129]

Second, and more concretely, "the warning may imply that human government was not well equipped to protect the rights [of widows and orphans] and that God was [thus] their only recourse."[130] This may also explain the ferocity of the threat: "Your own wives shall become widows and your children orphans." While God would obviously prefer that the widow and the orphan escape abuse because the powerful are kind and compassionate, God's first concern is to ensure that that mistreatment does not occur. So threats, even dire ones, also have their place.

What are we to make of these verses today, when, in some parts of the world at least, women are (blessedly) no longer as vulnerable and helpless when their spouses die? Sometimes biblical laws are meant to be illustrative rather than exhaustive. R. Abraham Joshua Heschel (1907–72) writes that "the prophets . . . tried to teach us how to think in the categories of God: His holiness, justice and compassion. The appropriation of these categories, far from exempting us from the obligation to gain new insights in our own time, is a challenge to look for ways of translating biblical commandments into programs required by our own conditions."[131]

As I have explained elsewhere, "Heschel does not spell out or offer examples of what he has in mind here, but I think he intends something like this: Biblical laws are to be understood not merely as concrete norms, but also as paradigms. In other words, they invite each generation to develop contemporary commitments that apply the eternal essence of the laws to particular times. Thus, for example, a modern reader who learns of the biblical requirement to build a parapet around one's roof (Deuteronomy 22:8) will discern from the concrete norm that the Torah is concerned with a broader commitment to public safety."[132] Similarly one who reads of God's (com)passionate concern for the plight of widows and orphans should perceive in the Torah's words a broader mandate to champion the cause of the vulnerable and powerless — whoever they may be in a particular society.[133]

To refuse to read biblical norms as paradigms is, willy-nilly, to destine significant swaths of the Torah to irrelevance. If there are no longer *almanot* in the biblical sense, after all, then the Torah's words may be beautiful but they are also inconsequential. If we do not read such norms as paradigms, in other words, we run the very real risk of domesticating the Torah by admiring it even as we rob it of its normative force.

Bible scholar Terence Fretheim suggests that readers of the Torah are "invited to extrapolate" from the specifics of biblical law "along the grain of the original formulations." Reading our verses, he insists, we are invited to extend our concern "to include any injustice that might occasion the cries of the disadvantaged."[134]

When the Israelites can no longer bear their oppression in Egypt, we learn, God both "hears" their moaning and "sees" them. To be a religious person is, in part, to follow God's example: To listen even when others will not, and to see even when others look away.

Terumah #1

Being Present While Making Space
Or, Two Meanings of *Tzimtzum*

The great Kabbalist R. Isaac Luria (known as the ARI, 1534–72) was troubled by a fundamental theological question. If God is truly everywhere, he wondered, how can the world exist? If God is infinite, how can anything finite exist? How, in other words, can there be anything that is not God?

His answer was radical, and it became enormously influential in later Kabbalah: Luria taught that the existence of the world is made possible by an act of contraction or withdrawal on God's part. God recoils or withdraws into Godself, leaving a space that is not God. This process of divine self-contraction, which Luria called *tzimtzum*, is what makes the existence of the world, of everything that is not God, possible. This idea, Gershom Scholem notes, is "one of the most amazing and far-reaching conceptions ever put forward in the whole history" of Kabbalah.[135]

The notion of *tzimtzum* is widely associated with Luria, so much so that the actual origins of the term are frequently forgotten. *Tzimtzum* is originally a Rabbinic term, and for the talmudic sages it means something very different—one is tempted to say antithetical—than it meant for Luria. At the beginning of Parashat Terumah, God directs Moses to "tell the Israelite people to bring Me gifts. . . . And let them make me a sanctuary (*mikdash*) that I may dwell among them" (Exod. 25:2,8)." A midrash imagines Moses's shock and confusion at God's instructions: "When God said to Moses, 'Let them make Me a sanctuary,' Moses responded, 'Master of the Universe, the highest heavens cannot contain You, and yet You say, Let them make Me a sanctuary?!'" God seeks to reassure Moses and replies, "Moses, not as you think. Rather, twenty boards to the north, twenty boards to the south, and eight to the west—and I will descend and contract (*metzamtzem*, from the same root as *tzimtzum*) My presence (*shekhinah*) among you below" (*Pesikta DeRav Kahana* 2:10).[136] For the sages, then, *tzimtzum* explains how a vast and uncontainable God can dwell in a finite space.

Note just how different these two conceptions are. They begin with disparate questions: Luria wonders how a world can exist apart from God, while the sages want to know how God can be intensely present in one place within the world. Not surprisingly, they arrive at conclusions that are poles apart. According to Luria, *tzimtzum* means that God moves *out from* the world; for the sages, it means that God moves profoundly *into* it—or into one part of it. For Luria, in other words, *tzimtzum* yields divine absence; for the sages, in contrast, it yields intensified presence.

On one level, these ideas are plainly contradictory. Scholem states simply that Luria inherited the Rabbinic idea and "stood it on its head."[137] And yet there is something powerful, I think, about holding the two conflicting images in mind at the same time. The idea of God's retreat, on the one hand, and God's intensified presence, on the other, tells us something important about who God is in relation to the world, and also about who we ought to be in relation to each other. Taken together these Rabbinic and Lurianic notions of *tzimtzum* convey the importance of being present while making space.

Traditional Jewish theology affirms that God is all-powerful, but also that God usually refrains from making use of this power. One of the premises of biblical thinking, for example, is that God makes space for human agency and allows us the freedom and the power to impact upon the world in significant ways. God is, a modern Bible scholar writes, a "power-sharing" rather than a power-hoarding God.[138] This means that we can obey God's will or thwart it. We can care for a person in pain or ignore her. We can cure illness or invent new ways of inflicting death and devastation. We can sanctify Shabbat or utterly profane it. God wants human beings to have meaningful freedom, and that means that God has to contract some—most, and sometimes all—of God's power.

The transcendent God is also immanent, meaning that God is beyond the world but also present in it. But in another form of divine self-restraint, God does not make the divine presence always and everywhere obvious. If human beings are to choose relationship with God rather than having it imposed upon them, if we are to discern God's presence rather than be bludgeoned by it, then God has to render the divine presence more subtle, and even elusive, than we would sometimes like. In order that there be space for us, God does not exercise all of God's power; in order that God's presence be discovered and freely embraced, God does not make God's presence manifestly obvious at all times. So God withdraws and pulls back—but at the same time, God remains radically present. God is "with us in our afflictions" (Ps. 91:15).

A real divine-human relationship depends on God making space for humanity. The covenants between God and Israel and between God and humanity thus depend upon a kind of *tzimtzum*. In order to summon us as partners, God needs to affirm and respect our independence. This is not absolute, ontological independence, to be sure—we still depend on God for our being—but it is a form of independence nevertheless. Jewish theology insists that God wants relationship, and the possibility of relationship emerges only when both partners are honored in their separateness, and then choose to come together.

God is radically present while still making space for us. Since the Torah commands us to "walk in God's ways," this paradox can teach us about the kind of human relationships to which we should aspire—we must be present while making space, make space while remaining present. So often in life, we are tempted to seize one pole at the expense of the other—to be present in such a way that we leave no space for the other, or to allow so much space that we cease to be present at all. Our goal, then, should be to steer a course between narcissism and abandonment. All deep human relatedness depends on a capacity to be present while making space.

One of the core challenges of loving a friend or a spouse is to learn to be completely present—available, attentive, loving, and nurturing—while also making space for our partner to be who he or she is, independent of us. Perhaps another way of saying this is that in loving other people, we are always there for them even as we always respect their freedom and remember that, close as we are, we are not the same person. Just as God makes space for a world that is other than God, we make space for a spouse or a friend who is other than we.[139] Too much presence suffocates our partner (there is a wonderful paradox here — too much presence ceases to be presence at all). Too little presence constitutes abandonment.

In his classic *I and Thou*, Martin Buber writes that "in the beginning is the relation."[140] Who and what we are is constituted in the moment of relating to another. But in his later writings, Buber emphasizes that in order for genuine relation to be possible, something else has to happen first.

Buber argues that "the principle of human life is not simple but two-fold." It begins with what he calls the "primal setting at a distance" and continues with "entering into relation." That first step — recognizing and affirming that the other is not me, and allowing him to be genuinely and fully other than me — is a precondition for the second, and makes it possible, since "one can enter into relation only with a being that has been set at a distance or, more precisely, has become an independent opposite."[141]

If all of this sounds too abstract, we can state it more simply: There can be no authentic relationship without a robust sense of two-ness. Both you and I need to realize — and to uphold in the ways we think and act — that although we are in relation, we are not one and the same. On the contrary, we can only be in relation because we are not one and the same. "Genuine conversation," Buber writes, "and therefore every actual fulfillment of relations between people, means acceptance of otherness."[142]

Of course we can recognize the otherness of the other and still remain indifferent to him. The first movement — "setting at a distance" — is thus no guarantee of the second — "entering into relation." As Buber puts it, "With the appearance of the first . . . nothing more than room for the second is given; if, when, and how the second manifests itself can no longer be determined by looking at the first."[143]

In other words *tzimtzum* makes authentic relationship possible, but it is not in itself enough. There must still be a second movement or gesture, of moving toward the person whose independence and otherness I recognize and affirm. I must make space and also actively choose to be present.

If at times there can be tension between presence and separateness, there can also be profound complementarity between them. Far from undermining a relationship, making space is actually what makes it possible. Or, to return to our own terms, *tzimtzum* and intensified presence go hand in hand. Presence and separateness are—or should be—central to our relationships with God and with one another.

Terumah #2

Returning to Eden?

An Island of Wholeness in a Fractured World

Biblical texts remember a perfect past and dream of a redeemed future. Jewish life offers us glimpses of those idealized moments in the hopes that they will nourish, sustain, and inspire us as we make our way through a far-less-than-perfect present.[144] Dreaming of a perfect world is deeply rooted in the Jewish psyche. And yet potent and powerful as they are, dreams of perfection also have their dangers: They can keep us so rooted in a longed-for future that we grow indifferent—or even oblivious—to the blessings and possibilities of the present.

A midrash teaches that Adam was created from the site where the Temple would one day stand (Genesis Rabbah 14:8). Another adds that he brought sacrifices on "the great altar in Jerusalem" (34:9). At the beginning of time, a third suggests, Adam donned the garments of the High Priest and offered sacrifices (Numbers Rabbah 4:8). When God expelled Adam from the Garden, still another avers, God showed him the destruction of the Temple (Genesis Rabbah 21:8). This array of midrashic images raises an obvious question: What do Adam in the Garden of Eden and the Temple have to do with one another?

The answer, as we shall see, is quite a lot.

During their time in Eden, Adam and Eve had everything they needed provided for them. It was a time devoid of want or fear. For the Torah "the Garden of Eden is the symbol of all good—birth and blessing, life and knowledge, order and communication—which can be found on earth."[145] The world in which we live, so suffused with suffering and predation, is a far cry indeed from the wholeness portrayed in Eden. Not surprisingly, although the place called Eden disappeared long ago, the dream it represents and hope for its restoration have had an enduring place in Jewish religious consciousness. "Set in the primordial past . . .

Eden imagery reflects a memory of human harmony on earth and so nurtures hope for its restoration."[146]

Longing in exile for a better day, the prophets imagined an utterly transformed status for the people and the land of Israel; in their visions "the 'Eden' motif ... emerged with singular force and clarity."[147] Thus, for example, Ezekiel foresees a radically new era: "Thus said the Lord God: 'When I have cleansed you of all your iniquities, I will people your settlements, and the ruined places shall be rebuilt; and the desolate land, after lying waste in the sight of every passerby, shall again be tilled.'" The transformation will be so profound that "men shall say: 'That land, once desolate, has become like the Garden of Eden; and the cities, once ruined, desolate, and ravaged, are now populated and fortified'" (Ezek. 36:33–35).

Isaiah dreams in similar terms: "Truly the Lord has comforted Zion, comforted all her ruins; [the Lord] has made her wilderness like Eden, her desert like the Garden of the Lord. Gladness and joy shall abide there, thanksgiving, and the sound of music" (Isa. 51:3). In strikingly evocative imagery, Ezekiel and Isaiah assure the people that the pains of the present will be erased in the future; the yearnings that seem so far away now will soon be fulfilled. A return to Eden is indeed within reach.

When God shows Ezekiel a rebuilt Temple, the prophet is reminded of Eden. Genesis tells us that "a river issues forth from Eden to water the garden" (Gen. 2:10).[148] Ezekiel sees water flowing eastward from under the Temple and is told that this water will give and renew life: "Every living creature that swarms will be able to live wherever this stream goes; the fish will be very abundant once these waters have reached there. ... All kinds of trees for food will grow up on both banks of the stream. Their leaves will not wither nor their fruit fail; they will yield new fruit every month, because the water for them flows from the Temple. Their fruit will serve for food and their leaves for healing" (Ezek. 47:1–12).

Bible scholar Michael Fishbane explains that for Ezekiel, "the new Temple, on a mountain, is an Eden: Waters of sustenance and life flow from the threshold and altar of the shrine." In Ezekiel's vision of the

Temple, "the rich power of [the Eden] motif is . . . fully evident. It arises from and taps the most primal of yearnings: A harmonious life on earth, with the grace of God."[149]

Eden thus features powerfully both in memories of the past and in hopes for the future, but what of the (biblical) present?

The *mishkan* (tabernacle) is intended to serve, I would suggest, as an island of Eden in a decidedly non-Edenic world.[150] Like Ezekiel's future Temple (though less dramatically), the *mishkan* is portrayed in terms strikingly reminiscent of the Garden. Like the Garden, the *mishkan* and the Temple in Jerusalem are entered from the east.[151] God commands Moses to make two cherubim of gold and station them on either side of the Ark of the Covenant in the Holy of Holies (Exod. 25:18–20). This, too, echoes the Garden, which was similarly guarded by two cherubim (Gen. 3:24).[152]

God commands Moses to erect a menorah (lampstand) in the *mishkan*. Bible scholar Carol Meyers points out that "the significance of the lampstand lies more in its iconic value than in its pragmatic function. . . . The various terms used for its constituent parts are replete with botanical imagery: calyxes, petals, branches and almond blossoms."

More than that, the form of the menorah—a central stand with three branches extending from each side of it—is itself suggestive of a tree. Such stylized "trees of life" were common in ancient times; they "connote the divine power that provides the fertility of plant life."[153] It hardly seems like a leap to conclude that the menorah in the *mishkan* was intended, at least in part, to evoke the tree of life in the Garden. Just as God's blessings and presence could be found there, the tree-like lampstand suggests, so also are they present here.

God places Adam in the Garden "to till and to tend it" (*le-ovdah u-le-shomrah*). This pair of verbs (*la'avod* and *lishmor*) is used together in only three other places in the Torah—all of them, tellingly, to describe the tasks of the Levites in guarding and doing the work of the *mishkan* (Num. 3:7–8, 8:26, 18:5–6). Linguistically, a strong link is thus implied between the Garden and the *mishkan*.

The holiest items in the Temple were fashioned from gold; Eden was in or near "the land of Havilah, where the gold is" (Gen. 2:11). That land also contains an abundance of *shoham* (likely either lapis lazuli or onyx) (Gen. 2:12); the same stone is used to adorn the priestly vestments (Exod. 25:7; 28:9,20).[154]

Cumulatively, all this suggests a deep connection between the Garden and the *mishkan*.[155] A number of scholars have argued that these links suggest that the Garden of Eden was the first Temple.[156] They are probably right—although that interpretation has recently been called into question[157]—but my interest is in the reverse: The *mishkan* is, as I have suggested, an attempt to re-create Eden, to erect "a microcosm of the only spotless point in creation, Eden."[158] As Bible scholar Daniel Block nicely puts it, "while functioning as replicas of [God's] heavenly residence, both tabernacle and Temple were also constructed as miniature Edens. Decorated with images of cherubim and palm trees, lit by the menorah—a symbol of the tree of life—and served by a priest decked out in royal colors and precious stones, these motifs hark back to the garden where God first put human beings."[159]

It seems reasonable to conclude that the "design and function [of the *mishkan*] intended to capture something of the original creation, perhaps even to represent in miniature the original environment in which human beings were placed."[160] But what was that environment really like?

Bible scholar Terence Fretheim warns against "overly romantic . . . descriptions of paradise." In describing Eden, he argues, Genesis actually "shows remarkable restraint. It emphasizes basics: life, freedom, food, a place to call home, a family, harmonious relationships, and a stable natural environment." It would be a mistake, Fretheim insists, to imagine that suffering emerges only in the broken, post-Edenic world; suffering is undoubtedly *intensified* after the expulsion from Eden, but it is not *introduced* then.[161] Some degree of suffering, at least, is constitutive of the human condition.

Christian theologian Douglas Hall writes about the ways that some suffering is simply built into life; it cannot be escaped, nor should it be. He mentions loneliness, which is not a good in itself, but which "provide[s] a background against which relationship with another might contain a dimension of wonder and ecstasy"; limits, which provide "graceful boundaries" within which we can pursue "the grandeur appropriate for our kind (e.g. we are embodied and mortal, conditions within which we strive to achieve our full humanity); temptation, which enables us to develop both "rational powers of discernment" and "moral capacities for goodness"; and anxiety, which "as a background awareness of our finitude, makes possible a depth of reflection and compassion without which neither wisdom nor art nor courage would be likely."[162]

It is important to tread carefully here, lest we fall into the temptation to glorify suffering or see it as inherently redemptive in some way. Hall is talking about the kind of suffering that serves life, not the kind that destroys it. The former is a kind of low-grade existential pain; this is "the suffering which is necessary to creaturely becoming (integrative suffering)," not "the suffering that detracts from life (disintegrative suffering)." Fretheim's suggestion is that "integrative suffering" existed even in Eden. After all, as Hall maintains, "life without suffering would be no life at all; it would be a form of death. Life—the life of the spirit like the life of the body—depends in some mysterious way on the struggle to be."[163]

Regardless of whether or not one accepts Fretheim's interpretation of life in the Garden, the point that both he and Hall raise is a crucial one: Overly romanticized dreams of what could be often prevent us from appreciating—or from being able to receive at all—the blessings already before us. The Eden-like *mishkan* holds out the possibility that greater degrees of wholeness are possible even in the midst of a (for now) irreparably broken world. The biblical people of Israel could enter an actual physical space; students of Torah are invited to enter it imaginatively, through reading.[164] But for the mini-Edens we enter to serve life, we must eschew illusory images of wholeness, which only sow more sorrow and discontent.

The dream of Eden represents another reality, but it is—still and always—a human reality. Jews dream of a world transformed, but we will not—we cannot—transcend the human condition. Our hope is for our humanity to be fulfilled, not overcome.

Tetsavveh #1

God in the Mishkan

Present but Not Domesticated

The hunger to be close to God can be one of the most powerful human desires, but it can also be among the most dangerous.

Some psalmists pine for God so intensely that they dream of living in the Temple, God's earthly abode. In one well-known psalm, the psalmist speaks of his longing to "dwell in the house of the Lord for many long years" (Ps. 23:6); in another, he asks "to dwell in the house of the Lord all the days of [his] life" so that he may "gaze upon the beauty of the Lord" (27:4). Such longing for proximity to the divine presence is arguably fundamental to God-centered religion. And yet such yearnings can also be perilous, because, consciously or not, people all too often try to domesticate God, to reduce God to something they can comprehend, predict, and even control.

Wandering through the desert and parched with thirst, the Israelites turn on Moses and ask, "Why did you bring us up from Egypt, to kill us and our children and our livestock?" (Exod. 17:3). Through Moses God provides water, and for the moment at least, calm returns. But the narrator adds a striking observation. What is really troubling the Israelites, he suggests, is their uncertainty: "Is the Lord present among us or not?" (17:7). In many ways the chapters about the tabernacle, or *mishkan*, at the end of Exodus are an attempt to answer the Israelites' question with a resounding yes: God is right here with us on our journey.[165]

At Mount Sinai Moses receives God's instructions for constructing the *mishkan*. But the connection between the mountain and the *mishkan* is deeper than it might at first seem. As Bible scholar Victor Hamilton notes (developing an insight already found in Nahmanides,[166] 1194–c. 1270), "It appears that Israel's experience of God at Sinai . . . is an archetype of the tabernacle. What the peak of Mount Sinai is in [chapters] 19–24," Hamilton writes, "the Holy of Holies is in [chapters] 25–40." Just as only Moses may ascend to the peak of Mount Sinai, so also only Aaron may enter the Holy of Holies (*kodesh ha-kodashim*). Just as seeing the top of Mount Sinai is a dangerous offense punishable by death (Exod. 19:21), so also is entering the Holy of Holies (Lev. 16:2). Just as, according to God's instructions, only Joshua, Aaron, Aaron's sons, and seventy of the elders may go part way up the mountain but no farther (Exod. 24:1), so, similarly, only the priests may enter the Holy Place (*ha-kodesh*), but they may go no farther. The foot of the mountain, where Moses builds an altar, is parallel to the forecourt area of the *mishkan*, where the people bring their sacrifices.[167]

According to Hamilton the *mishkan* "perpetuates" Mount Sinai: Just as "the Presence of the Lord (*kevod Hashem*) abode on Mount Sinai" (Exod. 24:16), so also "the Presence of the Lord filled the *mishkan*" (40:35). The *mishkan* also "intensifies" Mount Sinai: At Sinai "Moses went inside the cloud and ascended the mountain" (24:18), but by the time the *mishkan* is built, he can't enter the cloud: "Moses could not enter the Tent of Meeting because the cloud had settled upon it and the Presence of the Lord filled the *mishkan*" (40:35).

Further, the *mishkan* brings the formative moment at Sinai to fruition: If Sinai establishes the marriage between God and Israel, the *mishkan* represents God and Israel cohabitating: "I will abide (*veshakhanti*) among the Israelites, and I will be their God" (Exod. 29:45). Finally, the *mishkan* "extends" Mount Sinai. As Hamilton puts it, "The Israelites cannot take a mountain with them when it is time to break camp, but they can take along a portable tent. To leave Sinai behind is [thus] not to leave the God of Sinai behind."[168]

Exodus is not content to answer the Israelites' anxious query about God's presence with them in the affirmative. Parashat Tetsavveh goes much further, suggesting that God's presence among the people was the very purpose of the Exodus from Egypt: "I will dwell among the Israelites, and I will be their God. And they shall know that I the Lord am their God, *who brought them out from the land of Egypt to dwell in their midst*, I the Lord their God" (Exod. 29:45–46; emphasis mine). Note how startling this sentence is: These verses, at least, suggest that God's goal in liberating the slaves was not to bring them to the land so much as to dwell in their midst along the way. On this account intimacy with God, not inheritance of the land, is the goal of Exodus.

The revelation at Sinai was a once-in-history event, but now the Israelites are assured that God will continue to be present with them in an ongoing way. Indeed Numbers emphatically points out that God's presence, in a cloud by day and a fire by night, never leaves the Israelites (Num. 9:15–23). At Sinai Moses had encountered God's presence at the top of a mountain no one else could dare to approach, but now, all the restrictions on coming too close notwithstanding, God's presence will dwell at the very center of the Israelite camp. As Bible scholar Terence Fretheim puts it, "God comes down to be with the people at close, even intimate range; they no longer need to ascend to God."

More radically, with the erection of the *mishkan*, God's presence will no longer be limited to a fixed place. God's dwelling place, and hence God's presence, will be portable, moving with the people. When the *mishkan* is built, the Israelites' mode of worship changes, but crucially so also does God's mode of being present with them.[169]

Wherever the Israelites go, God will go with them. But as inspiring as having God close by can be, it is also fraught with peril. If a sense of God's immanence is not amply balanced with a robust awareness of God's transcendence, we run the risk of thinking we can domesticate God. We convince ourselves that we can truly know who God is, or worse, we come to think that we can simply get God to do our bidding. Under such circumstances religion becomes about God serving us rather than us serving God. Faith very quickly descends into idolatry.

The Torah worries about this problem. Will the *mishkan* facilitate the worship of God, or will it be abused so that it foments idolatry? Between the instructions for how the *mishkan* and its appurtenances are to be built (Exodus 25–31) and the description of how those instructions are executed (35–40), comes the harrowing story of the Golden Calf (chs. 32–34). As Fretheim points out, the contrasts between the *mishkan*, on the one hand, and the calf, on the other, are both profound and highly significant. While the *mishkan* is erected on God's initiative, the calf is built on the people's; whereas the people are asked to make gifts of their own free will for the *mishkan*, for the calf Aaron commands them to bring gold. While "painstaking preparations" are undertaken for the *mishkan*, for the calf there is no planning at all; whereas the *mishkan* is constructed slowly and deliberately, the calf is made extremely quickly, even wildly. Most crucially, while the *mishkan* safeguards God's holiness by setting limits and preserving a deep sense of divine mystery and otherness, the Golden Calf offers "immediate accessibility"—or at least the illusion thereof. The *mishkan* upholds an invisible God, but the calf presents a visible one. Ultimately the *mishkan* is constructed so that the Israelites may worship a transcendent, active, and personal God; the calf offers them an impersonal object, devoid of will, to bow down to.[170]

In the *mishkan* God is constantly present—yet God is still transcendent, and the Torah works hard to avoid a theology that could easily "deteriorate into a cozy over-familiarity."[171] Perhaps this is why the tabernacle is called both *mishkan*, literally dwelling place, and *ohel mo'ed*, or tent of meeting. As Bible scholar Menahem Haran notes, "The word *mishkan*, tabernacle, indicates the place where God dwells, i.e. his abode, whereas *ohel mo'ed* describes the place to which he comes at an appointed time, the tent to the entrance of which he comes in response to prophetic invocation, only to leave it when the communication with him is over."[172] This is a core tension in biblical theology (and not just there): God is radically present but also mysterious and transcendent; immanent but not willing to be localized or domesticated.

This may well be part of why it is so important to the Torah to emphasize both that God dictated every last detail of the plan for the *mishkan* and that the people executed it exactly according to God's instructions. The key point is that Israel is serving God rather than imagining that God is serving it.

The Torah details both the plans for the *mishkan* and their fulfillment, but in the middle it inserts the story of the Golden Calf as a kind of warning: God will be present, but God will not be your possession. Any god you think you can possess or control is merely an idol. God is present, the Torah reminds us, but God is still God.

Tetsavveh #2

Between Ecstasy and Constancy

The Dynamics of Covenantal Commitment

Rabbinic interpretation of parashat Tetsavveh paints a powerful portrait of covenantal mutuality—of God's commitment to Israel and of Israel's commitment to God. But it also claims, crucially, that covenantal mutuality depends less on ecstasy than on constancy. Covenant thrives, ultimately, less on high drama than on the day-to-day commitment to living with God.

As parashat Tetsavveh opens, God instructs Moses: "You shall further command the Israelites to bring you clear oil of beaten olives for lighting, for kindling lamps perpetually (*le-ha'alot ner tamid*)" (Exod. 27:20). Traditional commentators disagree over the meaning of the word "perpetually" (*tamid*). Rashi (1040–1105) understands it to mean that the lamps must be lit every evening and stay aflame until morning (commentary to Exod. 27:20). But a midrash insists that "perpetually" means that one lamp, the "western light" (*ner ma'aravi*), is to burn constantly, day as well as night; from this perpetually burning western light all the other lights are kindled each night (*Midrash Sifrei*, Beha'alotkha 59). It is this latter approach that gives rise to the later custom of having a *ner tamid*, an eternal light, burning in the synagogue.

What is odd about the midrash's position is that it seems to be directly contradicted by the very next verse: "Aaron and his sons shall set [the lamps] up in the Tent of Meeting, outside the curtain which is over [the Ark of] the Covenant, [to burn] *from evening to morning* before the Lord." (Exod. 27:21; emphasis added). The Torah thus makes explicit what "perpetually" means: evening to morning (as Rashi notes), and not constantly (as the midrash suggests). This is so obvious that one has to ask: What leads the midrash to its seemingly implausible reading of the biblical text?

One possibility is suggested by a striking passage from the Talmud. Puzzled by the commandment to kindle a lamp for God, R. Sheshet asks, "Does God then require its light—surely, during the entire forty years that the Israelites traveled in the wilderness they traveled only by God's light! But the light is a testimony to humanity that the Divine Presence (*Shekhinah*) rests in Israel" (BT, Shabbat 22b). If the light is intended to symbolize God's presence, then it stands to reason that the light must be kept constantly aflame. Just as God is always present, so must the light be always shining.

And yet the plain sense (*peshat*) of the text accords with Rashi's reading. In fact the cantillation marks make this clear: There is a pause between *ner* (light) and *tamid* (perpetually), indicating that a better translation would be "for kindling lamps, regularly." R. Yehoyada Amir explains that the focus of the commandment is not on the light always being aflame but on Israel's obligation to kindle it again and again. Accordingly the intention of the text is "not to give expression to . . . the presence of God in our midst, as the eternal light in our synagogues likely does. Rather, this is a light kindled always 'before the Lord,' by the Children of Israel. This is a light that we are commanded to kindle before God in order to express our presence before God, our standing ready to serve as partners in the work of holiness and the work of creation."[173] Over the course of Exodus, God has shown that God will be present for Israel; now God asks for reciprocity—Israel, too, must be present for God.

While the plain-sense meaning and the midrashic interpretation of the text seem clearly at odds with one another, taken together they form a potent symbol of God and Israel's life together: The light burning in the *mishkan* (tabernacle) makes the statement that God and the people are perpetually committed to, and present for, one another.[174]

Parashat Tetsavveh mandates another ritual of constancy in addition to "kindling lights regularly": Twice a day "the perpetual offering" (*korban tamid*) must be brought.[175] God tells Moses, "This is what you shall offer upon the altar: two yearling lambs each day, regularly (*tamid*). You shall offer the one lamb in the morning, and you shall offer the other lamb at twilight. . . . A regular burnt-offering throughout the generations" (Exod. 29:38–39,42). Bible scholar John Durham explains that the *korban tamid* was "offered in the morning, probably at the beginning of the day's activity, and in the evening just before nightfall; thus the day was opened and closed with gifts to [God], from whom all gifts were believed to come."[176]

Durham points to a fascinating "reversal" in Exodus: So much of the book—Exodus, desert journey, Sinai—has been concerned with God demonstrating God's presence by what *God* does; now, with these rituals of constancy, God's presence is demonstrated by what *Israel* does.[177] In kindling a light and offering sacrifices each day, Israel testifies to its confidence that God is really present, always—and in so doing, it meets God's presence with an affirmation of its own. Strikingly, the laws of the *korban tamid* are followed immediately—in the very same verse—by an affirmation that God will meet with Israel and speak with Israel at the very place that it brings these offerings (Exod. 29:42b–43). "It is in these ordinary, repetitious . . . [rituals on the part of the priests] that God promises to 'meet' with [God's] people."[178] According to these passages, then, the presence of God is both demonstrated and elicited not primarily through intense drama but through daily discipline.

R. Yehudah Brandes notices an important tension between the names of the two *parashiyot*, Terumah and Tetsavveh, that convey God's instructions for the building of the *mishkan*: Whereas the word *terumah* (gift) connotes voluntary giving, the word *tetsavveh* (command) connotes obligation. Parashat Terumah begins by appealing to the hearts of the Israelites: God instructs Moses to "tell the Israelite people to bring Me gifts; you shall accept gifts for Me from every person whose heart so moves him" (Exod. 25:2). In stark contrast, parashat Tetsavveh opens, as we have seen, with the command—not the request, but the command—that the people bring oil for kindling the lights regularly.

Brandes finds the meaning of this polarity in the fact that while Terumah deals with the construction of the *mishkan*, Tetsavveh is concerned with preparing the priests for their service: "The initial construction of the *mishkan* and its vessels is a one-time event; the one-time preparations are exciting. As for any important building project, it is relatively easy to enlist donors. . . . But the service in the *mishkan* is different. Service requires consistency and constancy; it does not contain the same excitement. There is an element of routine to it, which can sometimes be exhausting and dispiriting." For one-time events one can rely on passion and spontaneity; for enduring commitments, on the other hand, one needs steadiness and steadfastness.[179]

What is true of service of God is true of any relational commitment we make: We commit that we will be present even when the spirit does not so move us. Consider love between spouses. The initial phase of a relationship is often a "Terumah moment," a time of freely flowing passion. But no one lives in an unwavering state of fierce ardor. At a certain point in the unfolding of a relationship, we discover that love is not only an emotion but also an existential commitment. We decide that we will love even in moments when we are not overcome with feeling. To be sure, in order for existential commitment to endure, there need to be moments of fervor. But it is an illusion—and a prescription for profound unhappiness—to imagine that heightened passion is possible, or even desirable, at all times. Robust marriages do have "Terumah moments," but what enables them to endure is the mutual commitment implied by Tetsavveh.

R. Jacob Ibn Habib (1460–1516) reports a Rabbinic debate about what constitutes the "great (or perhaps: the most encompassing) principle in the Torah (*kelal gadol ba-torah*). Ben Zoma argues that the Shema— "Hear, O Israel! The Lord is our God, the Lord alone" (Deut. 6:4) is the most encompassing; Ben Nannas, in contrast, advocates for "You shall love your neighbor as yourself" (Lev. 19:18). Each position has much to recommend it: Affirming our utter loyalty to the one God and striving to love others are both fundamental to what it means to serve God and take Torah seriously.

But Shimon b. Pazi insists that a very different verse is in fact the most encompassing one in the Torah: "You shall offer the one lamb in the morning, and you shall offer the other lamb at twilight" (Exod. 29:39). An anonymous sage stands up and declares: The law is like Shimon b.

Pazi (Ein Ya'akov, Introduction). This is, on the surface, an astonishing midrash: How can such a seemingly pedestrian verse compete with—and even outweigh—two of Judaism's most fundamental, compelling, and inspiring teachings? Shimon b. Pazi's point is crucial, and as I have suggested, it lies at the very heart of parashat Tetsavveh: In serving God consistency and constancy may just be the most important things in the world. The point is not really that the twice-daily sacrifice is more important than affirming God or learning to love; the point, rather, is that in order to affirm God with the totality of who we are and in order to love others in all that we do, regularity and steadfastness are essential.

We should not overinflate the point: Total inattention to experience (or to what is "meaningful") can all too easily reduce religion to sterile and lifeless rote, practices we habitually repeat but that express nothing real, deep, or important. And yet obsessive focus on experience and meaning can reinforce narcissism and self-absorption, which are perennial dangers in the spiritual life. Like romantic passion, religious experience does matter (though we should be careful not to assume that only ecstatic, "high-voltage" religious experiences count as experience). In serving God, as in loving another person, never "feeling it" can be disastrous. But covenant, like marriage, is not built on experience alone but also on loyalty, faithfulness, and "showing up."

This is what the rituals of constancy in Parashat Tetsavveh serve to remind us: There is no spiritual life without discipline and commitment. This may just be the most encompassing—and for many of us, the most challenging—principle in the Torah.

Ki Tissa' #1

The Importance of Character

Or, Why Stubbornness Is Worse Than Idolatry

God's response to the sin of the Golden Calf is perplexing. God is so angry with the Israelites' unfaithfulness that God wants to wipe them out. But the explanation God gives for why God wants to destroy them is baffling. And yet God's anomalous response is actually a crucial window into the world of Jewish ethics.

As the Israelites worship the calf, God bids Moses to go witness their appalling behavior: "The Lord spoke to Moses, 'Hurry down, for your people, whom you brought out of the land of Egypt, have acted basely. . . . They have made themselves a molten calf and bowed low to it and sacrificed to it, saying: This is your god, O Israel, who brought you out of the land of Egypt!'" (Exod. 32:7–8). The Israelites are guilty of the ultimate theological transgression: They have engaged in the crudest form of idol worship. And yet God's desire to smite them is rooted in something else. God says: "I see that this is a stiff-necked people. Now, let Me be, that My anger may blaze forth against them and that I may destroy them, and make of you a great nation" (32:9–10).

R. Nosson Tzvi Finkel (the Alter of Slabodka, 1849–1927) expresses profound surprise at what transpires here. The Israelites commit the crime of idolatry, and yet God wants to punish them . . . *for their stubbornness?!* If someone did something truly awful, R. Finkel asks, why would we discipline that person for a far smaller, seemingly insignificant offense? After the worst breach of the covenant imaginable, how can God want to punish the Israelites for something other than the sin itself? There is something deeply odd, he insists, about the Israelites committing idolatry and being condemned to death on account of their stiff-neckedness.

"From here we see," Finkel argues, "that a defect in character is even worse than a defect in action—more serious even," he adds, "than a grave sin like idolatry." A transgression, Finkel explains, is at bottom just a mistake, and the reality of human free will means that one who sins today can choose to behave differently tomorrow. But a character flaw is far more insidious: It alters who we are at the deepest level, and the divine image in us is damaged in the process.[180]

What Finkel is suggesting—in the most dramatic possible terms—is that Judaism is concerned not just with *what we do*, but also with *who we are*. Jewish ethics is focused not just on conduct but also on character.[181] From a Jewish perspective, character matters, and the cultivation of good character lies at the heart of the religious life. In other words, Judaism is deeply invested in virtue ethics.

Now, to be clear, good behavior and good character are thoroughly intertwined. Good character is manifested in good behavior, and good behavior, in turn, helps instill good character. If you want to train yourself to be more compassionate, for example, start by doing compassionate things. Compassionate character yields compassionate behavior, which in turn deepens compassionate character, and so on in a virtuous cycle. (I have always wondered what it says about our culture that we talk about vicious cycles but rarely mention virtuous ones.)

So far so good. But for many thinkers, good character is important not just because it is the best guarantee of good behavior. It has its own intrinsic value.[182] Who we are matters, and not just because it plays such a major role in determining how we act in concrete situations.

Maimonides (also known as Rambam, 1135–1204) insists that the cultivation of good character—as opposed merely to the performance of good actions—is utterly central to the religious life. The Torah requires us to "walk in God's ways," but it does not specify precisely what this entails. In his extended enumeration of the 613 mitzvot, Maimonides states unequivocally that the obligation to walk in God's ways (what philosophers call *imitatio dei*) includes both concrete actions ("good deeds") and character traits ("fine attributes") (*Sefer Ha-Mitzvot*, Positive Commandments, #8). On Maimonides's account, then, the Torah mandates that we focus both on what we are commanded *to do*—compassionate action—and on who we are commanded *to become*—compassionate beings.

In turning our attention both to actions and to character traits, Maimonides seems to be following a highly significant rabbinic precedent. Let's consider the two most influential rabbinic interpretations of the mitzvah "to walk in God's ways." The first offers a list of godly character traits we ought to emulate: "As God is called merciful, so should you be merciful; as God is called gracious, so should you be gracious. As God is called righteous, so you too should be righteous; as God is called merciful, so too should you be merciful" (*Midrash Sifrei*, 'Ekev 49). The second, in contrast, lays out a program of actions: "As God clothes the naked, so you, too, clothe the naked; the Blessed Holy One visited the sick, so you, too, visit the sick. The Blessed Holy One comforted mourners, so you, too, comfort the mourners; the Blessed Holy One buried the dead, so you, too, bury the dead" (BT, Sotah 14a). Taken together these two classic sources seem to bolster Maimonides's point: If we want to become godly, we have to behave in compassionate ways, but crucially we also have to develop a compassionate personality.

As Maimonides grew older, he came to see the pursuit of virtue as a greater and greater priority for Jewish ethics. As R. Walter Wurzburger (1920–2002) argues, Maimonides likely worried that readers would think that character development is only instrumental in value—that is, they would think that character matters solely because it generates good actions, which are what is ultimately important.[183]

Maimonides dealt with this anxiety in a strikingly innovative way. In the *Mishneh Torah*, his colossal code of Jewish law, he interprets the directive to walk in God's ways to be focused exclusively on character: "As God is called gracious, so should you be gracious; as God is called merciful, so should you be merciful; as God is called holy, so should you be holy, etc." (*Mishneh Torah*, Hilkhot De'ot 1:6). There is a critical difference between the Maimonides of *Sefer Ha-Mitzvot* and the Maimonides of the *Mishneh Torah*: Whereas the former holds that the mandate to walk in God's ways includes both actions and character traits, the latter limits it to character traits alone—presumably in order to make sure we realize that virtue is important on its own terms. (Troubling as this may be to some, if anything for Maimonides, it seems more important that actions lead to instilling virtue than that being virtuous leads to moral action.)

What happens to good behavior, to concrete actions in the world aimed at helping those in need? Maimonides now interprets them as part of another commandment, the obligation to love our neighbor as ourself (*Mishneh Torah*, Laws of Mourning 14:1). According to Maimonides, then, walking in God's ways, the obligation and aspiration to be like God, is about who we are; loving our neighbor, in contrast, is about what we do. Of course, as we've seen, what we do flows from who we are (just as surely as who we are flows from what we do), but Maimonides is clear and unequivocal: Character matters, and not just as a means to an end.

Maimonides is aware that not everyone will agree with how much weight he places on the cultivation of virtue. In offering his instructions in the ways of repentance (*teshuvah*), Maimonides at once emphasizes the centrality of character development and admits that not everyone agrees. He writes: "Do not think that repentance is only necessary for those sins that involve a deed such as promiscuity, robbery, or theft. Rather, just as a person is obligated to repent from these, similarly, he must search after the bad character traits he has. He must repent from anger, hatred, envy, frivolity, the pursuit of money and honor, gluttony, and the like. He must repent for all of these" (*Mishneh Torah*, Hilkhot Teshuvah 7:3). When a thinker warns us not to think something, it is usually evidence that he is aware of at least some people who think just that. Maimonides implicitly acknowledges that some people think that conduct is all that matters. But character matters, too, he tells us, and doing *teshuvah* requires us to work on who we are, not just on what we do.

God's surprising response to the idolatrous infidelity of the Israelites, then, teaches us a crucial lesson about Jewish ethics: As we make our way through the world, Judaism asks us to take careful stock not just of the things we do, but also of the kind of human beings we are. From a religious perspective, character really does matter.

Ki Tissa' #2

God's Expansive Mercy

Moses's Praise and Jonah's Fury

Parashat Ki Tissa' culminates in a stirring—and enormously influential—proclamation of God's mercy. The appropriate response to this rousing affirmation of God's grace and benevolence would seem to be praise and thanksgiving. But for one embittered biblical prophet, these words elicit pain, desperation, and indignation instead. To understand why is to learn a powerful lesson about the vastness of God's love—and about our own dogged but ill-fated attempts to cut God down to size.

Still reeling from the people's apostasy at the Golden Calf and afraid that God will abandon them, Moses beseeches God to let him "know God's ways" (Exod. 33:13). In response God recites the divine attributes to Moses: "The Lord passed before him and proclaimed: 'The Lord! the Lord! a God compassionate and gracious, slow to anger, abounding in kindness and faithfulness, extending kindness to the thousandth generation, forgiving iniquity, transgression, and sin; yet by no means does [the Lord] wholly acquit, but visits the iniquity of parents upon children, and children's children, upon the third and fourth generations'" (34:6-7). These verses, known in Jewish tradition as "the thirteen attributes of God" (*shelosh esreh middot*), are recited on holidays when the ark is opened for the taking out of the Torah and are chanted aloud during the Torah reading on fast days. This latter practice is rooted in a startling image evoked by the talmudic sage R. Yohanan: "The Blessed Holy One drew his robe around Himself like the leader of a congregation and showed Moses the order of prayer. God said to him: 'Whenever Israel sins, let them carry out this service before Me, and I will forgive them'" (BT, Rosh HaShanah 17b). Our verses are anticipated in the Ten Commandments, where God, warning Israel not to bow down to or worship idols, declares, "For I the Lord your God am a jealous God, visiting the guilt of the parents upon the children, upon the third and fourth generations of those who reject Me (son'ai), but showing kindness to the thousandth generation of those who love Me and keep my commandments" (Exod. 20:5–6).

Note the dramatic shift in emphasis: Whereas in laying down the law, God begins with the threat of punishment, in the wake of apostasy, God leads with the possibility of forgiveness. "Emphasis and priority here are given to God's magnanimous qualities rather than [God's] judgmental actions."[184] Moreover, in stark contrast to the formulation in the Ten Commandments, the recitation here contains no reference at all to divine jealousy.

But the two texts differ in an even more powerful way. In Exodus 20 God speaks of showing kindness (hesed) to those who love God and keep God's commandments; after the Golden Calf, however, God sets no limits on who may be the beneficiary of divine grace and compassion. The point, Bible scholar Walter Moberly notes, is that God's "mercy towards Israel is independent of their responding in the right way. Even when Israel is disobedient it is still the recipient of the divine goodness."[185] God's love, it seems, is unconditional. But the text goes further in emphasizing God's radically forgiving nature: "When speaking of God's forgiveness, [it] seems to search the Hebrew lexicon exhaustively to make sure to miss no 'sin' family word"—God, we are told, forgives "iniquity, transgression, and sin." Nothing is beyond the reach of God's mercy.[186]

And yet the heavy emphasis on God's mercy should not blind us to the fact that although divine judgment takes the backseat in the enumeration of the thirteen attributes, it is still very much present. Focusing exclusively on divine mercy would run the risk of creating the insidious illusion that "one can just get away with anything." So God reminds us that even in the context of divine mercy, "there is still justice."[187]

In other words, the Torah worries about what the Christian theologian Dietrich Bonhoeffer refers to as "cheap grace": "Cheap grace is the preaching of forgiveness without requiring repentance. . . . Grace alone does everything . . . and so everything can remain as it was before."[188]

The message of these verses in Exodus—and of Jewish theology more broadly—is that although compassion, mercy, and forgiveness are at the very heart of who God is in relation to the world, one may not simply assume that God will forgive. Faith is striving, and although forgiveness is available when we fail, judgment is real—and striving remains obligatory.[189] A reliance on cheap grace both belittles God and demeans the worshipper, treating the sovereign Creator of all as an automatic forgiveness dispenser.

Strikingly, when the prophet Joel calls upon the people to turn back to God, "for [God] is gracious and compassionate, slow to anger, abounding in kindness, and renouncing punishment" (Joel 2:13), he immediately adds, "who knows—perhaps [God] may return and relent" (2:14). Joel's uncertainty is instructive. "God is indeed merciful and responsive," he asserts, "but although this can be relied upon, it should not be presumed upon. God's mercy remains [God's] to give, and [God] interacts sovereignly and relationally but not mechanically."[190]

Not surprisingly the language of the thirteen attributes, which is "the fullest statement about the divine nature in the whole Bible,"[191] reappears in a variety of biblical texts.[192] Most of them quote only the first part, about God's mercy, and leave out the second part, about punishment. As we would expect, in most cases these verses are invoked in praise of God and/or in anticipation of divine mercy and forgiveness. But one case is different, even antithetical to the rest.

The prophet Jonah has been summoned to call the Assyrian city of Nineveh to repentance and has resisted mightily; when he finally does do as he has been commanded, the people of Nineveh repent. Ordinarily one would expect a prophet to rejoice at such a turn of events. Prophecy that generates a genuine change of heart is tragically rare; Jonah may just be the most successful prophet of all time. And yet when God renounces the punishment that God had intended to bring upon Nineveh, the prophet's reaction is not joy but indignation. Exasperatedly he announces that his hesitations in fulfilling his mission have been vindicated: "O Lord! Isn't this just what I said when I was still in my own country? That is why I fled beforehand. . . . For I know that You are a compassionate and gracious God, slow to anger, abounding in kindness, renouncing punishment" (Jon. 4:2). What so many biblical texts find wondrous and worthy of praise, the prophet Jonah finds contemptible.

It is clear that Jonah is angry about God's mercy. What is less clear, however, is why God's mercy — or perhaps better, God's mercy in this situation — so upsets him.

Some scholars condemn Jonah for his purported "theological parochialism"; on their interpretation, Jonah consistently displays "a shocking antipathy toward non-Israelites and an aversion to seeing God's mercy extend to them." They find the alleged "incongruity between Jonah's mission and his unchanging antipathy for displays of grace to non-Israelites . . . alarming" and denounce the prophet for his "xenophobia" and the "deviant nature of [his] attitudes and beliefs."[193] The book of Jonah, on their telling, is a tale of a stubborn and arrogant prophet who refuses to learn the lesson of God's universal love. The problem with such interpretations is that there is simply nothing in the text to support them. Jonah is indeed profoundly troubled by the mercy God extends to Nineveh, but the assumption that the Ninevites somehow represent all non-Israelites is entirely unfounded.

So why does Jonah grow so sullen at the thought of God forgiving the people of Nineveh?

In order to understand Jonah, "the reader must bear in mind that Nineveh or Assyria would one day destroy Jonah's homeland and carry its people off into exile."[194] Bible scholar Elizabeth Achtemeier notes that in biblical times, "Nineveh was the symbol of the overwhelming and ruthless power of [the Assyrian] empire"; it was, in the words of the prophet Nahum, a "city of blood" (*ir damim*) (Nah. 3:1) and a bastion of "endless cruelty" (3:19). "It was the Assyrian Empire that first carried out a systematic policy of deporting captured peoples and of replacing them with foreigners, a policy that led to the disappearance from history of the ten northern tribes of Israel when they were defeated by Assyria in 721 B.C.E."[195] Assyria was thus a place of unprecedented brutality and barbarism.

On one level Jonah may be afraid that in showing mercy to the Ninevites, God is making a mistake. As R. Isaac Abravanel (1437–1508) writes, Jonah "knew the evils and exiles that [Nineveh] would bring on the tribes of Israel in the future; hence he yearned for the nation of Assyria to be destroyed and Nineveh its capital to be utterly smitten. This is why he fled instead of going there" (commentary on Jonah, introduction). The issue Abravanel raises is both important and difficult: Perhaps Jonah struggles with "the recognition that the bestowal of mercy may be costly, even potentially or actually fatal, for the one who bestows it (or the one who is the agent of divine bestowal). For even a repentant recipient of mercy may only be repentant in the short term. What is to prevent that recipient from turning against the benefactor in the longer term?"[196] And indeed, as we have seen, this is in fact what ends up happening.

Still, I wonder whether something deeper and even more fundamental may also be at play. Jonah understandably finds Assyria detestable, and he desperately wants God to share his assessment. After all is not an enemy of God's people also an enemy of God? But God will not play along with Jonah's script. Instead God constructs a living parable for the prophet. God prepares a plant to provide Jonah with shade, and Jonah is delighted. But God soon sends a worm to attack the plant, which promptly withers. God then sends an east wind, and the sun beats down on Jonah's head, leaving him faint. Jonah is devastated and expresses a wish to die (Jon. 4:5–9), whereupon God responds: "You cared about the plant, which you did not work for and which you did not grow, which appeared overnight and perished overnight. And should I not care about Nineveh, that great city, in which there are more than a hundred twenty thousand persons who do not know their right hand from the left, and many beasts as well?" (4:10–11).

There are many ways to understand what God does and says in this part of the story, but it seems that God wants Jonah to understand that he cannot have it both ways: He cannot be the recipient of God's mercy while adamantly begrudging it to others. Divine mercy cannot be hoarded; part of its very purpose is to be shared.

And God may also be telling Jonah something else: You cared about a mere plant, which you had no hand in making; all the more so must I care about Nineveh, filled as it is with people and beasts that I Myself created. God's care and concern—and God's openness to forgiving—extend even to "the whole sinful wicked world of violence and wrong."[197] The people of Nineveh are not angels, God effectively tells Jonah, but they are still My creations—one is tempted to say "My children"[198]—and because of that, when they repent, I will respond.

It is a very difficult lesson to learn: God may well love even people whom we cannot stand—even people who have behaved wickedly and may one day do so again. God's love and mercy will not be constrained by our (human and therefore inherently limited) capacity for love and mercy. In other words God's concern is not confined by the boundaries we all too often seek to set for it. A God whose mercy was determined by us would not be God at all, but simply a projection of ourselves. And so God tells Jonah—and by extension Jonah's readers—that "God's mercy is upon all God's works" (Ps. 145:9).

The question God implicitly asks Jonah—and the rest of us—is whether we can accept, and worship, and celebrate a God whose love and mercy extend far beyond our comprehension.

Va-yak'hel #1

Whom Do We Serve?

The Exodus toward Dignified Work

At the beginning of Exodus, God's people are enslaved to a false god; by the book's end, they have been liberated to serve the real One.

The king of Egypt is not just a brutal taskmaster; he is a brazen and delusional despot: "My Nile is my own," he declares; "I made it for myself"[199] (Ezek. 29:3). A medieval midrash imagines him insolently declaring: "I have no need of God; I created myself" (*Midrash Ha-Gadol* to Exod. 5:2). For Pharaoh grandiosity and cruelty go hand in hand. In response to the request Moses and Aaron make for a brief opportunity to worship God in the wilderness, Pharaoh places more and more onerous burdens on his increasingly desperate slaves. He disdainfully condemns Moses and Aaron for wanting to cause the Israelites to desist from their labors—and tellingly, the word the narrator places in his mouth is *hishbatem* (Exod. 5:5), from the same root as the word Shabbat, a day of rest. The reader knows (as Pharaoh and the slaves do not yet) that Shabbat is intended to acknowledge that God, and God alone, is the Creator (Exod. 20:11). Thus, in upbraiding Moses and Aaron for wanting to give the Israelites a Sabbath, Pharaoh unwittingly reveals the vast gulf separating enslavement to a human master from dignified service of the God of Israel.

Exodus begins with the Israelites forced to build cities for a human king who views them as a potential threat to his rule and treats them accordingly; it ends with the people engaged in building a tabernacle (*mishkan*) in which the God who has redeemed them can dwell. This trajectory is crucial to Jewish theology: In Bible scholar Ellen Davis's words, the people move from "perverted work, designed by Pharaoh to destroy God's people ... [to] divinely mandated work, designed to bring together God and God's people, in the closest proximity possible in this life."[200] As slaves in Egypt, the Israelites work without respite against their will. When they build the *mishkan* in this week's parashah, in stark contrast, Moses asks for voluntary contributions: "Take from among you gifts to the Lord; everyone whose heart so moves him shall bring them" (Exod. 35:5). Finally freed from slavery, the Israelites are slowly being taught that there is a form of service radically different from slavery, one that honors and nurtures one's sense of agency rather than degrading it and whittling it away.

Not surprisingly, then, as Moses lays out instructions for how to build the *mishkan* (tabernacle), he starts by invoking Shabbat: "On six days work may be done, but on the seventh day you shall have a sabbath of complete rest (Shabbat *Shabbaton*), holy to the Lord" (Exod. 35:2). An unbridgeable chasm divides enslavement to a human tyrant and service of the God of creation and covenant: Whereas the tyrant prohibits even a moment of Shabbat, God actually mandates and regularizes it.

Whereas serving Pharaoh had stripped the Israelites of their dignity, serving God will now affirm it. Moreover, and critically, God commands them to take their own dignity seriously.

Is Shabbat about affirming that God, and God alone, is God, or is Shabbat a testimony to human dignity and the importance of rest? The biblical answer is that it is both. The Torah sees no contradiction between a day aimed at affirming God as sovereign over the entirety of creation, on the one hand, and a day aimed at insisting that everyone, including slaves male and female, is entitled and obligated to rest (Exod. 20:10), on the other. Observing Shabbat is a dramatic statement about Who the Israelites serve, and also, crucially, about how the One they serve understands and treats them.

Herein lies a key difference between service of God and enslavement to a human pretender: Whereas the latter systematically dehumanizes his subjects, the former values and cherishes them. Work and service come in dignified and degrading versions; the Torah is about a journey from the latter toward the former.

The Torah captures the transition the Israelites undergo linguistically as well. In Egypt their mode of labor is called *avodah*, from the same root as *eved*, or slave. In building the *mishkan*, in contrast, the word predominantly used to describe their work is *melakhah*, from the same root as *mal'akh*, or messenger. The word *melakhah* conveys immense dignity, since it is the same term used to depict God's work in creation (Gen. 2:2–3). The Israelites, in building the *mishkan*, are in some sense mirroring God's work in creating the world. So far from degrading slave labor, *melakhah* is godly work.

What do the two terms *melakhah* and *avodah* actually mean? According to contemporary commentator Moshe Sokolow, "*Melakhah* appears to be work done by an independent agent, while *avodah* is (the same) work done by a servant. The former implies a measure of equality between the principal and his agent, while the latter just as clearly implies the subordination of the laborer to a master." Furthermore, Sokolow adds, one who engages in *melakhah* commits to completing a task "guided and informed by his own experience and expertise," whereas one who performs *avodah* contracts to complete his task only "according to the instructions and specifications of the principal." The work of constructing a dwelling place for God is referred to again and again (twenty-five times in Exodus) as *melakhah*, which Sokolow in this context renders "agency," and it calls for the participation of artisans and those expert in "every kind of designer's craft" (*melekhet mahashevet*—literally, work that requires knowledge) (Exod. 35:33).[201] In leaving Egypt, therefore, the Israelites leave behind slave labor for work inextricably linked to dignity, wisdom, and skill.

The journey the Israelites take is, crucially, from one building project to another. They are transformed from slaves of an earthly ruler to servants of a Heavenly One. Freedom, as imagined by Exodus, is decidedly not about casting off the burdens of service altogether. In fact it says a great deal about our secularized society that while we often cite the demand that Pharaoh "let my people go!" we usually omit the telos of that call, "that they may serve Me." The Torah is passionately concerned with a journey from slavery to freedom, but it imagines freedom in ways that are different from (one is tempted to say antithetical to) the ways freedom is commonly spoken of in contemporary consumerist

America. Doing whatever I want, whenever I want, is arguably not freedom at all, but enslavement to impulse. The depths of freedom are discovered not in self-assertion but in rare moments of authentic self-transcendence. Authentic freedom, Jewish theology insists, is found in service of something (and Someone) greater than oneself.

And yet we should tread carefully here, because as Isaiah Berlin famously warned, invocations of "positive liberty" are a favored tool of totalitarians—and, we ought to add, of religious bullies of all stripes. We need to talk not just about freedom *from* external constraint ("let my people go"), but also about freedom *for* a sacred purpose ("that they may serve Me"). But we also need to be mindful of the political dangers of that way of talking: Once some people presume to know who other people really are deep down, and thus to have greater insight than they into what they truly want, the very real danger of political oppression in the name of "self-mastery" or some purportedly higher freedom emerges in full force.

This sobering fact, all too often ignored by rabbis and preachers, points to a critical line we ought to uphold: Invocations of self-transcendence and of realer, deeper, truer selves must rely on persuasion rather than force. We should allow people the freedom and dignity to discover what we insist is their true freedom.

Va-yak'hel #2, Pekudei #1

(A) Building with Heart

In conveying instructions for the building of the *mishkan* (tabernacle), God instructs Moses, "Tell the Israelite people to bring Me gifts (*terumah*); you shall accept gifts for Me from every person whose heart so moves him (*yidvenu libo*). . . . And let them make Me a sanctuary that I may dwell among them" (Exod. 25:2,8). These opening words make two crucial points. First, God does not simply seek a place to dwell; God seeks, rather, a place constructed by human hands. Second, God has no interest in a structure erected through coercion or taxation; what God wants is an edifice built from freely bestowed gifts. As Bible scholar Walter Brueggemann puts it: "Constructing an adequate place for the holiness of God is indeed human work, wrought in generosity."[202]

Sure enough, when Moses transmits God's word to the people, he announces, "This is what the Lord has commanded: 'Take from among you gifts to the Lord; everyone whose heart so moves him shall bring them'" (Exod. 35:4–5). The Torah then narrates the bringing of gifts at great length (35:4–36:8).

Strikingly, the phrase "one whose heart so moves him" (*nediv libo* or a variant), which appears nowhere else in the Torah, appears three times over the course of just forty verses; within these verses the root *n-d-v*, meaning to donate, appears no fewer than six times. These repetitions underscore just how important it is to God that gifts for the *mishkan* come freely and without any hint of coercion.

Another word occurs even more frequently than *n-d-v* in the narration of the bringing of gifts: The word "heart" (*lev*) appears fourteen times—a multiple of seven, the biblical symbol of completion or totality.[203] While the contributors must be "generous of heart," the actual builders must be "wise of heart" (*hakham lev*). The Torah seems to go out of its way to emphasize that both the giving and the constructing must be done with "heart."[204]

The question, of course, is why. What is it about the construction of the *mishkan* that makes giving from the heart so fundamental? The answer, I think, lies in the fact that the heart is the great equalizer.

R. Meir Leibush Weiser (Malbim, 1809–79) makes the beautiful observation that in the construction of the *mishkan*, "the essence of the gift (*terumah*) . . . is the generosity (*nedavat ha-lev*); the spirit's desire to donate is the very essence of the donation." This requires emphasis, Malbim writes, because "there were poor people among the children of Israel who did not have anything at all to donate, but they gave in spirit (*hitnadvu be-ruham*) — that is, they thought that if only they had great wealth, they would give enough for the whole *mishkan* and all of its utensils just from their own possessions. God, who knew what was in their heart, received this as if they had given concretely" (commentary to Exod. 35:21).

Why the special concern in this context to include those who cannot afford to contribute materially? The *mishkan* is a magnificent structure; in constructing it, the Torah tells us, the Israelites make use of "gold, silver, and copper; blue, purple, and crimson yarns; fine linen and goats' hair; tanned ram skins, dolphin skins, and acacia wood . . . lapis lazuli and other stones" (Exod. 25:3–5,7). In any massive capital campaign, the temptation is for people to lavish attention and admiration upon those with means; after all it is their generosity that makes the project feasible. In such moments those without wealth or "capacity" can quickly be rendered invisible. Yet something about that possibility undercuts the very purpose of the construction: If the *mishkan* is to be erected so that God can dwell in and with the entire people, then manifesting — and even deepening — divisions of status and class in the process of building it represents a spiritual contradiction in terms. So God stresses that all gifts count — even the smallest of the small,[205] even the purely internal gift of wishing one had the means to contribute materially. As a talmudic dictum puts it, "It is the same whether one offers much or one offers little, as long as one directs one's heart to Heaven" (BT, Menahot 110a).

A similar logic underlies a memorable midrash about those who led the construction efforts. The Torah highlights the great wisdom and skill of Bezalel, from the tribe of Judah, who directed all aspects of the building (Exod. 35:30–35). Alongside him, we learn, stood Oholiab, from the tribe of Dan (35:34). R. Hanina b. Pazi observes that "there was no more elevated tribe than the tribe of Judah and no more lowly tribe than the tribe of Dan, who was from among the sons of Jacob's concubines. . . . The Blessed Holy One said, 'Let Oholiab come and work with Bezalel, lest the latter grow haughty—for the great and the lowly are equal before the Blessed Holy One'" (*Midrash Tanhuma*, Ki Tissa' 13). Expanding on this midrash, Rashi (1040–1105) cites a description of God from the book of Job: "The noble are not preferred to the wretched" (Job 34:19, cited in Rashi's commentary to Exod. 35:34). In appointing those who will manage the massive construction project, in other words, God carefully ensures that the whole people is represented. The *mishkan* is to be built together, without some being glorified and others erased.

From beginning to end, the construction process is animated by overflowing generosity. So responsive are the people to Moses's call for donations that he eventually has to call a halt to the proliferation of gifts; the people's efforts "had been more than enough for all that had to be done" (Exod. 36:4–7). The Torah spends several verses discussing how much has already been brought—not just brought, but brought freely and generously (35:20–28)—and then, somewhat oddly, stops to note—again—that "every man and woman whose hearts so moved them" brought these gifts (35:29). R. Isaac Abravanel (1437–1508) explains that the text is emphasizing that "each and every one of them donated for the proper reason, to serve God and fulfill God's will"; they had no ulterior motives, like pride or the pursuit of grandeur. According to Abravanel, then, the people did not just give freely; they also gave for the right reasons, without thought of status or recognition (commentary to Exodus 35).

Implicit in Abravanel's words is a (gentle? stinging?) critique of those whose generosity is motivated by a desire for attention and approbation. While in most instances it is better to give for less-than-ideal reasons than not to give at all, we can take Abravanel's comments as a subtle reminder of what giving at its best looks like: It is about the cause, not the donor. Or, in this (and many) context(s), it is about serving God, not our own ego or lust for prestige. So pure was Israel's giving in this paradigmatic building project, Abravanel suggests, that for a moment at least, the people forget themselves and achieve a state of unadulterated generosity.

According to some commentators, the generosity extended still further. The Torah describes Bezalel and Ohaliab as being endowed by God with the skills necessary to work "in every kind of designer's craft," but also, crucially, with the "the heart to instruct others (*lehorot natan be-libo*)" (35:31–35). R. Abraham Ibn Ezra (1089–1164) notes tersely that "there are many wise people who find it hard to teach others" (longer commentary to Exod. 35:34). On one level, of course, Ibn Ezra may simply be referring to the fact that some people find it difficult to communicate what they know. Yet he may also be pointing to something deeper, namely that some people hoard their expertise and are reluctant to share what they know.[206] If that is what Ibn Ezra means, then Israel's two master craftsmen are credited here with being openhearted enough to share their talents and abilities with others.

At first glance Bezalel and Ohaliab's eagerness to teach may seem like an insignificant detail. Upon closer examination, though, it helps us discern the larger thrust of the narrative: God wants God's dwelling place to be wrought in generosity both toward God and toward one another. After all, as God makes clear, God wishes to dwell among the people, and not (merely) in the *mishkan* (Exod. 25:8).

For many of us, it may be difficult to imagine genuine selflessness and generosity flowing so freely among flesh-and-blood people in the "real world." But consider: If the *mishkan* is intended to serve as a "counterworld,"[207] an oasis of Eden in a decidedly non-Edenic world,[208] then it makes sense that the construction process is described in ideal(ized) terms. Through its portrayal, the Torah offers us a window on what the ideal communal project would look like: generous, egoless, and motivated by the sacredness of the cause itself.

Pekudei #2

Building a Home for God

After reporting on all that had been done in erecting the *mishkan* (tabernacle), the Torah declares: "And Moses saw (*vayar*) all the tasks (*kol ha-melakhah*), and behold (*ve-hinei*), they had done it (*asu*) — as the Lord had commanded, so had they done — and Moses blessed them" (Exod. 39:43). To the attentive reader, the links to the creation story are unmistakable: "And God saw (*vayar*) all (*kol*) that God had done (*asah*), and, behold (*ve-hinei*), it was very good" (Gen. 1:31). In the one case God looks and sees, while in the other Moses does; in both cases everything has been completed just as God wants. There seems to be a deep connection between God's creation of the world on the one hand, and the Israelites' construction of the *mishkan* on the other.[209] But just what is that connection, and what is it intended to suggest?

The literary links between creation and the *mishkan* are both abundant and striking. Immediately after God looks and sees that the world is good, Genesis tells us that "the heaven and the earth were finished (*vayekhulu*) (Gen. 2:1). Similarly, when the *mishkan* is completed, Exodus says that "all the work of the tabernacle of the tent of meeting was finished" (*vatekhel*) (Exod. 39:32). In the creation story, we learn that "on the seventh day God finished (*vayekhal*) His work (*melakhto*) which He had done" (Gen. 2:2); in the story of the *mishkan*, we discover that "Moses finished (*vayekhal*) the work (*ha-melakhah*)" (Exod. 40:33). After God evaluates the world, we are informed that "God blessed (*vayeva-rekh*) the seventh day" (Gen. 2:3); after Moses sees that the *mishkan* has been built according to plan, we hear that "Moses blessed" (*vayevarekh*) the Israelites (Exod. 39:43).

In Exodus there are six days of preparation for receiving God's revelation, and God's instructions are given to Moses on the seventh day.

These instructions are presented in seven distinct divine speeches, each of which begins with "the Lord spoke (*vayedaber*) or "the Lord said" (*vayomer*) (Exod. 25:1; 30:11,17,22,34; 31:1,12). These seven speeches mirror Genesis's description of God's utilization of speech to create the world in seven days. The seventh and final speech enjoins the Israelites to keep Shabbat (Exod. 31:12–17), just as the seventh day of creation introduces the seventh day as God's day of rest. Lest we miss the point, this seventh divine communication concludes: "[The Shabbat] shall be a sign for all time between Me and the people of Israel, for in six days the Lord made heaven and earth, and on the seventh day, He ceased from work and was refreshed" (31:17). The instructions for the construction of the *mishkan* thus not only allude to God's creation of the world, but also explicitly culminate by invoking it.

But there are even more literary connections. Exodus describes Bezalel, the *mishkan*'s chief craftsman. as endowed with a "divine spirit" (*ruach Elohim*) (Exod. 31:3; 35:31). That Hebrew phrase, *ruach Elohim*, has occurred only twice before in the Torah: Just as God is about to begin creating the world, Genesis tells us that a "divine spirit" (*ruach Elohim*) was sweeping over the water (Gen. 1:2; see also Gen. 41:38). By now, I trust, the point is clear: The Torah wants us to know that God's creation of the world and Israel's construction of the *mishkan* are intertwined in a highly significant way. To return to where we started: Precisely how and why are world creation and *mishkan* construction so intimately connected?

On one level the implication of the coupling of the construction of the *mishkan* and the creation of the world is that the *mishkan* is intended to serve as a microcosm, a world in miniature. To understand what this means, we ought to consider one more literary link between *mishkan* in Exodus and creation in Genesis. The final chapter of Exodus contains seven instances of the expression "just as the Lord had commanded Moses" (Exod. 40:19,21,23,25,27,29,32), which serves a similar function to the sevenfold repetition of the phrase "And God saw that is was good" in Genesis (Gen. 1:4,10,12,18,21,25,31).

Bible scholar Jon Levenson helpfully draws out the relationship between the two repeating formulas: "The theological substance of the two similar refrains is a pointed insistence upon the correspondence of the object constructed with the intentions of God. The [*mishkan*] and the world both result from the perfect realization of divine commandments, and nothing that God has commanded falls short of his expectations."[210] The *mishkan*, like the world, is a perfect realization of God's plans.

Except that in reality—and according to the Torah itself—the world as we find it falls far short of God's hopes and expectations. Instead of a world in which human dignity is real, we live in a world in which barbarism and cruelty all too often rule the day, in which unspeakable suffering pervades every corner of the globe, and in which all talk of human dignity can thus sound like so much Pollyanna nonsense. Instead of a world in which God's presence is manifest and almost tangible, we live in a world in which God all too often seems utterly absent, so much so that talk of God can seem like little more than wishful fantasy. One way to think about the Torah—and, for that matter, about human history as a whole—is as a story of divine disillusionment and disappointment. The best laid plans of God, too, often go awry.

In a world overrun by chaos, the *mishkan*, I'd like to suggest, is intended to serve as one place in which everything unfolds according to the divine plan—"just as the Lord had commanded Moses." In Levenson's apt formulation, the *mishkan* is meant to be a world, "an ordered, supportive, and obedient environment."[211] Amid all the world's brokenness, then, there is to be one place, at least, in which God really is present and God's word really is authoritative. It is as if God says to Moses and the Israelites: I made you a place to live, now you make one for Me.

But Judaism could never rest content with one small pocket of order and goodness in a world otherwise utterly adrift. If the correspondence between *mishkan* and world is meant to suggest that the *mishkan* is supposed to be a miniature world, it is equally supposed to remind us that the world is intended to be a very large tabernacle—that is, a place in which God's word is obeyed, God's presence felt, and God's dreams for the world fulfilled. Like the *mishkan* the world is supposed to be "a place in which the reign of God is visible and unchallenged, and his holiness is palpable, unthreatened, and pervasive." Just as the *mishkan* is a microcosm, so the world is—or is supposed to be—what Levenson calls a "macro-temple."[212]

Jewish theology often wrestles with the tragic sense that although God brought the world into being, it has run so totally amok that God's presence seems to be in exile. In a world so filled with callousness and inhumanity, so enamored of idols both insipid and insidious, where is there room for God? In a world so permeated by selfishness and indifference, where can the God who shatters our indifference and commands us to love the stranger dwell? As we read the thirteen chapters in Exodus about the *mishkan* (25–31, 35–40), we are challenged to ask: How can I live my life in a way that makes space for God—not just in the forms and rituals of religion, which can so easily become shallow or corrupt—but also in the most fundamental ways I carry myself in the world? How can we—my community and the Jewish people as a whole—live in such a way as to let God in?

For the religious person, what R. Abraham Joshua Heschel (1907–72) writes about prayer applies to life as a whole as well: "God is in exile; the world is corrupt. The universe itself is not at home. To pray means to bring God back into the world, to establish His kingship for a second at least. To pray means to expand His presence. . . . To worship, therefore, means to make God immanent, to make Him present. His being immanent in the world depends upon us."[213]

The challenge before us, in other words, is to transform the idea that the world is a temple, a home for God's presence, from a pretty but potentially banal notion into a tangible reality and a life's project. Even in a world in which God seems so far, it is possible to create moments when God's presence is brought intimately near.

Notes

INTRODUCTION

1. Heschel, *God in Search of Man*, 250. Emphasis in the original. Heschel goes on to make a stronger claim: "It is the sense for the presence that leads us to a belief in its origin."
2. Heschel, *Torah Min Ha-Shamayim Be-Aspaklaryah Shel Ha-Dorot*, vol. 3, 30. Translation from *Heavenly Torah as Refracted through the Generations*, 667.
3. See Hos. 11:8–9 and "God's Unfathomable Love," Parashat Be-har-Be-ḥukkotai #2.
4. See Hos. 11:1.
5. V. Hamilton, *Exodus*, 258. And see "Bread from the Sky: Learning to Trust," Parashat Be-shallaḥ #2; and "God's Unfathomable Love," Parashat Be-har-Be-ḥukkotai #2.
6. See especially Deut. 7:6–8. And see also Hos. 11:1 and Simundson, *Hosea-Joel-Amos-Obadiah-Jonah-Micah*, 84.
7. Moreover, God's love for the people is entwined with—and may even be a simple consequence of—God's love for their ancestors (Deut. 7:8).
8. Hubbard, *Joel and Amos*, 147. See especially Amos 3:2. See also "A Bolt from the Blue: Or, When God Falls in Love," Parashat Devarim #2; and "Election and Service: What Joseph Learned," Parashat Va-yeshev #2.
9. See "Are Jews Always the Victims?," Parashat Lekh Lekha #1.
10. Miller, "Wilderness Journey in Deuteronomy," 57. See Deut. 2:4–5,9,19.
11. See Gen. 8:21 and "Before and After the Flood: Or, It All Depends on How You Look," Parashat Noaḥ #1.
12. See "God's Expansive Mercy: Moses's Praise and Jonah's Fury," Parashat Ki Tissa' #2.
13. See PT, Makkot 2:6 and "Between God and Torah: Judaism's Gamble," Parashat Toledot #2. See also Heschel, *God in Search of Man*, 262, 262, 268.
14. See Deut. 30:19.
15. See "Pharaoh: Consumed by the Chaos He Sows," Parashat Bo' #1.
16. See especially "Order amid Chaos: Connecting to Leviticus," Parashat Va-yikra' #1. And see, for example, Isa. 27:1, and Levenson, *Creation and the Persistence of Evil*.

17. Davis, "Slaves or Sabbath-Keepers?," 30–31. See, at length, "Whom Do We Serve? The Exodus toward Dignified Work," Parashat Va-yak'hel #1.

18. See Lev. 26:13 and "Standing Tall: Serving God with Dignity," Parashat Be-ḥukkotai #1.

19. "Yom Kippur: Purifying the Tabernacle and Ourselves," Parashat 'Aḥarei Mot #1.

20. R. Abraham Noah Paley, "Enthroning Your Creator and Enthroning Your Fellow," 8.

21. R. Yeruham Levovitz, *Da'at Hokhmah UMusar*, vol. 2, #13, 38. I hasten to add that the God of Israel *prioritizes* the ethical but is not *reducible* to the ethical. For the Torah God is not a metaphor or a way of talking about ethical obligations. God is God, the Creator of heaven and earth and the Redeemer of Israel. To employ philosophical terms that are foreign to its world, Tanakh is unequivocally committed to theological realism, the view that God exists independently of human beings.

22. "The Holiness of Israel and the Dignity of the Disabled," Parashat 'Aḥarei Mot-Kedoshim #2.

23. See "Are Jews Always the Victims?," Parashat Lekh Lekha #1; and see also "Isaac's Search: On the *Akedah* and its Aftermath," Parashat Ḥayyei Sarah #1.

24. "Hearing the Cries of the Defenseless: Or, We Are All Responsible," Parashat Mishpatim #2.

25. See E. Fox, *Five Books of Moses*, 393; and "God in the *Mishkan*: Present but Not Domesticated," Parashat Tetsavveh #1.

26. "God in the *Mishkan*: Present but Not Domesticated," Parashat Tetsavveh #1. See also "The Lampooned Prophet: On Learning From (and With) Balaam," Parashat Balak #1; and "Hearing the Whisper: God and the Limits of Language," Parashat Ha'azinu #2.

27. Klein, "Back to the Future," 275.

28. Frymer-Kensky, *In the Wake of the Goddesses*, 108.

29. See especially Gen. 4:17–26 and "What Can Human Beings Do, and What Can't They? Or, Does the Torah Believe in Progress?," Parashat Bere'shit #1.

30. See "Leaving Slavery Behind: On Taking the First Step," Parashat Be-shallaḥ #1.

31. Middleton, *Liberating Image*, 59, 60. See also the commentary of R. Saadia Gaon (882–942) to Gen. 1:26.

32. See "Created in God's Image: Ruling for God," Parashat Bere'shit #2.

33. See "No Excuses: Jacob's Sin and Its Consequences," Parashat Va-yetse' #2.

34. See "People Are Complicated: Or, Sensitivity Is a Dangerous Thing,"
    Parashat Ḥayyei Sarah #2.
35. "No Excuses: Jacob's Sin and Its Consequences," Parashat Va-yetse' #2.
36. Towner, *Genesis*, 62. And see "His Brother's Brother: Judah's Journey,"
    Parashat Mikkets #1.
37. "His Brother's Brother: Judah's Journey," Parashat Mikkets #1.
38. "Why Moses? Or, What Makes a Leader?," Parashat Shemot #1.
39. "In Praise of Protest: Or, Who's Teaching Whom?," Parashat Va-yera' #2.
40. "Hearing the Cries of the Defenseless: Or, We Are All Responsible,"
    Parashat Mishpatim #2.
41. "The Tragedy (and Hope) of the Book of Numbers," Parashat Shelaḥ #1.
    And see also "Will and Grace: Or, Who Will Circumcise Our Hearts?,"
    Parashat 'Ekev #1.
42. See Gen. 4:8 and 4:17.
43. "What Can Human Beings Do, and What Can't They? Or, Does the Torah
    Believe in Progress?," Parashat Bere'shit #1. On the complexity of human
    nature, see "People Are Complicated: Or, Sensitivity Is a Dangerous
    Thing," Parashat Ḥayyei Sarah #2.
44. See especially "Turning Memory into Empathy: The Torah's Ethical
    Charge," Parashat Mishpatim #1; and "Hearing the Cries of the Defense-
    less: Or, We Are All Responsible," Parashat Mishpatim #2.
45. Nelson, *Deuteronomy*, 190. And see "Opening Our Hearts and Our Hands:
    Deuteronomy and the Poor," Parashat Re'eh #1.
46. See Tigay, *Deuteronomy*, 12, and see also "'Do Not Be Afraid of Anyone':
    On Courage and Leadership," Parashat Devarim #1; "Opening Our Hearts
    and Our Hands: Deuteronomy and the Poor," Parashat Re'eh #1; and "Give
    the People (Only Some of) What They Want: Deuteronomy and the King,"
    Parashat Shofetim #2.
47. I develop this at length in "Turning Memory into Empathy: The Torah's
    Ethical Charge," Parashat Mishpatim #1.
48. See "The Beginning and End of Torah," Parashat Ve-zo't ha-berakhah.
49. See the remarkable words of R. Benno Jacob (1862–1945) in "Receiving Gifts
    (and Learning to Love?): The 'Stripping' of the Egyptians," Parashat Bo' #2.
50. See especially "No Leftovers: The Meaning of the Thanksgiving Offering,"
    Parashat Tsav #1.
51. "The Importance of Character: Or, Why Stubbornness Is Worse Than
    Idolatry," Parashat Ki Tissa' #1.

52. George Santayana, *Reason in Religion*, cited in Geertz, "Religion as a Cultural System," 87.
53. "Another World to Live In: The Meaning of Shabbat," Parashat Be-har #1.
54. Brueggemann, *Theology of the Old Testament*, 664.
55. See "Order amid Chaos: Connecting to Leviticus," Parashat Va-yikra' #1. And see also "Returning to Eden? An Island of Wholeness in a Fractured World," Parashat Terumah #2.
56. See "Struggling with Stigma: Making Sense of the *Metzora*," Parashat #2 Tazria'-Metsora' #1.
57. See "Women in Deuteronomy—and Beyond," Parashat Re'eh #2.
58. See "Combating Cruelty: Amalek Within and Without," Parashat Ki Tetse' #2.
59. See, for example, "Struggling with Stigma: Making Sense of the *Metzora*," Parashat Tazria'-Metsora' #1.
60. See, for example, "Combating Cruelty: Amalek Within and Without," Parashat Ki Tetse' #2.
61. Moshe Unna, "Education in Our Lives" (Hebrew), in *Ha-Kehilah Ha-Hadashah: Iyyunim Be-Mishnat Ha-Kevutzah Ha-Datit*, 264.
62. See especially "The Face of Guests as the Face of God: Abraham's Radical and Traditional Theology," Parashat Va-yera' #1.
63. For some examples see "The Face of Guests as the Face of God: Abraham's Radical and Traditional Theology," Parashat Va-yera' #1; "In Praise of Isaac: The Bible's Paragon of Marital Empathy," Parashat Toledot #1; and "The Power of Compassion: Or, Why Rachel's Cries Pierce the Heavens," Parashat Va-yishlaḥ #2.
64. For some examples see "Are Jews Always the Victims?," Parashat Lekh Lekha #1; "People Are Complicated: Or, Sensitivity Is a Dangerous Thing," Parashat Ḥayyei Sarah #2; and "No Excuses: Jacob's Sin and Its Consequences," Parashat Va-yetse' #2.
65. See "The Lampooned Prophet: On Learning From (and With) Balaam," Parashat Balak #1.

GENESIS

1. Frymer-Kensky, *In the Wake of the Goddesses*, 111.
2. Lambert, "Destiny and Divine Intervention in Babylon and Israel," 67, 70.
3. Frymer-Kensky, *In the Wake of the Goddesses*, 108.
4. Middleton, *Liberating Image*, 219–20.

5. Kidner, *Genesis*, 78.

6. Blenkinsopp, *Creation, Un-Creation, Re-Creation*, p 88.

7. R. Eliyahu Dessler, *Mikhtav Me-Eliyahu*, vol. 1, 32.

8. Middleton, *Liberating Image*, 26. For our purposes here, it doesn't matter all that much whether representing God's rule in the world is the *purpose* or *meaning* of being created in God's image or merely the *consequence* thereof. Middleton, for example, argues for the former. For examples of the latter, see Weinfeld, "Creator God in Genesis 1 and in the Prophecy of Deutero-Isaiah," 113; and Goldingay, *Old Testament Theology*, 109.

9. Middleton, *Liberating Image*, 59, 60.

10. For some accessible examples from the ancient world, see Levenson, *Creation and the Persistence of Evil*, 114.

11. Middleton, *Liberating Image*, 108–22.

12. Levenson, *Creation and the Persistence of Evil*, 114.

13. Middleton, *Liberating Image*, 121. See also, for example, Levenson, *Creation and the Persistence of Evil*, 111–17; and Sarna, *Genesis*, 12.

14. More familiar to some readers, perhaps, is the King James Bible's rendering: "Be fruitful, and multiply, and replenish the earth, and subdue it; and have dominion over the fish of the sea, and over the fowl of the air, and over every living thing that moveth upon the earth."

15. White, "Historical Roots of Our Ecologic Crisis," 1205.

16. Presumably the blessing from day 5 (1:22) extends to the land animals created on day six as well, although the text does not make this explicit.

17. Limburg, "Who Cares for the Earth?," 50.

18. Welker, "Creation and the Image of God," 447. See also Tosefta Bava Metzia 11:33.

19. David Ehrenfeld and Philip J. Bentley write: "As Jews and Christians have found, to their sorrow, the practice of stewardship, under the intoxicating influence of the power that comes with science and technology, is easily twisted and distorted so that stewardship becomes subjugation. When this occurs, as it does all around us, the vision of a power higher than humanity, which gave the original sanction and limit to the idea of stewardship, is itself washed away in a flood of collective egomania." Ehrenfeld and Bentley, "Judaism and the Practice of Stewardship," 302.

20. Mays, "What Is a Human Being?," 518.

21. Hall, "Stewardship as Key to a Theology of Nature."

22. Wirzba, *Paradise of God*, 135.

23. Bernstein, "Rereading Genesis," 59.

24. Brueggemann, *Genesis*, 85.

25. Moberly, "On Interpreting the Mind of God," 61.

26. See Deut. 1:28 and 9:1.

27. V. Hamilton, *Book of Genesis, Chapters 1–17*, 356. See also Klitsner, *Subversive Sequels in the Bible*, 35.

28. Smith, "'What Hope after Babel?,'" 179. See also, for example, Jacob, *First Book of the Bible*, 79.

29. Rachel Anisfeld insightfully connects the fact that the same sounds (B, V, N, L, S, SH) keep repeating over and over again throughout the story to the predicament of oppressive uniformity: "All of these repetitions create a throbbing, hypnotizing rhythm and a grating sense of sameness. All the people speak in the same manner, saying the same things with the same words because this is the communal refrain that has been inculcated into their consciousness through mesmerizing repetition." Anisfeld, "Generation of Bavel," 43.

30. Translation adapted slightly from Klitsner, *Subversive Sequels*, 39–40.

31. Note that when they speak of making a name, it is "for themselves"—the name they dream of refers to a collective rather than an individual. See, by way of comparison, God's promise to Abraham in Gen. 12:2.

32. Klitsner, *Subversive Sequels*, 47–48.

33. Middleton, *Liberating Image*, 225.

34. On the irreducible significance of individuals in Jewish theology, see also "Divine Love and Human Uniqueness," Parashat Be-midbar #1.

35. Middleton, *Liberating Image*, 225.

36. At this point in the story, Abram and Sarai have not yet had their names changed to Abraham and Sarah. But for ease of reading, I will refer to them as Abraham and Sarah throughout.

37. Frymer-Kensky, *Reading the Women of the Bible*, 233–34.

38. Or perhaps: "storage cities"—*arei miskenot*.

39. The three terms—*gerut, innui*, and *avdut*—are so fundamental to biblical theology that R. David Silber refers to them simply as "the covenantal formula." Silber, *Go Forth and Learn*, 16–19.

40. Sarah, of course, is not technically an Israelite—there are not yet any Israelites at this point—but the point, I trust, is clear.

41. Genesis itself does not suggest that Sarah is punished for her behavior, but see, by way of comparison, Nahmanides (Ramban, 1194–c. 1270) to Gen. 16:6.

42. But see, by way of comparison, the talmudic sage R. Elazar's interpretation of Hannah's words in 1 Sam. 1:11 in BT, Berakhot 31b. I am grateful to

Avital Hazony and Judy Richman for reminding me of a talmudic passage I had forgotten.

43. Sarna, *Genesis*, 97. See also N. Leibowitz, *New Studies in Bereshit*, 122, who notes: "The order of words in the verse is not accidental. Changes in emphasis, approval and disapproval and shades of meaning are not imparted, in the Torah, through long-winded psychological explanations or verbose analysis, but by a subtle syntactical device or seemingly insignificant but definitely unusual turn of phrase, combination, order or choice of words."

44. For an interpretation of Abram and Lot that dovetails in some ways with my own, see Touito, "'Property' as a Test of Abraham Our Father," 42–46.

45. See Cohen, "Abraham's Separation from Lot," esp. 12, 16.

46. Sarna, *Genesis*, 98. See Exod. 17:7; Num. 20:13,24; 27:14; Deut. 32:57, 33:8; Ezek. 47:19, 48:28; Ps. 81:8; 95:8; 106:32.

47. Brueggemann, *Genesis*, 130–31.

48. Brueggemann, *Genesis*, 131.

49. Joseph B. Soloveitchik, *Halakhic Man*, 100.

50. On the land as gift, see also "Against Entitlement: Why Blessings Can Be Dangerous," Parashat Ki Tavo' #1.

51. V. Hamilton, *Book of Genesis, Chapters 1–17*, 392.

52. Jon D. Levenson, personal communication, October 12, 2014. Levenson's comments are in some ways reminiscent of Kierkegaard's *Fear and Trembling*.

53. See Wenham, *Genesis 1–15*, 299–301. Passage cited is on 300. See also Waltke, *Genesis*, 218. For a very different understanding of what God's words mean, see, by way of comparison, Cohen, "Abraham's Separation," 19–20.

54. R. Shmuel Binyomin Sofer (1815–1871), *Ketav Sofer* to Gen. 13:3. See also Arnold, *Genesis*, 140.

55. See Cohen, "Abraham's Separation," 13–14.

56. On Reuben and Gad, see also "Cattle, Cattle Everywhere: The Failure of Reuben and Gad," Parashat Mattot #1.

57. For a similar interpretation of the connection between Lot and the Reubenites and Gadites, see Cohen, "Abraham's Separation," 20–22.

58. Sarna, *Genesis*, 99. Some scholars insist that Lot had no inkling of the character of the Sodomites. See, e.g., V. Hamilton, *Book of Genesis, Chapters 1–17*, 394. But it seems to me—and to most scholars—that vv. 10 and 13 suggest otherwise, that Lot's choice is at best foolish and at worst "wicked." For the latter characterization, see Waltke, *Genesis*, 221.

59. Arnold, *Genesis*, 140. Lot's single-minded pursuit of what he regards as the best land serves to explain an otherwise puzzling dimension of the text: We hear of a conflict between Abram's herdsmen and Lot's (13:8) and then of Abram speaking of (and trying to heal) a conflict between him and Lot (13:9). Does conflict between herdsmen necessarily entail conflict between their employers? The text evidently assumes that Lot's herdsmen accurately reflected his values, such that the conflict between the herdsmen is in fact a manifestation of a deeper characterological divide between Abram and Lot. See Genesis Rabbah 40:8 and Cohen, "Abraham's Separation," 12n9.

60. R. Alter, *Five Books of Moses*, 68.

61. A comparison with the use of the same Hebrew phrase in Gen. 19:8 makes the KJ version less likely, though still very much in character with Abraham.

62. For the Maharal, in order for welcoming guests to have this truly elevated spiritual status, it is crucial that the guest we receive be a stranger to us. An analysis of this claim is beyond the scope of this essay.

63. R. Abraham Noah Paley, "Enthroning Your Creator and Enthroning Your Fellow," 8.

64. Paley, "Enthroning Your Creator and Enthroning Your Fellow," 8.

65. Brueggemann, *Genesis*, 168, 176.

66. See MacDonald, "Listening to Abraham—Listening to YHWH," 36.

67. The logic of the verse would thus be that two of the three men journeyed on to Sodom, but the Lord (the third "man") stayed behind to talk to Abraham. This would also make sense of the literal meaning of the Hebrew: "The men went on from there to Sodom, but the Lord—He remained standing before Abraham." See Pröbstle, "YHWH Standing before Abraham," 173.

68. Bible scholar Carmel McCarthy notes that throughout Rabbinic literature, "there is almost unanimous agreement . . . that Genesis 18:22 is a *tiqqun sopherim*." McCarthy, *Tiqqune Sopherim and Other Theological Corrections*, 73, cited in Pröbstle, "YHWH Standing before Abraham," 174. And yet there is a long-standing scholarly debate over whether these Scribal revisions should be understood as claims about the original text or as midrashic interpretations. For a comprehensive and illuminating discussion of this purported Scribal revision, and of Scribal revisions more generally, see Pröbstle's careful and judicious study.

69. Brueggemann, *Genesis*, 168.

70. Pröbstle, "YHWH Standing before Abraham," 175–76, 187. In a similar vein,

Bruce Waltke contends that in waiting for Abraham, "the Lord is challenging Abraham to play the role of a righteous judge." I would quibble with the word "judge," but Waltke's point is well taken. More broadly, Waltke writes, "this dialogue between the Lord and Abraham is for Abraham's benefit, to challenge him to act wisely and nobly for justice" (268). Waltke, *Genesis*, 270, 269.

71. Pröbstle, "YHWH Standing before Abraham," 187.

72. Hartman, *Living Covenant*, 29.

73. See how R. Isaac Abravanel (1437–1508) explains the seemingly superfluous *"vayomru"* in his comments to Num. 32:5.

74. Reis, "Numbers XI," 213.

75. Indeed here (for the first time?) God's promises to Abraham are presented as conditional. Compare Gen. 17:2 with Gen. 18:19, and see Gen. 22:15–18 and 26:4–5.

76. See, in a somewhat similar vein, Waltke, *Genesis*, 269.

77. Maimonides (Rambam, 1135–1203), *Mishneh Torah*, Laws of Idolatry 11:4.

78. Sternberg, *Poetics of Biblical Narrative*, 137.

79. Sasson, "Servant's Tale," 251.

80. Sarna, *Genesis*, 164.

81. See, for example, Waltke, *Genesis*, 325.

82. Sternberg, *Poetics of Biblical Narrative*, 137.

83. Sternberg, *Poetics of Biblical Narrative*, 138.

84. See Sternberg, *Poetics of Biblical Narrative*, 138. See also Shkop, "Rivka," 50.

85. Fretheim, "Book of Genesis," 509. In a similar vein, Shkop writes that "both Abraham and [Rebekah] come from a common source and both are called to wander to a place unknown, leaving their paternal homes . . . and abandon all that is familiar to pursue a future veiled in mystery." Shkop, "Rivka," 55.

86. See Rashi to Gen. 24:60.

87. Fretheim, "Genesis," 510.

88. Jon D. Levenson, "Genesis," in A. Berlin and Brettler, *Jewish Study Bible*, 48–49. Psychotherapist Menorah Rotenberg posits that Rebekah is Abraham's "double and inheritor of his spiritual mantle"; although I do not agree with every part of her analysis (I have serious doubts about whether the Torah sees Rebekah and Abraham as "ruthless"), she insists, correctly, that "the textual literary links between [Rebekah] and Abraham are numerous, deliberate, and unmistakable." Rotenberg, "Portrait of Rebecca," 46.

89. Recall that Jacob is a journeyer like Abraham and Rebekah before him. See Turner, "Rebekah," 43.
90. Turner, "Rebekah," 42.
91. In the interests of space, I will not recount the details of Rebekah's plan here. In order to fully understand what follows, the reader may wish to consult Genesis 27.
92. Waltke, *Genesis*, 374.
93. Waltke, *Genesis*, 377.
94. Gerhard von Rad, *Genesis*, 277.
95. Levenson, "Genesis," 55–56.
96. See, by way of comparison, Gen. 23:1–2.
97. Waltke, *Genesis*, 373.
98. On Isaac's virtues, see also "In Praise of Isaac: The Bible's Paragon of Marital Empathy," Parashat Toledot #1.
99. My interpretation of Isaac in this brief essay intersects with, and at a few points is directly derived from, chapters 5 and 6 of Judy Klitsner, *Subversive Sequels*.
100. See, e.g., the comments of R. Samuel b. Meir Rashbam (1085–1158) to Gen. 25:21, as well as the NJPS translation of the verse.
101. My point, needless to say, is not to imply that Abraham did not love Sarah, but to suggest that perhaps the text subtly implies that Isaac displays and acts on his love more deeply and consistently than does his father.
102. Note the very understated comment of R. Vidal HaTzarfati (1540–1619), *Imrei Yosher*, on the midrash we will consider in the next paragraph: "This is the meaning of '*lenokhakh* his wife': His intention in turning to God and praying was only for children from that righteous woman (Rebecca), *and not like Abraham*" (emphasis mine).
103. See Gen. 27:20,21–23, and 27:27 in light of 27:15.
104. Hartley, *Genesis*, 184, cited in Fleming, "'She Went to Inquire of the Lord,'" 1. In a similar vein, Terence Fretheim asserts that the language of Gen. 25:22 "suggests a trip to a sanctuary." Fretheim, "Book of Genesis," 521.
105. Tamara Cohn Eskenazi, in Eskenazi and Weiss, *Torah*, 136. For a similar insistence that Rebekah consults God "directly, not through an intermediary," see V. Hamilton, *Book of Genesis, Chapters 18–50*, 177. Bible scholar Gordon Wenham takes a third path, suggesting that the text is simply not interested in the details of how Rebekah communicates with God; what matters, Wenham avers, is only that "the prophetic message is given." Wenham, *Genesis 16–50*, 175.

106. Fleming, "'She Went to Inquire of the Lord,'" 5, 3.

107. Sarna, *Genesis*, 179. But see, by way of comparison, Fleming, "Independent Divination," who argues that independent divination was not as rare in the Bible and the ancient Near East as many scholars suggest.

108. Sarna. *Exodus*, 100.

109. Durham, *Exodus*, 250.

110. Bible scholar Joseph Blenkinsopp notes that "these three activities—study, observance, instruction . . . lay the basis, first adumbrated in Deuteronomy, of the kind of religion Judaism was to remain thereafter." Blenkinsopp, *Ezra-Nehemiah*, 139.

111. David Stern, "Midrash and Midrashic Interpretation," in A. Berlin and Brettler, *Jewish Study Bible*, 1863. See also David Weiss Halivni, who writes that "*Drash* in the Bible does not, as a rule, mean exegesis, exposition of a text. Rather, it means seeking information—theological or otherwise—without reference to a text. However, the combination of *drash* and *torah* [in Ezra 7:10] connotes an exegetical activity similar to that engaged in by the rabbis of the Talmud." Halivni, *Midrash, Mishnah, and Gemara*, 15.

112. In the present context, I leave aside the question of precisely what the psalmist has in mind when he speaks of Torah—whether a canonized text or, more generally, the teachings of the wise. For two very different approaches to this question, see, by way of comparison, Amir, "Place of Psalm 119 in the History of the Religion of Israel," 57–81, and Levenson, "Sources of Torah." See also the brief but judicious comments of Adele Berlin and Marc Brettler, "Psalms," in A. Berlin and Brettler, *Jewish Study Bible*, 1414.

113. All the examples that follow are discussed in M. Greenberg, "Three Conceptions of the Torah in Hebrew Scriptures," 11–24; relevant passage is on 21–22. For a more extensive cataloging and analysis of such expressions in the psalm, see Amir, "Psalm 119," 60–64.

114. M. Greenberg, "Three Conception of the Torah in Hebrew Scriptures," 21.

115. Understandably nervous about this bold image, traditional commentators tend to offer "softer" interpretations. To take but two examples: R. Abraham Ibn Ezra (1089–1167) takes raising one's palms here to suggest not a prayer but a display of honor and a willingness to obey. R. Isaiah Di Trani (thirteenth to fourteenth century), for his part, sees raising one's palms as symbolizing one's commitment to fulfill the commandments. Some modern scholars find this image so disconcerting that they emend

the text to "I raise my palms to You (*eilekha*)." Gunkel, *Die Psalmen*, 512, cited in Amir, "Psalm 119," 60. Even Amir, who clearly finds the psalm extremely compelling, worries that this expression "goes too far." Amir, "Place of Psalm 119," 66.

116. In Ps. 63:5 raising one's palms is part of a song of praise; in Lam. 2:19 it is a part of a petition and a cry.

117. M. Greenberg," Three Conceptions of the Torah," 21–22. I agree with Jeffrey Tigay that David Noel Freedman's suggestion that in Psalm 119 we encounter a "apotheosis of Torah" is an "overstatement"—and, I would add, a very misleading one at that. Compare Freedman, *Psalm 119*, 88, with Tigay, "Torah Scroll and God's Presence," 330.

118. Tigay, "Torah Scroll and God's Presence," 333.

119. To be clear, I use "Torah" here not to refer not merely to the Five Books of Moses but also to the sum total of God's teachings and the Jewish people's ever-growing discussion and interpretation thereof.

120. Heschel, *God in Search of Man*, 261, 262. See also 268.

121. I am grateful to R. David Hoffman, whose essay "Why Religion?" planted some of the seeds of my own thinking about Leah. See: http://www.jtsa .edu/why-religion.

122. See Gen. 16:11–13.

123. I am grateful to Eli Gordon for this point.

124. Zakovitch, *Jacob*, 23.

125. Waltke, *Genesis*, 363.

126. On Rebekah's generosity (and complexity), see "People Are Complicated: Or, Sensitivity is a Dangerous Thing," Parashat Ḥayyei Sarah #2.

127. Zakovitch, *Jacob*, 24.

128. Translation adapted very slightly from Zakovitch, *Jacob*, 23.

129. See R. Alter, *Five Books of Moses*, 144.

130. R. Mecklenberg notes that: (1) Jacob says, "Perhaps (*ulai*) my father will touch me" (27:12) rather than "lest (*pen*) he touch me," thus suggesting that he wants the plot to be foiled; (2) Jacob does what his mother orders, but since there are no verbs in the text to suggest eagerness or alacrity, Jacob's heart must not be in it; (3) the text says that Rebekah dressed Jacob (27:16), not that he dressed himself. Clearly, then, according to R. Mecklenberg, Jacob is only a very reluctant participant in the goings-on.

131. V. Hamilton, *Book of Genesis, Chapters 18–50*, 217.

132. Zakovitch, *Jacob*, 64.

133. Fretheim, "Book of Genesis," 553. Fretheim adds rather tartly that Jacob "has met in Laban someone not unlike himself."

134. Zakovitch, *Jacob*, 64. Note, as does R. Eliezer Ashkenazi (1512-85), that in contrast to the narrator, who refers to Leah as *"ha-gedolah,"* the big one, Laban speaks of her as *"ha-bekhirah,"* the older one—an allusion to Esau's status in Gen. 25:33. Laban is mocking Jacob, as if to say, "You are the younger, yet you took the birthright from your brother—but that is not the practice in our place." R. Eliezer Ashekanzi, *Gedolim Ma'asei HaShem*, Ma'sei Avot, 32, cited in Frisch, "'Your Brother Came with Guile,'" 294n28.

135. Zakovitch, *Jacob*, 156. See also R. Abraham Saba (1440–1508), *Tzror Ha-Mor* to Gen. 37:29.

136. The wonderful alliteration of the aphorism cannot be captured in translation: *"B'BeGeD BaGaD Ya'akov, u-ve-BeGeD BaGDu bo banav."* Cited in Rotenberg, "Portrait of Rebecca," 61n31.

137. For a provocative historical-critical discussion of Jacob's name(s), see Shinan and Zakovitch, *From Gods to God*, 149–56.

138. Deut. 32:15; 33:5,26; and see especially Isa. 44:2.

139. R. Shmuel Yaffa Ashkenazi (1525–95), *Yefe To'ar* to Genesis Rabbah 76:2.

140. See R. Yissachar Berman HaKohen (late sixteenth to early seventeenth century), *Matnot Kehunah* to Genesis Rabbah 76:2.

141. Playing on the word *"mekhoroteihem,"* their weapons, the midrash links weapons to Esau, the one who sold (*makhar*) his birthright.

142. R. Abraham ben Aryeh Loeb Schick (nineteenth century), *Eshed HaNe-halim* to Genesis Rabbah 98:5.

143. Just how and why Rabbinic tradition travels so far from the plain meaning of the biblical text is a topic for another day.

144. R. Isaac Jacob Reines, *Orah VeSimchah*, 22.

145. R. Abraham Isaac Kook, "HaMilhamah," 3, in *Orot*, 14.

146. A. Kook, "HaMilhamah," 14.

147. R. Zvi Yehudah Kook, "Eretz Yisrael VeHaGe'ulah HaSheleimah," 120.

148. R. Zvi Yehudah Kook, "Lihiyot Yehudi Tov—Kodem Kol Lihyot BeEretz Yisrael," 212.

149. Actually both names are ambiguous. "Ben-Oni" could mean "son of my misfortune/affliction," but it could also plausibly mean "son of my vigor." The latter meaning, however, would make it difficult to understand Jacob's decision to change the child's name. "Benjamin," in turn, could mean "son of my good fortune," but also "son of the south." Other possi-

ble meanings have also been suggested. For a fairly thorough discussion of the two names, see V. Hamilton, *Book of Genesis, Chapters 18–50*, 383n8 and 384–86.

150. Brueggemann, *Genesis*, 284.

151. I leave aside the two seemingly disparate biblical traditions about just where Rachel died and was buried. According to 1 Sam. 10:2, Rachel's tomb was in or near the territory of Benjamin, rather than near Bethlehem, which is in the territory of Judah. See also Jer. 31:15.

152. Shawna Dolansky and Rina Levitt Kohn, in Eskenazi and Weiss, *Torah*, 197.

153. Ramah is likely a reference to the town from which the Judeans were taken into exile (Jer. 40:1). Some prefer to render Ramah not as a place name but as meaning "on high." If the link to Jeremiah 40 is apt, then the prophet seems to associate Rachel's burial place with the tribal region of Benjamin, as in 1 Sam. 10:2.

154. See Miller, "Jeremiah," 815n178, and Hoffman, *Jeremiah, Introduction and Commentary*, 594.

155. It is difficult to capture this in English, but Rachel's lament ends with the cry that her children "are not" (*einenu*). In responding and offering hope and consolation, God, in turn, twice affirms that "there is" (*yesh*). See Miller, "Jeremiah," 810; and L. Allen, *Jeremiah*, 348n251.

156. Brueggemann, *Jeremiah 26–52*, 64.

157. The source for Rashi's version of this story is not clear. Another midrash explains why Jacob chooses to bury Rachel on the road to Efrat: "Jacob foresaw that the exiles were destined to pass through there in the future [as they were being sent into exile by the Babylonians]. For that reason, he buried Rachel there, so that she could plead for mercy on their behalf" (Genesis Rabbah 82:10).

158. See Mishnah Ta'anit 1:4, which serves as an implicit backdrop to the story.

159. For the Rabbinic attempt to create distance between former spouses, see BT, Ketubot 27b–28a.

160. Frankel, *Aggadic Story*, 310.

161. See Frankel, *Aggadic Story*, 312, and Faust, *Aggadeta: Stories of Talmudic Drama*, 67–68.

162. See also Leviticus Rabbah 34:8.

163. See R. Jacob Moshe Hellin Ashkenazi, *Yedei Moshe* to Leviticus Rabbah 34:8

164. See R. Vidal HaTzarfati (1540–1619), *Imrei Yosher* to Leviticus Rabbah 34:8.

165. R. Yeruham Levovitz, *Da'at Torah*, 151–53.

166. R. Chaim Ephraim Zaitchik, *Or HaNefesh*, 228.

167. Num. 13:32 and 14:36–37. In those two instances, NJPS renders *dibah* as calumny.

168. Wenham, *Genesis 16–50*, 350. Based on Prov. 10:18, Bruce Waltke suggests that *dibah* means "news slanted to damage the victim." Waltke, *Genesis*, 499.

169. Others suggest: a robe with long sleeves and skirts. The common rendering, "a coat of many colors," is based on the Septuagint and the Vulgate.

170. Wenham, *Genesis 16–50*, 354.

171. Kaminsky, "Reclaiming a Theology of Election," 138. As will be obvious from following the notes, this essay owes a great deal to Kaminsky's rich study.

172. Fretheim, "Book of Genesis," 601.

173. Kaminsky, "Reclaiming a Theology of Election," 137. All of Jacob's sons are God's elect, but Joseph, it seems, is the elect among the elect. See Kaminsky, "Reclaiming a Theology of Election," 137n6.

174. Rashi seems to combine aspects of *Midrash Tanhuma*, Va-yeshev 8 and Genesis Rabbah 87:4. Midrash scholar James Kugel suggests that some Rabbinic interpretations take 39:6b to be saying not that "Joseph *was* well-built and handsome" but that he "*became* well-built and handsome"; the Hebrew *vayehi* can yield either. The implication, of course, is that Joseph was preoccupied with his looks and spent a great deal of time and energy "primping." Kugel, "Case against Joseph," 278.

175. As often, the Rabbinic reading relies on a real textual problem. Kugel contends that the Rabbinic presentation of Joseph as at least somewhat complicit in the situation that develops between him and Potiphar's wife is "subtly rooted in the biblical text, or texts, themselves." Kugel, "Case against Joseph," 272. And Kaminsky suggests similarly that "even the biblical text leaves one wondering whether Joseph, who is in charge of Potiphar's house (Genesis 39:4), knew that no servants were in the house on the day Potiphar's wife accosted [him]." Kaminsky, "Reclaiming a Theology of Election," 139.

176. See also the statement of R. Yohanan, ad loc. Rashi cites both; but see, by way of comparison, the comments of Radak and R. Abraham Ibn Ezra (1089–1164), who find no hint of anything untoward in Joseph's behavior.

177. Note also the *shalshelet*, the long cantillation mark over the word "*va-yema'en*"—but he refused [her advances] (39:8). The mark, itself an interpretation, may suggest Joseph's ambivalence and uncertainty, a push-pull going on inside of him. See Kaminsky, "Reclaiming a Theology of Election," 139.

178. Kaminsky, "Reclaiming a Theology of Election," 139.

179. Kaminsky, "Reclaiming a Theology of Election," 139–40.

180. Kaminsky, "Reclaiming a Theology of Election," 140.

181. Another fascinating dimension of the text, which I cannot explore here for reasons of space, is the role of subtle but ever-present divine providence in the Joseph story. Part of what enables Joseph to reconcile with his brothers is the realization that, badly as they behaved, their actions were used by God to preserve life.

182. Kaminsky, "Reclaiming a Theology of Election," 152.

183. I am not suggesting that this conceptual link is the reason Amos 2:6–3:8 was chosen as the haftarah for this parashat. The connection between the Torah reading and haftarah is the fact that the prophet condemns Israel for selling "for silver those whose cause was just" (Amos 2:6), which calls to mind Joseph's brothers' sale of him "for twenty pieces of silver" (Gen. 37:28); and the fact that the prophet castigates Israel because "father and son go to the same girl" (Amos 2:7), which calls to mind Judah's sexual encounter with his sons' wife (Genesis 38). The association between Amos's words and Joseph's story is so strong—and evidently so ancient—that in the noncanonical *Testament of the Twelve Patriarchs* (which likely reached its final form in the second century CE), Zebulun says that he and his brothers bought shoes for themselves and their families with the money they received for Joseph (3:2). This very odd statement makes sense when we recall Amos's words denouncing Israel for "selling the needy for a pair of shoes" (Amos 2:6, the opening verse of the haftarah). See also *Targum Yonatan* as well as *Midrash Eileh Ezkerah*, 2:64. And see the discussion in Fishbane, *Haftarot*, 61–67, esp. 66–67.

184. Hubbard, *Joel and Amos*, 147. Note that Amos seeks to clarify and purify Israel's shallow and self-serving understanding of chosenness; nowhere does he suggest is abandoning it.

185. Kaminsky, "Reclaiming a Theology of Election," 140. It should be emphasized that being called to serve does not exhaust the meaning of election in the Torah. As Walter Moberly writes, "Even if [divine] love brings with it a call to serve, that service is a corollary to being loved, not the core of being loved." Speaking of the election of Israel as a whole, Moberly argues that "the Israelites are loved for themselves, prior to any impact for good they may have on others." Moberly, *Old Testament Theology*, 48. Needless to say this does not undermine the centrality of service in a biblical understanding of covenant; it merely introduces nuance and complexity to the discussion.

186. On receiving and becoming givers, see "No Leftovers: The Meaning of the Thanksgiving Offering," Parashat Tsav #1.

187. Towner, *Genesis*, 62.

188. Devora Steinmetz, "Three Themes in the Book of Exodus," Lecture Series at Mechon Hadar, Lecture 1, January 11, 2011, online at: https://www.mechonhadar.org/torah-resource/three-themes-book-exodus.

189. Waltke, *Genesis*, 603. Waltke feels impelled to add that "in terms of the nation's destiny these anti-blessings are a blessing. By demoting Reuben for his turbulence and uncontrolled sex drive, Jacob saves Israel from reckless leadership. Likewise, by cursing the cruelty of Simeon and Levi, he restricts their cruel rashness from dominating." Note the parallel to Noah's curse of Ham for the latter's sexual violation (9:22–27). As will become clear, I am not persuaded that Reuben's purportedly "uncontrolled sexual drive" is really the issue at stake here.

190. Levenson, "Genesis," 96.

191. Noting that the word "*reishit*," meaning "first," often appears in sacrificial contexts, Gordon Wenham proposes that Jacob's reference to Reuben as "first fruit" is intended to "suggest the holy calling that Reuben ought to have followed." Wenham, *Genesis 16–50*, 472. See, e.g., Lev. 2:12; 23:10; Num. 15:20; 18:12; Deut. 18:4; 26:10. This may be an overreading, but in any case, as the next paragraph makes clear, Jacob's words make clear that Reuben was destined to be exalted and has fallen far indeed.

192. See Num. 12:2.

193. Note also that this is a case of *piska be-emtza pasuk*, a paragraph in the biblical text that ends in the middle of a verse. It is not entirely clear what purpose this device serves, but perhaps in this context it is meant to draw attention to Jacob's anomalous silence. Of course it may also point to the fact that "there is certainly much more to the story than is here revealed." Sarna, *Genesis*, 245.

194. Wenham, *Genesis*, 471.

195. See, for example, Jubilees 33:2; Testament of Reuben 3:11. See also Genesis Rabbah 98:4, as well as the subtle analysis in Kugel, *Bible As It Was*, 272–74.

196. Sarna, *Genesis*, 244. And see *Midrash Sifrei, Devarim* 347.

197. But notice how the story is softened by the insistence that what Reuben actually did was move his father's bed, not mount it.

198. Sarna, *Genesis*, 244.

199. See Songs 7:14 (and note the connection of the word *duda'im* with the

word for love—*dod*). When Reuben brings the mandrakes to his mother, she has stopped bearing children (Gen. 29:35 and 30:9) while Rachel remains childless altogether—hence the difficult scene between the two sisters in 30:14–15. As the following verses demonstrate, the Torah is skeptical about the effectiveness of mandrakes—Rachel, who has the mandrakes, remains barren for three additional years; Leah, who gives them up, proceeds to bear three more children. For the Torah it is God who opens and closes wombs. See Sarna, *Genesis*, 209.

200. I explore Leah's naming of her children, and her spiritual evolution, in "Can We Be Grateful and Disappointed at the Same Time? Or, What Leah Learned," Parashat Va-yetse' #1.

201. Brueggemann, *Genesis*, 284.

202. V. Hamilton, *Book of Genesis, Chapters 18–50*, 387. Note also that when David succeeds Saul as king of Israel, he inherits his wives (2 Sam. 12:8).

203. Zakovitch, *Jacob*, 111.

204. Sarna, *Genesis*, 333.

205. Kidner, *Genesis*, 316.

206. It is also possible that Reuben hopes that in saving Joseph, he will be able to win (back) his father's love. If so his failure takes on another tragic dimension.

207. See Lev. 18:8; 20:11.

208. R. Alter, *Art of Biblical Narrative*, 8.

209. R. Alter, *Art of Biblical Narrative*, 9.

210. But see, by way of comparison, the very different interpretation of the story attributed to the same sage in Genesis Rabbah 93:9. In significant ways Joseph's story can serve as a useful counterpoint to Tamar's. Some readers may understandably be uneasy with the sages celebrating Tamar, a socially vulnerable woman, for choosing to die rather than defend herself against the powerful man about to cause her execution. (As we have learned from cases of sexual abuse, for example, we should be extremely careful about warning the powerless never to humiliate the powerful.) Joseph's case is entirely different—it is an instance of the powerful refusing to humiliate the powerless. Joseph has all the power in this scene, and yet he actively chooses not to use it. I am grateful to Aryeh Bernstein for refining my understanding of this point. Along similar lines see "The Majesty of Restraint: Or, Joseph's Shining Moment," Parashat Va-yeḥi #1.

211. R. Isaac Alfasi (Rif, 1003–1103) to Bava Metzia 33a; Tosafot to Sotah 10b,

s.v. Noah; and R. Yonah (d. 1263), *Sha'arei Teshuvah*, 3:139. But see, by way of comparison, R. Menachem HaMeiri (1249-1310) to Berakhot 43b.

212. Technically, as will become evident in the next paragraph, R. Yonah subsumes humiliation under the broader category of murder.

213. R. Eliyahu HaKohen, *Midrash Eliyahu*, ch. 8.

214. I borrow the phrase "saving and enslaving" from Levenson, "Genesis," 93.

215. Gordon Wenham notes that the Egyptians' use of "our corpses" "vividly anticipates their state if Joseph does not provide them with food." Wenham, *Genesis 16-50*, 448.

216. Sarna, *Genesis*, 321.

217. See Wenham, *Genesis 16-50*, 438. It seems to me that the plausibility of this interpretation depends on Gen. 45:7 being taken as illustrative of Joseph's meaning in 45:5 but not exhaustive of it.

218. According to the Masoretic text, Joseph "'removed' (*he'evir*) the population town by town (*le-arim*)" (or perhaps: he transferred them into cities); the Septuagint, in contrast, reads: "He made slaves (*he'evid*) of them (*le-avadim*)." The Septuagint version does more closely follow the logical flow of the text, since the people have just said they would be Pharaoh's serfs (47:19). That seems to be the version accepted by most—though by no means all—modern scholars.

219. See also *Midrash Seikhel Tov* and *Midrash Lekah Tov* as well as the comments of R. Joseph b. Isaac Bekhor Shor (twelfth century) to Gen. 47:21.

220. I am grateful to Professor Martin Lockshin for our exchange on this point.

221. Following Radak (but without mentioning him) Robert Alter explains Joseph's dislocation of the people as follows: "The purpose would be to sever them from their hereditary lands and locate them on other lands that they knew were theirs to till only by the grace of Pharaoh, to whom the land now belonged." R. Alter, *Five Books of Moses*, 275.

222. V. Hamilton, *Book of Genesis, Chapters 18-50*, 618.

223. Wenham, *Genesis 16-50*, 449.

224. V. Hamilton, *Book of Genesis, Chapters 18-50*, 618.

225. Lowenthal, *Joseph Narrative in Genesis*, 193, cited in V. Hamilton, *Book of Genesis, Chapters 18-50*, 618n41. Bruce Waltke notes that "by ancient Near Eastern standards, 20 percent interest is low; the average was $33\frac{1}{3}$ percent." Waltke, *Genesis*, 591.

226. Levenson, "Genesis," 93.

227. R. Alter, *Five Books of Moses*, 275. In a similar vein, Nahum Sarna main-

tains that the story is included here precisely because "it provides examples of Joseph's wisdom and leadership capabilities." Sarna, *Genesis*, 321.

228. Levenson, "Genesis," 93. Terence Fretheim comments that "as Joseph makes 'slaves' of the Egyptians (though not to himself), so the later pharaohs—who do not have the wisdom and commitments of Joseph—will make 'slaves' of his family. . . . While we cannot be certain, this reversal raises the question of whether later pharaohs extend Joseph's economic policy to include the Israelites." Fretheim, "Book of Genesis," 655.

229. See, in a similar vein, Waltke, *Genesis*, 589.

230. See Brueggemann, *Genesis*, 356. Moreover, contemporary interpreter Berel Dov Lerner notes, Joseph misses an opportunity to "walk in God's ways": "During their sojourn in the desert," Lerner writes, "God gave manna freely to the Children of Israel and did not use food to extort power." The same, obviously, cannot be said of Joseph. More expansively Lerner insists that "the Torah's condemnation of Joseph's administration is complete." Lerner, "Joseph the Unrighteous," 279, 281. I am not convinced that the Torah's view is clear and unequivocal: When Genesis wishes to register its disapproval of Sarah's mistreatment of her Egyptian slave, it describes her as "oppressing" Hagar (*va-te'aneha*) (Gen. 16:6)—the key word the Torah later uses to characterize Pharaoh's treatment of Israel; I find it interesting that there is no obvious linguistic parallel here. See the comments of Ramban and Radak to Gen. 16:6, and see also "Are Jews Always the Victims?," Parashat Lekh Lekha #1. While I think Lerner's position needs some nuancing, his provocative essay is worth reading carefully. For another critical perspective on Joseph's actions, see Graetz, "From Joseph to Joseph," 45.

231. See, e.g., the struggle between Navoth and King Ahab in 1 Kings 21.

232. Nelson, *Deuteronomy*, 190. And see "Opening Our Hearts and Our Hands: Deuteronomy and the Poor," Parashat Re'eh #1.

233. See Exod. 21:2.

234. Again with the exception of the priests—Gen. 47:22.

235. Brueggemann, *Deuteronomy*, 169. Brueggemann points to our verses as a counterexample to Deuteronomy's vision. In struggling with a text like this, it can be difficult to discern definitively what is the Torah's perspective and what may be imported by modern readers. Perhaps we can put the question raised by this essay in one other way: In the ancient world, "slavery was the accepted way of bailing out the destitute." Wenham, *Genesis 16–50*, 449. But the Torah clearly worries about the implications

of long-term debt slavery. Is our story about a man doing the best he can within a fixed economic system or about a man who too readily plays along with—and even amplifies—a fundamentally problematic system? Or is the ambiguity of our story a function of the fact that on some level, it is about both?

236. Brueggemann, *Genesis*, 356.

237. Societies are commonly tempted to take measures meant to cope with emergencies and render them permanent. The temptation is no less hazardous for being widespread.

238. For Joseph's remarkable exercise of restraint in another situation in which he has the power to do great damage, see "Majesty of Restraint: Or, Joseph's Shining Moment," Parashat Va-yeḥi #1.

239. Soloveitchik, *Halakhic Man*, 101.

240. See, e.g., the comments of R. Obadiah Seforno (c. 1475–1550) to Gen. 16:6 (*Commentary to the Torah*).

241. Schlimm, *From Fratricide to Forgiveness*, 173. While I do not agree with him on every point, and while the conclusion I will draw is different, my interpretation of the dynamics between Joseph and his brothers is heavily indebted to Schlimm's fine analysis.

242. Broadie, *Genesis as Dialogue*, 387.

243. Schlimm, *From Fratricide to Forgivenes*, 175.

244. Schlimm, *From Fratricide to Forgivenes*, 176.

245. Scholars are at a loss to translate "*mekhoroteihem.*" Bruce Waltke avers that "the data is too meager to decide the meaning, and no scholarly consensus has been reached"; Nahum Sarna adds that "any translation of this unique word is guesswork." Waltke, *Genesis*, 606; and Sarna, *Genesis*, 334. For a useful discussion of the various ways the word has been translated and the problems with each proposal, see Wenham, *Genesis 16–50*, 473–74.

246. Some suggest: "They tear down [the city's] walls" (reading *shur* for *shor*). Some scholars worry that neither action—hamstringing animals or knocking down ramparts—is mentioned in Genesis 34. But the point of the text may simply be to convey a sense of wanton, unrestrained violence and aggression.

247. Fretheim, "Book of Genesis," 665.

248. Waltke, *Genesis*, 606.

249. A number of scholars have raised the possibility that Genesis 34 is in fact a story about seduction rather than rape. To take but one example,

Richard Elliott Friedman points out that the verb *"inah"* (which I have rendered above as "violated") is used once in Deuteronomy to describe a case which is ruled not to be a rape (Deut. 22:23–34); in the following case, where rape is clearly in view, the phrase "he forced her" (*hehezik bah*) appears, as it does in an unambiguous story of rape in 2 Samuel (*vayehezak mimenah*) (2 Sam. 13:14). Since what he regards as "the determining verb in Deuteronomy and in [2 Samuel] is not present in here in the Dinah story," Friedman concludes that "it may be a rape, but we cannot be sure. What we can say, at minimum, is that whether it is a rape, a seduction, or even consensual intercourse, Shechem's act, taking place before the request for marriage, is regarded as disgraceful by Dinah's family." R. Friedman, *Commentary on the Torah*, 116. For an extended argument that Dinah was not raped, see Bechtel, "What If Dinah Is Not Raped? (Genesis 34)"; for a rebuttal of such approaches, see Shemesh, "Rape Is Rape Is Rape." Be all this as it may, in this essay I follow the conventional interpretation, still held (I think) by a majority of scholars, that we are dealing here with Dinah's being raped by Shechem. I leave it to readers to decide whether and how the analysis would need to change if seduction rather than rape were the issue in question.

250. This in obvious contrast to Amnon in 2 Samuel, who, after raping his sister Tamar, immediately detests her (2 Sam. 13:15).

251. Interestingly, however, David too fails to act in response to the scandal.

252. Wenham, *Genesis 16–50*, 308, 311. Wenham adds that "Jacob's indifference to his daughter's humiliation here stands in sharp contrast to his passionate attachment to Joseph and Benjamin, the sons of Rachel his favorite wife. . . . It seems likely that it is Jacob's indifference to his daughter's plight that prompts the violent overreaction of her brothers in this story" (311, 308). See also V. Hamilton, *Book of Genesis, Chapters 18–50*, 356.

253. Waltke, *Genesis*, 463. See also V. Hamilton, *Book of Genesis, Chapters 18–50*, 356. But see, by way of comparison, Genesis Rabbah 80:6, where the sage R. Tanhuma insists that the text is ambiguous and that we therefore cannot definitively discern whether or not the brothers were summoned home by their father. It is difficult to capture the ambiguity in translation, but R. Tanhuma asks, in effect, whether Gen. 34:7 means that the brothers rushed home as soon as they heard (*ba'u . . . ke-shom'am*) or whether they were distressed when they heard (*keshom'am va-yit'atzvu*). For a similar interpretation of the verse, see Wenham, *Genesis 16–50*, 311.

254. But see, by way of comparison, Terence Fretheim, who insists that the

text "understands [Jacob's] reticence positively," as a sign of his com-
mendable "prudence." Fretheim, "Genesis," 578.

255. The Hebrew *"va-yavo'u al ha-ir beitah"* is ambiguous: It may mean that
they entered the city confidently and facing no resistance (*beitah* in that
instance would describe the manner of their arrival at the city) or that
they entered the city while it was unsuspecting and caught off guard
(*beitah* in that case would characterize the city upon their arrival). See
Sarna, *Genesis*, 238.

256. Waltke, *Genesis*, 465. In addition to the passage cited in the next sentence, see Jer. 5:27.

257. Fretheim, "Genesis," 578. Walter Brueggemann comments that through
the brothers' behavior, "the most precious symbol of faith has now
become a tool of inhumanity." Brueggemann, *Genesis* 278.

258. Waltke, *Genesis*, 467.

259. Wenham, *Genesis 16–50*, 315.

260. Sarna, *Genesis*, 238.

261. Sternberg, *Poetics of Biblical Narrative*, 472. Victor Hamilton writes that "Simeon and Levi came upon a living enemy, albeit one in pain. Their brothers
came upon the slaughtered, like vultures landing on lifeless corpses." V.
Hamilton, *Book of Genesis, Chapters 18–50*, 370. See, by way of comparison,
the ambivalent approach taken by Wenham in *Genesis 16–50*, 316.

262. Arnold, *Genesis*, 298.

263. N. Leibowitz, *New Studies in Bereshit*, 380.

264. Wenham, *Genesis 16–50*, 316.

265. Sternberg, *Poetics*, 474–75. It is striking that, as Victor Hamilton puts it,
"throughout all of this violence and vendetta, not one word has been
heard from Dinah. She is abused, avenged, spoken about, delivered, but
she never talks." V. Hamilton, *Book of Genesis, Chapters 18–50*, 372. In a
more explicitly feminist vein, Shawna Dolansky and Risa Levitt Kohn
write that "Dinah is not granted a voice in the story; instead her body
and her life form a site for settling issues between men." Dolansky and
Kohn, *Torah*, 191.

266. Wenham, *Genesis 16–50*, 317.

267. Waltke, *Genesis*, 468.

268. Waltke, *Genesis*, 458.

269. Kidner, *Genesis*, 174.

270. According to Herbert Haag, *hamas* means "cold-blooded and unscrupulous infringement of the personal rights of others, motivated by greed

and hate, often making use of physical violence and brutality." Haag, "*Hamas*." According to Gordon Wenham, *hamas* "denotes any antisocial, unneighborly activity. Very often it involves the use of brute force, but it may just be the exploitation of the weak by the powerful or the poor by the rich or the naive by the clever." Wenham, *Genesis 1–15*, 171.

EXODUS

1. Jeffrey H. Tigay, "Exodus," in A. Berlin and Brettler, *Jewish Study Bible*, 109.
2. Even Moses, one can easily argue, falls short on this last count.
3. The meaning of the Hebrew word *hasit* is not clear.
4. R. Chanokh Zundel ben Joseph (d. 1867), *Etz Yosef* to Exodus Rabbah 1:27.
5. R. Alter, *Five Books of Moses*, 321.
6. R. Alexander Zusia Friedman, *Ma'ayanah Shel Torah*, vol. 2, 18. Attributed to "Avnei Ezel," which is thought to be R. Friedman's way of introducing his own insights.
7. On the centrality and meaning of gratitude in Jewish theology and spirituality, see "No Leftovers: The Meaning of the Thanksgiving Offering," Parashat Tsav #1; "Against Entitlement: Why Blessings Can Be Dangerous," Parashat Ki Tavo' #1; and "Can We Be Grateful and Disappointed at the Same Time? Or, What Leah Learned," Parashat Va-yetse' #1.
8. Exod. 2:23 indicates a different Pharaoh is spoken of in each case (1:8 and 5:2), a fact of which the midrash makes no mention. The midrash seems to assume that it can equate all those who hold the title of Pharaoh (at least in Exodus). I am grateful to Professor Jon Levenson for our exchange on this point.
9. I have argued elsewhere that Joseph's treatment of the Egyptians is in fact quite complicated—he saves them, but he also enslaves them. Accordingly their attitude toward him might understandably have been more complicated than simple gratitude. See "Saving and Enslaving: The Complexity of Joseph," Parashat Va-yiggash #2. Nevertheless the midrash works from the assumption that immense (and unambivalent) gratitude should have been the Egyptian posture toward Joseph.
10. See also Mishnat R. Eliezer, parashat 7, 137. Why is this midrash so confident that even contemporary Egyptians know about Joseph? *Midrash Ha-Gadol* originates in Islamic countries, and all Quran-reading Muslims know of Joseph thanks to the twelfth Sura. I am grateful to Professor Burton Visotzky for this insight.

11. For the idea of juxtaposing Moses and Pharaoh as paragons of gratitude and ingratitude; for many of the references cited in this essay; and for much of the flow of the argument, I am indebted to Moshe Yehiel Tsuriel, *Otzrot Ha-Musar*, 498–501.

12. For an interpretation along similar lines, see R. David Dov Levanon, "Hakarat Ha-tov—Sod Ge'ulat Mitzrayim" (Hebrew), http://www.yeshiva.org.il/midrash/3113, October 31, 2016.

13. It is painfully ironic, in light of this, that the Israelites' entire sojourn in the wilderness is marked by such stubborn ingratitude, both to Moses and to God. The people seem to have learned the wrong lesson from Pharaoh, making Moses's countermodel all the more urgent and necessary. I am grateful to Jeremy Tabick for this insight.

14. Moreover, as my colleague R. Jason Rubenstein points out, Moses's deep sense of gratitude is also a crucial "part of what enables him to escape the trap of becoming a new Pharaoh to the liberated Israelites." Personal correspondence, January 24, 2012.

15. I suspect that something even more profound is also at work: The fact that part of what it means to live a life of faith is the need to endure a prolonged period of "not yet." We live in the (often excruciatingly vast) space between God's promises and their fulfillment. I am grateful to Jon Levenson for our discussion of this point, which I hope to take up at length in my next book.

16. Fretheim, *Pentateuch*, 54.

17. Fretheim, *Pentateuch*, 54.

18. See the comments of R. Samuel b. Meir (Rashbam, 1085–1158) to Exod. 7:5.

19. Durham, *Exodus*, 87. Bible scholar Peter Enns writes that for the Torah, "Pharaoh is God's plaything. God will do as [God] wishes to the king. God will not only act mightily and sovereignly in delivering Israel, [God] will also dictate Pharaoh's response. . . . The deliverance of Israel from Egypt is entirely God's doing and under [God's] complete control." Enns, *Exodus*, 130–31. Jon Levenson offers a more nuanced—and, I think, more compelling—view: In Exodus, he maintains, "we are dealing with a narrative need for a worthy and formidable antagonist to the protagonist, on the one hand, and the need to make the protagonist incomparably powerful, on the other. The resolution? The formidability of the antagonist is itself owing to the incomparable power of the protagonist." Personal correspondence, December 31, 2014.

20. Among Maimonides scholars, see Kadari, *Studies in Repentance*, 187–91.

Among contemporary teachers of biblical interpretation, see Hattin, *Passages*, 111–12.

21. I hasten to clarify that Maimonides's naturalism should not in any way be confused with the naturalism of Mordecai Kaplan. Maimonides's entire religious universe is built around the acknowledgment and worship of a transcendent Creator.

22. Shatz, "Divine Intervention and Religious Sensibilities," 155. Maimonides makes this move explicit in *Guide of the Perplexed*, 2:48.

23. I am grateful to Professor Bernard Septimus, who emphasized this last point in personal conversation.

24. See, for example, Schweid, *Iyunim BiShemonah Perakim LaRambam*, 121 (commenting on the eighth of the Eight Chapters); and, more expansively, Shatz, "Freedom, Repentance, and Hardening of the Hearts."

25. On this interpretation, Maimonides would endorse what Aristotle writes in the Nicomachean Ethics: "It is irrational to suppose that a man who acts unjustly does not wish to be unjust or a man who acts self-indulgently to be self-indulgent. But if without being ignorant a man does the things which will make him unjust, he will be unjust voluntarily. Yet it does not follow that if he wishes he will cease to be unjust and will be just. For neither does the man who is ill become well on those terms. We may suppose a case in which he is ill voluntarily, through living incontinently and disobeying his doctors. In that case it was then open to him not to be ill, but not now, when he has thrown away his chance, just as when you have let a stone go it is too late to recover it; but yet it was in your power to throw it, since the moving principle was in you. So, too, to the unjust and to the self-indulgent man it was open at the beginning not to become men of this kind, and so they are unjust and self-indulgent voluntarily; but now that they have become so it is not possible for them not to be so." Aristotle, *Nicomachean Ethics*, 3:5.

26. More precisely: After the seventh plague (hail), we hear both that Pharaoh hardened his own heart (9:34–35) and that God hardened it (10:1).

27. Nahum M. Sarna, *Exodus*, 23. Sarna notes that the motif of hardening, or stiffening, occurs twenty times in Exodus; exactly half of the occurrences are attributed to Pharaoh and half to God. For a full cataloging, see Sarna, *Exodus*, 241nn22–23.

28. Keil and Delitzsch, *Commentary on the Old Testament*, 456.

29. The ambiguity some find in the text—is God engaged in permissive hardening or effective?—is encapsulated well in Robert Alter's observation that

"Pharaoh is presumably manifesting his own character: callousness, resistance to instruction, and arrogance would all be implied by the toughening of the heart. God is not so much pulling a marionette's strings as *allowing, or perhaps encouraging*, the oppressor-king to persist in his habitual willfulness and presumption." R. Alter, *Five Books of Moses*, 330 (emphasis mine). "Allowing" is permissive hardening; "encouraging" is effective.

30. Fromm, *You Shall Be as Gods*, 81.
31. Soloveitchik, *On Repentance*, 143.
32. Wolbe, *Alei Shur*, 155.
33. Schmid, "Creation, Righteousness, and Salvation," 105.
34. Schmid, "Creation Righteousness, and Salvation," 106. A version of this insight will later be critical to Maimonides's understanding of how a non-interventionist God nevertheless "acts" in the natural world.
35. Fretheim, "Plagues as Ecological Signs of Historical Disaster," esp. 385n4.
36. Or perhaps: "I made myself" (*Ani asitini*).
37. See also Ezek. 32:2.
38. See, for example, Ps. 74:13–14.
39. Fretheim, *Exodus*, 166.
40. Fretheim, *Exodus*, 111.
41. Zevit, "Three Ways to Look at the Ten Plagues," 22.
42. Zevit, "Three Ways to Look at the Ten Plagues," 23.
43. Zevit, "Three Ways to Look at the Ten Plagues," 23.
44. Zevit, "Three Ways to Look at the Ten Plagues," 23.
45. Fretheim, *Exodus*, 106.
46. For an important scholarly interpretation of Exodus that expresses skepticism about the plagues as a case of uncreation or anticreation, see Propp, *Exodus 1–18*, 345–46.
47. Childs, *Book of Exodus*, 175.
48. Leibowitz, *Studies in Shemot-Exodus*, 183.
49. See also, for example, Philo, *Life of Moses*, 141.
50. V. Hamilton, *Exodus*, 67–68.
51. The connection between the Exodus narrative and the Deuteronomic law was noticed, but not developed, by R. Hezekiah ben Manoah (Hizkuni, thirteenth century) in his comments to Exod. 3:21. On the law of the manumitted slave, see "Opening Our Hearts and Our Hands: Deuteronomy and the Poor," Parashat Re'eh #1.
52. See, e.g., Daube, *Exodus Pattern in the Bible*, 55–61.
53. Cassuto, *Commentary on the Book of Exodus*, 44. Walter Brueggemann finds

here a "decisive redefinition" of the drama of the Exodus: "No longer is this a desperate, frantic, forced escape. For an instant [at least], the exodus is pictured as an ordered, proper, regulated 'letting go.'" Brueggemann, "Exodus," 770.

54. M. Greenberg, *Understanding Exodus*, 71. R. Bahya ben Asher (1255–1340) combines the two interpretations—fair wages coupled with a parting gift: "There was no fraud in God's command, God forbid. The act was totally permissible to [the Israelites], since the labor they had done for [the Egyptians] was incalculable, and its wages [which they had never received] beyond measure. Now the Torah lays it down that a slave who has served his master for seven years must be given a parting bounty" (commentary to Exod. 11:2; translation adapted from M. Greenberg, *Understanding Exodus*, 70). Penina Galpaz-Feller finds in our story a reflection of an ancient Egyptian practice of giving gold, silver, and garments to people as a token of their having achieved a new status in society. Galpaz-Feller, "And I Will Give This People Favour in the Sight of the Egyptians (Exodus 3:22)."

55. Daube, *Exodus Pattern*, 59.

56. M. Greenberg, *Understanding Exodus*, 71.

57. See also the comments of R. Samson Raphael Hirsch (1808–88) to Exod. 3:22. Among academic scholars see, for example, Victor Hamilton, who renders Exod. 3:22, "A woman will ask a gift of her neighbor." V. Hamilton, *Exodus*, 61; and Jeffrey Tigay, who translates *sha'al* as "request." Tigay, "Exodus," 112. In a similar vein, John Durham maintains that to speak of "borrowing" in this text is to misapprehend the story: "There is," he argues, "no hint of any deception, any 'borrowing' with even an implied promise of return of the borrowed items." Durham, *Exodus*, 148. Note also that the older JPS translation (1917) renders *sha'al* as "ask."

58. Childs, *Exodus*, 176. For a different perspective, see, by way of comparison, James Kugel's remarks in *Bible As It Was*, 322–24. In any case Childs is careful to add that "the traditional way of putting the question—permanent gift or temporary loan—runs into an impasse which cannot be answered from the text itself" (176).

59. Childs, *Exodus*, 177.

60. See my discussion of the hardening of Pharaoh's heart in the text and the history of exegesis, in "Cultivating Freedom: When Is Character (Not) Destiny?," Parashat Va-'era' #2.

61. Durham, *Exodus*, 40, 147, 148. In a similar vein, Douglas Stuart comments

that in the plundering of the Egyptians, "God's beneficent foreknowledge was operating: [God] knew that [the Israelites'] sojourn in the wilderness would be very long and that a poor group hardly could expect to survive without supplies and financial reserves. So from their former persecutors [God] would supply those needs, further demonstrating [God's] power and control over all people and circumstances." Stuart, *Exodus*, 127. Stuart's formulation requires significant nuancing—much of biblical theology is about God *not* using all of God's power in order to make space for others to exercise agency—but his interpretation of this story is insightful and proceeds along similar lines to Durham's.

62. Fretheim, *Exodus*, 67, 131. Fretheim emphasizes that as the narrative progresses, the contrast between Pharaoh and his people serves to accentuate one dramatic fact: "Pharaoh stands alone! . . . One is prompted to wonder: If it had not been for Pharaoh, what would the effect of [the plagues] have been? History has shown that this picture of the difference between a country's leaders and its people are not uncommon" (131).

63. Victor Hamilton wonders "what people who just had the daylights smacked out of them are going to be so philanthropic to those who have caused so much agony and turmoil?" V. Hamilton, *Exodus*, 67. Samuel David Luzzatto (Shadal, 1800–1865) suggests that prosperous, successful people generally "see the wretched poor as belonging to a different species from them, and so they think that adding to their misery is no crime. But when these unfortunates begin to rise from the depths of their lowliness, the prosperous and successful begin to have regard, sympathy, and love for them" (commentary to Exod. 11:3).

64. Janzen, *Exodus*, 36–37. But note that to sustain his interpretation, Janzen feels compelled to soften the meaning of the word "plunder," and perhaps even to intimate that the word is used ironically. After all, if people willingly and generously give things to you, you can hardly be said to be "plundering" them.

65. Jacob, *Second Book of the Bible*, 339, 343.

66. Jacob, *Second Book of the Bible*, 344, 345.

67. Jacob worked on his Exodus commentary between 1934 and 1939 and worked on revisions thereafter. I am grateful to R. Walter Jacob for our exchange on this biographical point.

68. Moreover, as R. Hayyim Ibn Attar (d. 1696) points out, it isn't clear in what direction the Israelites are supposed to move, with the pursuer behind them and the sea in front of them (Or Ha-Hayyim to Exod. 14:15). Of

course another anomaly in the text is that we never hear anything explicit about Moses's crying out, and yet God lambasts him for doing just that.

69. See, e.g., Jer. 46:4 and 1 Sam. 17:16.

70. Exod. 13:18. But see, by way of comparison, Rashi's (1040–1105) second explanation there.

71. Margalit, "Day the Sun Did Not Stand Still," 474.

72. See also BT, Shabbat 32a and Pesahim 64b.

73. I borrow the phrase "between bondage and well-being" from Brueggemann, "Exodus," 812.

74. R. Alter, Five Books of Moses, 405.

75. For a very different Rabbinic understanding of the narrative, see, by way of comparison, the words of R. Eliezer the Moda'ite in Mekhilta DeR. Shimon b. Yohai, 16:3.

76. Walzer, Exodus and Revolution, 34, 33.

77. Goldingay, Old Testament Theology, 455.

78. Brueggemann, "Exodus," 812.

79. Scholars have long attempted to offer naturalistic explanations for what the manna might be. As Jeffrey Tigay explains, "If [the manna] has a natural explanation, it is probably the sweet, edible honeydew (still called 'manna' in Arabic) found in parts of the Sinai in June and July. Scale insects and plant lice ingest the sap of tamarisk trees and excrete it onto the branches, from which it crystallizes and falls to the ground as sticky solids. Bedouin use it as a sweetener." But Tigay immediately adds that "if this was the manna, the miracle was that it arrived just when the Israelites needed it, that enough was produced to feed the entire people but never more than an *omer* per person daily, that it doubled on the sixth day and did not appear on the Sabbath, and that contrary to its natural pattern it appeared year-round." Tigay, "Exodus," 140. It should be noted that some scholars are dismissive of the search for naturalistic explanations of the manna (seemingly even nuanced ones). Carol Meyers, for example, states simply that "manna should be considered a non-natural substance, a miracle provided by God." Carol Meyers, in Eskenazi and Weiss Torah, 396.

80. Tigay, "Exodus," 141.

81. See, similarly, R. Hayyim Ibn Attar (1696–1743), Or Ha-Hayyim to Exod. 16:4.

82. On the danger of growing entitled while living in the land, see "Against Entitlement: Why Blessings Can Be Dangerous," Parashat Ki Tavo' #1.

83. See also the comments of R. Samuel ben Meir (Rashbam, 1085–1158).

84. Brueggeman, "Exodus," 813.

85. Durham, *Exodus*, 226.

86. Just how difficult the transition is from oppressive slavery to dignified relationship to God is evidenced by the fact that of the whole first generation to experience freedom, only two people, Caleb and Joshua, make it to the Promised Land. On the recalcitrance of that generation, see "Tragedy (and Hope) of the Book of Numbers," Parashat Shelaḥ #1.

87. Brueggemann, "Exodus," 814.

88. Janzen, *Exodus*, 116–17. See Exod. 5:13,19; and 6:4.

89. Fretheim, *Exodus*, 187.

90. Brueggemann, "Exodus," 812. See also "Whom Do We Serve? The Exodus toward Dignified Work," Parashat Va-yak'hel #1.

91. See, for example, R. Friedman, *Commentary on the Torah*, 225.

92. V. Hamilton, *Exodus*, 258.

93. On Amalek in the Torah and in Jewish thought more broadly, see "Combating Cruelty: Amalek Within and Without," Parashat Ki Tetse' #2.

94. Cassuto, *Commentary on the Book of Genesis*, 211–12.

95. Wright, *Deuteronomy*, 87, and Brueggemann, "Exodus," 847. These same verbs occur in a single verse to describe the antithetical ways people respond to God (and the consequences of each way): "For I honor those who honor Me (*mekhabdai*), but those who dishonor Me (*mekallelai*) will be dishonored" (1 Sam. 2:30). See Wright, *Deuteronomy*, 87; and V. Hamilton, *Exodus*, 340.

96. Tigay, *Deuteronomy*, 69–70.

97. Childs, *Book of Exodus*, 418.

98. Childs, *Book of Exodus*, 418.

99. Fretheim, *Exodus*, 231.

100. Tigay, *Deuteronomy*, 69.

101. Nelson, *Deuteronomy*, 83.

102. Brueggemann, "Exodus," 847.

103. Fretheim, *Exodus*, 231.

104. Enns, *Exodus*, 421.

105. Yuval Cherlow makes a strong case for their being no such obligation in "Dignity of the Child in the Commandment to Honor Parents — Must the Child Obey His Parents?" My analysis in the next two paragraphs is heavily indebted to his.

106. In a similar vein, Bible scholar Tremper Longman writes, "It is interesting that the law uses the term 'honor' and not the word 'obey.' This choice may be intentional since not all parents desire their children to obey God's law." Longman, *How to Read Exodus*, 124.

107. I am aware that one could couch even these cases as instances of conflict between two religious obligations, but I am not sure that such interpretations are convincing, let alone necessary.

108. See, for example, Nahmanides (Ramban, 1194–c. 1270), Hiddushei Ha-Ramban to BT, Yevamot 6a, s.v. *Mah Le-Hanakh*; and R. Yom Tov b. Avraham Asevilli (Ritva, 1250–1330), Hiddushei Ha-Ritva to Yevamot 6a, s.v. *Mah*; and see Yuval Sherlo's analysis in "Dignity of the Child," 323–24.

109. I am not speaking here of situations involving severely abusive parents. There are times when a child is not only permitted but arguably even obligated to separate from a parent. There is no halakhic obligation to become sick or incapacitated (physically or psychologically) in attempting to placate an abusive parent. For two useful and accessible discussions, see Benzion Sorotzkin, "Honoring Parents Who Are Abusive," http://drsorotzkin.com/wp-content/uploads/2014/09/eng-honoring -abusive-parents.pdf; and Dratch, "Honoring Abusive Parents," 1–15.

110. Childs, *Exodus*, 418. See also Fretheim, *Exodus*, 231.

111. Miller, *Deuteronomy*, 84.

112. Like most Christian interpreters (but unlike Jewish ones), Brueggemann assumes that Exod. 20:2 ("I am the Lord your God . . .") serves a prologue to the Ten Commandments and does not itself constitute the First Commandment.

113. Brueggemann, *Deuteronomy*, 69.

114. Gawande, *Being Mortal*, 17.

115. Scarry, "Difficulty of Imagining Other People," 103.

116. Hiebert, "'Whence Shall Help Come to Me?,'" 137. Victor Hamilton suggests that the fact that not every widow is an *almanah* "may explain why some women in Scripture who are widows are never called [*almanot*] — Naomi, Orpah, Ruth, Abigail, Bathsheba. Even without their spouses, they have some means of support." V. Hamilton, *Exodus*, 413. For a dissenting view that resists limiting the meaning of *almanah* in this way, see, by way of comparison, Fensham, "Widow, Orphan, and the Poor in Ancient Near Eastern Legal and Wisdom Literature," 136.

117. Brueggemann, "Exodus," 868.

118. Bible scholar Pietro Bovati argues that "this '[out]cry' is not just a personal outburst or a simple instinctive reaction to suffering: It is essentially addressed to someone (*el* . . .) and demands to be heard in the name of right. . . . In this way a complaint reveals another aspect of what constitutes it; it is request for help addressed to an 'authorized' person,

juridically bound by the actual cry." Bovati, *Re-establishing Justice*, 317, cited in M. Jacobs, "Toward an Old Testament Theology of Concern for the Underprivileged," 221. On the surface at least, there is some tension between Bovati's words and those of James Kugel, *God of Old*, 110.

119. Ibn Ezra states that one who oppresses and one who witnesses oppression and says nothing have the very same status. Among modern scholars, Ibn Ezra's interpretation is "tentatively accepted" by Joe Sprinkle. See Sprinkle, "*Book of the Covenant*," 169.

120. See, for example, Psalm 72 and Ezekiel 34.

121. See Fensham, "Widow, Orphan, and the Poor."

122. On the democratization of ancient Near Eastern royal ideology in the Torah, see also "Created in God's Image: Ruling for God," Parashat Bere'shit #2.

123. Enns, *Exodus*, 452.

124. Brueggemann, "Exodus," 868.

125. I have explored the prohibition on oppressing the stranger as well as the mandate to love him in "Turning Memory into Empathy: The Torah's Ethical Charge," Parashat Mishpatim #1.

126. See Lev. 19:33–34; Deut. 10:19.

127. Enns, *Exodus*, 452.

128. God says of the poor person having his lone garment taken in pledge overnight, "It is his only clothing, the sole covering for his skin. In what else shall he sleep? Therefore, if he cries out to Me, I will pay heed, for I am compassionate (*hanun*)" (Exod. 22:26). In these verses, it seems, "it is the oppressed human's cry . . . that will unleash the chain of events that will ultimately result in [Israel] being punished. I am powerless *not* to react, God seems to say, once the abused party cries out to Me." Kugel, *God of Old*, 110. For a discussion of "the cry of the victim" in biblical theology more broadly, see 109–36. The Torah wants to protect the vulnerable, but also, it seems, to teach something fundamental about the nature of God: Compassion is at the very core of who God is.

129. See also my discussion of Ps. 145:9 in "Power of Compassion: Or, Why Rachel's Cries Pierce the Heavens," Parashat Va-yishlaḥ #2.

130. Tigay, "Exodus," 157. More expansively, Nahum Sarna writes: "The exploitation of these unfortunates was so tempting, and apparently so widespread, and seemingly beyond the reach of the law, that the Torah amplifies the ordinary apodictic formulation with a passionate emphasis on the gravity of the sin in the eyes of God. The absence of a human pro-

tector of the widow and the orphan should not delude the unscrupulous or the society that tolerates them. God Himself champions the cause of the downtrodden." Sarna, *Exodus*, 138. See also Prov. 22:22–23 and 23:10–11. And see the analysis of Deut. 15:7–11 in "Opening Our Hearts and Our Hands: Deuteronomy and the Poor," Parashat Re'eh #1.

131. Heschel, *God in Search of Man*, 273.

132. Held, *Abraham Joshua Heschel*, 123. I have suggested there that "this principle [of reading paradigmatically] should apply to theological commandments, and not just to ethical or interpersonal ones. Thus one who understands that to observe the Sabbath is to offer testimony that God is creator, while human beings are mere creatures, may conclude that in a time of unprecedented technological power, additional forms of Sabbath-like acknowledgment of the divine-human divide are called for. And so on."

133. See, by way of comparison, the related but different thrust of R. Akiva's and R. Ishmael's "paradigmatic" understanding of our verses in *Mekhilta de-Rabbi Yishmael, Nezikin*, ch. 18.

134. Fretheim, *Exodus*, 249, 248. Fretheim's comments focus primarily on Exod. 22:24–26 (the laws about not acting like a merciless creditor in dealing with the poor), but he has a much broader perspective in mind—and alludes to our verses as illustration.

135. Scholem, *Major Trends in Jewish Mysticism*, 260.

136. See, by way of comparison, the version in Exodus Rabbah 34:1, according to which God contracts the divine presence even more intensely, into one small square cubit.

137. Scholem, *Major Trends in Jewish Mysticism*, 260.

138. Fretheim, "Book of Genesis," 346.

139. The same logic—and the same challenges—apply, mutatis mutandis, in the relationship between parents and their children.

140. Martin Buber, *I and Thou*, 69. 78.

141. Martin Buber, "Distance and Relation," 207.

142. Martin Buber, "Distance and Relation," 211.

143. Martin Buber, "Distance and Relation," 208.

144. See my analysis of Shabbat in "Another World to Live in: The Meaning of Shabbat," Parashat Be-har #1.

145. Fishbane, *Text and Texture*, 112.

146. Fishbane, *Text and Texture*, 112.

147. Fishbane, *Text and Texture*, 116.

148. Of course this verse raises the question of the exact relationship

between "Eden" and "the garden," which are clearly not synonymous, since one is said to water the other.

149. Fishbane, *Text and Texture*, 119.

150. On the *mishkan* as "counterworld," see "Order amid Chaos: Connecting to Leviticus," Parashat Va-yikra' # 1.

151. See Wenham, "Sanctuary Symbolism in the Garden of Eden Story," 21.

152. According to Wenham, in the ancient Near East, cherubim "were the traditional guardians of holy places." Wenham, "Sanctuary Symbolism," 21. Gregory Beale suggests that the cherubim serve to replace Adam as guardians of God's garden; when he failed, they took over. Beale, *Temple and the Church's Mission*, 70.

153. Meyers, *Exodus*, 232. See also Meyers, *Tabernacle Menorah*.

154. See also 1 Chron. 29:2.

155. Some find another strong tie between Eden and the *mishkan* in God's promise of a blessed life to an obedient Israel: "I will establish my abode (*mishkani*) in your midst, and I will not spurn you. I will walk about (*ve-hithalakhti*) in your midst; I will be your God and you shall be My people" (Lev. 26:11–12). Arguing that *mishkani* should be rendered here—as often—as "my tabernacle," they suggest that we find here a close connection between the *mishkan* and Genesis's description of God's voice "moving about (*mithalekh*) in the garden" (Gen. 3:8): "The Lord walked in Eden as he subsequently walked in the tabernacle." Wenham, "Sanctuary Symbolism," 20; see also Wenham, *Book of Leviticus*, 329–30. But Jacob Milgrom has convincingly shown that in this context, *mishkani* cannot refer to the *mishkan*—as he explains, "the verb ve-natati (I will establish) would testify that there is no sanctuary building at the moment, which patently is not the case [in Leviticus]." In Leviticus 26, then, *mishkani* refers to God's presence, not God's tabernacle. To be clear: The allusion to Eden may well be intended, but the point would be that "in the paradisiacal conditions of the blessed land. . . . God himself (not his voice) will move about." The land, and not the *mishkan* in particular, is here connected to the Garden. Milgrom, *Leviticus 23–27*, 2299, 2301. See Ezekiel 36 and Isaiah 51, discussed earlier in the essay.

156. For two important and influential examples, see Wenham, "Sanctuary Symbolism," and Beale, *Temple and the Church's Mission*, 66–80.

157. Block, "Eden." Block readily acknowledges that in arguing against the idea that the Garden is a Temple, he is "swimming against an overwhelming current of scholarly opinion" (3).

158. Enns, *Exodus*, 553.

159. Block, "Eden," 4.

160. Block, "Eden," 21.

161. Fretheim, "Book of Genesis," 366.

162. Hall, *God and Human Suffering*, 64–65.

163. Hall, *God and Human Suffering*, 68, 60.

164. See also "Order amid Chaos," Parashat Va-yikra' #1.

165. See E. Fox, *Five Books of Moses*, 393.

166. Nahmanides (Ramban, 1194–c. 1270), Commentary to Exod. 25:2.

167. V. Hamilton, *Handbook on the Pentateuch*, 220.

168. V. Hamilton, *Handbook on the Pentateuch*, 220–21.

169. Fretheim, *Exodus*, 264.

170. Fretheim, *Exodus*, 267.

171. Klein, "Back to the Future," 275.

172. Haran, *Temples and Temple-Service in Ancient Israel*, 269.

173. Yehoyada Amir, "To Kindle a Lamp: Thoughts on Parashat Tetzaveh," http://www.reform.org.il/Heb/holidays/WeeklyPortionArticle.asp?ContentID=144 (accessed February 17, 2015).

174. In reality even the midrashic interpretation alone gives expression both sides of the relationship: Six candles are lit each night (Israel), and one stays burning always (God). In a sense this pair of images is reminiscent of a classic Rabbinic debate about the meaning of the sukkot (booths) in which Jews are charged to dwell for one week each year. God commands Israel to live in booths "in order that future generations may know that I made the Israelite people live in booths when I brought them out of the land of Egypt, I the Lord your God" (Lev. 23:43). R. Akiva explains that "booths" refers to the real booths the people made for themselves in the desert, but R. Eliezer insists that it refers to the "clouds of divine glory" (*ananei kavod*) that traveled with the people (BT, Sukkah 11b). R. Akiva's position seems to capture the plain sense of the text, but R. Eliezer cannot help but notice that God is the main actor in our verse: God made the people dwell in booths when God brought them out of Egypt. The Torah's mandate, he concludes, is for us to remember what God did for the people and to build sukkot as symbols of God's providential love and concern. The two images together paint another potent picture of divine-human connection: Dwelling in booths for seven days, we recall and celebrate both God's presence for the people and the people's presence for God.

175. More precisely parashatTetsavveh mandates three such rituals: the regular kindling of the light, the *korban tamid*, and the twice-daily burning of incense (30:7–8).

176. Durham, *Exodus*, 396.

177. Durham, *Exodus*, 397. The word "demonstrated" is Durham's. More nuanced terms such as "evoked," "affirmed," or "testified to" might be more appropriate—and more insightful about how ritual works.

178. V. Hamilton, *Exodus*, 505.

179. Brandes, "Generous-Hearted People," 211.

180. R. Nosson Zvi Finkel, "Kashyut Oref," 187.

181. I borrow the pairing of "conduct" and "character" from the subtitle of Alan Mittleman's recent work, *Short History of Jewish Ethics: Conduct and Character in the Context of Covenant*.

182. See also "Coveting, Craving . . . and Being Free," Parashat Va-etḥannan #1.

183. See, for example, Wurzburger, "*Imitatio Dei* in Maimonides' Sefer Hamitzvot and the Mishneh Torah." The analysis that follows is heavily indebted to Wurzburger's.

184. Sarna, *Exodus*, 216.

185. Moberly, *At the Mountain of God*, 88.

186. V. Hamilton, *Exodus*, 576. Bible scholar Richard Elliot Friedman reminds us that "those who speak of the 'Old Testament God of wrath' focus disproportionately on the episodes of anger in the Bible and somehow lose this crucial passage and the hundreds of times that the divine mercy functions in the Hebrew Bible." R. Friedman, *Commentary on the Torah*, 291.

187. R. Friedman, *Commentary on the Torah*, 291.

188. Bonhoeffer, *Cost of Discipleship*, 44, 43.

189. All of this said, it does seem that a tension remains in the text—and in Jewish theology as a whole: God forgives sinners and God also punishes them. There is mercy, but there is also judgment. (Perhaps we can put this differently: Working out a perfect synthesis of judgment and mercy is so difficult that according to Jewish theology even God struggles with it.)

190. Moberly, *Old Testament Theology: Reading the Hebrew Bible as Christian Scripture*, 195.

191. Moberly, *Old Testament Theology*, 192.

192. See Num. 14:18; Neh. 9:17; Ps. 86:15, 103:8, and 145:8; Joel 2:13; and Nah. 1:3.

193. Timmer, *Gracious and Compassionate God*, 119, 123, 124, 123.

194. Sweeney, *Twelve Prophets*, 328.

195. Achtemeier, *Minor Prophets I*, 257.

196. Moberly, *Old Testament Theology*, 200.

197. Achtemeier, *Minor Prophets I*, 282.

198. In a similar vein, Marvin Sweeney observes that at the end of Jonah, God's "role as creator and master of the world comes once more into play, as the Ninevites were understood to be a people that only a parent could love in biblical tradition. . . . Nevertheless, [God] is their creator and loves them." Sweeney, *Twelve Prophets*, 332.

199. Or perhaps: "I made myself" (*asitini*).

200. Davis, "Slaves or Sabbath-Keepers?," 30–31. My own analysis is heavily indebted to Davis's provocative study of the nature of work in Exodus.

201. Sokolow, *Hatzi Nehamah*, 135.

202. Brueggemann, "Exodus," 888.

203. See also the astute analysis of "leading words" in the text in Sharon Rimon, "Generosity of Heart and Wisdom of Heart in the Construction of the *Mishkan*" (Hebrew), available at www.etzion.org/vbm.

204. As I have written elsewhere, "Scholars have long struggled to understand just what the heart symbolizes in biblical thinking." Some think it refers primarily to intelligence, others to the will. More persuasive, in my view, is a more expansive interpretation, according to which "the heart in Hebrew thought is the preeminent metaphor for the inner being of a person, the seat of intelligence; the seat of emotions; and the seat of volition, i.e., the will." Lundbom, *Deuteronomy*, 391. See "Will and Grace? Or, Who Will Circumcise Our Hearts," Parashat 'Ekev #1. In any case, where connected to the root *n-d-v*, the word *lev* undoubtedly suggests something very close to what we tend to mean by "heart," namely emotion and feeling.

205. Malbim reads the phrase "*kol ish asher yidvenu libo*," rendered above as "every person whose heart so moves him," to mean something more like "every person whatever he is able to contribute," to which he comments, "Even one string" (commentary to Exod. 25:1).

206. In his shorter commentary to our verse, Ibn Ezra writes that "there are wise people and craftsmen who are not capable of teaching well," which seems to support the first interpretation, but in his longer commentary, he employs an odd locution: *yesh hakhamim rabim she-hem kashim le-horot*, which I have rendered above as "there are many wise people who find it hard to teach others." I would tentatively suggest that either interpretation of these words is plausible—that some are pedagogically unskilled, or that some are circumspect about sharing their wisdom, or

both. I am grateful to Professor Martin Lockshin for our exchange about Ibn Ezra's remarks.

207. See "Order amid Chaos: Connecting to Leviticus," Parashat Va-yikra' #1. I borrow the term "counterworld" from Brueggemann, *Theology of the Old Testament*, 664.

208. See "Returning to Eden? An Island of Wholeness in a Fractured World," Parashat Terumah #2.

209. In exploring the connection between the *mishkan* and the world in biblical theology, two useful places to start are Levenson: *Creation and the Persistence of Evil*, 78–99, and Balentine, *Torah's Vision of Worship*, 136–41.

210. Levenson, *Creation and the Persistence of Evil*, 84.

211. Levenson, *Creation and the Persistence of Evil*, 86.

212. Levenson, *Creation and the Persistence of Evil*, 86.

213. Heschel, *Insecurity of Freedom*, 258.

A Note on Bible Commentaries

Readers who wish to engage with Rabbinic interpretation of the Torah can turn to the classic midrashic compilations: the Mekhiltot on Exodus; Sifra on Leviticus; Sifre on Numbers and Deuteronomy; and the Rabbah collections and Tanhuma on all Five Books.

Louis Ginzberg's astonishingly learned *Legends of the Jews* casts a wide net in gathering interpretations of major biblical figures and stories. The one major drawback of *Legends* is that erases the textual bases that make many of these stories possible; in other words, reading Ginzberg one can lose sight of the fact that Rabbinic interpretation is midrash, commentary on texts, rather than just "legends."

To understand how Jews have read biblical texts, the medieval commentators who traditionally appear in the Mikra'ot Gedolot are indispensable. I also recommend the work of Rabbi Isaac Abravanel, whose commentaries are verbose but filled with literary and theological insight. Among modern Rabbinic interpreters, I find the (very different) commentaries of Rabbi Naftali Zevi Yehudah Berlin (Netziv), Rabbi Samson Raphael Hirsch, and Rabbi Meir Leibish Malbim extremely useful. For a sure-handed guide through classical discussions of important issues in each parashah, readers may wish to consult Nehama Leibowitz.

The scholars mentioned below all share a view of the Torah as a composite document composed over time; these volumes are not recommended for readers who would find such perspectives alienating (or religiously unacceptable). Many are also believing Christians; I recommend them highly to readers open to learning from them.

GENESIS

Terence Fretheim, "Genesis: Introduction, Commentary and Reflections," in the *New Interpreter's Bible*, volume 1 (Abingdon, 1994). A distinguished biblical theologian, Fretheim focuses readers' attention not just on the God of history but also on the God of creation; his commentaries combine keen literary sensitivity with subtle theological interpretation.

Jon D. Levenson, "Genesis," in Adele Berlin and Marc Zvi Brettler, eds., *Jewish Study Bible* (Oxford, 2004). Levenson's extremely brief commentary is studded with theological and interpretive insights and makes good use of classical Jewish interpretation.

Also worth noting: Umberto (Moshe David) Cassuto, *A Commentary on the Book of Genesis* (Magnes, 1961–64), who offered astute literary interpretations of the Bible long before literary approaches to the text were popular; four evangelical scholars—Bill Arnold, *Genesis* (Cambridge, 2008); Victor Hamilton, *The Book of Genesis* (2 volumes) (Eerdmans, 1990, 1995); Bruce Waltke, *Genesis: A Commentary* (Zondervan, 2001); and Gordon Wenham, *Genesis* (2 volumes) (Thomas Nelson, 1987, 1994)—bring together mastery of Semitic philology, knowledge of the ancient Near Eastern context, and genuine sensitivity to matters of biblical theology (and ethics).

EXODUS

Terence Fretheim, *Exodus* (Westminster John Knox, 1991). In a very accessible and extremely astute commentary, Fretheim pays a great deal of attention to how God's concern with nature and God's involvement in history intersect.

Walter Brueggemann, "Exodus: Introduction, Commentary and Reflections," in the *New Interpreter's Bible*, volume 1 (Abingdon, 1994). Brueggemann is an exceptionally prolific and enormously influential biblical theologian. His commentary on Exodus combines careful literary interpretations with fascinating (and often bold) claims about biblical theology.

Also worth noting: Cassuto, *A Commentary on the Book of Exodus* (Magnes, 1967) (see above); Moshe Greenberg, *Understanding Exodus: A Holistic Commentary on Exodus 1-11*, second edition (Cascade, 2013);

Victor Hamilton, *Exodus: An Exegetical Commentary* (Baker, 2011) (see above); and Peter Enns, *Exodus* (Zondervan, 2000), a Christian scholar who focuses heavily on the implications of the text for devout Christians, but who offers many theological insights also pertinent to Jews.

LEVITICUS

Baruch Levine, *Leviticus* (JPS, 2003). Levine helps the reader navigate a text whose assumptions can seem utterly foreign to many modern readers. His commentary makes judicious use of philology and of ancient Near Eastern parallels; it is somewhat weaker where big ideas are concerned.

Samuel Balentine, *Leviticus* (Westminster John Knox, 2003). Balentine is a careful reader with a keen eye for the theological assumptions and implications of the text. Pays less attention to the details of temple ritual.

Also worth noting: Jacob Milgrom's massive three-volume *Leviticus* (Yale, 1998, 2000, 2001) is a monumental scholarly achievement, but it is extremely dense and not for the faint of heart (the one-volume abridgment, *Leviticus: A Book of Ritual and Ethics* [Augsburg Fortress, 2004] is idiosyncratic and not very helpful); Roy Gane's *Leviticus, Numbers* (Zondervan, 2004) is devoutly Christian, but it offers an abundance of literary and theological insights from which Jewish readers can benefit. Frank Gorman's very brief *Leviticus: Divine Presence and Community* (Eerdmans, 1997) is extremely accessible and makes good use of anthropological approaches to make sense of ritual.

NUMBERS

Jacob Milgrom, *Numbers* (JPS, 2003). Less overwhelming than Milgrom's commentary on Leviticus, this is an extremely solid work: Milgrom is sensitive to literary issues and theological implications and makes extremely productive use of classical Jewish commentaries.

Dennis Olson, *Numbers* (Westminster John Knox, 1996). A brief but extremely insightful commentary from a highly regarded Christian scholar. Focuses on the stark contrasts between the first, failed generation, and the second, hope-filled one.

Also worth noting: Gordon Wenham's *Numbers* (IVP, 2008) is very short but theologically suggestive; Roy Gane *Leviticus, Numbers* (Zondervan, 2004).

DEUTERONOMY

Jeffrey Tigay, *Deuteronomy* (JPS, 2003). A model of a rigorous, methodical commentary. Makes productive use of ancient Near Eastern parallels and does a fine job elucidating the unique religious vision of Deuteronomy.

Patrick Miller, *Deuteronomy* (Westminster John Knox, 1990). Miller's work tends to combine careful attention to ancient Near Eastern parallels with real theological insight, and this volume is no exception. This short commentary is a wonderful resource — Miller's interpretations are always solid and often arresting.

Also worth noting: Richard Nelson's *Deuteronomy: A Commentary* (Westminster John Knox, 2002) is methodical and careful but also willing to make big theological claims; Walter Brueggeman's *Deuteronomy* (Abingdon, 2001) is classic Brueggemann — beautifully written, bold, and always eager to make connections between the text and contemporary American realities; Moshe Weinfeld's *Deuteronomy 1–11* (Yale, 1995) is a remarkable achievement (though it is not light reading).

ON THE FIVE BOOKS AS A WHOLE

Robert Alter, *The Five Books of Moses: A Translation with Commentary* (Norton, 2004) offers consistently insightful (and sometimes downright stunning) literary interpretations of biblical passages; his comments on biblical religion and theology tend to be weaker.

Adele Berlin and Marc Zvi Brettler, eds., *Jewish Study Bible* (Oxford, 2004), is a remarkable resource. Renowned scholars offer short but often extremely insightful commentaries on each of the Five Books of Moses.

Also worth noting: Each parashah in Tamara Cohn Eskenazi and Andrea L. Weiss, eds., *The Torah: A Women's Commentary* (URJ, 2008) is treated by a different scholar. Not surprisingly, then, the contents are of uneven quality. But many of the commentaries are provocative and insightful.

Bibliography

Abravanel, Isaac. *Commentary to the Torah*. Venice: 1579.

Achtemeier, Elizabeth. *Minor Prophets I*. Peabody MA: Hendrickson, 1996.

Adler, Rachel. "Those Who Turn Away Their Faces: Tzara'at and Stigma." In *Healing and the Jewish Imagination: Spiritual and Practical Perspectives on Judaism and Health*, edited by William Cutter, 142–59. Woodstock VT: Jewish Lights, 2007.

Albo, Joseph. *Sefer Ha-Ikkarim*, 1485. Philadelphia: Jewish Publication Society, 1929.

Alfasi, Isaac (Rif). *Sefer Ha-Halakhot*. Jerusalem: Mossad HaRav Kook, 1969.

Allen, Leslie C. *The Books of Joel, Obadiah, Jonah, and Micah*. Grand Rapids MI: Eerdmans, 1976.

———. *Ezekiel 1–19*. Nashville TN: Thomas Nelson, 1994.

———. *Jeremiah: A Commentary*. Louisville KY: Westminster John Knox, 2008.

Allen, Ronald B. "Numbers." In *Expositor's Bible Commentary — Revised Edition*. Vol. 2, edited by Tremper Longman and David E. Garland. Grand Rapids MI: Zondervan, 2012.

Alsheikh, Moshe. *Torat Moshe*. Venice: 1601.

Alter, Robert. *The Art of Biblical Narrative*. New York: Basic Books, 1981.

———. *The David Story: A Translation with Commentary of 1 and 2 Samuel*. New York: W. W. Norton, 1999.

———. *The Five Books of Moses: A Translation with Commentary*. New York: W. W. Norton, 2004.

Alter, Yehudah Aryeh Leib. *Sefas Emes*. Merkaz Shapira, Israel: Ha-Makhon Ha-Torani Yeshivat Or-Etzion, 2000.

Althann, Robert. "Mwl, 'Circumcise' with the Lamedh of Agency." *Biblica* 62, no. 2 (1981): 239–40.

Altschuler, David, and Hillel Altschuler. *Metzudat David*. Livorno: 1782.

———. *Metzudat Tziyon*. Livorno: 1782.

Amiel, Moshe Avigdor. *Derashot El Ami*. Vol. 3. Tel Aviv: Va'ad Le-hotsa'at Sifre Ha-Rav 'Ami'el, 1964.

———. "The Prohibition 'Do Not Murder' in Relation to Arabs" (Hebrew). *Tehumin* 10 (1989): 148–50.

Amir, Yehoshua. "The Place of Psalm 119 in the History of the Religion of Israel" (Hebrew). *Te'udah* 2 (1982): 55–81.

Amit, Aaron. "The Death of Rabbi Akiva's Disciples: A Literary History." *Journal of Jewish Studies* 56 (2005): 265–84.

Anisfeld, Rachel. "The Generation of Bavel: A Misguided Unity." *Bikkurim: Midreshet Lindenbaum Torah Journal*, May 1990, 7–17.

Arama, Isaac. *Akeidat Yitzhak*. Thessaloniki: 1522.

Aristotle. *Nicomachean Ethics*. Edited by David Ross.

Arnold, Bill T. *Genesis*. Cambridge: Cambridge University Press, 2009.

———. "The Love-Fear Antinomy in Deuteronomy 5–11." *Vetus Testamentum* 61 (2011): 551–69.

Asevilli, Yom Tov. *Novellae on the Talmud*. Warsaw: 1839.

Ashkenazi, Eliezer. *Gedolim Ma'asei Hashem: Sermons on Genesis and Exodus and a Commentary on the Passover Haggada, with the Haggada Text*. Hague: 1777.

Ashley, Timothy. *The Book of Numbers*. Grand Rapids MI: Eerdmans, 1993.

Auld, A. Graeme. *I and II Samuel: A Commentary*. Louisville KY: Westminster John Knox, 2011.

Baldwin, Joyce G. *1 and 2 Samuel: An Introduction and Commentary*. Leicester, England: Inter-varsity, 1988.

———. *Haggai, Zechariah, and Malachi: An Introduction and Commentary*. Downers Grove IL: Inter-varsity, 1972.

Balentine, Samuel E. *Leviticus*. Louisville KY: John Knox, 2003.

———. "The Prophet as Intercessor: A Reassessment." *Journal of Biblical Literature* 103 (1984): 161–73.

———. *The Torah's Vision of Worship*. Minneapolis: Fortress, 1999.

Bar Shaul, Elimelekh. *Mitzvah Va-Lev*. Tel Aviv: A. Tsiyoni, 1956.

Barton, John. *Joel and Obadiah: A Commentary*. Louisville KY: Westminster John Knox, 2001.

Beale, G. K. *The Temple and the Church's Mission: A Biblical Theology of the Dwelling Place of God*. Downers Grove IL: Inter-varsity, 2004.

Bechtel, Lyn M. "What If Dinah Is Not Raped? (Genesis 34)." *Journal for the Study of the Old Testament* 62 (1994): 19–36.

Beck, John A. "Why Did Moses Strike Out? The Narrative-Geographical Shaping of Moses' Disqualification in Numbers 20:1–13." *Westminster Theological Journal* 65 (2003): 135–41.

Bekhor Shor, Joseph. *Commentary to the Torah*. 1520.

Bellinger, W. H., Jr. *Leviticus, Numbers*. Peabody MA: Hendrickson, 2001.

Ben Adert, Solomon (Rashba). *Novellae on the Talmud*. Warsaw: 1922.

Ben Amram, David. *Midrash Ha-Gadol.* c. 1300.

Ben Asher, Bahya. *Commentary to the Torah.* Soncino, 1524.

———. *Midrash Rabbeinu Bahya.* c. 1291.

Ben Asher, Jacob. *Arba Turim.* Piove de Sacco: 1475.

Ben Avraham, Dov Ber of Mezeritch. *Or Torah.* Korets: 1804.

Ben Elijah, Aaron. *Keter Torah.* Yevpatoriya: 1866.

Ben Husiel, Hananel. *Commentary to the Talmud.* Jerusalem: Mekhon Lev Sameah, 1995.

Ben Manoah, Hezekiah. *Hizkuni.* Venice: 1524.

Ben Meir, Samuel (Rashbam). *Commentary to the Torah.* Breslau: David Rosin, 1881.

Ben Shlomo, Menahem. *Midrash Seikhel Tov.* Berlin: Buber, 1901.

Benstein, Jeremy. *The Way into Judaism and the Environment.* Woodstock VT: Jewish Lights, 2006.

Berezovsky, Shalom Noah. *Netivot Shalom.* Jerusalem: Yeshivat Beit Avraham Slonim, 1994.

Bergman, Samuel Hugo. *Faith and Reason: Modern Jewish Thought.* New York: Schocken Books, 1961.

Berkovits, Eliezer. *God, Man and History.* 4th ed. Jerusalem: Shalem, 2004.

Berlin, Adele, and Marc Brettler. *Jewish Study Bible.* Oxford: Oxford University Press, 2004.

Berlin, Naftali Zvi Yehuda. *Ha-amek Davar.* Jerusalem: Bamberger et Vaherman, 1936.

Berman, Yissahar Ha-Kohen. *Matanot Kehunah.* Krakow: 1587.

Bernstein, Ellen. "Rereading Genesis: Human Stewardship of the Earth." In *Righteous Indignation: A Jewish Call for Justice,* edited by Or N. Rose, Jo Ellen Green Kaiser, and Margie Klein, 55–59. Woodstock VT: Jewish Lights, 2008.

Bickerman, Elias J. *Studies in Jewish and Christian History.* Part 1. Leiden: E. J. Brill, 1976.

Biddle, Mark E. *Deuteronomy.* Smyth and Helwys Bible Commentary. Macon GA: Smyth & Helwys, 2003.

Blenkinsopp, Joseph. *Creation, Un-Creation, Re-Creation: A Discursive Commentary on Genesis 1–11.* London: T & T Clark, 2011.

———. *Ezra-Nehemiah.* Philadelphia: Westminster, 1988.

Blidstein, Gerald (Yaakov). "HaSimhah BeMishnato HaMusarit Shel HaRambam." *Eishel Be'er Sheva* 2 (1980): 145–63.

Blidstein, Gerald J. "Capital Punishment—the Classic Jewish Discussion." *Judaism* 14, no. 2 (Spring 1965), 159–71.

Block, Daniel I. "Eden: A Temple? A Reassessment of the Biblical Evidence."

In *From Creation to New Creation: Biblical Theology and Exegesis*, edited by D. M. Gurtner and B. L. Gladd, 3–29. Peabody MA: Hendrickson, 2013.

Blum, Lawrence. "Compassion." In *Explaining Emotions*, edited by Amelie Oksenberg Rorty, 507–17. Berkeley: University of California Press, 1980.

Bonhoeffer, Dietrich. *The Cost of Discipleship*. Translated by R. H. Fuller. New York: Macmillan, 1959.

Bovati, Pietro. *Re-establishing Justice: Legal Concepts, Terms and Procedures in the Hebrew Bible*. London: Continuum International, 1997.

Boyarin, Daniel. *A Radical Jew: Paul and the Politics of Identity*. Berkeley: University of California Press, 1997.

Boyce, Richard N. *Leviticus and Numbers*. Louisville KY: Westminster John Knox, 2008.

Bracke, John M. *Jeremiah 1–29*. Louisville KY: Westminster John Knox, 2000.

Brandes, Yehudah. "Generous-Hearted People." (Hebrew) In *Torat Imekha: Derashot Le-Farashat Ha-Shavua*. Jerusalem: Sifre Magid, 2008. 211–13.

Braulik, Georg. "Wisdom, Divine Presence and Law: Reflections on the Kerygma of Deut 4:5–8." In *The Theology of Deuteronomy: Collected Essays of Georg Braulik, O.S.B.*, translated by Ulrika Lindblad. N. Richland Hills TX: Bibal, 1994.

Brettler, Marc Zvi. "Predestination in Deuteronomy 30.1–10." In *Those Elusive Deuteronomists: The Phenomenon of Pan-Deuteronomism*, edited by Linda S. Schearing and Steven L. McKenzie, 171–88. Journal for the Study of the Old Testament Supplement Series 268. Sheffield: Sheffield Academic, 1999.

Brown, William P. *Ecclesiastes*. Louisville KY: John Knox, 2000.

Brueggemann, Walter. *1 and 2 Kings*. Macon GA: Smyth & Helwys, 2000.

———. *A Commentary on Jeremiah: Exile and Homecoming*. Grand Rapids MI: W. B. Eerdmans, 1998.

———. *Deuteronomy*. Nashville TN: Abingdon, 2001.

———. "Exodus: Introduction, Commentary, and Reflections." In *The New Interpreter's Bible*, vol. 1. Nashville TN: Abingdon, 1994.

———. *Genesis*. Atlanta: John Knox, 1982.

———. *Isaiah 1–39*. Louisville KY: Westminster John Knox, 1998.

———. *Isaiah 40–66*. Louisville KY: Westminster John Knox, 1998.

———. *Jeremiah 26–52: To Build, to Plant*. Grand Rapids MI: Eerdmans, 1991.

———. *The Land: Place as Gift, Promise, and Challenge in Biblical Faith*. 2nd ed. Minneapolis: Fortress, 2002.

———. *Old Testament Theology: An Introduction*. Nashville TN: Abingdon, 2008.

———. *The Theology of the Book of Jeremiah*. Old Testament Theology. New York: Cambridge University Press, 2007.

———. *Theology of the Old Testament: Testimony, Dispute, Advocacy*. Minneapolis: Fortress, 1997.

Brümmer, Vincent. *The Model of Love: A Study in Philosophical Theology*. Cambridge: Cambridge University Press, 1993.

Buber, Martin. "Distance and Relation." In *The Martin Buber Reader*, edited by Asher Biemann, 206–13. New York: Palgrave Macmillan, 2002.

———. *I and Thou*. Translated by Walter Kaufmann. New York: Charles Scribner's Sons, 1970.

———. *Moses: The Revelation and the Covenant*. New York: Harper & Row, 1958.

———. "The Prayer of the First Fruits." In *On the Bible: Eighteen Studies*. New York: Schocken Books, 1968.

Buber, Salomon. *Agadat Bereshit*. Krakow: Fisher, 1902.

Burnside, Jonathan. *God, Justice, and Society: Aspects of Law and Legality in the Bible*. Oxford: Oxford University Press, 2011.

Cassuto, Umberto. *A Commentary on the Book of Exodus*. Translated by Israel Abrahams. Jerusalem: Magnes, 1967.

———. *A Commentary on the Book of Genesis*. 2 vols. Translated by Israel Abrahams. Jerusalem: Magnes, 1961–64.

Chaney, Marvin L. "You Shall Not Covet Your Neighbor's House." *Pacific Theological Review* 15 (1982): 3–13.

Chapman, Stephen B. "Perpetual War: The Case of Amalek." In *The Bible and Spirituality: Exploratory Essays in Reading Scripture Spiritually*, edited by Andrew T. Lincoln, J. Gordon McConville, and Lloyd K. Pietersen, 1–19. Eugene OR: Cascade Books, 2013.

Cherlow, Yuval. "The Dignity of the Child in the Commandment to Honor Parents—Must the Child Obey His Parents?" (Hebrew). In *Ahavat Ha-Adam U-Khevod Ha-Beriyot*, edited by Shlomo Niss and Tzviyah Schiff, 318–28. Ramat Gan: Shlomo Nes, 2006.

Childs, Brevard S. *The Book of Exodus: A Critical, Theological Commentary*. Philadelphia: Westminster, 1974.

———. "On Reading the Elijah Narratives." *Interpretation* 34 (1980): 128–37.

Claassens, L. Juliana. "'I Kill and I Give Life': Contrasting Depictions for God in Deuteronomy 32." *Old Testament Essays* 18 (2005): 35–46.

Clifford, Richard J. *Deuteronomy: With an Excursus on Covenant and Law*. Old Testament Message 4. Wilmington DE: Michael Glazier, 1982.

———. *Proverbs: A Commentary*. Louisville KY: Westminster John Knox, 1999.

Clines, D. J. A. "Social Responsibility in the Old Testament." Shaftesbury Project Working Paper 8. Quoted in Christopher J. H. Wright, *Old Testament*

Ethics for the People of God: A Fully Revised, Updated and Integrated Edition of "Living as the People of God" and "Walking in the Ways of the Lord," 336. Leicester: Inter-varsity, 2004.

Coats, George W. "Balaam: Sinner or Saint?" *Biblical Research* 18 (1973): 21–29.

Cogan, Mordechai. *1 Kings*. New York: Doubleday, 2001.

———. *Yoel*. Tel Aviv: 'Am 'oved, 1994.

Cohen, Hezi. "Abraham's Separation from Lot: Genesis 13" (Hebrew). *Megadim* 52 (2011): 9–22.

Cole, R. Dennis. *Numbers*. Nashville TN: Broadman & Holman, 2000.

Collins, John J. "The Zeal of Phinehas: The Bible and the Legitimation of Violence." *Journal of Biblical Literature* 122, no. 1 (2003): 3–21.

Condie, Keith. "Narrative Features of Numbers 13–14 and Their Significance for the Meaning of the Book of Numbers." *Reformed Theological Review 60*, no. 3 (December 2001): 123–37.

Craigie, Peter C. *The Book of Deuteronomy*. New International Commentary on the Old Testament. Grand Rapids MI: Eerdmans, 1976.

Crenshaw, James L. *Ecclesiastes: A Commentary*. Philadelphia: Westminster, 1987.

———. *Joel*. New York: Doubleday, 1995.

Da'at Zekenim. Leghorn: 1783.

Davis, Ellen F. *Proverbs, Ecclesiastes, and Song of Songs*. Louisville KY: Westminster John Knox, 2000.

———. "Slaves or Sabbath-Keepers? A Biblical Perspective on Human Work." *Anglican Theological Review* 83, no. 1 (Winter 2001): 25–40.

Daube, David. *The Exodus Pattern in the Bible*. London: Faber & Faber, 1963.

Dearman, J. Andrew. *Jeremiah, Lamentations*. Grand Rapids MI: Zondervan, 2002.

Dessler, Eliyahu. *Mikhtav Me-Eliyahu*. Jerusalem: Feldheim, 1978.

Douglas, Mary. "The Abominations of Leviticus." In *Purity and Danger*, 41–57. London: Routledge & Paul, 1966.

Dozeman, Thomas. "The Book of Numbers: Introduction, Commentary, and Reflections." In *New Interpreter's Bible*, vol. 2. Nashville TN: Abingdon, 1998.

Dratch, Mark. "Honoring Abusive Parents." *Hakirah* 12 (2011): 1–15.

Driver, S. R. *A Critical and Exegetical Commentary on Deuteronomy*. International Critical Commentary on the Holy Scriptures of the Old and New Testaments. Edinburgh: T. & T. Clark, 1895.

Durham, John I. *Exodus*. Waco TX: Word Books, 1987.

Ehrenfeld, David, and Philip J. Bentley. "Judaism and the Practice of Stewardship." *Judaism* 34 (1985): 301–11.

Eisenstadt, Abraham Tzvi Hirsch. *Pithei Teshuvah*. Vilna: Widow and Brothers
Rom, 1895.

Emmons, Robert. "Gratitude." In *Encyclopedia of Positive Psychology*, edited by
Shane J. Lopez, 442. Malden MA: WileyBlackwell, 2009.

Enelau, Hillel Gershon. *Mishnat Rebbi Eliezer*. New York: Bloch, 1933.

Enns, Peter. *Exodus*. Grand Rapids MI: Zondervan, 2000.

Epstein, Barukh Ha-Levi. *Torah Temimah*. Jerusalem: Hotza'at Va'ad Ve-Halak,
1904.

Eskenazi, Tamara Cohn, and Andrea L. Weiss, eds. *The Torah: A Women's Commentary*. New York: URJ, 2008.

Faust, Shmuel. *Aggadeta: Stories of Talmudic Drama* (Hebrew). Or Yehuda,
Israel: Devir, 2011.

Fensham, F. Charles. "Widow, Orphan, and the Poor in Ancient Near Eastern Legal and Wisdom Literature." *Journal of Near Eastern Studies* 21 (1962):
129–39.

Finkel, Nosson Zvi. "Kashyut Oref." In *Or HaTzafun*. Jerusalem: Mossad
Haskel al yedei Yeshivat Hevron, 1959.

Fiser, Karen. "Philosophy, Disability, and Essentialism." In *Defending Diversity:
Contemporary Philosophical Perspectives on Pluralism and Multiculturalism*,
edited by Lawrence Foster and Patricia Herzog, 83–101. Amherst: University of Massachusetts Press, 1994.

Fishbane, Michael. *Haftarot*. JPS Bible Commentary. Philadelphia: Jewish
Publication Society, 2002.

———. *Text and Texture: Close Readings of Selected Biblical Texts*. New York:
Schocken Books, 1979.

Fleming, Erin E. "'She Went to Inquire of the Lord': Independent Divination in
Genesis 25:22." *Union Seminary Quarterly Review* 60, nos. 3–4 (2007): 1–10.

Fokkelman, J. P. *Narrative Art and Poetry in the Books of Samuel*. Vol. 1, *King
David*. Assen, The Netherlands: Van Gorcum, 1993.

Fox, Everett. *The Five Books of Moses: A New Translation with Introductions, Commentary, and Notes*. New York: Schocken Books, 1995.

Fox, Michael V. *Ecclesiastes*. JPS Bible Commentary. Philadelphia: Jewish Publication Society, 2004.

Frankel, Yonah. *The Aggadic Story: Unity of Content and Form* (Hebrew). Tel
Aviv: Hakibbutz Hameuchad, 2001.

Freedman, David Noel, with Jeffrey C. Geoghegan and Andrew Welch. *Psalm
119: The Exaltation of Torah*. Winona Lake IN: Eisenbrauns, 1999.

Fretheim, Terence E. "The Book of Genesis: Introduction, Commentary, and

Reflections." In *The New Interpreter's Bible*, vol. 1. Nashville TN: Abingdon, 1994.

———. *Exodus*. Louisville KY: John Knox, 1991.

———. *Jeremiah*. Smyth and Helwys Bible Commentary. Macon GA: Smyth & Helwys, 2002.

———. *The Pentateuch*. Nashville TN: Abingdon, 1996.

———. "The Plagues as Ecological Signs of Historical Disaster." *Journal of Biblical Literature* 110 (1991): 385–96.

Friedman, Alexander Zusia. *Ma'ayanah Shel Torah*. Vols. 2–3. Bene Berak: Mishor, 1996.

Friedman, Richard Elliot. *Commentary on the Torah: With a New English Translation of the Hebrew Text*. San Francisco: Harper San Francisco, 2003.

Frisch, Amos. "'Your Brother Came with Guile': Responses to an Explicit Moral Evaluation in the Bible." *Prooftexts* 23 (2003): 271–96.

Fromm, Erich. *You Shall Be as Gods: A Radical Interpretation of the Old Testament and Its Tradition*. New York: Holt, Rinehart & Winston, 1966.

Frymer-Kensky, Tikva. "Deuteronomy." In *The Women's Bible Commentary*, edited by Carol A. Newsom and Sharon H. Ringe, 57–69. London: SPCK, 1992.

———. "The Image, the Glory, and the Holy: Aspects of Being Human in Biblical Thought." In *Humanity before God: Contemporary Faces of Jewish, Christian, and Islamic Ethics*, edited by William Schweiker, Michael A. Johnson, and Kevin Jung, 118–38. Minneapolis: Fortress, 2006.

———. *In the Wake of the Goddesses: Women, Culture, and the Biblical Transformation of Pagan Myth*. New York: Free Press, 1992.

———. *Reading the Women of the Bible: A New Interpretation of Their Stories*. New York: Schocken Books, 2002.

———. *Studies in Bible and Feminist Criticism*. JPS Scholar of Distinction Series. Philadelphia: Jewish Publication Society, 2006.

Galpaz-Feller, Penina. "And I Will Give This People Favour in the Sight of the Egyptians (Exodus 3:22)" (Hebrew). *Beit Mikra* 47 (2002): 133–42.

Gane, Roy. *Leviticus, Numbers*. NIV Application Commentary. Grand Rapids MI: Zondervan, 2004.

Gaon, Saadia. *Commentary to the Bible*.

———. *The Book of Beliefs and Opinions*. Treatise 8. Translated by Samuel Rosenblatt. New Haven CT: Yale University Press, 1976.

Gawande, Atul. *Being Mortal: Medicine and What Matters in the End*. New York: Henry Holt, 2014.

Geertz, Clifford. "Religion as a Cultural System." In *The Interpretation of Cultures*, 87–125. New York: Basic Books, 1973.

Gerondi, Yonah (Rabbeinu Yonah). *Sha'arei Teshuva*. Fano, Italy: 1500.

Gersonides, Levi (Ralbag). *Milhamot Ha-Shem*. Riva di Trenta: 1560.

Ginzberg, Louis. *Legends of the Jews*. Philadelphia: Jewish Publication Society, 1969.

Gombiner, Abraham. *Magen Avraham*. c. 1683.

Goldin, Judah. "The Death of Moses: An Exercise in Midrashic Transposition." In *Love and Death in the Ancient Near East: Studies Presented to Marvin H. Pope*, edited by John Marks and Robert Good, 219–25. Guilford CT: Four Quarters, 1987.

Goldin, Shmuel. *Unlocking the Torah Text: An In-Depth Journey into the Weekly Parshah — Devarim*. Jerusalem: Gefen, 2014.

———. *Unlocking the Torah Text: An In-Depth Journey into the Weekly Parshah — Vayikra*. Jerusalem: Gefen, 2010.

Goldingay, John. *Old Testament Theology*. Vol. 1, *Israel's Gospel*. Downers Grove IL: Academic, 2003.

Gordis, Robert. *Koheleth: The Man and His World*. New York: Bloch, 1951.

Gorman, Frank H., Jr. *Leviticus: Divine Presence and Community*. Grand Rapids MI: Wm. B. Eerdmans, 1997.

Greenberg, Irving. *The Jewish Way: Living the Holidays*. New York: Summit Books, 1988.

Greenberg, Moshe. "Some Postulates of Biblical Criminal Law." In *Studies in the Bible and Jewish Thought*, 25–41. JPS Scholar of Distinction Series. Philadelphia: Jewish Publication Society, 1995.

———. "Three Conceptions of the Torah in Hebrew Scriptures." In *Studies in the Bible and Jewish Thought*, 11–24. JPS Scholar of Distinction Series. Philadelphia: Jewish Publication Society, 1995.

———. *Understanding Exodus: A Holistic Commentary on Exodus 1–11*. 2nd ed. Eugene OR: Cascade Books, 2013.

Gruber, Mayer I. "Fear, Anxiety, and Reverence in Akkadian, Biblical Hebrew, and Other North-West Semitic Languages." *Vetus Testamentum* 90 (1990): 411–22.

Gunkel, Hermann. *Die Psalmen*. Gottingen: Vandenhoeck & Ruprecht, 1926.

Haag, Herbert. "*Hamas*." In *Theological Dictionary of the Old Testament*, vol. 4, edited by G. Johannes Botterweck and Helmer Ringgren, 482. Grand Rapids MI: Eerdmans, 1981.

Ha-Darshan, Shimon. *Yalkut Shimoni*. Salonika, 1521.

Ha-hinukh. Venice: 1523.

Ha-Itamari, Eliyahu Ha-Kohen. *Midrash Eliyahu*. Izmir: 1759.

Hall, Douglas J. *God and Human Suffering: An Exercise in the Theology of the Cross*. Minneapolis: Augsburg, 1986.

———. "Stewardship as Key to a Theology of Nature." In *Environmental Stewardship: Critical Perspectives—Past and Present*, edited by R. J. Berry, 129–44. London: T & T Clark, 2006.

Ha-Meiri, Menahem. *Beit HaBehirah*. Zichron Yaakov, Israel: Mekhon L'Hotzaat Sefarim V'Kitvei Yad, 1977.

Hamilton, Jeffries M. *Social Justice and Deuteronomy: The Case of Deuteronomy 15*. Society of Biblical Literature Dissertation Series 136. Atlanta: Scholars Press, 1992.

Hamilton, Victor P. *The Book of Genesis, Chapters 1–17*. Grand Rapids MI: W. B. Eerdmans, 1990.

———. *The Book of Genesis, Chapters 18–50*. Grand Rapids MI: W. B. Eerdmans, 1995.

———. *Exodus: An Exegetical Commentary*. Grand Rapids MI: Baker Academic, 2011.

———. *Handbook on the Pentateuch: Genesis, Exodus, Leviticus, Numbers, Deuteronomy*. 2nd ed. Grand Rapids MI: Baker Academic, 2005.

Haran, Menahem. *Temples and Temple-Service in Ancient Israel*. Oxford: Clarendon, 1977.

Hartley, John E. *Genesis*. Peabody MA: Hendrickson, 2000.

———. *Leviticus*. Dallas TX: Word Books, 1992.

Hartman, David. *A Living Covenant: The Innovative Spirit in Traditional Judaism*. New York: Free Press, 1985.

Hartman, David, and Charlie Buckholtz. *The God Who Hates Lies: Confronting and Rethinking Jewish Tradition*. Woodstock VT: Jewish Lights, 2011.

Harvey, Warren Zev. "Yirat Shamayim in Jewish Thought." In *Yirat Shamayim: The Awe, Reverence, and Fear of God*, edited by Marc D. Stern, 1–26. Jersey City NJ: Ktav, 2008.

Hattin, Michael. *Passages: Text and Transformation in the Parasha*. Jerusalem: Urim, 2012.

Ha-Tzarfati, Vidal. *Imrei Yosher*. In *Midrash Rabbah Im Kol Ha-Mefarshim*. Jerusalem: Vagshal, 2001.

Held, Shai. *Abraham Joshua Heschel: The Call of Transcendence*. Bloomington: Indiana University Press, 2013.

———. "Wonder and Indignation: Abraham's Uneasy Faith." *Jewish Review of Books* 3, no. 4 (Winter 2013): 36–37.

Hellin, Jacob Moshe Ashkenazi. *Yedei Moshe*. Frankfurt (Oder): 1692.

Heschel, Abraham Joshua. *God in Search of Man: A Philosophy of Judaism*. New York: Farrar, Straus & Giroux, 1955.

——. *Heavenly Torah: As Refracted through the Generations*. Translated by Leonard Levin and Gordon Tucker. New York: Continuum, 2005.

——. *The Insecurity of Freedom: Essays on Human Existence*. New York: Farrar, Straus & Giroux, 1966.

——. *Man's Quest for God: Studies in Prayer and Symbolism*. New York: Scribner, 1954.

——. *Torah Min HaShamayim Be-Aspaklaryah Shel Ha-Dorot*. New York: Defus Shontsin, 1995.

——. *The Sabbath*. New York: Farrar, Straus & Young, 1951.

Hess, Richard S. "The Distinctive Value of Human Life in Israel's Earliest Legal Traditions." In *The Ancient Near East in the 12th–10th Centuries BCE: Culture and History: Proceedings of the International Conference Held at the University of Haifa, 2–5 May, 2010*, edited by Gershon Galil et al., 221–28. Alter Orient und Altes Testament, 392. Münster: Ugarit-Verlag, 2012.

Hibbard, J. Todd. "True and False Prophecy: Jeremiah's Revision of Deuteronomy." *Journal for the Study of the Old Testament* 35, no. 3 (March 2011): 339–58.

Hiebert, Paula S. "'Whence Shall Help Come to Me?': The Biblical Widow." In *Gender and Difference in Ancient Israel*, edited by Peggy L. Day, 125–41. Minneapolis: Fortress, 1989.

Hirsch, Samson Raphael. *Pirkei Avot/Chapters of the Fathers: Translation and Commentary by Samson Raphael Hirsch*. Translated by Gertrude Hirschler. New York: Feldheim, 1967.

Hirshman, Marc. "Rabbinic Universalism in the Second and Third Centuries." *Harvard Theological Review* 93 (2000): 101–15.

Hoffman, Yair. *Jeremiah, Introduction and Commentary*. Vol. 2, *Chapters 26–52* (Hebrew). Mikra Leyisra'el. Tel Aviv: Am Oved, 2001.

Holzer, Elie. *A Double-Edged Sword: Military Activism in the Thought of Religious Zionism* (Hebrew). Judaism and Israel. Shalom Hartman Institute; Keter Publishing House; Faculty of Law, Bar Ilan University, 2009.

Horowitz, Isaiah. *Shenei Luhot Ha-berit (Shelah)*. Amsterdam: 1649.

Houston, Walter. "'You Shall Open Your Hand to Your Needy Brother': Ideology and Moral Formation in Deut. 15,1–18." In *The Bible in Ethics: The Second Sheffield Colloquium*, edited by John W. Rogerson, Margaret Davis, and Daniel Carroll, 296–314. Journal for the Study of the Old Testament Supplement Series 240. Sheffield: Sheffield Academic, 1995.

Houtman, Cornelius. *Exodus*. Vol. 2. Historical Commentary on the Old Testament. Kampen: Kok, 1996.

Hubbard, David Allan. *Joel and Amos: An Introduction and Commentary*. Leicester, England: Inter-varsity, 1989.

Hutner, Yitzhak. *Pahad Yitzhak: Iggerot Ukhtavim*. Brooklyn NY. Gur Aryeh Institute for Advanced Jewish Studies, 1980.

Ibn Ezra, Abraham. *Commentary to the Torah, 1488*. Jerusalem: Makor, 1978.

Ibn Attar, Hayyim. *Or Ha-hayyim*. B'nei Brak: Meshor, 2001.

Isaac of Corbeil. *Sefer Mitzvot Katan*. Constantinople, 1510.

Ish Shalom, Meir. *Tanna De-Bei Eliyahu*. Vienna: 1900.

Janzen, J. Gerald. *Exodus*. Louisville KY: Westminster John Knox, 1997.

———. *Job*. Atlanta: John Knox, 1985.

Jacob, Benno. *The First Book of the Bible: Genesis*. Translated and edited by Ernest I. Jacob and Walter Jacob. New York: Ktav, 1974.

———. *The Second Book of the Bible: Exodus*. Translated by Walter Jacob and Yaakov Elman. Hoboken NJ: Ktav, 1992.

Jacobs, Louis. *The Book of Jewish Values*. Chappaqua NY: Rossel Books, 1960.

Jacobs, Mignon R. "Toward an Old Testament Theology of Concern for the Underprivileged." In *Reading the Hebrew Bible for a New Millennium: Form, Concept, and Theological Perspective*, edited by Wonil Kim et al., 205–29. Harrisburg PA: Trinity Press International, 2000.

Kadari, Adiel. *Studies in Repentance: Law, Philosophy and Educational Thought in Maimonides' Hilkhot Teshuvah* (Hebrew). Be'er Sheva': Hotsa'at ha-sefarim shel Universitat Ben Guryon ba-Negev, 2010.

Kaminsky, Joel S. "Reclaiming a Theology of Election: Favoritism and the Joseph Story." *Perspectives in Religious Studies* 31, no. 2 (Summer 2004): 135–52.

Karo, Josef. *Shulkhan Arukh*. Venice: c. 1564.

Kasser, Tim. "Materialistic Value Orientation." In *The Palgrave Handbook of Spirituality and Business*, edited by Luk Bouckaert and Laszlo Zsolnai, 204–10. New York: Palgrave Macmillan, 2011.

Katznellbogen, Mordechai Lev. *Torat Hayyim: Hamishah Humshei Torah; Vayikra*. Jerusalem: Mossad Harav Kook, 1990.

Keil, C. F., and F. Delitzsch. *Commentary on the Old Testament: The Pentateuch, Genesis, Exodus 1–11*. Translated by James Martin. Peabody MA: Hendrickson, 1989.

Kidner, Derek. *Genesis: An Introduction and Commentary*. Leicester: Inter-varsity, 1967.

———. *The Message of Jeremiah: Against Wind and Tide*. Leicester: Inter-varsity, 1987.

———. *Proverbs: An Introduction and Commentary*. Tyndale Old Testament Commentaries. Downers Grove IL: Inter-varsity, 1985.

Kimelman, Reuven. "Prophecy as Arguing with God and the Ideal of Justice." *Interpretation* 68 (2014): 17–27.

———. "The Shema' Liturgy: From Covenant Ceremony to Coronation." In *Kenishta: Studies of the Synagogue World*, edited by Joseph Tabory, 9–105. Ramat-Gan, Israel: Bar-Ilan University Press, 2001.

Kimhi, David (Radak). *Commentary to the Torah*. Soncino, Italy: Soncino, 1486.

Klein, Ralph. "Back to the Future: The Tabernacle in the Book of Exodus." *Interpretation* 50 (1996): 264–76.

Klitsner, Judy. *Subversive Sequels in the Bible: How Biblical Stories Mine and Undermine Each Other*. Jerusalem: Maggid Books, 2011.

Knowles, Michael P. "'The Rock, His Work Is Perfect': Unusual Imagery for God in Deuteronomy XXXII," *Vetus Testamentum* 39 (1989): 307–22.

Kook, Abraham Isaac. "Be-Khol Derakhekha Da'ehu." In *Musar avikha u-Midot ha-Re'iyah*, 39–40. Jerusalem: Mosad Harav Kook, 1971.

———. *Orot*. Jerusalem: Mosad Harav Kook, 1961.

Kook, Zvi Yehudah. "Eretz Yisrael VeHaGe'ulah HaSheleimah." In *BaMa'arakhah HaTziburit*, edited by Yosef Abramson. Jerusalem: Agudat Zahav Ha'aretz, 1986.

———. "Lihiyot Yehudi Tov—Kodem Kol Lihyot BeEretz Yisrael." In *The State in Jewish Thought: Sources and Studies* (Hebrew), edited by Aryeh Strikovsky. Jerusalem: Midrad Hahinukh veHatarbut, Ha-agaf le-Tarbut Toranit, 1982.

Kugel, James L. *The Bible as It Was*. Cambridge MA: Belknap Press of Harvard University Press, 1997.

———. "The Case against Joseph." In *Lingering over Words: Studies in Ancient Near Eastern Literature in Honor of William L. Moran*, edited by Tzvi Abusch et al., 272–87. Atlanta: Scholars Press, 1990.

———. *The God of Old: Inside the Lost World of the Bible*. New York: Free Press, 2003.

Kynes, William L. "Follow Your Heart and Do Not Say It Was a Mistake: Qoheleth's Allusions to Numbers 15 and the Story of the Spies." In *Reading Ecclesiastes Intertextually*, edited by Katherine Dell and Will Kynes, 15–27. London: Bloomsbury, 2014.

Lambert, W. G. "Destiny and Divine Intervention in Babylon and Israel." *Outtestamentische Studiën* 17 (1972): 65–72.

Lamott, Anne. *Bird by Bird: Some Instructions on Writing and Life*. New York: Anchor Books, 1995.

Lapsley, Jacqueline. "Am I Able to Say Just Anything? Learning Faithful Exegesis from Balaam." *Interpretation* 60 (2006): 22–31.

———. "Feeling Our Way: Love for God in Deuteronomy." *Catholic Biblical Quarterly* 65 (2003): 350–69.

Lear, Jonathan. *Open-Minded: Working Out the Logic of the Soul*. Cambridge MA: Harvard University Press, 1998.

Leibowitz, Nehama. *New Studies in Bereshit*. Jerusalem: Eliner Library, Joint Authority for Jewish Zionist Education, Dept. for Torah Education and Culture in the Diaspora, 1995.

———. *Studies in Bamidbar-Numbers*. Translated by Aryeh Newman. Jerusalem: World Zionist Organization, Dept. for Torah Education and Culture in the Diaspora, 1993.

———. *Studies in Devarim-Deuteronomy*. Translated by Aryeh Newman. Jerusalem: World Zionist Organization, Dept. for Torah Education and Culture in the Diaspora, 1993.

———. *Studies in Shemot-Exodus*. Translated by Aryeh Newman. Jerusalem: World Zionist Organization, Dept. for Torah Education and Culture in the Diaspora, 1981.

Leibowitz, Yeshayahu. *Judaism, Human Values, and the Jewish State*. Edited by Eliezer Goldman. Cambridge MA: Harvard University Press, 1995.

———. *Sheva Shanim Shel Sichot Al Parashat HaShavua*. Jerusalem: Keter, 2000.

Lerner, Berel Dov. "Joseph the Unrighteous." *Judaism* 38 (1989): 278–81.

Levenson, Jon D. *Creation and the Persistence of Evil: The Jewish Drama of Divine Omnipotence*. San Francisco: Harper & Row, 1988.

———. *Inheriting Abraham: The Legacy of the Patriarch in Judaism, Christianity, and Islam*. Princeton: Princeton University Press, 2012.

———. "Is There a Counterpart in the Hebrew Bible to New Testament Anti-semitism?" *Journal of Ecumenical Studies* 22 (1985): 242–60.

———. *Sinai and Zion: An Entry into the Jewish Bible*. Minneapolis: Winston, 1985.

———. "The Sources of Torah: Psalm 119 and the Modes of Revelation in Second Temple Judaism." In *Ancient Israelite Religion: Essays in Honor of Frank Moore Cross*, edited by Patrick D. Miller Jr. et al., 559–74. Philadelphia: Fortress, 1987.

———. "The Universal Horizon of Biblical Particularlism." In *Ethnicity and the Bible*, edited by Mark R. Brett, 143–69. Biblical Interpretation Series 19. Leiden: E. J. Brill, 1996.

Levin, B. M., ed. *Otzar Ha-Geonim*. Jerusalem: Mossad Harav Kook, 1936.

Levine, Baruch A. *Leviticus*. JPS Torah Commentary. Philadelphia: Jewish Publication Society, 1989.

———. *Numbers 21–36: A New Translation with Introduction and Commentary*. New York: Doubleday, 2000.

———. "Silence, Sound, and the Phenomenology of Mourning in Biblical Israel." *Journal of the Ancient Near Eastern Society* 22 (1993): 89–106.

Levi Yitzhak of Berditchev. *Kedushat Levi*. Lviv: 1858.

Levovitz, Yeruham. *Da'at Hokhmah UMusar*. Brooklyn NY: Daas Chochmo Umussar, 1966.

———. *Da'at Torah*. In R. Moshe Ibgui, *Hokhmat HaMatzpun*, Genesis, vol. 3. Bene-Berak: M. ben Y. Ibgi, 1993.

Licht, Haim. "On the Death of R. Akiva's Students" (Hebrew). *Tura* 1 (1989): 119–34.

Lichtenstein, Eliezer Lipman. *Shem Olam*. Warsaw: 1877.

Limburg, James. "Who Cares for the Earth? Psalm Eight and the Environment." In *All Things New: Essays in Honor of Roy A. Harrisville*, edited by Arland J. Hultgren, Donald H. Juel, and Jack D. Kingsbury. St. Paul MN: Word & World, Luther Northwestern Theological Seminary, 1992.

Lipton, Diana. "Remembering Amalek: A Positive Biblical Model for Dealing with Negative Scriptural Types." In *Reading Texts, Seeking Wisdom: Scripture and Theology*, edited by David F. Ford and Graham Stanton, 140–53. Grand Rapids MI: Eerdmans, 2004.

Loew, Judah of Prague. *Hiddushei Aggadot*. Jerusalem: Henig and Sons, 1964.

———. *Netivot Olam*. Prague: c. 1595.

Lohfink, Norbert. *Qoheleth: A Continental Commentary*. Minneapolis: Fortress, 2003.

Lohr, Joel N. "Taming the Untamable: Christian Attempts to Make Israel's Election Universal." *Horizons in Biblical Theology* 33 (2011): 24–33.

Longman, Tremper, III. *The Book of Ecclesiastes*. Grand Rapids MI: W. B. Eerdmans, 1998.

———. *How to Read Exodus*. Downers Grove IL: IVP Academic, 2009.

Lowenthal, Eric I. *The Joseph Narrative in Genesis*. New York, Ktav, 1973.

Lundbom, Jack R. *Deuteronomy: A Commentary*. Grand Rapids MI: William B. Eerdmans, 2013.

Luntschitz, Shelomo Ephraim. *Keli Yakar*. Lublin: 1602.

Luzzatto, Moshe Hayyim. *Mesillat Yesharim* (The path of the just). Northvale NJ: Jason Aronson, 1995.

Luzzatto, Samuel David. *Commentary to the Five Books of the Torah*. Padua: 1871.

MacDonald, Nathan. "The Book of Numbers." In *A Theological Introduction to the Pentateuch: Interpreting the Torah as Christian Scripture*, edited by Richard S. Briggs and Joel N. Lohr, 113–44. Grand Rapids MI: Baker Academic, 2012.

———. "Listening to Abraham—Listening to YHWH: Divine Justice and Mercy in Genesis 18:16–33." *Catholic Biblical Quarterly* 66, no. 1 (January 2004): 25–43.

Mack, Hananel. "The Zealotry of Pinhas the Son of Elazar the Son of Aaron the Priest" (Hebrew). *Mahanayim* 5 (1993): 122–29.

Maimonides, Moses (Rambam). *Guide of the Perplexed*. 1190.

———. *Mishneh Torah*. Italy: 1480.

———. *Sefer Ha-Mitzvot*. 1421.

Magid, Shaul. *American Post-Judaism: Identity and Renewal in a Postethnic Society*. Bloomington: Indiana University Press, 2013.

Malamat, Abraham. "Love Your Neighbor as Yourself: What It Really Means." *Biblical Archaeology Review* 16, no. 4 (July/August 1990): 50–51.

———. "You Shall Love Your Neighbor as Yourself: A Case of Misinterpretation?" (German). In *Hebräische Bibel und ihre zweifache Nachgeschichte: Festschrift für Rolf Rendtorff zum 65. Geburtstag*, edited by Erhard Blum et al., 111–15. Neukirchen-Vluyn, Germany: Neukirchener Verlag, 1990.

Margalit, Baruch. "The Day the Sun Did Not Stand Still: A New Look at Joshua X: 8–15." *Vetus Testamentum* 42 (1992): 466–91.

Marmorstein, Arthur. *Studies in Jewish Theology*. London: Oxford University Press, 1950.

Mayes, A. D. H. *Deuteronomy: Based on the Revised Standard Version*. New Century Bible Commentary. 2nd ed. Grand Rapids MI: Wm. B. Eerdmans, 1981.

Mays, James L. *Hosea: A Commentary*. Philadelphia: Westminster, 1969.

———. "What Is a Human Being? Reflections on Psalm 8." *Theology Today* 50, no. 4 (January 1994): 511–20.

McCarthy, Carmel. *The Tiqqune Sopherim and Other Theological Corrections in the Masoretic Text of the Old Testament*. Göttingen, Germany. Vandenhoeck & Ruprecht, 1981.

McFague, Sallie. *Metaphorical Theology: Models of God in Religious Language*. Philadelphia: Fortress, 1982.

McKane, William. *Proverbs: A New Approach*. Old Testament Library. Philadelphia: Westminster, 1970.

Mecklenberg, Ya'akov Zvi. *Ha-Ketav V-ha-Kabbalah*. 1839.

Menahem Mendel of Rimanov. *Ilana De-Hayyei*.

Merton, Thomas. *Contemplative Prayer*. New York: Herder & Herder, 1969.

Meyers, Carol L. *Exodus*. Cambridge: Cambridge University Press, 2005.

———. *The Tabernacle Menorah*. Missoula MT: Published by Scholars Press for the American Schools of Oriental Research, 1976.

Middleton, J. Richard. *The Liberating Image: The Imago Dei in Genesis 1*. Grand Rapids MI: Brazos, 2005.

Midrash Eileh Ezkerah. In *Beit HaMidrash*, edited by Adolf Jellinek, 64. Vienna: Bruder Winter vorm Herzfeld & Bauer, 1873.

Milgrom, Jacob. "Concerning Jeremiah's Repudiation of Sacrifice." *Zeitschrift für die altetestamentliche Wissenschaft* 89 (1977): 273–75.

———. *Cult and Conscience: The Asham and the Priestly Doctrine of Repentance*. Leiden: Brill, 1976.

———. *Leviticus 1–16: A New Translation with Introduction and Commentary*. New York: Doubleday, 1991.

———. *Leviticus 23–27*. New York: Doubleday, 2001.

———. *Leviticus: A Book of Ritual and Ethics*. Minneapolis: Fortress, 2004.

———. *Numbers*. Philadelphia: Jewish Publication Society, 1990.

———. "Of Hems and Tassels." *Biblical Archaeology Review* (May/June 1983): 61–65.

———. "Repentance in the OT." In *The Interpreter's Dictionary of the Bible — Supplementary Volume*, 736–38. Nashville: Abingdon, 1976.

———. "Sin-Offering or Purification-Offering?" *Vetus Testamentum* 21, no. 2 (1971): 237–39.

———. "The Tassel and the Tallith." Fourth Annual Rabbi Louis Fineberg Memorial Lecture. University of Cincinnati, 1981.

Miller, Patrick D., Jr. *Deuteronomy*. Louisville KY: J. Knox, 1990.

———. "God's Other Stories: On the Margins of Deuteronomic Theology." In *Israelite Religion and Biblical Theology: Collected Essays*. Journal for the Study of the Old Testament Supplement Series 267. Sheffield: Sheffield Academic, 2000.

———. "Jeremiah: Introduction, Commentary, and Reflections." In *New Interpreter's Bible*, vol. 6. Nashville TN: Abingdon, 2001.

———. "'Moses My Servant': The Deuteronomic Portrait of Moses." *Interpretation* 41 (July 1987): 245–55.

———. *The Ten Commandments*. Interpretation: Resources for the Use of Scripture in the Church. Louisville KY: Westmister John Knox, 2009.

———. "The Way of Torah." *Princeton Seminary Bulletin* 8, no. 3 (1987): 17–27.

———. "The Wilderness Journey in Deuteronomy: Style, Structure and Theology in Deuteronomy 1–3." *Covenant Quarterly* 55 (August 1997): 50–68.

Mittleman, Alan. *A Short History of Jewish Ethics: Conduct and Character in the Context of Covenant*. Chichester: Wiley-Blackwell, 2012.

Moberly, R. W. L. *At the Mountain of God: Story and Theology in Exodus 32–34.* Sheffield: JSOT, 1983.

———. *Old Testament Theology: Reading the Hebrew Bible as Christian Scripture*. Grand Rapids MI: Baker Academic, 2013.

———. "On Interpreting the Mind of God: The Theological Significance of the Flood Narrative (Genesis 6–9)." In *The Word Leaps the Gap: Essays on Scripture and Theology in Honor of Richard B. Hays*, edited by J. Ross Wagner, C. Kavin Rowe, and A. Katherine Grieb, 44–66. Grand Rapids MI: William B. Eerdmans, 2008.

———. "On Learning to Be a True Prophet: The Story of Balaam and His Ass." In *New Heaven and New Earth Prophecy and the Millennium: Essays in Honour of Anthony Gelston*, edited by Peter J. Harland and Robert Hayward, 1–17. Leiden: Brill, 1999.

———. *Prophecy and Discernment*. Cambridge Studies in Christian Doctrine 14. Cambridge: Cambridge University Press, 2006.

Moran, William. "The Ancient Near Eastern Background of the Love of God in Deuteronomy." *Catholic Biblical Quarterly* 25 (1963): 77–87.

Morgensztern, Menahem Mendel, of Kotzk. *Amud Ha-Emet*. Tel Aviv: c. 1950.

Muffs, Yohanan. "Covenant Traditions in Deuteronomy." In "Readings in the History of Biblical Thought," vol. 3, "Lectures at the Jewish Theological Seminary (1965)." Unpublished.

Murphy, Roland E. *Proverbs*. Word Biblical Commentary 22. Nashville TN: T. Nelson, 1998.

Nahmanides, Moses (Ramban). *Commentary to the Torah*. Rome: 1480.

———. *Novellae on the Talmud*. Jerusalem: 1928.

Nelson, Richard D. *Deuteronomy: A Commentary*. Louisville KY: Westminster John Knox, 2002.

———. *First and Second Kings*. Atlanta: John Knox, 1987.

———. *Raising Up a Faithful Priest: Community and Priesthood in Biblical Theology*. Louisville KY: Westminster John Knox, 1993.

Nissim of Gerona. *Derashot Ha-Ran*. Constantinople: 1533.

Noth, Martin. *Numbers: A Commentary*. Philadelphia: Westminster, 1968.

Ollenburger, Ben. "Zechariah: Introduction, Commentary, and Reflections." In *The New Interpreter's Bible*, vol. 7. Nashville TN: Abingdon, 1998.

Olson, Dennis T. *Deuteronomy and the Death of Moses: A Theological Reading*. Overtures to Biblical Theology. Minneapolis: Fortress, 1994.

———. "Judges: Introduction, Commentary, and Reflections." In *The New Interpreter's Bible*, vol. 2. Nashville TN: Abingdon, 1998.

———. "Negotiating Boundaries: The Old and New Generations and the Theology of Numbers." *Interpretation* 51 (July 1997): 229–40.

———. *Numbers*. Louisville KY: John Knox, 1996.

Orhot Tzaddikim. Prague: 1581.

Oswalt, John. *Isaiah: The NIV Application Commentary; From Biblical Text to Contemporary Life*. Grand Rapids MI: Zondervan, 2003.

"Otiot De-Rabbi Akiva." In *Otzar Midrashim*. Vol. 2, edited by J. D. Eisenstein. New York: J. D. Eisenstein, 1915.

Otto, Eckart. "False Weights in the Scales of Biblical Justice? Different Views of Women from Patriarchal Hierarchy to Religious Equality in the Book of Deuteronomy." In *Gender and Law and the Hebrew Bible and the Ancient Near East*, edited by Victor H. Matthews, Bernard M. Levinson, and Tikva Frymer-Kensky, 128–46. Journal for the Study of the Old Testament Supplement Series 262. Sheffield: Sheffield Academic, 1998.

Paley, R. Abraham Noah. "Enthroning Your Creator and Enthroning Your Fellow." *Ha-Ne'eman*, Kislev 5710, 8.

Perry, T. A. *Dialogues with Kohelet: The Book of Ecclesiastes — Translation and Commentary*. University Park: Pennsylvania State University Press, 1993.

Philo of Alexandria. "Life of Moses." In *The Works of Philo Judaeus, the Contemporary of Josephus*, translated by Charles Duke Yonge. London: H. G. Bohn, 1854–55.

Piekarz, Mendel. *Hasidut Polin Bein Shtei Milhamot Ha-Olam*. Jerusalem: Mosad Bialik, 1990.

Pinto, Yoshiyahu. *Me'or Enayim*. Amsterdam: 1754.

Pressler, Carolyn. "Deuteronomy." In *Women's Bible Commentary, Twentieth Anniversary Edition: Revised and Updated*, edited by Carol A. Newsom, Sharon H. Ringe, and Jacqueline E. Lapsley. 3rd ed. Louisville KY: Westminster John Knox, 2012.

———. *The View of Women Found in the Deuteronomic Family Laws*. Beihefte zur Zeitschrift für die alttestamentliche Wissenschaft 216. Berlin: de Gruyter, 1993.

Pröbstle, Martin. "YHWH Standing before Abraham: Genesis 18:22 and Its Theological Force." In *Inicios, Paradigmas y Fundamentos: Estudios teológicos y exegéticos en el Pentateuco*, edited by Gerald Klingbeil. Libertador San Martín, Enre Ríos, Argentina: Editorial Universidad Adventista del Plata, 2004.

Propp, William H. C. *Exodus 1–18: A New Translation with Introduction and Commentary*. New York: Doubleday, 1999.

Provan, Iain W. *1 and 2 Kings*. Peabody MA: Hendrickson, 1995.

Reines, Isaac Jacob. *Orah VeSimchah*. Vilna: Ha-Almana Ve-Ha-Ahim Rom, 1898.

Reis, Pamela Tamarkin. "Numbers XI: Seeing Moses Plain." *Vetus Testamentum* 55, no. 2 (2005): 207–31.

Rendsburg, Gary A. "The Vegetarian Ideal in the Bible." In *Food and Judaism*, edited by L. J. Greenspoon, R. A. Simkins, and G. Shapiro, 319–33. Omaha NE: Creighton University Press, 2005. Distributed by the University of Nebraska Press.

Rosenberg, Shimon Gershon. *Ba-Yom Ha-Huh: Derashot UMa'amarim Le-Mo'adei Iyyar*. Alon Shevut: Mekhon kitve ha-Rav Shagar, 2012.

Rotenberg, Menorah. "A Portrait of Rebecca: The Devolution of a Matriarch into a Patriarch." *Conservative Judaism* 54, no. 2 (2002): 46–62.

Saba, Abraham. *Tzeror Ha-Mor*. Venice: 1523.

Safrai, Samuel. *R. Akiva b. Joseph and His Teaching* (Hebrew). Jerusalem: Mossad Bialik, 1970.

Sagi, Avi. "The Punishment of Amalek in the Jewish Tradition: Coping with the Moral Problem." *Harvard Theological Review* 87 (1994): 323–46.

Santayana, George. *Reason in Religion*. New York: Dover, 1982.

Sarna. Nahum M. *Exodus*. Philadelphia: Jewish Publication Society, 1991.

———. *Genesis*. Philadelphia: Jewish Publication Society, 1989.

Sasson, Jack M. "The Servant's Tale: How Rebekah Found a Spouse." *Journal of Near East Studies* 65, no. 4 (2006): 241–65.

Scarry, Elaine. "The Difficulty of Imagining Other People." In *For Love of Country: Debating the Limits of Patriotism*, edited by Martha C. Nussbaum et al., 98–110. Boston: Beacon, 1996.

Schick, Abraham ben Aryeh Loeb. *Eshed Hanechalim*. Tel Aviv: Mekhon "Yad Mordechai," 1985.

Schlimm, Matthew R. *From Fratricide to Forgiveness: The Language and Ethics of Anger in Genesis*. Winona Lake IN: Eisenbrauns, 2011.

Schmid, H. H. "Creation, Righteousness, and Salvation: 'Creation Theology' as the Broad Horizon of Biblical Theology." In *Creation in the Old Testament*, edited by Bernhard W. Anderson, 102–17. Philadelphia: Fortress, 1984.

Scholem, Gershom G. *Major Trends in Jewish Mysticism*. New York: Schocken Books, 1941.

Schwartz, Baruch J. "The Ultimate Aim of Israel's Restoration in Ezekiel." In *Birkat Shalom: Studies in the Bible, Ancient Near Eastern Literature, and Post-biblical Judaism Presented to Shalom M. Paul on the Occasion of His Seventieth Birthday*, edited by Chaim Cohen et al., 305–19. Winona Lake IN: Eisenbrauns, 2008.

Schweid, Eliezer. *Iyunim BiShemonah Perakim LaRambam*. Jerusalem: Akademon, 1989.

Sefer Ha-Yashar. New York: K'tav, 1973.

Seforno, Obadiah. *Commentary to the Torah*. Venice: 1567.

Sennott, Charles. *Broken Covenant: The Story of Father Bruce Ritter's Fall from Grace*. New York: Simon & Schuster, 1992.

Seow, Choon-Leong. "1 and 2 Kings: Introduction, Commentary, and Reflections." In *New Interpreter's Bible*, vol. 3. Nashville TN: Abingdon, 1999.

———. *Ecclesiastes: A New Translation with Introduction*. New York: Doubleday, 1997.

Shatz, David. "Divine Intervention and Religious Sensibilities." In *Divine Intervention and Miracles in Jewish Theology*, edited by Dan Cohn-Sherbok, 153–94. Lewiston NY: E. Mellen, 1996.

———. "Freedom, Repentance, and Hardening of the Hearts: Albo vs. Maimonides." *Faith and Philosophy* 14 (1997): 478–509.

Shemesh, Yael. "Rape Is Rape Is Rape: The Story of Dinah and Shechem (Genesis 34)." *Zeitschrift für die alttestamentliche Wissenschaft* 119 (2007): 2–21.

Sherwin, Byron L. *Toward a Jewish Theology: Methods, Problems, and Possibilities*. Lewiston, NY: Edwin Mellen, 1992.

Shinan, Avigdor, and Yair Zakovitch. *From Gods to God: How the Bible Debunked, Suppressed, or Changed Ancient Myths and Legends*. Translated by Valerie Zakovitch. Philadelphia: Jewish Publication Society, 2012.

Shkop, Esther. "Rivka: The Enigma behind the Veil." *Tradition* 36, no. 3 (2002): 46–59.

Shmuelevitz, Chaim. *Sihot Musar*. Brooklyn NY: Mesorah Publications in conjunction with Alumni Association of Yeshivas Mir Yerushalayim, 1998.

Shneur Zalman of Liadi. *Likkutei Torah: Devarim*. Brooklyn NY: Kehot Publication Society, 2011.

Silber, David, with Rachel Furst. *Go Forth and Learn: A Passover Haggadah*. Philadelphia: Jewish Publication Society, 2011.

Simha, Meir, of Dvinsk. *Meshekh Hokhmah*. Riga, Lativa: 1927.

Simundson, Daniel J. *Hosea-Joel-Amos-Obadiah-Jonah-Micah*. Nashville TN: Abingdon, 2005.

Sklar, Jay. *Leviticus*. Downers Grove IL: Inter-varsity, 2014.

Smith, David. "What Hope after Babel? Diversity and Community in Gen 11:1–9, Exod 1:1–14, Zeph 3:1–13 and Acts 2:1–13." *Horizons in Biblical Theology* 18, no. 2 (1996): 169–91.

Soelle, Dorothee. *Against the Wind: Memoir of a Radical Christian*. Minneapolis: Fortress, 1999.

Sofer, Shmuel Binyomin. *Ketav Sofer*. Pressburg: 1883.

Sokolow, Moshe. *Hatzi Nehamah: Studies in the Weekly Parashah Based on the Lessons of Nehama Leibowitz*. Jerusalem: Urim, 2008.

Soloveitchik, Joseph B. "The Community." *Tradition* 17, no. 2 (1978): 7–24.

——— . *Fate and Destiny: From the Holocaust to the State of Israel*. Hoboken NJ: KTAV, 2000.

——— . *Halakhic Man*. Philadelphia: Jewish Publication Society of America, 1983.

——— . *On Repentance: The Thought and Oral Discourses of Rabbi Joseph Dov Soloveitchik*. Edited by Pinchas H. Peli. New York: Paulist Press, 1984.

——— . "Redemption, Prayer, Talmud Torah." *Tradition* 17, no. 2 (1978): 55–72.

——— . "Shelihut." In *Yemei Zikaron*. Jerusalem: Ha-Reshut Hameshutefet Le-Hinukh Yehudi Tzioni, Ha-mahlakah Le-Hinukh ULe-Tarbut Toraniim Ba-Golah, 1996.

Sperling, S. David. "Miriam, Aaron and Moses: Sibling Rivalry." *Hebrew Union College Annual* 70–71 (1999–2000): 39–55.

Sprinkle, Joe M. *"The Book of the Covenant": A Literary Approach*. Sheffield: JSOT, 1994.

Sternberg, Meir. *The Poetics of Biblical Narrative: Ideological Literature and the Drama of Reading*. Bloomington: Indiana University Press, 1985.

Stuart, Douglas K. *Exodus: An Exegetical and Theological Exposition of Holy Scripture*. Nashville TN: Broadman & Holman, 2006.

Sturdy, John. *Numbers*. Cambridge: Cambridge University Press, 1976.

Sweeney, Marvin A. *The Twelve Prophets*. Vol. 1. Collegeville MN: Liturgical Press, 2000.

Thompson, J. A. *The Book of Jeremiah*. Grand Rapids MI: Eerdmans, 1980.

Tigay, Jeffrey H. *Deuteronomy*. Philadelphia: Jewish Publication Society, 1996.

——— . "The Torah Scroll and God's Presence." In *Built by Wisdom, Established by Understanding: Essays on Biblical and Near Eastern Literature in Honor of Adele Berlin*, edited by Maxine L. Grossman, 323–40. Bethesda: University Press of Maryland, 2013.

Timmer, Daniel C. *A Gracious and Compassionate God: Mission, Salvation, and Spirituality in the Book of Jonah*. Nottingham: Apollos, 2011.

Touito, Hazoniel. "'Property' as a Test of Abraham Our Father" (Hebrew). In *Mi-Peirot Ha-Ilan: Al Parshat Hashavua me-et hokrei Universitat Bar Ilan*, edited by Leib Moskowitz. Ramat-Gan: Universitat Bar-Ilan, 1997.

Towner, W. Sibley. *Genesis*. Louisville KY: Westminster John Knox, 2001.

Tsuriel, Moshe Yehiel. *Otzrot Ha-Musar*. Jerusalem: Yerid ha-Sefarim, 2000.

Turner, Mary Donovan. "Rebekah: Ancestor of Faith." *Lexington Theological Quarterly* 20, no. 2 (1985): 42–50.

Tuviyah ben Eliezer. *Midrash Lekah Tov*. Vilna: Buber, 1880.

Twersky, Isadore. *Introduction to the Code of Maimonides*. New Haven CT: Yale University Press, 1980.

Unna, Moshe. "Education in Our Lives" (Hebrew). In *Ha-Kehilah Ha-Hadashah: Iyyunim Be-Mishnat Ha-Kevutzah HaDatit*. Tel Aviv: Hakibbutz Hameuchad, 1984.

Van Leeuwen, Raymond C. "What Comes Out of God's Mouth: Theological Wordplay in Deuteronomy 8." *Catholic Biblical Quarterly* 47, no. 1 (January 1985), 55–57.

Volf, Miroslav. *Free of Charge: Giving and Forgiving in a Culture Stripped of Grace*. Grand Rapids MI: Zondervan, 2005.

Von Rad, Gerhard. *Deuteronomy: A Commentary*. Old Testament Library. Philadelphia: Westminster, 1966.

———. *Genesis*. Translated by J. H. Marks. Philadelphia: Westminster, 1972.

Vital, Hayyim. "Sha'ar Hag HaSukkot, Chapter 4." In *Sha'ar HaKavvanot*. Krakow: 1782.

Walker, A. D. M. "Gratefulness and Gratitude." *Proceedings of the Aristotelian Society*, n.s., 81 (1980–81): 49.

Waltke, Bruce K. *Proverbs, Chapter 15–31*. Grand Rapids MI: William B. Eerdmans, 2005.

Waltke, Bruce K., with Cathi J. Fredricks. *Genesis: A Commentary*. Grand Rapids MI: Zondervan, 2001.

Walzer, Michael. *Exodus and Revolution*. New York: Basic Books, 1985.

Weinfeld, Moshe. "The Creator God in Genesis 1 and in the Prophecy of Deutero-Isaiah" (Hebrew). *Tarbitz* 37, no. 2 (1968): 105–32.

———. *Deuteronomy 1–11: A New Translation with Introduction and Commentary*. Anchor Bible 5. New York: Doubleday, 1991.

———. *Deuteronomy and the Deuteronomic School*. Oxford: Clarendon, 1972.

———. *Devarim (Olam HaTanakh)*. Tel-Aviv: Davidzon-'Iti, 1995.

———. "The Universalist Trend and the Isolationist Trend in the Period of the Return to Zion" (Hebrew). *Tarbitz* 33 (1964): 228–42.

Weiser, Meir Libush. *Malbim, Commentary to the Bible*. B'nei Brak: Mishor, 1990.

Weiss Halivni, David. *Midrash, Mishnah, and Gemara: The Jewish Predilection for Justified Law*. Cambridge MA: Harvard University Press, 1986.

Welker, Michael. "Creation and the Image of God: Their Understanding in Christian Tradition and the Biblical Grounds." *Journal of Ecumenical Studies* 34, no. 3 (Summer 1997): 436–48.

Wenham, Gordon J. *The Book of Leviticus*. Grand Rapids MI: W. B. Eerdmans, 1979.

———. "The Gap between Law and Ethics in the Bible." *Journal of Jewish Studies* 48, no. 1 (Spring 1997): 17–29.

———. *Genesis 1–15*. Waco TX: Word Books, 1987.

———. *Genesis 16–20*. Waco TX: Word Books, 1994.

———. "Law and Ethical Ideals in Deuteronomy." In *For Our Good Always: Studies on the Message and Influence of Deuteronomy in Honor of Daniel J. Block*, edited by Jason S. DeRouchie, Jason Gile, and Kenneth J. Turner, 81–92. Winona Lake IN: Eisenbrauns, 2013.

———. *Numbers*. Leicester: Inter-varsity, 1981.

———. "Sanctuary Symbolism in the Garden of Eden Story." *Proceedings of the World Congress of Jewish Studies* 9 (1986): 19–25.

Wessely, Naphtali Hirz. *Biur to Sefer Vayikra*. Vilna: 1894.

Westphal, Merold. "Prayer as the Posture of the Decentered Self." In *The Phenomenology of Prayer*, edited by Bruce Ellis Benson and Norman Wirzba, 13–31. New York: Fordham University Press, 2005.

White, Lynn Townsend, Jr. "The Historical Roots of Our Ecologic Crisis." *Science* 155, no. 3767 (March 10, 1967): 1203–7.

Wirzba, Norman. *The Paradise of God: Renewing Religion in an Ecological Age*. Oxford: Oxford University Press, 2003.

Wright, Christopher J. H. *New International Biblical Commentary: Deuteronomy*. Old Testament Series. Peabody MA: Hendrickson, 2003.

Wolbe, Shlomo. *Alei Shur*. Vol. 1. Be'er Ya'akov: Otsar Ha-sefarim, 1977.

Wolff, Hans Walter. *Anthropology of the Old Testament*. Philadelphia: Fortress, 1974.

Wurzburger, Walter S. "*Imitatio Dei* in Maimonides' Sefer Hamitzvot and the Mishneh Torah." In *Tradition and Transition: Essays Presented to Chief Rabbi Sir Immanuel Jakobovits to Celebrate Twenty Years in Office*, edited by Jonathan Sacks, 321–24. London: Jews' College Publications, 1986.

Yaffa Ashkenazi, Shmuel. *Yefe To'ar*. Venice, 1597.

Yitzhaki, Solomon (Rashi). *Commentary to the Bible*. Rome: 1470.

Yoder, Christine Roy. *Proverbs*. Abingdon Old Testament Commentaries. Nashville TN: Abingdon, 2009.

Zaitchik, Chaim Ephraim. *Or HaNefesh*. Vol. 1. New York: Bi-defus Balshan, 1958.

Zakovitch, Yair. *Jacob: Unexpected Patriarch*. Translated by Valerie Zakovitch. New Haven CT: Yale University Press, 2012.

———. "A Still, Small Voice: Form and Content in I Kings 19" (Hebrew). *Tarbitz* 51 (1982): 329–46.

Zevit, Ziony. "Three Ways to Look at the Ten Plagues." *Bible Review* 6, no. 3 (June 1990): 16–24.

Zohar He-hadash. Thessaloniki: 1597.

Zuenz, Aryeh Leib. *Melo Ha-omer*. Tel Aviv: A. Borzhikovsky, 1964.

Zundel, Hanokh. *Etz Yosef*. Warsaw: 1867.

Subject Index

Aaron: blessings and, **2**:103, 106; commanded to place jar of manna before the ark, **1**:xxii, 162–63; **2**:xxiv; confronting Pharaoh with Moses, **1**:80, 213; crown of priesthood and, **2**:99; death before reaching promised land, **2**:146–50, 186, 285, 324n123; divinely bestowed nature of elevated status, **2**:142; encroachment on *mishkan*, responsibility for, **2**:141; Golden Calf incident and, **1**:197; **2**:122; Korah challenging, **2**:136, 139; love and peace associated with, **2**:106; *mishkan* and, **1**:195, 198; Nile turned into blood and, **1**:147; ordination of, **2**:44; Pinhas as descendant of, **2**:168; rebellion against Moses, **2**:119–22, 320nn47–48; skin disease suffered by Miriam and, **2**:43, 51, 120; sons, death of, **2**:31–36; spies sent to survey the land and, **2**:126, 281; water struck from rock and, **2**:146–50

Aaron b. Elijah, **2**:155

R. Abba b. Hanina, **2**:348n208

Abel, **1**:88–90; **2**:194

abolition of slavery, **2**:253–54

Abraham: as Abram, **1**:26–30, 135, 230n36; **2**:18; *Akedah*, **1**:xiii, 28, 32, 40–42, 45, 76; **2**:xv; blessed by God, **2**:18; burial site of, **1**:62; Caleb compared to, **2**:284; circumcision and, **2**:221; conditional nature of God's promises to, **1**:233n75; covenant with, **1**:21–22, 28, 36, 39, 45, 49–50,

135; **2**:82, 204, 205, 207, 286; directly communicating with God, **1**:54; in Egypt, **1**:26–27, 28, 29; election of, **2**:204, 205, 207; God's lovingkindness for, **2**:296; Hagar, treatment of, **1**:xxv, 23–24, 40; **2**:xxvii; hospitality of, **1**:xiii, 31–34, 45; **2**:xv; human responsibility as theme of Torah and, **1**:xxvii; **2**:xxix; and Isaac, announcement of birth of, **1**:36, 39, 49; Isaac's life recapitulating, **1**:52; Jacob contrasted with, **1**:64; as journeyer, **1**:234n89; Lot, conflict with, **1**:26–30, 231n44; Manasseh, pleading for, **1**:75, 76; marriage to Sarah, **1**:49–50, 234n101; promises of God on inheritance and descendants of, **1**:21–22, 28, 36, 39, 45, 135; **2**:127; Rebekah paralleling, **1**:45–46, 233n88; servant sent to find wife for Isaac, **1**:43–45; Sodom, efforts to save, **1**:xiii, 35–39; **2**:xv, 89; wealth of, **1**:26–30

Abravanel, R. Isaac: on construction of *mishkan*, **1**:219–20; on dietary laws, **2**:26–27, 28, 306n54, 306n58; disabled, on treatment of, **2**:311n131, 312n139; on Edom's hostility to Israelites, **2**:152; on Jacob's theft of Esau's birthright, **1**:64–65; on Jonah, **1**:211; on kings and kingship, **2**:343n148; on Moses in Golden Calf incident, **1**:233n73; on priests, **2**:318n19; on recounting of rest stops in wilderness in Numbers, **2**:186; on repentance,

Abravanel, R. Isaac (*continued*)
2:351n243; on silence of Aaron after death of sons, 2:32–33; as source, 1:265; 2:359; on thanksgiving offering, 2:16
Absalom, 1:95; 2:246
Achtemeier, Elizabeth, 1:210
action and emotion, 1:xxx; 2:xxxii, 61–65, 113
Adam: cherubim replacing, as guardian of Garden, 1:259n152; clothing of, 2:295–96; created from site of future Temple, 1:189; direct access to God, 1:54; forbidden fruit consumed by, 1:111; in Garden of Eden, 1:189, 191; gratitude of, 1:63; speech as breath of God and, 2:47; value of each individual life and single creation of, 2:93, 317n2
Adler, Rachel, 2:309n99, 309n103
Admah, 2:84
Adonijah, 2:246
adultery, 1:91, 172; 2:12–13, 212
Agag (Amalekite ruler), 2:257
aggadah, 2:296
Ahab, 2:176, 212, 247
Ahitophel, 1:95
Ai, 1:29
Akedah (binding of Isaac), 1:xiii, 28, 32, 40–42, 45, 76; 2:xv
R. Akiva, 1:xxxiii, 142, 258n133, 260n174; 2:xxxv, 61, 72–73, 75, 93, 320n50, 331n227
Albo, R. Joseph, 2:266–68, 271, 351n244
Alfasi, R. Isaac, 1:242n211
Allen, Ronald, 2:149–50, 324n128
almanah, meaning of, 1:179, 256n116
Alsheikh, R. Moshe, 2:107
Alter, Robert: on circumcision of the heart, 2:223; on dividing in Leviti-

cus, 2:6, 42; *The Five Books of Moses: A Translation with Commentary* (2004), 1:268; 2:362; on God hardening heart of Pharaoh, 1:250n29; on injuries/insults to persons with disabilities, 2:57; on Joseph's enslavement of Egyptians, 1:106, 243n221; on kings and kingship, 2:344n157; on laws and obedience to them, 2:337n90; on Nathan and David, 2:303n16; on seventy elders appointed by Moses, 2:115; on Song of the Sea, 2:73; on stiff-neckedness, 2:336n55; on Tamar and Judah, 1:99; translations of, 1:xix; 2:xxi
Alter, R. Yehudah Leib, of Ger, 2:67–68
Alter of Slabodka (R. Nosson Tzvi Finkel), 1:203–4
Altschuler, R. David, 2:320n44, 332n9
Amalek and Amalekites, 1:xii, xxxi, 165–66; 2:xiv, xxxiii, 156, 255–59, 347nn196–204, 348n214
Amidah, 2:48–49, 67, 75, 78
Amiel, R. Moshe Avigdor, 2:195, 258
Aminadav, 1:157
Amir, Yehoshua, 1:236n115
Amir, R. Yehoyada, 1:199
Ammon and Ammonites, 1:29; 2:170–71, 206–7
Amnon, 1:246n250
Amos (prophet), 1:xxiii, 86–87, 240nn183–84; 2:xxv, 120, 206
anavim, 2:120
ancient Near East. *See* Near Eastern myth and society
anger of God, 1:261n186
Anisfeld, Rachel, 1:230n29
anthropocentrism, 1:11
Ar, 2:206
Arab-Jewish relations, 2:195

Aram, **2**:177

Arama, R. Isaac, **2**:95

ARI, the (R. Isaac Luria), **1**:184–85

Aristotle, *Nichomachean Ethics*, **1**:250n25

Ark of the Covenant: Aaron commanded to place jar of manna before, **1**:xxii, 162–63; **2**:xxiv; cherubim as guardians of, **1**:191

Arnold, Bill, *Genesis* (2008), **1**:266; **2**:360

Asevilli, R. Yom Tov b. Avraham (Ritva), **1**:256n108

Asherah, **2**:247

Ashkenazi, R. Eliezer, **1**:237n134

Ashkenazi, R. Shmuel Yaffa, **1**:237n139

Ashley, Timothy, **2**:179

Assyrian empire, **1**:105, 210–11; **2**:243–44

avdut (being oppressed), **1**:22, 23, 230n39

Avihu, **2**:31–36

Avimelech (king of Gerar), **1**:50

avodah, **1**:214–15

awe, **2**:265–69, 349–50nn229–30, 350n233

Baal, **2**:22, 84, 174, 177, 247

Baal-peor, **2**:125

Ba'al Shem Tov, R. Israel, **2**:165, 349n229

ba'al teshuvah (person committed to mending his ways), **2**:12

Baal-zephon, **2**:185

Babel, Tower of, **1**:16–20, 230n29, 230n31

Babylon and Babylonia, **2**:74, 193

Babylonian Talmud, as core text of Jewish culture, **1**:136. *See also Classical Sources Index*

R. Bahya ben Asher, **1**:151, 252n54; **2**:10

Balaam, **1**:xiii–xiv, 67; **2**:xv–xvi, 85, 158–65

Balak (Moabite king), **2**:158–60, 163

Balentine, Samuel, **2**:6–7, 40, 315n191; *Leviticus* (2003), **1**:267; **2**:361

Bar Kappara, **2**:187

Bar-Kokhba revolt, **2**:72–73, 75

barrenness: of Rachel, **1**:50–51, 61, 62, 242n199; of Rebekah, **1**:51; of Sarah, **1**:49–50

Bar Shaul, R. Elimelekh, **2**:111–12

Bathsheba, **2**:12, 13, 303n14, 303nn18–19, 304n20

Beale, Gregory, **1**:259n152

Be'er-lahai-roi, **1**:40–41

Beer-sheba, **1**:40; **2**:174, 176

Bekhor Shor, R. Joseph b. Isaac, **1**:242n219; **2**:152

Benjamin (son of Jacob and Rachel): birth of, **1**:74; favoritism of Jacob regarding, **1**:100, 246n252; Joseph in Egypt requiring brothers to bring, **1**:90–91, 96, 97, 100, 110; name of, **1**:74, 237n149; silver cup placed in bag of, **1**:110, 112–13

Benjamin (tribe), **1**:157, 238n151, 238n153

Ben Nannas, **1**:201

Ben-Oni (birth name of Benjamin), **1**:74, 237n149

Ben Sira, **2**:131

Benstein, Jeremy, **2**:26

Bentley, Philip J., **1**:229n19

Ben Zoma, **1**:201

Berezovsky, R. Shalom Noah, **2**:106, 273–74

Berkovits, R. Eliezer, **2**:316n210

Berlin, Adele, and Marc Zvi Brettler, eds., *Oxford Jewish Study Bible* (2004), **1**:268–69; **2**:362–63

Berlin, Isaiah, **1**:216

Berlin, R. Naftali Tzvi Yehudah (Netziv), **1**:18, 47, 265; **2**:105, 169, 265, 359; *Ha'amek Davar* (1937), **1**:18, 47; **2**:10, 304n22

Bethel, **1**:29

Bethlehem, **1**:238n151

Bezalel, **1**:219–20, 222

Bible. *See* Tanakh

Bickerman, Elias, **2**:352n257

Bilhah, **1**:93, 94, 98

Blenkinsopp, Joseph, **1**:235n110

blessings: Abraham blessed by God, **2**:18; entitlement and, **2**:260–64; Esau's loss of birthright and blessing, **1**:46–47, 53, 64–68, 116, 237n134; Jacob blessed after dream, **1**:89; priests as channels of, **2**:106, 318n19; threefold priestly blessing, **2**:103–7

Blidstein, Gerald, **2**:17

blind and deaf persons, respect for, **2**:57–60, 310–11nn126–27, 311n131, 311n134, 312nn138–40

Block, Daniel, **1**:192, 259n192

blood: innocent blood, prohibition on shedding, **2**:191–95; prohibition on eating, **2**:27, 192; purity laws and, **2**:38

Blum, Lawrence, **2**:278

Bonhoeffer, Dietrich, **1**:208

booths and Feast of Booths. *See* Sukkot

Bosnian War (1990s), **2**:156

Bovati, Pietro, **1**:256n118

Boyarin, Daniel, **2**:100–101

Boyce, Richard, **2**:150, 324n128

Bracke, John, **2**:21–22

Brandes, R. Yehudah, **1**:200–201

bread alone, not living by, **2**:225–29

Brettler, Marc Zvi, **2**:336n63, 350n237

Broadie, Thomas, **1**:111

brothers: concept of, in Deuteronomy, **2**:341n132; Israelites as, **2**:248–49, 344n165; prophets as, **2**:341n132; treating vulnerable and oppressed as, **2**:231

Brueggemann, Walter: on Abraham's attempt to save Sodom, **1**:35–37; on Amalek, **2**:255; on departure from Egypt, **1**:251n53; *Deuteronomy* (2002),

1:268; **2**:362; on Elijah, **2**:177; "Exodus: Introduction, Commentary and Reflections" in *New Interpreter's Bible* (1994), **1**:266; **2**:360; on Fifth Commandment, **1**:170, 173; on the Flood, **1**:14; on fugitive slaves, **2**:345n173; on Isaiah's treatment of Exodus/return from Babylon, **2**:74; on Job, **2**:316n218; on Joseph's enslavement of Egyptians, **1**:108, 244n235; on kings and kingship, **2**:344n168; on laws, **2**:216; on loans and debt, **2**:233; on manna in the desert, **1**:161; on *mishkan*, **1**:217; **2**:77; on nostalgia for Egypt, **1**:160; on obedience to God, **2**:88, 89; on repentance, **2**:270; on Reuben sleeping with Jacob's concubine, **1**:95; on Simeon and Levi's destruction of Shechem's city, **1**:247n257; on Ten Commandments, **1**:256n112; on Tent of Meeting, **2**:353n273; on women as slaves, **2**:236, 339n114

Brümmer, Vincent, **2**:292

Buber, Martin, **2**:24, 112–13, 115, 117, 264; *I and Thou* (1970), **1**:187

burning bush, **1**:126, 130, 149–50

burnt offerings (*korban olah*), **2**:20, 22, 37

Bush, George H. W., **2**:252

Cain, **1**:xxvii, xxviii, 3–5, 54, 88–90, 92, 111; **2**:xxix, xxx, 194

Caleb, **1**:255n86; **2**:127–28, 134, 281–84, 354n279, 354n282

camels, watering, **1**:43, 44

Canaan and Canaanites: Abraham in, **1**:26–27; burning of gods of, **2**:209; famine in, **1**:90, 96; as land of milk and honey, **1**:135, 138; **2**:124, 126, 134, 227, 260, 263, 281; rape of Dinah and, **1**:114–19; Rebekah agreeing to go to,

1:45; Reubenites' and Gadites' desire to stay in Transjordan rather than enter, 1:29; 2:179–84; spies sent to survey, 2:126–29, 130, 134, 148, 281–82, 321n70

cantillation marks, 1:199, 239n177

capital punishment/death penalty, 2:192–93, 331n227

captive brides, 1:xxi; 2:xxiii, 236–38, 340–41nn124–31

Caro, R. Joseph, 1:171; 2:308n72, 313n161

Cassuto, Moshe David (Umberto), 1:150–51, 166; 2:27, 29; *A Commentary on the Book of Exodus* (1967), 1:266; 2:360; *A Commentary on the Book of Genesis* (1961–64), 1:266; 2:360

cattle of Reubenites and Gadites, 1:29; 2:179–84

census of Israelites, 2:93, 95, 96

Chaney, Marvin, 2:212

change, effecting, 2:270–74

chaos, order out of: Creation as, 2:3, 6; defeat of Pharaoh as cosmic victory of, 1:xxiii–xxiv, 144–48, 222–24; 2:xxv–xxvi, 256; Exodus from Egypt as, 2:73–74; rules of Leviticus as means of, 2:3–8

Chapman, Stephen, 2:256, 347n196, 348n214

character: Abraham's servant testing Rebekah's, 1:43–45; behavior versus, 1:203–6; focus of Jewish ethics on, 1:xxx, 203–6; 2:xxxii, 336n54; free will and destiny, 1:139–43; Jacob's censure of sons' character flaws, 1:70, 93, 114, 241n189, 241n191; of Reuben, 1:93–98; Jacob's name(s) reflecting, 1:65, 67–68

charity: compassion and, 1:77–78; as social ethic, 2:230–34, 338n95; Torah commandments requiring, 1:xii, 2:xiv

Cherlow, Yuval, 1:255n105

cherubim as guardians of holy places, 1:191, 259n152

childbirth and purity laws, 2:37–41, 308nn89–91, 329n195

Childs, Brevard, 1:149, 170, 252n58; 2:122, 177, 211

chosenness. *See* election

Christian tradition, 1:xii, xxxiii, 177, 256n112, 265; 2:xiv, xxxv, 101, 333n23, 359

circumcision, 1:49, 115–16, 118, 177; 2:221, 222, 336n68

circumcision of the heart, 2:82, 220–24, 336n64, 351n247

Claassens, Juliana, 2:293

Clifford, Richard, 2:217

Clines, D. J. A., 2:346n182

Cogan, Mordechai, 2:176, 178

Cole, Dennis, 2:121

Collins, John, 2:169

community, making, 2:275–79

compassion, 1:42, 64; of God, 1:42; Jacob's lack of, 1:64; of Moses, 1:125–26; pity compared, 2:278–79; of Rachel, 1:74–78, 238n155, 238n157; for vulnerable and oppressed, 1:xxx, 181–82; 2:xxxii

concubines: of Jacob, 1:93, 94, 95, 98, 219; kings' multiple marriages and foreign wives, dangers of, 2:246, 247; sons sleeping with concubines of fathers, 1:93–96. *See also specific concubines by name, e.g. Hagar*

confession, 2:82, 108–13

corpses: discovered but killer's identity unknown, 2:331n232; purity laws and, 2:38; skin disease and, 2:43

cosmic victory of order over chaos. *See* chaos, order out of

courage, 2:199–203

covenant: with Abraham, **1**:21–22, 28, 36, 39, 45, 49–50, 135; **2**:82, 204, 205, 207, 286; action and emotion required by, **1**:xxx; **2**:xxxii; circumcision as sign of, **2**:221; Elijah on, **2**:176–77; with Isaac, **2**:82, 204, 286; with Jacob, **2**:82, 204, 286; kings and, **2**:249; with Moses and Israelites at Sinai, **1**:135–36, 195–96, 198–202; **2**:35; mutual commitment of, **1**:198–202; Noahide, **2**:102; repentance and forgiveness, dependent on, **2**:70, 81–85; with Sarah, **1**:49–50. *See also* election

Covenant House (New York City), **2**:252

covetousness, Tenth Commandment forbidding, **2**:209–14, 236, 239

Craigie, Peter, **2**:338n107, 343n157

Creation: *creatio ex nihilo*, concept of, **2**:3; Exodus narrative and, **2**:73–74; goodness in its own right, **1**:8–9; human stewardship over, **1**:8–11, 229n19; image of God, human creation in, **1**:xxvi, 7–11, 229n8; **2**:xviii, 192–94; *mishkan*, construction of, **1**:221–24; of order out of chaos, **2**:3, 6; plagues of Egypt and, **1**:146–47; *tzimtzum* (divine self-contraction) and, **1**:184; words, power of, **2**:47

crimes against property versus crimes against the person, **2**:193–94

crowns, **2**:98–99

cultural progress, **1**:xxviii, 3–6; **2**:xxx

culture of the book versus culture of the sword, **2**:71–72, 258

cursing others, **2**:57–58

Cushite woman, Moses' marriage to, **2**:50, 119

Dan (tribe), **1**:219

David: Absalom sleeping with concubines of, **1**:95; adultery with Bathsheba, **2**:12–14, 212, 303n16, 303n19, 304n20; covetousness of, **2**:212; crown of royalty and, **2**:99; kingship of, **2**:245, 246; as leader, **2**:11–14; Nahshon as forebear of, **1**:158; as old man, **1**:174; rape of Tamar and, **1**:115, 246n251; wives of Saul inherited by, **1**:242n202

Davis, Ellen, **1**:213–14

Day of Atonement (Yom Kippur), **2**:52–56, 69–70

Days of Awe (Yamim Noraim), **2**:270

deaf and blind persons, respect for, **2**:57–60, 310–11nn126–27, 311n131, 311n134, 312nn138–40

death: of Aaron before reaching promised land, **2**:146–50, 186, 285, 324n123; of disciples of R. Akiva, **2**:72–73, 75; of Jacob, **1**:112; Joseph, supposed death of, **1**:67, 75, 91; maternal mortality fears and purity laws, **2**:37–41, 308nn89–90; *metzora* laws and, **2**:42–43, 309nn94–95; of Moses before reaching promised land, **1**:138; **2**:146–51, 280, 285–89, 295–96, 353n271; for non-Jews studying Torah, **2**:99–100; purity laws and, **2**:38; Rachel, death and burial of, **1**:74–75, 238n151, 238n153, 238n157; Rebekah, death and burial of, **1**:47, 62; of Sarah, **1**:41; of sons of Aaron, **2**:31–36; speech, power of, **2**:49–51. *See also* corpses

death penalty/capital punishment, **2**:192–93, 331n227

debts, remission of, **2**:230, 276, 338n98

debt slavery, **1**:244n235; **2**:230, 232, 276

Decalogue. *See* Ten Commandments

Delitzsch, Franz, **1**:142

dependence, embracing, **1**:159–64; **2**:225–29

ends not justifying means, 1:xxvii; 2:xxix

enjoyment and pleasure, Kohelet apparently advocating, 2:130–35, 313n159

Enns, Peter, 1:170, 249n19; 2:191; *Exodus (2000)*, 1:267; 2:361

Enosh, 1:3

entitlement, 2:260–64

environmentalism, 1:8–9

Ephraim (tribe), 1:75; 2:84, 172

Epstein, R. Barukh Ha-Levi, 2:201

Er, 1:91, 99

Esau: coarse nature of, 1:64–65, 68; descent of Amalek from, 2:348n214; Edom's hostility to Israel and, 2:152, 154–56; land designated by God for, 2:206; loss of birthright and blessing, 1:46–47, 53, 64–68, 116, 237n134; 2:154–55; as paradigmatic enemy of Jews, 1:70; reunion with Jacob, 1:69, 70, 71, 76, 95; 2:154; weapons associated with, 1:70, 237n141

escaped slaves, 2:250–54, 345n173, 345n177, 346n182

Eskenazi, Tamara Cohn, 1:54; 2:44; *The Torah: A Women's Commentary* (ed., with Andrea L. Weiss, 2008), 1:269; 2:363

Etham, 2:185

ethics. *See* morality and ethics

Eve, 1:54, 111, 189; 2:295–96

evil, equation of Amalek with, 2:255–59, 348n214

ex nihilo nihil fit, 2:3

Exodus, 1:176; 2:231, 232, 235–36, 239, 257

Exodus from Egypt: Amalek and Amalekites, 1:xii, xxxi, 165–66; 2:xiv, xxxiii, 156, 255–59, 347nn196–204, 348n214; complaining of Israelites in wilderness, 2:124–26; Creation narrative and, 2:73–74; fruitfulness of Isra-

elites in Egypt and God's commitment to life, 1:145, 146; generation of Exodus not reaching promised land, 1:255n86; 2:125, 147, 285; God hardening heart of Pharaoh and, 1:139–43, 249n19; gratitude and ingratitude, as tale of, 1:128–33; 2:124–29, 148–49; journey rather than arrival, stress on, 1:134–38; 2:262–63; manna in the desert, 1:xxii, 159–64, 244n230, 254n79; 2:xxiv, 225, 227, 306n54; Moses confronting Pharaoh, 1:80, 126, 128–33; nostalgic view of Egypt during, 1:xi–xii; 2:xiii–xiv; Omer and, 2:73–74; as orienting event for Jewish people, 2:275; Passover as reenactment of, 1:128; plagues and, 1:141, 144–48, 150, 250n26; plundering of Egyptians, 1:149–54; preparation of Israelites for, 2:124–25; recounting of resting places in Numbers, 2:185–90; Sea of Reeds, pursuit of Israelites by Pharaoh at, 1:155–58; 2:256; spies sent to survey the land, 2:126–29, 130, 134, 148, 281–82, 321n70; standing upright and, 2:82, 86–89; stubbornness and "stiff-neckedness" of Israelites, 1:13, 38, 203–6, 249n13; 2:124–29, 220, 336n55; Transjordan, Reubenites and Gadites desiring to stay in, 1:29; 2:179–84. *See also mishkan*; Sinai

eye for an eye (*talion*), 1:5

eyes and hearts, following, 2:130–35

Ezekiel (prophet), 1:9–10, 130, 146, 190–91; 2:43, 73, 87–89, 316n210

Ezra the Scribe, 1:55

false prophecy, 2:241, 243, 244

famine: Abraham going to Egypt due to, 1:26–27; Jacob's sons going to Egypt due to, 1:90, 96, 110; Joseph's handling of, in Egypt, 1:104–8, 112; offenses causing, 1:144

father and mother. *See* parents

fear: courage and, 2:199–203; of God, 2:265–69, 349–50nn229–30, 350n233; Jacob's fear of killing, violence, and military force as ethical legacy, 1:69–73

Fifth Commandment (honor your father and mother), 1:xi, 68, 169–74; 2:xiii

Finkel, R. Nosson Tzvi (the Alter of Slabodka), 1:203–4

First and Second Commandments (I am the Lord your God, thou shalt have no other Gods before me), 1:208, 256n112

first fruits, 1:22, 93, 134, 241n191; 2:71, 260, 262–63, 349nn218–19

Fiser, Karen, 2:59

Fishbane, Michael, 1:190–91; 2:313n168, 314n170, 314n172

Fleming, Erin, 1:54–55, 235n107

fleshpots of Egypt, nostalgic view of, 1:xi–xii, 155, 159–60; 2:xiii–xiv, 125, 148

Flood, the, 1:12–15; 2:26–27, 192

following hearts and eyes, 2:130–35

forgiveness: confession and, 2:82, 108–13; covenant dependent on repentance and, 2:70, 81–85; *teshuvah* (repentance) and, 1:206; 2:69–70, 111–12, 128, 224, 243–44, 270–74, 315n191, 350–52nn237–51. *See also* mercy

Fourth Commandment (Sabbath observance), 1:172–73

Fox, Everett, 2:39, 319n37

Frankel, R. Neta, of Kelm, 2:303n12

Freedman, David Noel, 1:236n117

freedom: authentic, 1:215–16; gratitude, relationship to, 1:128–33; liberation

from slavery and human responsibility, 1:155–58, 255n86; lost via sin, 1:140–43; love and respect for, 1:186–88; manumission of slaves, 1:150–51, 252n54; 2:232–33, 338–39n107; as spiritual project, 1:143; *tzimtzum* (divine self-contraction) and, 1:185–86

free will, 1:139–43, 185; 2:243–44

Fretheim, Terence: on Amalek and Amalekites, 2:256, 347n198; on commandment not to oppress widows and orphans, 1:183, 258n134; on Egypt as embodiment of chaos, 1:146; on ending of Torah before arrival in promised land, 1:136, 138; *Exodus* (1991), 1:266; 2:360; on extrapolating from specifics of biblical law, 1:183; on Fifth Commandment, 1:170; "Genesis: Introduction, Commentary and Reflections" in *New Interpreter's Bible* (1994), 1:265–66; 2:359–60; on holiness of Israel, 2:323n107; on Jacob, 1:66, 246n254; on Jeremiah and the Temple, 2:305n48; on Jewish and non-Jewish sources, dialogue between, 1:xxxiii; 2:xxxv; on Joseph, 1:84, 244n228; on manna in the desert, 1:162; on *mishkan* and Golden Calf incident, 1:196–97; on paradise, 1:192; on plundering of Egyptians, 1:152–53, 253n62; on preparation for wilderness sojourn, 2:124; on Rebekah inquiring of God, 1:234n104; on suffering, 1:193

Friedman, R. Alexander Zusia, 1:126

Friedman, Richard Elliot, 1:246n249, 261n186; 2:121, 340n125

fringes (tzitzit), 2:130–31, 133–34, 136–40, 322n99

Frisch, Amos, 2:153

Fromm, Erich, **1**:142, 143
fruitfulness of Israelites in Egypt and
   God's commitment to life, **1**:145, 146
Frymer-Kensky, Tikva, **1**:3, 21; **2**:43, 193, 235
fugitive slaves, **2**:250–54, 345n173,
   345n177, 346n182
future, openness of, **2**:242–44

Gad (tribe), **1**:29; **2**:179–84
Galpaz-Feller, Penina, **1**:252n54
Gane, Roy, **2**:36, 45, 120, 320n49; *Leviticus,*
   Numbers (2004), **1**:267, 268; **2**:361, 362
Gaonic period, **2**:72
Garden of Eden, **1**:189–93, 220, 258n148,
   259n155
Gawande, Atul, **1**:173–74
Gebiha b. Pesisa, **1**:150
Geertz, Clifford, **2**:8
genealogies, biblical, **1**:18–19
generosity: gift from the heart, importance of *mishkan* as, **1**:217–20; Jacob's
   lack of, **1**:64; paschal and thanksgiving sacrifices as part of, **1**:xii; **2**:xiv,
   16–19; of Rebekah, **1**:44, 46, 236n126
gentiles: God's love for, **2**:317n3; holiness of Israel versus, **2**:323n107;
   human responsibility of all nations,
   2:347n204; permitted to worship
   celestial bodies, **2**:317n11; universalism of Torah and, **2**:98–102; wisdom
   amongst, **1**:xii, 167–68; **2**:xiv
Gerondi, R. Nissim, **2**:262
Gerondi, R. Yonah (Rabbeinu Yonah/R.
   Jonah Gerondi), **1**:102; **2**:265
Gershom (son of Moses), **1**:22
Gersonides (Ralbag), **2**:202, 303n1
gerut (being a stranger), **1**:22, 23, 230n39
get (writ of divorce), issued by soldiers to
   their wives, **2**:13, 303n20
Gideon, **2**:245

gifts: Egyptian gift of hard labor, **2**:264;
   election as gift of love, **2**:143, 204–8;
   God as giver of, **2**:260; land of Israel
   as, **2**:264; leadership status as gift,
   2:141–45; *mishkan* as gift from the
   heart, **1**:217–20; priestly service as
   gift, **2**:141–45, 323n111
Ginzberg, Louis, *Legends of the Jews*
   (1969), **1**:265; **2**:359
God: anger of, **1**:261n186; blood of innocent victims crying out to, **2**:194;
   closeness and presence of, **1**:xxv–xxvi,
   184–88, 194–97; **2**:xvii–xviii, 216–17,
   218; commandment to love, **2**:63–65;
   compassion of, **1**:42; fear and awe of,
   2:265–69, 349–50nn229–30, 350n233;
   fugitive slaves compared to, **2**:251,
   346n179; gentiles, love for, **2**:317n3;
   gifts, as giver of, **2**:260; hardening
   heart of Pharaoh, **1**:139–43, 249n19,
   250n26, 250n29; human activities,
   service to God in, **2**:186–90; human
   creation in image of, **1**:xxvi, 7–11,
   229n8; **2**:xxviii, 192–94; *imitatio*
   dei, **1**:xxx, 124, 204; **2**:xxxii, 48, 233;
   inquiring directly of, **1**:54–55; interdependence, divine-human, **1**:164; judgment of, **1**:207–9, 261n189; **2**:242–44,
   291–92; life and human dignity,
   commitment to, **1**:xxiii–xxv, 145, 146;
   2:xxv–xxvii, 244; love of, **1**:xxii–xxiii,
   42, 57, 225n7; **2**:xxiv–xxv, 81–85, 204–
   8, 292, 299n7, 315n200; mercy of,
   1:12–15, 207–12; not reducible to ethics, **1**:226n21; parental role of, **2**:293–
   94, 300n21, 315n199; as personal God
   with a will who can make choices,
   2:207–8; providence of, Israel living by, **2**:225–29; as Rock, **2**:290–91,
   294, 355n296, 355n299; sanctifica-

tion of, **2**:31, 307n64; self-limitation attributed to, **1**:38; Shekhinah (Divine Presence) of, **1**:31–33, 37, 85, 99; **2**:195; as spouse, **2**:293; thanks and praise to, **2**:269, 350nn234–35; thirteen attributes of, **1**:207–9; Torah, seeking God's will through, **1**:54–59; trust in, learning, **1**:159–64; *tzimtzum* (divine self-contraction), **1**:184–88; vulnerable and oppressed, care for, **1**:xxiv–xxv, 177–83; **2**:xxvi–xxvii; words/breath of, **2**:47–48. *See also* obedience to God; relationship to God and fellow human beings; theophany

Golden Calf incident, **1**:xiv, 13, 38, 196–97, 203–6, 208; **2**:xvi, 122, 125, 220, 321n70, 336n55

Gombiner, R. Avraham Aveli, *Magen Avraham* (c. 1683), **1**:33

Gomorrah, **1**:29, 35, 36; **2**:84

Goodfriend, Elaine, **2**:39–40

Gordis, Robert, **2**:132–33

Gorman, Frank, **2**:38; *Leviticus: Divine Presence and Community* (1997), **1**:267; **2**:361

grain offering (*minhah*), **2**:15, 20

Granot, R. Tamir, **2**:354n282

gratitude: entitlement versus, **2**:260–64; Exodus as story of ingratitude and, **1**:128–33; **2**:124–29, 148–49; Leah's disappointment not precluding, **1**:62–63; for love, **2**:333n12; of Moses, **1**:249n14; thanksgiving offering and, **2**:16–19

Gray, John, **1**:5

Greenberg, Moshe, **1**:56–57, 151; **2**:194; *Understanding Exodus: A Holistic Commentary on Exodus 1–11* (2013), **1**:266; **2**:360

Greenberg, R. Yitz, **1**:xi, xvi; **2**:xiii, xviii, 68–70, 77, 352n252

grief and sorrow: death of Aaron's sons and expression of, **2**:31–36; Omer and, **2**:71–75

Gruber, Mayer, **2**:58–59

grudges, holding, **2**:152–57

Haag, Herbert, **1**:247n270

Ha-Darshan, R. Moshe, **2**:186

haftarah, **1**:86, 240n183; **2**:20, 22, 54, 163, 174, 178

Hagar, **1**:xxv, 23–24, 40–42, 49–50, 54, 61, 109, 244n230; **2**:xxvii

hak'hel, **2**:275–79, 353n264

hakhnasat orchim. See hospitality

HaKohen, R. Eliyahu, of Izmir, **1**:102

HaKohen, R. Yissachar Berman, **1**:237n140

halakhah, **1**:170–71, 256n109; **2**:296

halfheartedness, **1**:79–82

Halivni, David Weiss, **1**:235n111

Hall, Douglas, **1**:192–93

R. Hama b. Abba, **2**:72

R. Hama b. Hanina, **2**:49–50

Haman, **2**:181–82, 257, 258

hamas, **1**:114, 119, 247n270

HaMeiri, R. Menachem, **1**:243n211

Hamilton, Victor, **1**:28, 65–66, 150, 194–95, 247n261, 247n265, 252n57, 252n63, 256n116; *The Book of Genesis* (1995), **1**:266; **2**:360; *Exodus: An Exegetical Commentary* (2011), **1**:267; **2**:361

Hamor, **1**:114, 116

R. Hananel, **1**:151

hands, raising, as prayer gesture, **1**:56, 235–36nn115–16

R. Hanina b. Hama, **2**:77

R. Hanina b. Pazi, **1**:219

Hannah, **1**:230n42

Haran, Menahem, **1**:197

Hartman, David, **1**:37–38

Hasidic masters, **1**:137; **2**:67, 96, 166, 170, 259, 272, 277, 283

Hasidic thought, **2**:335n53, 348n213

HaTazarfati, R. Vidal, **1**:234n102, 238n164

"Hatikvah" (Israel's national anthem), **2**:167

Hazael, **2**:177–78

heart: biblical motif of hardening, **1**:250n27; in biblical thinking, **1**:262n204; **2**:221; circumcision of, **2**:82, 220–24, 336n64, 351n247; following eyes and, **2**:130–35; God hardening heart of Pharaoh, **1**:139–43, 249n19, 250n26, 250n29; halfheartedness and wholeheartedness, **1**:79–82; *mishkan* as gift from, **1**:217–20; Ten Commandments intended to straighten, **1**:xxx, **2**:xxxii

heaven: *mishkan* and Garden of Eden, parallels between, **1**:189–93; origins of Torah in, **1**:xxi, **2**:xxiii; Shabbat as anticipatory glimpse of, **1**:xxxi; **2**:xxxiii, 76–80

Hebron, **2**:126–27

Held, Shai: *Abraham Joshua Heschel: The Call of Transcendence* (2013), **1**:xvi, **2**:xviii; *The Heart of Torah* (2017), **1**:xi–xvi; **2**:xiii–xviii

Heschel, R. Abraham Joshua: on commandment not to oppress widows and orphans, **1**:182; on covetousness, **2**:213; "a Jew without the Torah is obsolete," **2**:96; on love of God, **1**:58; on pious abuse, **2**:106; on prayer, **1**:224; on presence of God in Bible, **1**:xxi, 225n1; **2**:xxiii, 299n1; on "way of expediency" and "way of wonder," **2**:143–44; on words creating worlds, **2**:47

Hezekiah, **2**:242

R. Hezekiah b. Manoah (Hizkuni), **1**:251n51; **2**:142, 303n11

Hiebert, Paula, **1**:179

High Priest, **1**:189; **2**:35, 44, 138–40, 142, 171–72, 194, 323n109, 327n169

Hirsch, R. Samson Raphael, **1**:265; **2**:56, 116, 142–43, 310n127, 359

Hirshman, Marc, **2**:99

R. Hiyya b. Abba, **1**:58–59

R. Hiyya b. Avin, **2**:72

Hizkuni (R. Hezekiah b. Manoah), **1**:251n51; **2**:142, 303n11

Holdin, Judah, **2**:355n288

holiness: call to, **2**:136–40, 323n107; egalitarian versus hierarchical vision of, **2**:323n109; of Israel versus all peoples, **2**:323n107

Holocaust (Shoah), **1**:72, 176; **2**:258

Honi, **2**:288

honoring parents (Fifth Commandment), **1**:xi, 68, 169–74; **2**:xiii

hope in a hopeless world, **1**:xxx–xxxi, 76–80, 223–24; **2**:xxxii–xxxiii, 124–29

Horeb, **2**:176, 199, 275–76, 328n182. *See also* Sinai

Horowitz, R. Isaiah (the Shelah), **2**:96

horses, prohibition on excess of, **2**:246–47, 343n157

Hosea (prophet), **1**:xxii, 67; **2**:xxiv, 83–85, 292

Hosea (son of Nun). *See* Joshua

hospitality (*hakhnasat orchim*): of Abraham, **1**:xiii, 31–34, 45; **2**:xv; Edom's failure of, **2**:152–57; Jacob's lack of, **1**:64; Moses and requirements of, **1**:130–32; religious weight of, **1**:xii–xiii; **2**:xiv–xv

Houston, Walter, **2**:231, 338n95

Houtman, Cornelius, **2**:256

human activities, service to God in, **2**:186–90

human complexity, **1**:43, 47–48

human creation in image of God, 1:xxvi, 7–11, 229n8; 2:xxviii, 192–94

human dignity: absence of missionary thrust in Judaism and, 2:102; *Akedah* and, 1:xxiii; 2:xxv; of children, 2:252; God's affirmation of life and, 1:xxiii–xxv, 145, 146; 2:xxv–xvii, 244; hope in a hopeless world for, 1:xxx–xxxi, 76; 2:xxxii–xxxiii; ingratitude blinding us to, 1:132; memory and empathy intensifying commitment to, 1:175; of persons with disabilities, 2:57–60, 310–11nn126–27, 311n131, 311n134, 312nn138–40; Shabbat reinforcing, 1:xxiv, 214; 2:xxvi; slaves' recovery of, 1:151, 156; speech and, 2:50; standing upright and, 2:82, 86–89, 316n208, 316n210; of women, 2:235–39; of work versus slavery, 1:213–16

human equality, 2:79–80, 230–31, 248–49, 279

human imperfection, 2:161–62, 163–67

humanism, Jewish, 1:xxxii; 2:xxxiv

human progress, 1:3–6

human responsibility, 1:xxvi–xxix; 2:xxviii–xxx; of all nations, 2:347n204; in Cain and Abel story, 1:88–90, 92; Creation, stewardship over, 1:8–11; election and service, relationship between, 1:83–87, 240n185; Jacob's betrayal of Esau and, 1:64–68; Judah's moral and spiritual development and, 1:90–93; kingship, biblical view of, 1:9–10; liberation from slavery and, 1:155–58, 255n86; memory and empathy fueling, 1:174–78; 2:325n141; of Miriam, 1:92; for the poor, 2:234; radical democratization of, 1:181; in Torah and Torah commentary, 1:xxvi–xxix; 2:xxviii–xxxi;

for vulnerable and oppressed, 1:xxvii, 175, 179–83; 2:xix

human rights, 1:xiv, xxiv–xxv; 2:xvi, xxvi–xxvii

human stewardship over Creation, 1:8–11, 229n19

human uniqueness and individuality, 1:16–20; 2:93–98, 317n2

humiliation: of Dinah, 1:115; Jewish ethical prohibition on, 1:99–103; Joseph and Tamar compared, 1:103, 242n210

humility of Moses, 2:119–20

R. Huna, 2:131

Hutner, R. Yitzhak, 2:166

hypocrisy, religious, and sacrifice, 2:20–25, 82, 163–64

Ibn Attar, R. Hayyim, 1:253n68; 2:249, 344n171

Ibn Ezra, R. Abraham: on ability to teach what one knows, 1:220, 262n206; on commandment not to oppress widows or orphans, 1:180–81, 257n119; on covetousness, 2:211; on dependence, 2:337n83; on following heart and eyes, 2:131; on God hardening heart of Pharaoh, 1:139–40; on human responsibility, 1:xxvii; 2:xix; on human sovereignty over Creation, 1:10; on Joseph and Potiphar's wife, 1:239n176; on Joshua, 2:353n272; on juxtaposition of Amalekites and visit of Jethro, 1:166; on kings and kingship, 2:343n148; on manna in the desert, 1:161; on *metzora*, 2:45; non-Jewish sources, in dialogue with, 1:xxxiii; 2:xxxv; on prayer of Moses, 2:320n54; on purpose of Ten Commandments, 1:xxx; 2:xxxii; on raising hands as prayer gesture, 1:235n115;

Ibn Ezra, R. Abraham (*continued*)
on sins of leaders, **2**:303n11; on tzitzit
and *sha'atnez*, **2**:137; on work left to do
after Creation, **2**:314n185
Ibn Gabirol, Solomon, **1**:109
Ibn Habib, R. Jacob, **1**:201
idolatry: Asherah, **2**:247; Baal and Baal-
peor, **2**:22, 84, 125, 174, 177, 247; burning of gods of Canaan, **2**:209; First
and Second Commandments (I am
the Lord your God, thou shalt have no
other Gods before me), **1**:208; Golden
Calf incident, **1**:xiv, 13, 38, 196–97,
203–6, 208; **2**:xvi, 122, 125, 220,
321n70, 336n55; Israel having no need
for, **2**:217; stubbornness worse than,
1:203–6; as taking metaphors for God
literally, **2**:293
image of God, human creation in, **1**:xxvi,
7–11, 229n8; **2**:xviii, 192–94
imitatio dei (imitation of God), **1**:xxx, 124,
204; **2**:xxxii, 48, 233
imperfection, human, **2**:161–62, 163–67
impulsiveness and recklessness, **1**:93–98
impurity. *See* purification and purity laws
incense burning, **1**:261n175
individuals, uniqueness of, **1**:16–20;
2:93–98, 317n2
innocent blood, prohibition on shedding, **2**:191–95
innui (being a slave), **1**:22, 23, 230n39
integrity, religious, and sacrifice, **2**:20–
25, 82, 163–64
interest rates, **1**:243n225
Isaac (son of Abraham): *Akedah*, **1**:xiii,
28, 32, 40–42, 45, 76; **2**:xv; birth,
announcement of, **1**:36, 39, 49; blindness of, **1**:46; burial site of, **1**:62; covenant with, **2**:82, 204, 286; Hagar
found by, **1**:40–42; Manasseh, plead-

ing for, **1**:75, 76; marriage of Rebekah
and, **1**:43–48, 51–53, 234n102; passivity
of, **1**:52–53; traumatized nature of,
1:41, 44; tricked into blessing Jacob
instead of Esau, **1**:46–47, 52, 65, 116
R. Isaac, **1**:137, 142
R. Isaac b. Marion, **1**:79–82
R. Isaac of Corbeil, **2**:210–11
R. Isaac of Worka, **2**:277
Isaiah (prophet): on defeat of sea mon-
sters, **2**:5, 73–74; on end of warring,
1:71, 72; **2**:27–28, 29, 306n59; on fast-
ing, **2**:54–55; on God's intentions,
2:293; on military force, **2**:246–47;
mission of, **2**:120; on return to Gar-
den of Eden, **1**:190; on ruler for Israel,
2:215; universalism and, **2**:100–102
R. Isaiah di Trani, **1**:235n115
Ishmael, **1**:49, 50
Ishmaelites, **1**:79
ISIS, **2**:258
Israel (as name for Jacob), **1**:67
Israel (land/people), **1**:89; **2**:152, 154, 163,
179–84, 204, 228–29, 251, 264, 319n44
Israel (state), **1**:71–73; **2**:167, 195
Isserles, R. Moses, **1**:172
Izhar, **2**:145

Jacob: barrenness of Rachel and, **1**:50–
51; blessed after dream, **1**:89; censure of sons, **1**:70, 93, 114, 241n189,
241n191; concubines of, **1**:93, 94, 95,
98, 219; covenant with, **2**:82, 204,
286; death and burial of Rachel and,
1:74–75, 238n157; death of, **1**:112;
directly communicating with God,
1:54; Edom's hostility to Israel and,
2:152, 154–56; Esau's birthright and
blessing taken by, **1**:46–47, 53, 64–
68, 236n130; **2**:154–55; favoritism

regarding children, **1**:83–84, 95–96, 100, 109, 246n252; fear of killing, violence, and military force as ethical legacy of, **1**:69–73; human responsibility as theme of Torah and, **1**:xxvii; **2**:xxix; as journeyer, **1**:234n89; Judah and Benjamin in Egypt and, **1**:90–91, 100; Manasseh, pleading for, **1**:75, 76; marriage to Leah, **1**:60–63, 66–67, 94–95; marriage to Rachel, **1**:50–52, 60–63, 66–67, 95–96; name(s) of, **1**:65, 67–68; rape of Dinah and, **1**:114–19, 246–47nn252–54; Reuben judged by, **1**:93–98, 241n189, 241n191; reunion with Esau, **1**:69, 70, 71, 76, 95; **2**:154; supposed death of Joseph and, **1**:67, 75, 91; wrestling with angel, **1**:118

R. Jacob b. Asher, **2**:313n161

Jacob, R. Benno, **1**:153–54, 227n49; **2**:301n49, 347n201, 347n203

Jacobs, R. Louis, **1**:137; **2**:349n228

Janzen, Gerald, **1**:152–53, 162, 253n64

Jephthah, **2**:170–72, 326–27nn167–69

Jephunneh, **2**:282

Jeremiah (prophet), **1**:41, 67, 75; **2**:20–25, 223–24, 242–44, 305n31, 330n213, 342n135, 342n138

Jerusalem, **2**:23, 241–42, 276

Jesus, **1**:177; **2**:101

Jethro, **1**:125, 130–31, 133, 165–68; **2**:153, 332n1

Jezebel, **2**:174, 175–76, 212

Job (biblical character), **2**:34, 123, 316n218

Joel (prophet), **1**:209; **2**:117

Jonah (prophet), **1**:209–12; **2**:150, 243–44, 342nn141–42

Jordan River, **2**:179, 180, 276, 280, 286

Jordan Valley, **1**:29–30

Joseph: appearance, attention to, **1**:84, 85, 239n174; birth of, **1**:74; brothers decid-ing to kill, **1**:79–80, 97; brothers in Egypt and, **1**:79–80, 100–103, 109–13; brothers selling into slavery, **1**:79, 84, 90, 91, 110; divine providence in story of, **1**:240n181; Egyptians enslaved by, **1**:104–8, 243n218, 244n230, 248n9; election of, **1**:84, 239n173; famine in Egypt, handling of, **1**:104–8; favoritism of Jacob regarding, **1**:83, 95–96, 246n252; Jacob's reaction to supposed death of, **1**:67, 75, 91; moral and spiritual development of, **1**:xv, 83–87, 109–13; **2**:xvii; ornamental tunic of, **1**:67, 83–84, 91; Pharaoh and, **1**:84, 86, 128–30; Potiphar and Potiphar's wife, **1**:84–85, 110, 239n175, 239n177; Quran, **1**:248n10; restraint, exercise of, **1**:109–13, 245n238; Tamar compared, **1**:103, 242n210; as viceroy in Egypt, **1**:90–91; **2**:215–16

Joshua: Amalekites, defeat of, **2**:255, 256; Caleb compared, **2**:281–84, 354n282; as leader after Moses, **2**:116–17, 170, 280–84, 288, 353n271, 353n273; name changed from Hosea son of Nun, **2**:283; reticence of, **2**:282–84, 354n283; seventy elders appointed by Moses and, **2**:114–18; significance of arrival in promised land, **1**:255n86; Sinai, allowed to go part way up, **1**:195; spies sent to survey the land and, **2**:127–28, 134, 281–82

R. Joshua b. Korhah, **2**:201

R. Joshua b. Levi, **2**:105–6

R. Joshua of Sikhnin, **1**:78

journey rather than arrival, stress on, **1**:134–38

joy and joyousness, **1**:81, 137; **2**:17, 66–70, 130–35

Judah (kingdom), **2**:241–43

Judah (son of Jacob and Leah), 1:62, 63,
    90–93, 97–98, 99–101, 110, 112
Judah (tribe), 1:157, 219, 238n151
R. Judah, 1:xv, 32, 157; 2:xvii
R. Judah b. Ilai, 1:69, 71
R. Judah the Patriarch, 2:297
judgment of God, 1:207–9, 261n189;
    2:242–44, 291–92
justice: importance of arguing for, 1:35–
    39; judges appointed by Moses and,
    2:199–203; of laws of Israel, 2:215,
    217; Moses' concern for, 1:123–25

Kabbalah, 1:184; 2:67, 96
Kaminsky, Joel, 1:84, 86, 239n171
Kamionkowski, Tamar, 2:62, 65
Kaplan, Mordecai, 1:250n21
Karaites, 2:155
kavod (respect), 2:60
Keil, Carl Friedrich, 1:142
Keturah, 1:41
Kiddush, 2:67
Kidner, Derek, 1:4–5; 2:21, 302n34,
    335n45
Kierkegaard, Søren, 1:xii–xiii, 32, 231n52;
    2:xiv–xv
kil'ayim (prohibition on mixing different
    kinds), 2:136
killel (insult), 2:60
killing. See murder, killing, violence, and
    military force
Kimelman, Reuven, 2:178, 314n172,
    329n193
Kimhi, R. David (Radak): on Joseph and
    Potiphar's wife, 1:85, 239n176; on
    Joseph's enslavement of Egypt, 1:105–
    6, 243n221, 244n230; on love of Isaac
    for Rebekah, 1:52; on meaning of "all
    flesh," 2:319n44; on work left to do
    after Creation, 2:314n185

King, Martin Luther, Jr., 2:288
King James Bible, 1:31, 229n14, 232n61
kings and kingship: biblical view of,
    1:9–10; 2:245–49; foreign kings over
    Israel, prohibition of, 2:247; law,
    faithfulness to, 2:247–49; military
    power and, 2:246–47, 343n157; mul-
    tiple marriages and foreign wives,
    dangers of, 2:246, 247; in Near East-
    ern myth and society, 1:7–8, 180;
    2:246, 248; wealth of, 2:247. See also
    specific kings
Klitsner, Judy, 1:19, 234n99
Knowles, Michael, 2:355n299
Kohath, 2:145
Kohelet, 2:70, 130–35, 313n159, 322n84,
    322n93
Kohn, Risa Levitt, 1:247n265
Kook, R. Abraham Isaac, 1:71–73; 2:188–
    90
Kook, R. Zvi Yehudah, 1:73
Korah, 2:136, 139–40, 145, 181–82, 323n109
korban hattat ("sin offering" or purgation
    offering), 2:37, 39
korban olah (burnt offerings), 2:20, 22, 37
korban tamid (perpetual offering), 1:199–
    200, 201–2
korban todah (thanksgiving offering),
    1:xii; 2:xiv, 15–19
Kotzker, the (R. Menaham Mendel of
    Kotzk), 1:137; 2:166, 170
Kugel, James, 1:239nn174–75, 257n128
Kynes, Will, 2:134

Laban, 1:60, 66–67, 116, 237n134
land of milk and honey, 1:135, 138; 2:124,
    126, 134, 227, 260, 263, 281
language. See words/speech
Lapsley, Jacqueline, 2:62–64, 161
Lauer, Levi, 1:xxi; 2:xxiii

laws and obedience to them: consequences of disobedience, **2**:265; *halakhah*, **1**:170–71, 256n109; **2**:296; imperfection of human laws, **2**:253; importance of king's faithfulness to, **2**:247–49; Moses on, **2**:215–19, 226–27; preoccupation with, **2**:335nn52–53

leadership: of Caleb, **2**:281–84; courage and, **2**:199–203; in Deuteronomy versus Exodus, **2**:332n1; failures of Moses and Aaron as failure of, **2**:150–51; as gift and as act of giving, **2**:141–45; Joshua appointed as leader after Moses, **2**:116–17, 170, 280–84, 288, 353n271, 353n273; of Moses, **1**:123–27, 132; **2**:114–18; power and sins, leaders dealing with, **2**:9–14; recklessness of Reuben disqualifying him for, **1**:93–98, 241n189; requirements for, **1**:xiii; **2**:xv; seventy elders appointed by Moses, **2**:114–18

Leah, **1**:60–63, 66, 75–78, 94–95, 116, 237n134, 242nn199–200; **2**:350n234

leftovers from thanksgiving offering, requirement to burn, **2**:15–19

Leibowitz, Nehama, **1**:117, 149, 231n43, 265; **2**:95, 163, 351n240, 359

Leibowitz, Yeshayahu, **2**:139–40, 323n107

Lemekh, **1**:xxviii, 4–5; **2**:xxx

leprosy, **2**:42, 43, 50

Lerner, Berel Dov, **1**:244n230

leshon hara (tongue of evil), **2**:50

Levenson, Jon D.: on Abraham, Lot, and *Akedah*, **1**:28; "Genesis" in *Oxford Jewish Study Bible* (2004), **1**:266; **2**:360; on Joseph's enslavement of Egypt, **1**:106; Kierkegaard and, **1**:231n52; on kingship, **2**:249, 343n155; on Leviticus making order out of chaos, **2**:3–5; on *mishkan*, **1**:222–24; on order out of

chaos, **2**:3–5; on Pharaoh of Exodus, **1**:249n19; on the Temple, **2**:305n44, 305n47; on universalism, **2**:102

Levi (son of Jacob and Leah), **1**:61, 70, 114–19, 241n185, 246–47nn252–57, 247n261; **2**:145

R. Levi, **1**:78

Leviathan, **2**:5

Levine, Baruch, **2**:15, 20, 29, 33, 38, 83, 307n64, 307n69; *Leviticus* (2003), **1**:267; **2**:361

Levinson, Bernard, **2**:236

Levirate marriage (brother required to marry widow of deceased brother), **1**:91, 99–100; **2**:303n20

Levites, **2**:141, 148

Levi Yitzhak of Berditchev, **2**:96–97, 259

Levovitz, R. Yeruham, **1**:xxiv, 82; **2**:xxvi, 56, 310n124

lex talionis (eye for an eye), **1**:5

liberation/liberty. *See* freedom

Lichtenstein, R. Eliezer Lipman, **2**:32

life and human dignity, God's commitment to, **1**:xxiii–xxv, 145, 146; **2**:xxv–xvii, 244

lifnim mishurat hadin, **2**:30

lighting in *mishkan*, **1**:191, 198–99, 260n174

linen and wool, cloth combining (*sha'atnez*), **2**:136–40

Lipton, Diana, **2**:348n205

loans, **2**:230

Loew, R. Judah, of Prague (Maharal), **1**:232n62; *Netivot Olam* (c. 1595), **1**:32–33

Lohr, Joel, **2**:334n23

Longman, Tremper, **1**:255n106; **2**:322n93

Lopatin, Jon, **2**:338n91

Lot, **1**:26–30, 231n44, 231–32nn58–59; **2**:206–7, 330n207 love: of Aaron, **2**:106; election as gift of, **2**:143; freedom of others, respect for, **1**:186–88; for God, **2**:63–65; of God, **1**:xxii–xxiii, 42, 57, 225n7; **2**:xxiv–xxv, 81–85, 204–8, 292, 299n7, 315n200; gratitude for, **2**:333n12; of Isaac for Rebekah, **1**:51–52; of Jacob for Rachel and not Leah, **1**:60–63; of neighbor, **1**:xiii, xxx, xxxii, 33–34, 177, 201, 206; **2**:xv, xxxii, xxxiv, 61–65; of strangers, **1**:xxix–xxx, 175–78; **2**:xxxi–xxxii, 62–63; willingness to express, **2**:318n32

lovingkindness (*hesed*), **1**:xiv, xxx, 43, 45, 76, 208, 295–98; **2**:xvi, xxxii, 189, 356n317

Lundbom, Jack R., **1**:262n204; **2**:335n43

Luntschitz, R. Shlomo Ephraim, **2**:53, 103, 278, 303n13, 351n243

Luria, R. Isaac (the ARI), **1**:184–85

Luther, Martin, **2**:350n235

Luzzatto, R. Moshe Chaim (Ramhal), **2**:267–68, 349n229, 350n230, 350n233

Luzzatto, Samuel David (Shadal), **1**:253n63; **2**:147

MacDonald, Nathan, **2**:154

Mack, Hananel, **2**:172–73

Maharal. *See* Loew, R. Judah, of Prague (Maharal)

Maimonides (Rambam): on action and emotion, **2**:64, 312n149; on commandment not to oppress widows or orphans, **1**:179–80; on confession, **2**:110–11; on covetousness, **2**:210, 211; on cultivating good character, **1**:204–6; on cursing the deaf, **2**:58, 60; on free will, **1**:139–43; on generosity at festivals, **2**:17; on God acting in natural world, **1**:251n34; *Guide of the Perplexed*, **1**:7, 8, 141; **2**:185–86;

on holiness, **2**:322n106; on Isaiah, **2**:306n59; on kings and kingship, **2**:343n148; *Mishneh Torah*, **1**:116, 139, 180, 205–6, 233n77; **2**:17, 110, 111, 188, 210, 268, 306n59, 322n106, 334n29, 340n123; naturalism of, **1**:250n21; on purpose in every story in Torah, **2**:185; on reasons for serving God, **2**:268, 350n232; on recounting of rest stops in wilderness in Numbers, **2**:185–89; on repentance, **2**:351n244; *Sefer HaMitzvot*, **1**:204, 205; **2**:60, 343n148; on Simeon and Levi's murder of Shechem and city residents, **1**:116; on use of non-Jewish sources, **1**:xxxii–xxxiii; **2**:xxxiv–xxxv

Makhpelah, cave of, **1**:74

Malamat, Abraham, **2**:61–62, 312n141

Malbim (R. Meir Leibush Weiser), **1**:218, 262n205, 265; **2**:228–29, 270–71, 351n240, 359

Manasseh, **1**:75

mandrakes, **1**:94–95, 242n199

manna, **1**:xxii, 159–64, 244n230, 254n79; **2**:xxiv, 225, 227, 306n54

manumission of slaves, **1**:150–51, 252n54; **2**:232–33, 338n107

Marmorstein, Arthur, **2**:317n10

marriage: of Abraham and Sarah, **1**:49–50, 234n101; captive brides, **1**:xxi; **2**:xxiii, 236–38, 340–41nn124–31; discouraged during Omer, **2**:72; *get* (writ of divorce) issued by soldiers to their wives, **2**:13, 303n20; God as spouse, **2**:293; of Isaac and Rebekah, **1**:43–48, 51–53, 234n102; of Jacob and Leah, **1**:60–63, 66–67, 94–95; of Jacob and Rachel, **1**:50–52, 60–63, 66–67, 95–96; kings, multiple marriages and foreign wives of, **2**:246, 247; Levirate (brother required

to marry widow of deceased brother),
1:91, 99–100; 2:303n20; of Moses to
Cushite woman, 2:50, 119; mutual
commitment in, 1:201; of woman
slaves, 1:xiv; 2:xvi, 236–38, 340n124
"La Marseillaise," 2:167
Masoretic text, 1:37, 243n218; 2:305n42,
315n201
material well-being versus materialism,
1:xiii, 26–30; 2:xv, 181–84
Mathys, H. P., 2:312n141
R. Mattena, 2:98
McCarthy, Carmel, 1:232n68
McFague, Sallie, 2:292
McKane, William, 2:335n45
means not justified by ends, 1:xxvii; 2:xix
Mecklenberg, R. Ya'akov Zvi, 1:236n130;
    Ha-Ketav V-ha-Kabbalah (1839), 1:65
Meidad, 2:114–15, 117–18, 320n46
R. Meir, 1:157
mekhoroteihem, 1:114, 237n141, 245n245
melakhah, 1:215
memory: as double-edged sword, 2:156;
    Edom's hostility to Israelites and,
    2:152–57; human responsibility,
    memory and empathy fueling, 1:174–
    78; 2:325n141; importance in biblical
    theology, 2:156
Mendel, R. Menahem, of Kotzk (the Kot-
    zker), 1:137; 2:166, 170
Mendel, R. Menahem, of Rimanov (the
    Rimanover), 2:283, 354n280
menorah, as tree of life, 1:191
mercy: of God, 1:12–15, 207–12; impor-
    tance of arguing for justice and, 1:35–
    39; Jonah's anger about, 1:207–12;
    judgment not precluded by, 1:207–9,
    261n189; as reward for compassion,
    1:75–78; thirteen attributes of God
    and, 1:207–9

Meribah, 2:150, 285
Merton, Thomas, 2:165–66
Mesopotamian myth and society. *See*
    Near Eastern myth and society
Messiah, 1:xxviii, 6; 2:xxx
metaphors, theological, 2:290–94
metzora (one afflicted with a scaly skin
    disease), 1:xxi; 2:xxiii, 42–46, 50–51,
    120–21, 308n99, 309n95, 309n103
Meyers, Carol, 1:191, 254n79
Micah (prophet), 2:163, 164–65, 212, 241–
    42, 247
Middle Eastern myth and society. *See*
    Near Eastern myth and society
Middleton, J. Richard, 1:229n8
Midian and Midianites, 1:79, 123, 130–31;
    2:168, 169, 174
Migdol, 2:185
Mikra'ot Gedolot, 1:265; 2:359
mikveh (gatherings), 1:147
Milgrom, Jacob: on Balaam, 2:159; on
    confession rather than sacrifice, 2:82;
    on efficaciousness of rituals, 2:109;
    on Garden of Eden and *mishkan*,
    1:259n155; on holiness, 2:323n109;
    on injuries/insults to persons with
    disabilities, 2:58; Jewish and non-
    Jewish sources, dialogue between,
    1:xxxiii; 2:xxxv; on *korban hattat* ("sin
    offering" or purgation offering),
    2:39; *Leviticus* (2001), 1:267; 2:361;
    *Leviticus: A Book of Ritual and Eth-
    ics* (2004), 1:267; 2:361; on love and
    action, 2:313n152; *Numbers* (2003),
    1:267; 2:361; on prayer of Moses for
    Miriam, 2:121; on Reubenites and
    Gadites, 2:330n200; on seventy elders
    appointed by Moses, 2:114–15; on
    sha'atnez, 2:137–38; on spies sent to
    survey the land, 2:130, 353n278; on

Milgrom, Jacob (*continued*)
threefold priestly blessing, **2**:103; on
wronged person as only person who
can forgive afflicted, **2**:320n51
military force. *See* murder, killing, violence, and military force
milk and honey, land of, **1**:135, 138; **2**:124,
126, 134, 227, 260, 263, 281
Miller, Patrick, **1**:xxxiii, 173; **2**:xxxv, 199,
207, 218, 227, 280, 285, 287, 334n23;
Deuteronomy (1990), **1**:268; **2**:362
minhah (grain offering), **2**:15, 20
Miriam, **1**:92; **2**:43, 50–51, 119–21, 320n47,
320n50
mishkan: as counterworld to lived reality, **1**:xxxi, 223–24; **2**:xxxiii, 7–8, 77;
covenantal mutuality and, **1**:198–202;
Creation, parallels between building of *mishkan* and, **1**:221–24; death
of Aaron's sons and, **2**:31–32, 34–35;
encroachment on, responsibility for,
2:141; as Garden of Eden, **1**:189–93,
220, 258n148, 259n155; as gift from the
heart, **1**:217–20; Golden Calf incident
and, **1**:196–97; *korban tamid* (perpetual
offering) in, **1**:199–200, 201–2; lights
in, **1**:191, 198–99, 260n174; Moses and
building of, **1**:184–85, 191, 194–96, 198–
200, 214, 217–19, 221; Nahshon bringing first sacrifice to, **1**:158; as ordered
space, **2**:7; proximity to God in, **1**:194–
97; purification of, **2**:52–56; Shabbat
and, **1**:214, 222; **2**:76–77, 80; Tent of
Meeting and, **1**:195, 197, 221; **2**:32, 114,
146, 149, 281, 353n273; *tzimtzum* (divine
self-contraction) and, **1**:184–85; work,
recovery of human dignity of, **1**:214–15
missionary thrust, Jewish absence of,
2:102
Mithra temple, Dura, **2**:352n257

mitzvot (commandments): as God's face,
1:56; good character versus good
behavior, **1**:203–6; Maimonides' enumeration (613) of, **1**:204; priority of
love over, **1**:xxii; **2**:xxiv; of procreation, incumbent on men but not
women, **2**:40; Shabbat as, **1**:xxiv;
2:xvi; spiritual dimensions not over-
riding or negating performance obligations, **2**:222; walking in God's ways,
what constitutes, **1**:205–6; wholeheartedness and joy in performing,
1:79, 81. *See also* Ten Commandments;
specific mitzvot
Moab and Moabites, **1**:29; **2**:158–59, 168,
206–7, 276
Moberly, Walter (R. W. L.), **1**:15, 208,
240n185; **2**:160–61, 333n12, 342n135
monarchy. *See* kings and kingship
money. *See* wealth and money
morality and ethics: as action and emotion, **1**:xxx; **2**:xxxii, 61–65, 113; character, focus on, **1**:xxx, 203–6; **2**:xxxii,
336n54; charity, as social ethic, **2**:230–
34, 338n95; cultural progress and,
1:xxviii, 3–6; **2**:xxx; development, moral
and spiritual, in Torah commentary,
1:xiv–xv; **2**:xvi–xvii; God not reducible to, **1**:226n21; **2**:300n21; humiliation, prohibition of, **1**:99–103; killing,
violence, and military force, **1**:69–73;
memory and empathy fueling human
responsibility, **1**:174–78; Musar (Jewish ethics and moral self-cultivation),
1:xxiv, 33, 81–82; **2**:xxvi; obedience to
God and ethical responsibilities, **1**:xiii,
32–34, 226n21; **2**:xv, 300n21; piety and,
2:55–56. *See also* human responsibility;
Ten Commandments
Moriah, **1**:40

Moses: Aaron setting out to meet, **1**:80; adjudication between fellow Israelites in Egypt, **1**:123; Amalekites, defeat of, **2**:255–56; beating of Israelite, interference with, **1**:123; burning bush and, **1**:126, 130, 149–50; census taken by, **2**:93, 95; on circumcision of the heart, **2**:220–22; compassion of, **1**:123–26; complaining of Israelites in wilderness and, **2**:124–26; covenant of God with, **1**:135; on covetousness, **2**:209; Cushite woman, marriage to, **2**:50, 119; death before arrival in promised land, **1**:138; **2**:146–51, 280, 285–89, 295–96, 353n271; death of Aaron's sons and, **2**:31–36; divine attributes of God recited to, **1**:207; divinely bestowed nature of elevated status, **2**:142; Edom's hostility to Israelites and, **2**:152–55; Elijah compared, **2**:176–77; Golden Calf incident and, **1**:xiv, 13, 38, 196–97, 203–6, 208; **2**:xvi, 122, 125, 220, 321n70, 336n55; gratitude of, **1**:128–33, 249n14; high priest, plate or frontlet for, **2**:138; human responsibility as theme of Torah and, **1**:xxvii; **2**:xxix; humility of, **2**:119–20; Joshua appointed as leader after, **2**:116–17, 170, 280–84, 288, 353n271, 353n273; judges appointed by, **2**:199–203; judicial system set up by, **1**:165–68; justice, concern for, **1**:123–25; Korah's challenge to, **2**:136, 139–40, 145; on laws and obedience to them, **2**:215–19; as leader, **1**:123–27, 132; **2**:114–18; Manasseh, pleading for, **1**:75, 76; manna in the desert and, **1**:159–62; mercy of God, appealing to, **1**:13, 38, 39; Miriam watching out for, **1**:92; *mishkan*, building of, **1**:184–85, 191, 194–96, 198–200,

214, 217–19, 221; moral and spiritual development of, **1**:xv; **2**:xvii; Moshe Rabbeinu as name for, **2**:97; on not living by bread alone, **2**:225–29; people inquiring of God through, **1**:55; Pharoah, sent to confront, **1**:80, 126, 128–33, 139–41, 213; plundering of Egyptians and, **1**:149–50, 153; practical fruits of encounter with God on Sinai, **1**:xxix; **2**:xxxi; prayer for those who hurt and disappoint him, **2**:119–23; presence of God, Israelite concern about, **1**:194; on prophets and prophecy, **2**:240–41; pursuit of Israelites by Pharoah, response to, **1**:155–57; on reading of the Teaching, **2**:275–77; Reubenites' and Gadites' request to stay in Transjordan and, **1**:29; **2**:179–84; self-doubt and anxiety of, **1**:80, 126, 130; seventy elders appointed by, **2**:114–18; on Shabbat, **2**:76; as shepherd, **1**:125; shepherds mistreating Midianite women, intervention in, **1**:123–24; skin disease suffered by Miriam and Aaron, **2**:43, 50–51, 120–21, 320n50; Song of, **2**:290–94; spies sent to survey the land by, **2**:126–29, 130, 134, 148, 281–82, 321n70; splitting the sea, **2**:256; standing upright and, **2**:87–89; stranger, self-recognition as, **1**:22; as teacher of Torah, **2**:96–97; threefold priestly blessing and, **2**:103; visit of Jethro juxtaposed with Amalekite conflict, **1**:165–68; "wandering Aramean" liturgy introduced by, **2**:262; warned not to harass Edomites and Moabites, **2**:206; water struck from rock by, **2**:146–51, 285, 324n132

Moses ben Maimon. *See* Maimonides (Rambam)

mother and father. *See* parents
Mount Carmel, **2**:174–76
Mount Nebo, **2**:286
Mount Sinai. *See* Horeb; Sinai
mourning, **2**:31–36, 43, 236–37
Mozart, Wolfgang Amadeus, **1**:6
Muffs, Yohanan, **2**:83, 315n195
murder, killing, violence, and military
   force: Amalek and Amalekites, **1**:xii,
   xxxi, 165–66; **2**:xiv, xxxiii, 156, 255–
   59; Arab-Jewish relations and, **2**:195;
   Cain and Abel, **1**:xxvii, xxviii, 3–5, 54,
   88–90, 92, 111; **2**:xxix, xxx, 194; capital
   punishment/death penalty, **2**:192–
   93, 331n227; corpse discovered but
   killer's identity unknown, **2**:331n232;
   culture of the book versus culture of
   the sword, **2**:71–72, 258; *get* (writ of
   divorce) issued by soldiers to their
   wives, **2**:13, 303n20; *hamas*, **1**:114, 119,
   247n270; humiliation compared to
   murder, **1**:102; kings, military power
   of, **2**:246–47, 343n157; money ransom for life of murderers, prohibition on, **2**:193; Pinhas, zealotry and
   vigilantism of, **2**:168–73; rape of
   Dinah and attitudes toward, **1**:114–19,
   246–47nn252–57; reluctance regarding, as ethical legacy of Jacob, **1**:69–
   73; Sixth Commandment (thou shalt
   not kill/do not murder), **2**:191–95;
   weapons, Rabbinic antipathy to, **1**:70–
   71; Zionism and acceptance of military force, **1**:71–73
Musaf Amidah, **2**:75
Musar (Jewish ethics and moral self-
   cultivation), **1**:xxiv, 33, 81–82; **2**:xxvi

Naboth, **2**:212
Nadav, **2**:31–36

R. Nahman, **2**:72
Nahmanides (Ramban): on circumcision of the heart, **2**:223, 336n64;
   on destruction of Shechem, **1**:116;
   on enjoyment of wealth as gift of
   God, **2**:337n89; on inquiring of God,
   1:256n108; on Joseph, **1**:85, 107; on
   Joshua, **2**:353n272; on plundering of
   Egyptians, **1**:244n230; on repentance,
   2:271; on Sarah, **1**:230n41; on seventy
   elders appointed by Moses, **2**:319n42;
   on Sinai and *mishkan*, **1**:194; on spies
   sent to survey the land, **2**:308n75; on
   treatment of blind and deaf people,
   2:58, 311nn129–30
Nahshon son of Aminadav, **1**:157–58
Nahum (prophet), **1**:210
Nathan, **2**:12–13, 303n16
nations, wisdom amongst, **1**:xii, 167–68;
   2:xiv
Near Eastern myth and society: crimes
   against property versus crimes
   against the person, **2**:193–94; fugitive slaves in, **2**:250–51, 252; God as
   Rock in, **2**:290; human culture given
   by gods in, **1**:xxvi, 3; **2**:xxvii; interest
   rates, **1**:243n225; Jewish democratization of royal ideology of, **1**:181; kings
   and kingship in, **1**:7–8, 180; **2**:246,
   248; money ransom for life of murderers, **2**:193; rituals, efficaciousness
   of, **2**:108; sacred texts in, **2**:352n257
negative theologies, **2**:356n310
Negev, **1**:27, 29
neighbor, commandment to love, **1**:xiii,
   xxx, xxxii, 33–34, 177, 201, 206; **2**:xv,
   xxxii, xxxiv, 61–65
Nelson, Richard: on Amalek and Amalekites, **2**:347n204; on circumcision
   of the heart, **2**:221; *Deuteronomy: A*

Commentary (2002), **1**:xix, 268; **2**:xxi,
362; on Fifth Commandment (honor-
ing parents), **1**:170; on God as Rock,
2:355n296; on *hak'hel*, **2**:352n254; on
Joshua chosen as leader after Moses,
2:281; on kings and kingship, **2**:247,
344n162; on laws of Israel, **2**:215–16,
226; on *mishkan*, **2**:7; on theophany of
Elijah, **2**:328n180; on women in the
Bible, **2**:236, 237, 340n124
ner tamid (eternal light), **1**:198, 199
Netziv. *See* Berlin, R. Naftali Tzvi Yehudah (Netziv)
Nile River, **1**:92, 130, 146–47, 213; **2**:73,
228, 229
Nimrod, **1**:3
Nimshi, **2**:177
Nineveh, **1**:209–12; **2**:243–44
Noah, **1**:3, 12, 17–19, 54, 118, 119; **2**:26, 102,
192
nostalgia for fleshpots of Egypt, **1**:xi–xii,
155, 159–60; **2**:xiii–xiv, 125, 148
Nun, **2**:281, 282

obedience to God: commandment to love
God and, **2**:63–64; ethical responsibilities and, **1**:xiii, 32–34, 226n21; **2**:xv;
manna in the desert and, **1**:161–62;
sacrifice and, **2**:20–25, 300n21; standing upright and, **2**:86–89
obedience to laws. *See* laws and obedience to them
obedience to parents, **1**:169–74
offerings. *See* sacrifice
ohel mo'ed, **1**:197
Oholiab, **1**:219–20
Ollenburger, Ben, **2**:274, 352n251
Olson, Dennis, **2**:147, 291, 294, 326n167,
341n132, 353n271, 355n291; *Numbers*
(1996), **1**:267–68; **2**:361–62

Omer, **2**:71–75
Onan, **1**:91, 99
Onkelos, **2**:47–48, 307n67
oppressed, the. *See* vulnerable and
oppressed
order out of chaos. *See* chaos, order out of
ordination ceremony, **2**:44
orphans and widows, commandment not
to oppress, **1**:xxv, xxx, 177, 178, 179–83;
2:xxvii, xxxii
Otto, Eckart, **2**:237

pacifism, **1**:71–73
Palestinian Arabs, **2**:195
Palestinian Talmud, preeminence of Babylonian Talmud over, **1**:136. *See also*
Classical Sources Index
Paley, R. Abraham Noah, **1**:xxiv, 33–34;
2:xxvi
R. Papa, **2**:34
paradise. *See* heaven
parashat ha-shavua (weekly Torah portion) commentary. *See* Torah and
Torah commentary
parents: abusive, **1**:256n109; God as
mother and father, **2**:293–94, 315n199;
honoring (Fifth Commandment), **1**:xi,
68, 169–74; **2**:xiii; threefold priestly
blessing, **2**:103–7; treatment of disabled and, **2**:312n140; *tzimtzum* and,
1:258n139
particularism, **2**:101–2
Passover: four cups of wine at, **1**:135–36;
generosity as part of paschal sacrifice,
1:xii; **2**:xiv, 18–19; Haggadah stressing
journey over arrival, **1**:134–38; **2**:263;
Omer between Shavuot and, **2**:71–75;
as reenactment of Exodus, **1**:128, 136;
sinning by eating leavened foods at,
2:55; Sukkot and, **2**:66–68

Paul, **2**:222

perfection, human lack of, **2**:161–62, 163–67

Perizzites, **1**:27, 117

perpetual offering (*korban tamid*), **1**:199–200, 201–2

Perry, Theodore, **2**:132

persecution of Jews, **1**:xii, 21–25, 165–68; **2**:xiv

Pesach. *See* Passover

peshat (plain-sense meaning), **1**:xi, 85, 153–54, 199; **2**:xiii

Pharaoh: cosmic victory of order over chaos and, **1**:xxiii–xxiv, 144–48, 222–24; **2**:xxv–xxvi, 256; Edom's king and, **2**:153, 155; famine in Egypt and Joseph's enslavement of Egyptians, **1**:104–7, 243n218, 243n221; God contrasted with, **1**:162, 163; God hardening heart of, **1**:139–43, 249n19, 250n29, 250n26; grandiosity and monstrousness of, **1**:130, 140, 146–47, 213; **2**:73; ignorance of Joseph and God, **1**:128–29; ingratitude of, **1**:128–33; Joseph and, **1**:84, 86, 128–30; **2**:215; Midrash's conflation of, **1**:248n8; moral and spiritual development of Moses and, **1**:xv; **2**:xvii; Moses and Aaron confronting, **1**:80, 126, 128–33, 139–41, 213; plundering of Egyptians and, **1**:149–53; pursuit of Israelites by, **1**:155; Sarah and, **1**:24, 26; serving God versus, **2**:142; treatment of Jews by, **1**:22, 213–15, 244n230; **2**:86–87, 124; trust, Israelite loss of ability to, **1**:159, 162, 163. *See also* Egypt; Exodus from Egypt

Philistines, **2**:127

Phineas (Pinhas), **1**:131; **2**:168–74, 327n169

Phoenicians, **2**:247

piety and ethics, **2**:55–56

Pi-hahiroth, **2**:185

Pinhas (Phineas), **1**:131; **2**:168–74, 327n169

R. Pinhas, **1**:19

Pinker, Steven, **1**:5

Pinto, R. Yoshiyahu, **2**:54, 55, 310n120

piska be-emtza pasuk (paragraph ending in mid-verse), **1**:241n193

pity compared to compassion, **2**:278–79

plague: death from, of last of generation who left Egypt, **2**:125; Pinhas's action stopping, **2**:168; ten plagues of Egypt, **1**:141, 144–48, 150, 250n26

plain-sense meaning (*peshat*), **1**:xi, 85, 153–54, 199; **2**:xiii

Plato and Platonism, **2**:303n1

pleasure and enjoyment, Kohelet apparently advocating, **2**:130–35, 313n159

pluralism, **2**:101–2

pollution of land with innocent blood, **2**:194–95

poor. *See* charity; vulnerable and oppressed

Potiphar and Potiphar's wife, **1**:84–85, 110, 239n175, 239n177

poverty. *See* charity; vulnerable and oppressed

praise and thanks to God, **2**:269, 350nn234–35

prayer: accepting lack of expertise in, **2**:165–66; *Amidah*, **2**:48–49, 67, 75, 78; of Isaac for Rebekah, **1**:51–52; as means of bringing God back into world, **1**:224; of Moses for Miriam and Aaron, **2**:50, 120–21; raising of hands as gesture of, **1**:56, 235–36n115–116; redemption and, **2**:48–49; *Shema*, **1**:33, 201; **2**:63, 75, 297; for those who hurt and disappoint us, **2**:119–23; threefold priestly blessing, **2**:103–7; verbal expression

of, 2:112; "wandering Aramean" passage, 1:134, 262–63
predators, prohibition on eating, 2:29
Pressler, Carolyn, 2:341n129
priests and priesthood: of all people, 2:136–40, 323n111; blessings as channel of, 2:106, 318n19; crown of, 2:98–99; as gift and as act of giving, 2:141–45, 323n111; High Priest, 1:189; 2:35, 44, 138–40, 142, 171–72, 194, 323n109, 327n169; ordination of, 2:44; *sha'atnez*, priestly garments made from, 2:137–38; threefold priestly blessing, 2:103–7
progress, cultural, 1:xxviii, 3–6; 2:xxx
promises of God and their fulfillment, living in space between, 1:249n15
property crimes versus crimes against the person, 2:193–94
prophets and prophecy: Balaam and, 2:161; brothers, prophets as, 2:341n132; Elijah, prophets slain by, 2:174; false, 2:241, 243, 244; female, 2:342n132; loneliness of, 2:119; Moses' wish that all the people were prophets, 2:114–18; Pinhas losing gift of, 2:171; role of, 2:240–44
prostitution and whoring, 1:77, 91, 99–100, 118; 2:168
Provan, Iain, 2:328n182, 329n189
purgation offering or "sin offering" (*korban hattat*), 2:37, 39
purification and purity laws: blood and, 2:38; childbirth and, 2:37–41, 308nn89–91; corpses and, 2:38; dietary rules, 2:26–30, 306n63; impurity not in and of itself sinful, 2:37–38; leaders, sins of, 2:15; *metzora*, 2:44, 309n103; *mishkan*, purification of, 2:52–56

Quohelet. *See* Kohelet

Rachel: barrenness of, 1:50–51, 61, 62, 242n199; compassion of, 1:74–78, 238n155, 238n157; death and burial of, 1:74–75, 238n151, 238n153, 238n157; Jacob favoring children of, 1:95–96; marriage to Jacob, 1:50–52, 60–63, 66–67, 95–96; Reuben sleeping with Billhah after death of, 1:93–94; substitution of Leah for, 1:66, 116; weeping for her children, 1:75
Radak. *See* Kimhi, R. David (Radak)
Rahab, 2:74
Ralbag (Gersonides), 2:202, 303n1
Ramah, 1:75, 238n153
Rambam. *See* Maimonides (Rambam)
Ramban. *See* Nahmanides (Ramban)
Rameses (place), 2:185
Ramhal (R. Moshe Chaim Luzzatto), 2:267–68, 349n229, 350n230, 350n233
rape: of Dinah, 1:70, 114–19, 245n249, 246n252; marital rape of captive brides, 1:xxi; 2:xxiii, 236–38, 340–41nn124–31; seduction versus, 1:245n249; of women captured in war, 2:237
Rashba (R. Shlomo ben Aderet), 2:13
Rashbam (R. Samuel b. Meir), 1:105–6, 151, 234n100, 249n18, 254n83; 2:228, 337n90
Rashi: on Amalek and Amalekites, 2:347n200; on community of Israelites, 2:277; on compassion of Rachel, 1:76; on construction of *mishkan*, 1:219; on covetousness, 2:211; on Elijah, 2:178; on fear, 2:332n9; on growth of Israelite numbers in Egypt, 1:145; on Jacob's fear of killing, 1:69–70; on Joseph and Potiphar's wife, 1:85,

Rashi (*continued*)
239n174, 239n176; on Joshua as leader after Moses, **2**:117, 353n272, 355n292; on judges, **2**:332n7; on lighting in *mishkan*, **1**:198–99; on manna in the desert, **1**:161; on Moses asking for a successor, **2**:170; non-Jewish sources, used in dialogue with, **1**:xxxiii; **2**:xxxv; on Pharaoh's pursuit of Israelites, **1**:254n70; on priestly service, **2**:141–42; on Rebekah tested by Abraham's servant, **1**:43; on recounting of rest stops in wilderness in Numbers, **2**:186; on repentance, **2**:271; on silence of Aaron after death of sons, **2**:32; on soldiers issuing a *get* to their wives, **2**:13, 303n20; on Sukkot, **2**:68; on threefold priestly blessing, **2**:105; on tzitzit and *sha'atnez*, **2**:137; words/ speech, on power of, **2**:48

Rav, **1**:32; **2**:133

Rebekah: Abraham, paralleling, **1**:45–46, 233n88; barrenness of, **1**:51; death and burial of, **1**:47, 62; emotional sensitivity and ability to manipulate Isaac, **1**:43–48; generosity of, **1**:44, 46, 236n126; inquiring of God, **1**:54–55, 59, 234n91; as journeyer, **1**:234n89; marriage of Isaac and, **1**:43–48, 51–53, 234n102; prayer of Isaac for, **1**:51–53; tested by Abraham's servant, **1**:43–45; tricking of Isaac by Jacob and, **1**:xxvii, 46–47, 64–68, 236n130; **2**:xxix

recklessness and impulsiveness, **1**:93–98

redemption: speech/prayer and, **2**:48–49; suffering and redemption, correlation between, **1**:22–24

Red Sea. *See* Sea of Reeds

Rehoboam, **2**:344n159

Reines, R. Isaac Jacob, **1**:71–73

Reis, Pamela, **1**:38

relationship to God and fellow human beings: at center of Torah commentary, **1**:xiv–xv, xxix–xxx, 130; **2**:xvi–xvii, xxxi–xxxii; confession and, **2**:108–13; divine-human interdependence, **1**:164; gratitude crucial for, **1**:132–33; *tzimtzum* (divine self-contraction) and presence/separateness in, **1**:184–88

religious integrity and sacrifice, **2**:20–25, 82, 163–64

remission, year of (seventh year or *shemittah* year), **2**:230–34, 275–79

Rendsburg, Gary, **2**:29–30

repentance (*teshuvah*), **1**:206; **2**:69–70, 111–12, 128, 224, 243–44, 270–74, 315n191, 350–52nn237–51

Rephidim, **2**:277

Resh Lakish (Shimon b. Lakish), **2**:171, 326n168

responsibility. *See* human responsibility

restraint: Joseph's exercise of, **1**:109–13, 245n238; *tzimtzum* (divine self-contraction) as form of, **1**:184–88

rest stops in wilderness, Numbers recounting, **2**:185–90

Reuben (son of Jacob and Leah): Benjamin and, **1**:96–97; Jacob's concubine, sleeping with, **1**:93–94, 242n197; Jacob's judgment of, **1**:93–98, 241n189, 241n191; Joseph, halfhearted effort to save, **1**:79–82, 242n206; leadership, reckless character not suited for, **1**:93–98, 241n189; mandrakes fetched for Leah by, **1**:94–95, 242n199; naming of, **1**:61

Reuben (tribe), **1**:29; **2**:179–84

riches. *See* wealth and money

righteousness, **1**:217–18, **2**:215, 216, 335n45

Rimanover, the (R. Menahem Mendel of Rimanov), **2**:283, 354n280

Rimon, Sharon, **1**:262n203

Rishonim, **2**:304n20

Ritter, Bruce, **2**:252

Ritva (R. Yom Tov b. Avraham Asevilli), **1**:256n108

Rock, God as, **2**:290–91, 294, 355n296, 355n299

Romans, Bar-Kokhba revolt against, **2**:72–73, 75

Rosenberg, R. Shimon Gershon (Shagar), **2**:167

Rosh Hashanah, **2**:270

Rotenberg, Menorah, **1**:233n88

royalty. *See* kings and kingship

ruach Elohim (divine spirit), **1**:222

Ruah HaKodesh (Holy Spirit), **2**:171

Rubenstein, R. Jason, **1**:249n14

runaway slaves, **2**:250–54, 345n173, 345n177, 346n182

R. Saadia Gaon, **1**:7, 151, 226n31; **2**:300n31, 306n59, 343n148, 353n272

Saba, R. Abraham, **1**:237n135; **2**:185

Sabbath. *See* Shabbat

sacrifice: *Akedah* (binding of Isaac), **1**:xiii, 28, 32, 40–42, 45, 76; **2**:xv; of Jephthah's daughter, **2**:171, 172; *korban hattat* ("sin offering" or purgation offering), **2**:37, 39; *korban olah* (burnt offerings), **2**:20, 22, 37; *korban tamid* (perpetual offering), **1**:199–200, 201–2; *korban todah* (thanksgiving offering), **1**:xii; **2**:xiv, 15–19; *minhah* (grain offering), **2**:15, 20; paschal sacrifice, **1**:xii; **2**:xiv, 18–19; religious integrity and, **2**:20–25, 82, 163–64; *zevah ha-shelamim* (sacrifice of well-being), **2**:15, 18, 20

Sagi, Avi, **2**:258

Samuel, **2**:247, 292–93

R. Samuel b. R. Isaac, **2**:131

R. Samuel b. Meir (Rashbam), **1**:105–6, 151, 234n100, 249n18, 254n83; **2**:228, 337n90

R. Samuel b. Nahman, **1**:101

sanctification of God, **2**:31, 307n64

sanctuary. *See mishkan*

Santayana, George, **1**:228n52; **2**:80, 302n52

Sarah: Avimelech, king of Gerar and, **1**:50; barrenness of, **1**:49–50; burial site of, **1**:62; death of, **1**:41; directly communicating with God, **1**:54; Hagar, treatment of, **1**:xxv, 23–25, 49–50, 109, 113, 244n230; **2**:xxvii; hospitality of Abraham and, **1**:31; Isaac, announcement of birth of, **1**:36, 39, 49; marriage to Abraham, **1**:49–50, 234n101; Pharaoh and, **1**:24, 26, 29; as Sarai, **1**:26, 29, 230n36

Sarna, Nahum, **1**:27, 117, 141–43, 243n227, 245n245, 257n130; **2**:79, 80, 314n185

Satmar anti-Zionism, **2**:28

Saul, **1**:242n202; **2**:292–93

Scarry, Elaine, **1**:178

Schick, R. Abraham ben Aryeh Loeb, **1**:237n142; **2**:327n169

Schlimm, Matthew, **1**:110, 111

Schmid, H. H., **1**:144–45

Scholem, Gershom, **1**:184, 185; **2**:348n213

Schwartz, Baruch, **2**:309n95

scribal revisions (*tiqqun sopherim*), **1**:232n68

Sea of Reeds, pursuit of Israelites by Pharaoh at, **1**:155–58; **2**:256

Sefer ha-Hinnukh, **2**:72

Seforno, R. Obadiah, **1**:161, 245n240; **2**:86, 105, 186, 303n12, 319n42, 320n54, 330n213, 351n243

Seir, land of, **2**:154, 206

self-doubt, **1**:82, 126

semikhut parshiyot, **2**:136

Sennacherib (Assyrian ruler), **1**:105

sensitivity, emotional, **1**:43, 48

Seow, Choon-Leong, **2**:133

Septuagint, **1**:239n169, 243n218; **2**:131, 353n272

service and election, relationship between, **1**:83–87, 240n185

Seth, **1**:3

seventh year (*shemittah* year or year of remission), **2**:230–34, 275–79

seventy elders appointed by Moses, **2**:114–18

sha'al, **1**:151–52

sha'atnez (cloth combining wool and linen), **2**:136–40

Shabbat: as anticipatory glimpse of heavenly reality, **1**:xxxi; **2**:xxxiii, 76–80; Fourth Commandment (Sabbath observance), **1**:172–73; human dignity reinforced by, **1**:xxiv, 214; **2**:xxvi; manna in the desert and, **1**:160–62; *mishkan* and, **1**:214, 222; **2**:76–77, 80; Moses and Aaron requesting Israelite opportunity for, **1**:213; weapons, Rabbinic antipathy to, **1**:70–71

Shadal (Samuel David Luzzatto), **1**:253n63; **2**:147

Shagar (R. Shimon Gershon Rosenberg), **2**:167

shalshelet, **1**:239n177

Shaphat, **2**:177

Shavuot, **1**:136–37; **2**:66, 68, 71–72, 98

Shechem son of Hamor, **1**:114–16, 118, 246n249

Shekhinah (Divine Presence), **1**:31–33, 37, 85, 99; **2**:195

Shelah (third son of Judah), **1**:91, 99

Shelah, the (R. Isaiah Horowitz), **2**:96

Shem, **1**:19

Shema, **1**:33, 201; **2**:63, 75, 297

Shemini Atzeret, **2**:68

shemittah year (seventh year or year of remission), **2**:230–34, 275–79

R. Sheshet, **1**:199

R. Shimon bar Yohai, **1**:21, 254n75

R. Shimon b. Gamiel, **2**:331n227

Shimon b. Lakish (Resh Lakish), **2**:171, 326n168

Shimon b. Pazi, **1**:201–2

Shkop, Esther, **1**:233n85

R. Shlomo ben Aderet (Rashba), **2**:13

Shmuelevitz, R. Chaim, **2**:51

Shoah (Holocaust), **1**:72, 176; **2**:258

Shor, Joseph Bekhor, **2**:152

sickness and stigma, **1**:xxi; **2**:xxiii, 42–46, 50–51, 308n99, 309n95, 309n103

Silber, R. David, **1**:230n39

silence: of Aaron at death of sons, **2**:31–36; slavery and, **2**:48

Simeon (son of Jacob and Leah), **1**:61, 70, 114–19, 246–47nn252–57, 247n261, 249n189

R. Simeon, **2**:117–18

R. Simeon b. Elazar, **1**:94

R. Simeon b. Lakish, **2**:99–101

R. Simeon b. Yohai, **1**:63

Simha, R. Meir, of Dvinsk: *Meshekh Hokhmah* (1927), **1**:7; **2**:40, 310n122, 351n243

Simhat Torah, **2**:295

R. Simlai, **1**:xxx; **2**:xxxii, 295

R. Simon, **1**:36–37

Simundson, Daniel, **2**:315n200

sin: confession of, **2**:82, 108–13; cosmic victory of order over chaos despite, **1**:144–48; impurity not in and of itself sinful, **2**:37–38; of Jacob, **1**:64–

68; of leaders, **2**:9–14; loss of freedom through, **1**:140–43; of Moses
and Aaron in striking water from the
rock, **2**:146–51, 324n132; parents not
able to command children to, **1**:171;
wisdom, prophecy, and God on punishment for, **1**:57–58; Yom Kippur
(Day of Atonement) and, **2**:52–56,
69–70

Sinai: census at, **2**:96; covenant with
Moses and Israelites at, **1**:135–36, 195–
96, 198–202; **2**:35; God revealed at,
1:xxix, 128, 194–97; **2**:xxxi, 176, 275;
Golden Calf incident, **1**:xiv, 13, 38,
196–97, 203–6, 208; **2**:xvi, 122, 125,
220, 321n70, 336n55; as Horeb, **2**:176,
199, 275–76, 328n182; *mishkan*, parallels with, **1**:194–95; as orienting event
for Jewish people, **2**:275; preparation
of Israelites for sojourn in, **2**:124–
25; revelation at, **1**:xxix, 128, 136–37,
194–97; **2**:xxxi, 68, 71, 72, 176, 275–79;
sacrificial laws ordained at, **2**:20, 21;
seventh year, reenactment of Sinai in,
2:275–79; Shavuot commemorating,
1:136–37; **2**:68, 71, 72; Ten Commandments received at, **1**:xiv, xxii; **2**:xvi,
xxiv; Torah given in wilderness of,
2:98–102; tragedy and hope of, **2**:124–
29; visit of Jethro introduced before
revelation at, **1**:165, 167. *See also mish-*
kan; Ten Commandments

"sin offering" or purgation offering (*kor-*
ban hattat), **2**:37, 39

Sixth Commandment (thou shalt not
kill/murder), **2**:191–95

skin diseases, **1**:xxi, 120–21; **2**: xxiii, 42–
46, 50–51, 308n99, 309n95, 309n103

Sklar, Jay, **2**:59

slaves and slavery: abolition of,
2:253–54; commandment to stand
upright and, **2**:86–89; debt slavery,
1:244n235; **2**:230, 232, 276; dignity of
work versus, **1**:213–16; fugitive slaves,
2:250–54, 345n173, 345n177, 346n182;
God's recognition of personhood
of, **1**:xxv, 24; **2**:xxvii; *innui* (being
a slave), **1**:22, 23, 230n39; Joseph's
enslavement of Egyptians, **1**:104–8,
243n218, 244n230, 248n9; Joseph sold
into slavery, **1**:79, 84, 90, 91, 110; liberation and gratitude, relationship
between, **1**:128–33; liberation from
slavery and human responsibility,
1:155–58, 255n86; manumission rules,
1:150–51, 252n54; **2**:232–33, 338n107;
marriage of woman sold into slavery,
1:xiv; **2**:xvi, 236–38, 340n124; modern slavery, **2**:250; permanent versus
temporary, **1**:107–8; Shabbat, slaves
required to rest on, **2**:79–80; silence
associated with, **2**:48; women as
slaves, **1**:xiv; **2**:xvi, 235–39, 339n115,
340n14. *See also* Hagar

social vision, Torah as, **1**:xxix–xxx;
2:xxxi–xxxii

Sodom and Sodomites, **1**:xiii, 26–27, 29,
35–39, 231n58; **2**:xv, 84, 89

Soelle, Dorothee, **2**:289

Sofer, R. Shmuel Binyomin, **1**:231n54;
2:169

Sokolow, Moshe, **1**:215; **2**:330n205

Solomon, **2**:131, 188, 215, 216, 247, 322n84,
330n214, 344n159

Soloveitchik, Joseph, **1**:109, 143; **2**:28–29,
48, 87–88, 97, 123, 223, 306n60

Song of Moses, **2**:290–94

Song of the Sea, **2**:73–75

sorrow. *See* grief and sorrow

speech. *See* words/speech

teshuvah (repentance), **1**:206; **2**:69–70, 111–12, 128, 224, 243–44, 270–74, 315n191, 350–52nn237–51

thanks and praise to God, **2**:269, 350nn234–35

thanksgiving offering (*korban todah*), **1**:xii; **2**:xiv, 15–19

theodicy, **1**:xxx–xxxi; **2**:xxxii–xxxiii, 355n288

theophany: of Elijah, **2**:175, 327–28nn179–80; Joshua confirmed as leader after Moses by, **2**:281; Sinai, revelation at, **1**:xxix, 128, 136–37, 194–97; **2**:xxxi, 68, 71, 72, 176, 275–79

thirteen attributes of God, **1**:207–9

Thompson, J. A., **2**:305n49

Tigay, Jeffrey: on accidental manslaying, **2**:331n220; on consequences of disobedience to laws, **2**:265; *Deuteronomy* (2003), **1**:268; **2**:362; on equality and fraternity, **2**:232, 344n165; on Fifth Commandment, **1**:170; on fugitive slaves, **2**:250–51, 345n173; on justice, **2**:200; on kingship, **2**:248, 249; on laws of Israel, **2**:335n44; on manna in the desert, **1**:254n79; on not living by bread alone, **2**:225; on presence of God, **1**:57; on Psalm 119 as apotheosis of Torah, **1**:236n117; on Sukkot, **2**:278; on women's social and legal status, **2**:339n115, 340n125, 341n128

tiqqun sopherim (scribal revisions), **1**:232n68

todah, **2**:269

Torah and Torah commentary (*parashat ha-shavua*), **1**:xi–xvi, xxi–xxxiii; **2**:xiii–xviii, xxiii–xxxv; beginning and ending of, **2**:295–98; death of Moses and, **2**:287, 289; difficult or disturbing readings, **1**:xxxi–xxxii; **2**:xxxiii–

xxxiv; end of Torah before arrival in promised land, **1**:136, 138; on God's love, care, and presence, **1**:xxii–xxvi; **2**:xxiv–xxviii; golden age of, **1**:xi; **2**:xiii; on hope in a hopeless world, **1**:xxx–xxxi, 223–24; **2**:xxxii–xxxiii; on human responsibility, **1**:xxvi–xxix; **2**:xxviii–xxxi; letter of Torah, every Jew viewed as, **2**:96; lovingkindness central to, **2**:295–98; origins of Torah in heaven, **1**:xxi; **2**:xxiii; overfamiliarity with, **2**:165; paradigmatic reading of, **1**:182–83, 258n132; *peshat* (plain-sense meaning), **1**:xi, 85, 153–54, 199; **2**:xiii; presence of God in, **1**:57; purpose in every story, **2**:185; on relationship to God and fellow human beings, **1**:xiv–xv, xxix–xxx; **2**:xvi–xvii, xxxi–xxxii; search favored over discovery in, **1**:137; seeking will of God through, **1**:54–59, 235nn110–12; seventh year, public reading of Torah in, **2**:275–77; as social vision, **1**:xxix–xxx; **2**:xxxi–xxxii; *tiqqun sopherim* (scribal revisions), **1**:232n68; Torah-centeredness and law-centeredness, **2**:335n52; traditional, nontraditional, and non-Jewish sources, use of, **1**:xii–xiii, xxxii–xxxiii; **2**:xiv–xv, xxxiv–xxxv; universalism regarding, **2**:98–102; use of term, **1**:236n119. *See also Classical Sources Index*

Tosafists, **2**:39

totalitarianism, **1**:16–20, 216, 230n29, 230n31; **2**:317n1

Tower of Babel, **1**:16–20, 230n29, 230n31

Transjordan, Reubenites and Gadites desiring to stay in, **1**:29; **2**:179–84

tree of life, menorah as, **1**:191

trust in God, learning, **1**:159–64

Turner, Mary Donovan, 1:46

Tuval-Cain, 1:3, 4

tzara'at (scaly skin disease), 1:xxi; 2:xxiii, 42–46, 50–51, 308n99, 309n95, 309n103

tzedakah, 1:77–78

tzimtzum (divine self-contraction), 1:184–88

Tzintz, R. Aryeh Leib, 2:142

tzitzit (fringes), 2:130–31, 133–34, 136–40, 322n99

uniformity of practice in Judaism, 2:95–96

uniqueness and individuality, human, 1:16–20; 2:93–98, 317n2

universalism, 2:98–102, 333n23

Unna, Moshe, 1:xxxii; 2:xxxiv

Uriah the Hittite, 2:12, 304n20

vegetarianism, 2:26–30

victimization of Jews, 1:xii, 21–25, 165–68; 2:xiv

vigilantism, of Pinhas, 2:168–73

violence. *See* murder, killing, violence, and military force

Vital, R. Hayyim, 2:313n154

Volf, Miroslav, 2:18

Vulgate, 1:239n169; 2:191

vulnerability: community and, 2:278–79; love, willingness to express, 2:318n32

vulnerable and oppressed: *avdut* (being oppressed), 1:22, 23, 230n39; brothers, to be treated as, 2:231; God's care for, 1:xxiv–xxv, 177–83; 2:xxvi–xxvii, 232; human responsibility for, 1:xxvii, 175, 179–83; 2:xix; memory of being, and empathy for, 1:174–78; Moses' concern for, 1:123–25; persons with disabilities as, 2:57–60, 310–11nn126–27, 311n131, 311n134, 312nn138–40; pity

compared to compassion, 2:278–79; widows and orphans, commandment not to oppress, 1:xxv, xxx, 177, 178, 179–83; 2:xxvii, xxxii. *See also* charity; slaves and slavery

Walker, A. D. M., 2:16, 17

"walking in God's ways," 1:205–6; 2:6, 48, 296, 357n318

Waltke, Bruce: *Genesis: A Commentary* (2001), 1:233n70, 239n168, 241n189, 243n225, 245n245, 266; 2:360

Walzer, Michael, 1:160

"wandering Aramean" passage, 1:134, 262–63

war. *See* murder, killing, violence, and military force

"way of expediency" and "way of wonder," 2:143–44

wealth and money: covetousness, Tenth Commandment forbidding, 2:209–14, 236, 239; entitlement, dangers of, 2:260–64; interest rates, 1:243n225; of kings, 2:247; loans, debts, and debt slavery, 1:244n235; 2:230, 232, 276, 338n98; material well-being versus materialism, 1:xiii, 26–30; 2:xv, 181–84; murderers, money ransom for life of, 1:193; plundering of Egyptians, 1:149–54; Reubenites' and Gadites' request to stay in Transjordan and, 1:29; 2:179–84; Shabbat, prohibition on handling money on, 2:79; silver/money in story of Joseph and his brothers, 1:110–11, 240n183

weapons, Rabbinic antipathy to, 1:70–71

weekly Torah portion commentary. *See* Torah and Torah commentary

Weeks, Feast of. *See* Shavuot

Weinfeld, Moshe, 2:100, 221, 226, 236,

261, 334n38, 334n43, 340n119; *Deuteronomy 1-11* (1995), **1**:268; **2**:362

Weiser, R. Meir Leibush (Malbim), **1**:218, 262n205, 265; **2**:228-29, 270-71, 351n240, 359

Weiss, Andrea L., **2**:237; *The Torah: A Women's Commentary* (ed., with Tamara Cohn Eskenazi, 2008), **1**:269; **2**:363

Welker, Michael, **1**:10

well-being, sacrifice of (*zevah hashelamim*), **2**:15, 18, 20

Wenham, Gordon: on Abraham and Lot, **1**:28; on Balaam, **2**:159; on following hearts and eyes, **2**:130; on Garden of Eden and *mishkan*, **1**:259n155; *Genesis* (1994), **1**:243n215, 266; **2**:360; on imperfection of laws, **2**:253; on Jacob and Reuben, **1**:94, 241n191; on Joseph, **1**:83-84; on *metzora*, **2**:45; *Numbers* (2008), **1**:268; **2**:362; on rape of Dinah and destruction of Shechem, **1**:117, 118; on Rebekah inquiring of God, **1**:234n105; on spies sent to survey the land, **2**:126, 130

Wessely, R. Naphtali Hirz, **2**:307n68

Westphal, Merold, **2**:350n235

Whitman, Walt, *Leaves of Grass* (1855), **1**:xvi; **2**:xviii

wholeheartedness, **1**:79-82

whoring and prostitution, **1**:77, 91, 99-100, 118; **2**:168

widows: *almanah*, meaning of, **1**:179, 256n116; commandment not to oppress orphans and, **1**:xxv, xxx, 177, 178, 179-83; **2**:xxvii, xxxii; Levirate marriage (brother required to marry widow of deceased brother), **1**:91, 99-100; **2**:303n20

Wieseltier, Leon, **1**:176

wilderness. *See* Exodus from Egypt; Sinai

Wirzba, Norman, **1**:11

wisdom amongst gentiles, **1**:xii, 167-68; **2**:xiv

Wolbe, Shlomo, **1**:143

women: childbirth and purity laws, **2**:37-41; as commodities, **2**:236, 334n31; concubines of fathers, sons sleeping with, **1**:93-96; direct access to God by, **1**:54-55; Frederick Douglass on rights of, **1**:124; fringes (tzitzit), wearing, **2**:322n99; God, maternal aspects of, **2**:294, 315n199; legal and social status of, **2**:235-39; longer impurity period for birth of girl versus boy, **2**:37, 39-40; mitzvah of procreation incumbent on men but not women, **2**:40; as prophets, **2**:342n132; prostitution and whoring, **1**:77, 91, 99-100, 118; **2**:168; as slaves, **1**:xiv; **2**:xvi, 235-39, 339n115, 340n14; *yir'ah* and, **2**:350n230. *See also* marriage; rape; widows

wool and linen, cloth combining (*sha'atnez*), **2**:136-40

words/speech: confession, **2**:82, 108-13; metaphors, theological, **2**:290-94; plays on, **2**:307n69; power of, **2**:47-51, 310n111; in Tower of Babel story, **1**:17-18, 230n29

World War I, **1**:72

wrath of God, **1**:261n186

Wright, Christopher, **2**:205, 226, 237, 246, 251, 333n23, 337n90, 345n173, 346n185

Wurzburger, R. Walter, **1**:205

Yakar, Keli, **2**:351n243

Yamim Noraim (Days of Awe), **2**:270

Yaval, **1**:3, 4

year of remission (seventh year or *shemittah* year), **2**:230-34, 275-79

Yehoshaphat, **2**:200

Classical Sources Index

Tanakh   1:261n186

TORAH			

Genesis	**1:** xxvi, 1–119, 135, 147, 190, 192, 221, 222, 228n1– 248n270, 244n230, 265–66; **2:** xxviii, 47, 191, 192, 204, 205, 359–60	1:31	**1:** 7, 8, 221, 222
		2	**2:** 47
		2:1	**1:** 221
		2:1–3	**1:** 161
		2:2	**1:** 221
		2:2–3	**1:** 215
		2:3	**1:** 221; **2:** 6, 80
1	**1:** 8, 9, 10, 11, 145, 147; **2:** 3, 6, 26, 27, 47	2:7	**2:** 47
1:2	**1:** 222	2:10	**1:** 190
1:3	**1:** 147; **2:** 47	2:11	**1:** 192
1:4	**1:** 8, 147, 222; **2:** 6	2:12	**1:** 192
1:6	**2:** 73	3:8	**1:** 259n155
1:6–7	**1:** 146	3:13	**1:** 111
1:7	**2:** 6	3:21	**2:** 295
1:9–10	**2:** 6	3:24	**1:** 191
1:10	**1:** 8, 222	4:2–11	**1:** 88
1:10–11	**1:** 147	4:7	**1:** 5
1:11	**1:** 9	4:8	**1:** 227n42; **2:** 301n42
1:12	**1:** 8, 222	4:9	**1:** 88
1:14	**2:** 6	4:10	**1:** 111; **2:** 194
1:18	**1:** 8, 222; **2:** 6	4:12	**2:** 194
1:21	**1:** 8, 9, 222	4:14–15	**1:** 5
1:22	**1:** 9, 229n16; **2:** 47	4:17	**1:** 3, 227n42; **2:** 301n42
1:25	**1:** 9, 222	4:17–26	**1:** xxviii, 226n29; **2:** xxx, 300n29
1:26	**1:** 7, 226n31; **2:** 300n31	4:20–22	**1:** 3
1:26–27	**1:** 7	4:23–24	**1:** xxviii, 4; **2:** xxx
1:28	**1:** 8, 17, 145; **2:** 39, 47	4:26	**1:** 3
1:29	**2:** 26	6	**1:** 12
1:30	**2:** 26	6:5	**1:** 12

6:6	**1**:118	13:3	**1**:231n54
6:11	**1**:12, 119	13:3–4	**1**:29
6:17	**2**:319–20n44	13:6–7	**1**:27
8	**1**:12	13:7	**1**:27
8:21	**1**:12, 225n11;	13:8	**1**:27, 232n59
	2:299n11	13:9	**1**:28, 232n59
9:1	**1**:17	13:10	**1**:29, 231n58
9:1ff	**2**:306n54	13:11	**1**:30
9:3	**2**:26	13:13	**1**:29, 231n58
9:5	**2**:192	13:14–17	**1**:28
9:5–6	**2**:192	13:14–18	**2**:127
9:6	**2**:93, 192	14:2	**2**:316n202
9:7	**2**:39, 40	14:8	**2**:316n202
9:20	**1**:3	14:12	**1**:27
9:22–27	**1**:241n189	15	**1**:21
10	**1**:19	15:5	**1**:21; **2**:199
10:1–32	**1**:19	15:13	**1**:21, 22
10:5	**1**:19	15:13–14	**1**:135
10:8–10	**1**:3	15:14	**1**:68
10:18	**1**:19	15:16	**1**:135
10:19	**2**:316n202	15:18	**1**:135
10:20	**1**:19	15:18–21	**1**:21
10:31	**1**:19	16	**1**:23
10:32	**1**:19	16:2	**1**:49
11	**1**:16, 19	16:5	**1**:50
11:1	**1**:17, 18	16:6	**1**:23, 25, 109, 230n41,
11:4	**1**:16, 17, 18		244n230, 245n240
11:8	**1**:16	16:8	**1**:xxv, 24; **2**:xxvii
11:9	**1**:16	16:10	**1**:24
11:10	**1**:19	16:11	**1**:40
11:10–30	**1**:19	16:11–12	**1**:40
12	**1**:26	16:11–13	**1**:236n122
12:1	**1**:45	16:13	**1**:xxv, 24; **2**:xxvii
12:2	**1**:230n31; **2**:18	16:15–16	**1**:49
12:5	**1**:26	17:2	**1**:233n75
12:10	**1**:26	17:9–14	**2**:221
12:14–15	**1**:24	17:10	**2**:336–37n68
13	**1**:26, 28	17:16	**1**:49
13:1	**1**:27	17:18	**1**:49
13:2	**1**:26, 28–29	17:19	**1**:49

18	1:36, 37, 39	24:64–65	1:47
18:1	2:296	24:67	1:51, 52
18:1–8	1:64	25:20	1:51
18:1–15	1:36, 39	25:21	1:47, 51, 52
18:2	1:32, 45	25:22	1:54, 234n104
18:5	1:31	25:23	1:46
18:6	1:45	25:26	1:51, 65
18:6–7	1:43	25:30	1:64
18:7	1:45	25:31	2:154
18:16–19	1:36	25:32–34	1:64
18:16–33	1:xxvii, 39; 2:xxix	25:33	1:237n134
18:17	1:36	26	1:52
18:19	1:xxvii, 36, 39,	26:4	2:199
	233n75; 2:xxix	26:4–5	1:233n75
18:22	1:36, 232n68	27	1:66, 69, 234n91
18:23	1:35	27:1	1:46
18:25	1:35	27:1–4	1:47
18:27	2:89	27:4	1:46
18:30–32	2:89	27:5–17	1:47
19:8	1:232n61	27:8	1:46
20:6	1:50	27:12	1:65, 236n130
20:7	2:320n51	27:13	1:46, 68
20:17	1:50	27:14	1:65
22:6	1:40	27:15	1:234n103
22:15–18	1:233n75; 2:333n16	27:16	1:65, 236n130
22:17	1:45; 2:199	27:20	1:234n103
22:19	1:40	27:21–23	1:234n103
23:1–2	1:234n96	27:27	1:234n103
24	1:46	27:30–40	1:47
24:10	1:44	27:34	1:65
24:14	1:43	27:35	1:66, 116
24:15	1:44	27:35–36	1:65
24:15–27	1:64	27:36	1:65
24:18	1:45	27:40	2:337n72
24:18–20	1:45	27:41–42	1:69
24:20	1:45	27:41–45	1:47
24:28	1:45	27:46	1:47
24:58	1:45	28:1–5	1:47
24:60	1:45, 233n86	28:15	1:89
24:62	1:40	29:17	1:60

29:20	1:60	36:12	2:348n214
29:25	1:60, 66, 116	37:2	1:83, 84
29:26	1:66	37:2–4	1:110
29:30	1:61	37:3	1:83
29:32	1:61, 94	37:3–4	1:84
29:33	1:61	37:4	1:112
29:34	1:61	37:5–9	1:83
29:35	1:62, 242n199; 2:350n234	37:5–11	1:113
		37:8	1:83
30:1	1:74	37:10	1:83
30:1–2	1:51	37:17–23	1:84
30:9	1:242n199	37:21–22	1:79, 97
30:14	1:94	37:23	1:83
30:14–15	1:242n199	37:26	1:112
30:24	1:74	37:26–27	1:97
31:14	2:320n50	37:26–28	1:90, 110
32:4	2:154	37:28	1:110, 240n183
32:5	2:154	37:29	1:237n135
32:7	1:69; 2:154	37:29–30	1:79
32:8	1:69	37:31–32	1:67
33:1–2	1:95	37:32	1:91
34	1:114, 245n246, 245–46n249	37:35	1:75
		38	1:99, 240n183
34:1	1:114	38:25	1:91
34:2	1:114	38:25–26	1:100
34:3–4	1:115	38:26	1:91
34:5	1:115	39:2	1:85
34:7	1:115, 246n253	39:2–6	1:84
34:13	1:116	39:3	1:85
34:14	1:115	39:4	1:239n175
34:15	1:116	39:5	1:85
34:25–26	1:116	39:6	1:85
34:27–29	1:117	39:8	1:239n177
34:30	1:117	39:11	1:85
34:30–31	1:70	39:12	1:85
34:31	1:118	39:17–20	1:110
35:8	1:47	40:8	1:86
35:16–18	1:74	41:15–16	1:86
35:20	1:74	41:16	1:86
35:22	1:94	41:25	1:86

1:13–14	1:22	7:13	1:141
2	1:123	7:19	1:147
2:4	1:92	7:22	1:141
2:11	1:125	7:26	2:71
2:11–12	1:123	8:11	1:141
2:13	1:123	8:15	1:141
2:16–17	1:123	8:20	1:153
2:22	1:22	8:28	1:141
2:23	1:107, 248n8	9:7	1:141
2:24	1:181	9:12	1:141
3:1	1:125	9:34–35	1:250n26
3:6	2:176	10:1	1:141, 250n26
3:8	1:124; 2:127, 348n216	10:7	1:153
3:10	1:126, 130; 2:87	10:20	1:141
3:11	1:126	10:21–23	1:147
3:12	1:126	10:23	1:147
3:17	2:127	10:27	1:141
3:21	1:150, 251n51	11:2	1:252n54
3:21–22	1:150	11:2–3	1:150
3:22	1:151, 252n54,	11:3	1:153, 253n63
	252n57	12:10	2:18
4:14	1:80	12:35–36	1:149
4:18	1:130	13:5	2:348n216
4:21	1:139	13:17	2:127, 343n153
5	1:162	13:18	1:254n70
5:2	1:129, 130, 140, 213,	14:6–9	1:155
	248n8	14:13–14	1:155
5:5	1:xxiv, 213; 2:xxvi	14:15	1:156, 253n68
5:13	1:255n88	14:16	2:256
5:19	1:255n88	14:21	2:347n197
6:1	2:155	14:21–22	1:146; 2:73
6:4	1:255n88	14:26–27	2:347n197
6:5	1:135	14:30	1:124
6:6–8	1:135	15	2:314n170
6:12	2:221	15:11	2:320n50
6:18	2:327n174	15:14	2:256
6:30	2:221	15:14–16	2:127
7:1–3	1:139	15:20	2:342n132
7:3	1:140	15:22–27	1:159
7:5	1:249n18	15:24	1:159

25:1	1:222, 262n205	32:9–10	1:38, 203
25:2	1:184, 200, 217, 260n166	32:10	2:321n70
		32:11–13	1:38
25:3–5	1:218	32:14	1:38
25:7	1:192, 218	32:21	2:122
25:8	1:184, 217, 220	32:22	2:122
25:18–20	1:191	32:24	2:122
27:20	1:198	32:25	2:122
27:21	1:198	33:3	1:13; 2:348n216
28:6	2:137	33:5	1:13
28:9	1:192	33:7–11	2:353n273
28:20	1:192	33:13	1:207
28:36	2:138	33:22	2:176
28:39	2:138	34:6–7	1:207
29:20–21	2:44	34:8–9	1:13
29:38–39	1:200	34:28	2:176
29:39	1:201	35	1:219
29:42	1:200	35–40	1:196, 224
29:42b–43	1:200	35:2	1:xxiv, 214; 2:xxvi, 76
29:45	1:195		
29:45–46	1:195	35:4–5	1:217
30:7–8	1:261n175	35:4–36:8	1:217
30:11	1:222	35:5	1:214
30:17	1:222	35:20–28	1:219
30:22	1:222	35:21	1:218
30:34	1:222	35:29	1:219
31:1	1:222	35:30–35	1:219
31:3	1:222	35:31	1:222
31:12	1:222	35:31–35	1:220
31:12–17	1:222	35:33	1:215
31:13	2:76	35:34	1:219, 220
31:16	2:76	36:4–7	1:219
31:17	1:222	38:37	2:138
32	2:125	39:29	2:137, 323n109
32–34	1:196; 2:321n70	39:32	1:221
32:1	2:122	39:43	1:221
32:1–6	2:35	40:19	1:222
32:2–4	2:122	40:21	1:222
32:7–8	1:38, 203	40:23	1:222
32:9	1:13	40:25	1:222

40:27	**1**:222	12:1–7	**2**:37
40:29	**1**:222	12:8	**2**:39
40:32	**1**:222	13	**2**:42, 50
40:33	**1**:221	13:45	**2**:43, 45
40:35	**1**:195	13:46	**2**:50
69:6–8	**1**:131	14	**2**:42, 44, 50
		14:14	**2**:44
Leviticus	**1**:171, 176, 178,	14:17	**2**:44
	259n155, 265, 267;	16	**2**:52
	2:1–89, 108, 109, 136,	16:2	**1**:195
	138, 278, 359, 361	16:21	**2**:315n190
1	**2**:15	16:29	**2**:53
1:9	**2**:22	16:30	**2**:53, 310n122
2:12	**1**:241n191	18:8	**1**:242n207
3	**2**:15	18:24–30	**2**:332n232
4	**2**:9	19	**2**:311n132, 312n139
4:2	**2**:9	19:2	**2**:138
4:3	**2**:9	19:13	**2**:311n131
4:13	**2**:9	19:14	**1**:xxiv, 46; **2**:xxvi–
4:20	**2**:303n13		xxvii, 57, 58, 311n127
4:22	**2**:9, 10	19:17–18	**2**:62
4:26	**2**:109	19:18	**1**:113, 177, 201; **2**:61
4:27	**2**:9	19:19	**2**:136
4:32	**2**:9	19:30	**2**:76
5:5	**2**:315n190	19:32	**2**:58
5:20–26	**2**:108	19:33	**2**:252–53
7:11ff	**2**:16	19:33–34	**1**:176, 257n126; **2**:62,
7:15	**2**:15, 304n22		325n140
7:37–38	**2**:20	19:34	**2**:252–53
7:38	**2**:20	20:11	**1**:242n207
9:24	**2**:88	20:24	**2**:348n216
10:1–2	**2**:31	20:24–25	**2**:6
10:3	**2**:31, 32, 33, 307n68	20:26	**2**:7, 138
10:6	**2**:33, 43, 308n75	21:1–2	**2**:35
10:6–7	**2**:32	21:10–12	**2**:35
10:8–11	**2**:32	22:29	**2**:304n22
10:10	**2**:37	22:31–32	**2**:307n64
11:13–19	**2**:29, 30	23	**2**:66
11:29–31	**2**:40	23:4–8	**2**:71
11:44	**2**:138	23:10	**1**:241n191
11:46–47	**2**:6		

20:24	**1**:231n46; **2**:150	30:3	**2**:226
21:4	**2**:155	31:2	**1**:131
22	**2**:325n143	31:6	**1**:131
22–24	**2**:158	32:1	**2**:181, 182
22:12	**2**:159	32:5	**1**:233n73; **2**:179
22:15	**2**:159	32:6	**2**:179
22:17	**2**:159	32:14	**2**:179
22:18	**2**:158, 159	32:15	**2**:180
22:23	**2**:159	32:16	**2**:180
22:28	**2**:158	32:17	**2**:180, 183
22:29	**2**:159	32:20	**2**:183
22:34	**2**:158	32:20–24	**2**:183
22:38	**2**:158	32:24	**2**:180
23:5	**2**:158	33	**2**:185, 186, 190
23:8	**2**:157	33:1	**2**:185, 186
23:10	**1**:67	33:5–7	**2**:185
23:12	**2**:158	34	**2**:329n198
23:16	**2**:158	35:25	**2**:195
23:19	**2**:85, 160	35:30	**2**:331n220
24:2	**2**:163	35:32	**2**:193
24:4	**2**:158	35:33	**2**:194
24:5	**2**:163	35:34	**2**:195
24:16	**2**:158		
24:17	**2**:158	Deuteronomy	**1**:xiv, xxix–xxx, 22,
25:1–3	**2**:168		56, 108, 135, 138, 139,
25:1–9	**2**:125		150, 151, 165–66,
25:4	**2**:168		168, 169, 177, 178,
25:6–9	**2**:168, 174		241n196, 244n235,
25:9	**2**:125		246n249, 265, 268;
25:10–13	**2**:168		**2**:xxxi–xxxii, 17, 63,
25:12	**2**:169		64, 66, 67, 79, 100,
26	**2**:129		101–2, 136, 137, 143,
27:14	**1**:231n46		153, 155, 197–298,
27:16–17	**2**:170		321n70, 321n71,
27:16–21	**2**:116		325n139, 332n1–
27:16–23	**2**:355n292		357n321, 359, 362
27:18	**2**:170	1:3	**2**:285
27:18–23	**2**:353n274	1:5	**2**:285
27:22–23	**2**:117	1:9	**2**:199
27:23	**2**:117, 355n292	1:9–15	**1**:168
		1:10	**2**:199

10:17–19	1:177
10:18	1:178; **2**:65
10:18–19	1:xxx; **2**:xxxii, 325n140
10:19	1:178, 257n126; **2**:62, 252–53
10:20	1:56
11:1	**2**:65
11:1–7	**2**:352n260
11:10	**2**:228, 229, 337n87, 337n89
11:10–12	**2**:228
11:12	**2**:337n90
11:13ff	**2**:337n90
11:14	**2**:228
11:14–15	**2**:260
11:17	**2**:228
12:15	**2**:251, 260
12:21	**2**:260
13:13	**2**:260
14:1	**2**:293, 339n107
15	**2**:230, 231, 234, 311n134, 339n115
15:1–3	**2**:233, 276
15:1–6	**2**:230
15:1–8	**2**:338n95
15:2	**2**:231, 277
15:3	**2**:231, 277
15:4	**2**:234
15:4–5	**2**:234
15:5	**2**:234
15:7	**2**:231, 277
15:7–11	1:258n130; **2**:230
15:9	**2**:231, 232, 277
15:11	**2**:231, 234, 277
15:12	1:108; **2**:231, 232, 235, 277, 339n115
15:12–15	**2**:276
15:12–18	**2**:230
15:13	1:150
15:13–14	**2**:232
15:14	1:151
15:15	**2**:233
15:17	**2**:235, 339n115
16:5	**2**:260
16:11	**2**:66
16:14	**2**:17
16:14–15	**2**:66
16:15	**2**:67
16:16	**2**:276
17	**2**:343n147
17:3	**2**:317n11
17:8	1:166
17:9	1:166
17:10	1:166
17:12	1:166
17:14	**2**:249
17:14–15	**2**:245
17:15	**2**:231–32, 248, 343n148
17:16	1:166
17:16–17	**2**:246
17:17	**2**:344n159
17:18–19	**2**:247
17:20	**2**:10, 232, 248, 344n166
18	**2**:240, 242, 244
18:4	1:241n191
18:7	1:166
18:9–14	**2**:240
18:13	1:166; **2**:240
18:15	**2**:240, 285
18:16–17	**2**:241
18:17–23	1:167
18:18	1:166; **2**:240, 285
18:19	**2**:241
18:20	**2**:241, 242
18:22	**2**:241, 342n136
18:23	1:166
18:24	1:167

18:25	**1**:166
21:1-9	**2**:331n232
21:10-14	**1**:xxxi; **2**:xxxiii, 237
21:11	**2**:237
21:12	**2**:340n124
21:13	**2**:237
21:22-23	**2**:332n232
22:8	**1**:182
22:9	**2**:137
22:11	**2**:136
22:12	**2**:137
22:23-34	**1**:246n249
23:8	**1**:153; **2**:156, 255, 256
23:16-17	**2**:250
25:17	**2**:348n211
25:17-19	**2**:257
25:18	**1**:166; **2**:346n196, 347n200
25:18-19	**2**:156
25:19	**1**:166; **2**:348n211
26:1	**2**:264
26:1-11	**2**:262
26:2	**2**:262, 264
26:3	**2**:264, 349n220
26:5	**2**:334n42
26:5-6	**1**:22
26:5-8	**1**:134
26:5-10	**2**:263
26:6	**2**:264
26:8	**2**:153
26:9	**1**:135; **2**:264
26:10	**1**:241n191; **2**:264
26:11	**2**:264
26:12	**2**:264
26:12-15	**2**:349n218
27:18	**1**:46
28:1-14	**2**:265
28:15	**1**:138
28:15-68	**2**:265

28:53	**2**:260
28:68	**2**:343n153
29:9-10	**2**:276
29:17	**1**:138
29:22	**2**:316n202
29:25	**2**:317n11
30	**2**:222-23, 336n63, 350n237
30:1-5	**2**:223
30:1-10	**2**:270, 336n63
30:2	**2**:271, 351n240
30:6	**2**:222, 223, 336n64, 351n247
30:10	**2**:271, 351n240
30:11	**2**:271, 351n243
30:11-14	**2**:218, 271, 273
30:12	**2**:271
30:15	**2**:337n79
30:17	**1**:138
30:19	**1**:139, 225n14; **2**:299n14
31:2	**2**:280, 355n287, 355n289
31:3	**2**:280, 353n274
31:6	**2**:280
31:7-8	**2**:281, 288, 353n271, 353n274
31:8	**2**:354n283
31:9	**2**:275, 352n254
31:10-12	**2**:275
31:12	**2**:278
31:13	**2**:276
31:14	**2**:286, 353n274
31:14-15	**2**:353n271, 353n272
31:15	**2**:281, 353n272
31:16	**1**:138
31:22	**2**:353n272
31:23	**2**:281, 353n271, 353n272, 353n274, 354n283

32	2:290, 291, 292, 293–94, 356n299	32:35	2:291, 356n306
		32:37	2:355n297, 356n300
32:4	2:290, 355n296, 355n297	32:47	2:337n79
		32:48–52	2:286
32:5	2:290	32:49	2:329n198
32:6	2:294	32:51	2:285
32:10–14	2:291	32:57	1:231n46
32:15	1:68, 237n138; 2:291, 355n297	33:4	2:99
		33:5	1:237n138
32:18	2:294, 355n297	33:8	1:231n46
32:18–19	2:290	33:26	1:237n138
32:23	2:290, 291	34:4	2:286
32:23ff	2:356n299	34:5	2:337n78
32:24	2:356n302	34:6	2:295
32:27	2:291	34:7	2:287
32:30	2:355n297	34:9	2:353n274
32:31	2:355n297	34:10–12	2:285

NEVI'IM

Joshua	1:138	8:11	2:247
3–5	2:314n169	10:2	1:238n151, 238n153
14:8	2:354n279	15:22	2:304n33
22:9–11	2:329n198	15:29	2:293
22:32	2:329n198	17:16	1:254n69
Judges	2:170	2 Samuel	1:246n249, 246n250
4:4	2:342n132	7:19	2:99
5:1	2:320n50	11	2:212
8:22–23	2:245	11:4	2:12
11:11	2:170	11:25	2:12
11:30–31	2:171	11:27	2:12
11:34	2:171	12:7	2:12
11:39	2:171	12:8	1:242n202
12:1–6	2:172	12:10	2:12
21:12	2:329n198	12:13	2:12
		13:14	1:246n249
1 Samuel		13:15	1:246n250
1:11	1:230n42	13:21	1:115
2:30	1:255n95; 2:55	15:1	2:246
8:5	2:344–45n171	16:20–22	1:95
8:10–18	2:342n144		

4:5–9	**1**:211	6:6–8	**2**:304n34
4:10–11	**1**:211	6:8	**2**:164

Micah

2:1–2	**2**:212
3:9	**2**:241
3:9–12	**2**:306n49
3:12	**2**:242
5:9	**2**:247
6:1–5	**2**:163
6:6–7	**2**:164

Nahum

1:3	**1**:261n192
3:1	**1**:210
3:19	**1**:210

Zechariah	**2**:352n251
1:3	**2**:274

Malachi 3:7	**2**:351n248

KETUVIM

Psalms	**1**:177; **2**:88, 89	72:12–13	**1**:9
2	**2**:245	74	**2**:4
2:7	**2**:245	74:10–11	**2**:4
4:5	**2**:307n69	74:13–14	**1**:251n38; **2**:4
16:8	**1**:56, 57	74:16–17	**2**:4
19:2	**2**:316n215	74:23	**2**:4
19:8	**2**:165	81:8	**1**:231n46
19:14	**1**:xxxiii; **2**:xxxv	86:15	**1**:261n192
19:15	**2**:356n299	91:15	**1**:170, 186
20:8	**2**:247	95	**2**:305n41
22	**2**:316n216	95:8	**1**:231n46
23:6	**1**:194	103:8	**1**:261n192
27:4	**1**:194	106:32	**1**:231n46
30:2	**2**:316n215	115	**1**:10
32	**2**:303n18	115:16	**1**:10
35:10	**1**:177	118:17	**2**:286
40:7–9	**2**:304n34	119	**1**:56, 58, 235n112,
44	**2**:316n216		235n113, 236n115,
51	**2**:303n18		236n117
63	**1**:58	119:19	**1**:56
63:5	**1**:236n116	119:30	**1**:56
63:7	**1**:58	119:31	**1**:56
63:9	**1**:56	119:48	**1**:56
71:9	**1**:174	119:54	**2**:316n215
72	**1**:10, 257n120	119:92	**1**:xxi, 58; **2**:xxiii
72:2	**1**:9	119:97	**1**:xxi, 58; **2**:xxiii
72:4	**1**:9	119:148	**1**:58
72:7	**1**:9	121:3–4	**1**:89

APOCRYPHA AND PSEUDEPIGRAPHA

Ben Sira 5:2	**2**:131	33:2	**1**:241n195
Jubilees	**1**:150	48:18	**1**:150

Testaments of the Twelve Patriarchs

Reuben 3:11	**1**:241n195	Zebulun 3:2	**1**:240n183

NEW TESTAMENT

Luke 10:29	**1**:177

QURAN

Sura 12	**1**:248n10

MISHNAH

Avot		Sanhedrin 4:5	**2**:93
1:2	**2**:189	Shabbat	
1:12	**2**:106		
3:14	**2**:93	6:4	**1**:70
4:1	**2**:55	7:2	**2**:77
Bava Kamma 2:6	**1**:xxvii, 64; **2**:xxix	Sotah 7:8	**2**:353n264
Berakhot 2:1	**1**:33	Sukkah 5:1	**2**:69
Mishnah Ta'anit 1:4	**1**:238n158	Yoma	
		8:8	**2**:53
Pesahim 10:4	**1**:135	8:9	**2**:53

TOSEFTA

Sanhedrin 4:5	**2**:345n171	to Deuteronomy	
Shabbat 16:7	**2**:354n280	22:12	**2**:136–37
		to Exodus	
Sotah 10b	**1**:242n211	6:18	**2**:327n174
Targum Yonatan		to Leviticus	
(Targum Pseudo-		13:45	**2**:43
Jonathan)	**1**:240n183; **2**:283, 316n206		

PARASHAT HA-SHAVUA (WEEKLY TORAH PORTION) COMMENTARY

CPSIA information can be obtained
at www.ICGtesting.com
Printed in the USA
LVHW040313291019
635622LV00001B/1